SAGE was founded in 1965 by Sara Miller McCune to support the dissemination of usable knowledge by publishing innovative and high-quality research and teaching content. Today, we publish more than 750 journals, including those of more than 300 learned societies, more than 800 new books per year, and a growing range of library products including archives, data, case studies, reports, conference highlights, and video. SAGE remains majority-owned by our founder, and after Sara's lifetime will become owned by a charitable trust that secures our continued independence.

Los Angeles | London | Washington DC | New Delhi | Singapore

LEADERS

contemporary critical perspectives

Edited by

Brigid Carroll, Jackie Ford & Scott Taylor

SAGE

Los Angeles | London | New Delhi
Singapore | Washington DC | Boston

Los Angeles | London | New Delhi
Singapore | Washington DC

SAGE Publications Ltd
1 Oliver's Yard
55 City Road
London EC1Y 1SP

SAGE Publications Inc.
2455 Teller Road
Thousand Oaks, California 91320

SAGE Publications India Pvt Ltd
B 1/I 1 Mohan Cooperative Industrial Area
Mathura Road
New Delhi 110 044

SAGE Publications Asia-Pacific Pte Ltd
3 Church Street
#10-04 Samsung Hub
Singapore 049483

Editor: Kirsty Smy
Production editor: Tom Bedford
Copyeditor: Neil Dowden
Proofreader: David Hemsley
Indexer: David Rudeforth
Marketing manager: Alison Borg
Cover design: Francis Kenney
Typeset by: C&M Digitals (P) Ltd, Chennai, India
Printed and bound in Great Britain by Ashford
Colour Press Ltd

Library of Congress Control Number: 2014952894

British Library Cataloguing in Publication data

A catalogue record for this book is available from
the British Library

ISBN 978-1-4462-9437-6
ISBN 978-1-4462-9438-3 (pbk)

At SAGE we take sustainability seriously. Most of our products are printed in the UK using FSC papers and boards.
When we print overseas we ensure sustainable papers are used as measured by the Egmont grading system.
We undertake an annual audit to monitor our sustainability.

CONTENTS

LIST OF CASE STUDIES

LIST OF EDITORS AND CONTRIBUTORS

Brigid Carroll is an Associate Professor of Organisation Studies in the Department of Management and International Business and Director of Research at the New Zealand Leadership Institute, both at the University of Auckland, New Zealand.

Jackie Ford is Professor of Leadership and Organization studies at the University of Bradford, School of Management.

Scott Taylor is a Reader in Leadership and Organization Studies at Birmingham Business School, University of Birmingham, UK.

Lucia Crevani is a Senior Lecturer in Business Administration with focus on Organisation Theory at the School of Business, Society and Engineering at Mälardalen university in Västerås, Sweden.

John G. Cullen is Senior Lecturer at Maynooth University School of Business, Maynooth University, Co. Kildare, Ireland.

Helen Delaney is a Lecturer in the Department of Management and International Business, University of Auckland, New Zealand.

Michelle Evans is a Senior Lecturer in Leadership at the School for Management and Marketing at Charles Sturt University, Australia.

Nancy Harding is a Professor of Organization Theory and Director at the Centre for Research in Organizations and Work (CROW) at Bradford School of Management, University of Bradford, UK.

Brad Jackson is Head of the School of Government and Professor of Public and Community Leadership at Victoria University of Wellington, New Zealand.

Simon Kelly is a Lecturer in HRM and Organisational Behaviour at the Bradford University School of Management, University of Bradford, UK.

Donna Ladkin is Professor of Leadership and Ethics at the Graduate School of Management, Plymouth University, UK.

Annie Pye is Professor of Leadership and Organization Studies at the Centre for Leadership Studies at the University of Exeter Buisness School, UK.

Amanda Sinclair is a Professorial Fellow at the Melbourne Business School, The University of Melbourne, Australia.

Owain Smolović-Jones is a Lecturer in Management at the Open University Buisness School, UK.

Sverre Spoelstra is an Associate Professor at the Department of Business Administration, Lund University, Sweden.

Neil Sutherland is a Lecturer in Organisation Studies, based at the University of the West of England in Bristol.

FOREWORD

Why are you reading this book? My guess is that it is prescribed reading as part of a course on leadership, right? But as a student myself, I know that there's course reading and there's course reading: there's the stuff you read in order to pass, and then there's the stuff you read because you're genuinely interested. Which is this book for you?

A few years ago this book would have fallen into the first category for me, because – quite frankly – I found leadership to be a bit of a turn-off. I'd run into far too many power-hungry egotists who exploited positions of so-called leadership to force their opinions on to others. Sure, not all leaders are like that, but on the whole leadership seemed tied up with images of being in the spotlight and taking charge. I can remember being in countless different seminars on *how to be a leader*, which all seemed to offer a sort of Swiss Army knife version of leveraging power via means such as manipulation, fear, charisma and so on. But far from being motivational, I found myself thinking: 'Well if this is leadership then I want nothing to do with it'. It just felt so narcissistic, like it was anchored around a sort of worship of individual people (usually men) who trampled on the weak in order to lead their helpless followers to 'success'. Well, no thanks.

But if there's two kinds of reading, there's also (at least) two kinds of thinking about leadership. There's the so-called mainstream approach, which tends to focus on heroic individuals who dazzle and inspire their followers to achieve unquestionably good deeds – the sort of heroic leadership for which I have absolutely no appetite. But there's also this other kind of leadership thinking, the kind that characterises the chapters in this book. This thinking has redeemed leadership for me and given it a depth and richness that I now find surprisingly engaging. So much so in fact, the more I've encountered this sort of thinking, the more gravitational pull it has on me. I now work at the New Zealand Leadership Institute (along with Brigid Carroll, one of the editors of this book), and in my work there I've been involved in helping put this book together. I'm also now pursuing my own postgraduate studies in – believe it or not – leadership. So what is about this other kind of leadership that has brought about such a marked change?

I think there are two main reasons why the kind of leadership thinking in this book is exciting and different. The first is that again and again the authors in this book will challenge the notion that leadership is something individual 'special' people possess. Forget about leadership positions. They're more or less irrelevant: they're just titles that, as some critics suggest, upsize people's egos more than their actual jobs. What they don't do though is make anyone a leader, nor do they necessarily afford anyone a set of followers. Instead, leadership is something quite a bit more mysterious, and certainly a lot less grandiose. A simple thoughtful question asked by the most junior member of a team might in that moment produce a spark of unexpected leadership. Or a moment in which someone confesses that they are confused, admitting that they were picturing the problem in a radically different way may spur a shift in meaning for everyone else. Or perhaps everyone else *is* thinking something similar but struggling to put words to an inchoate jumble and then, like a lightning rod, someone manages to give voice to what needs to be said and thus stands, for that moment at least, as an ethereal leader. None of these are the possession of the leader; instead they emerge out of an interaction in unique and surprising ways.

Of course to call these actions leadership though they lack position or authority does open up the criticism of calling everything leadership. Certainly we would be loath to go that far. Similarly we are not suggesting that leadership is trivial, nor is it (usually) accidental. However, the murky ambiguity in which this places leadership is precisely the right home for it, and it's part of what has reanimated my interest in it. I like that it's surprising and mysterious. But more than that, what it really does is bring leadership down from the lofty heights of corporate superstars like Jack Welch or Steve Jobs and turns it into something that could come from anyone, anywhere, anytime. This is important. As the following chapters will argue, it's not only inaccurate to reduce complex organisational success or failure to the actions of one person; it's actually a disempowering excuse for apathy. But when leadership is wrestled into the realm of the mundane, so too follows responsibility, accountability and possibility. This is precisely the take on leadership about to unfold in this book, and the first reason leadership excites me.

The second reason is the way this other kind of leadership engages with the reality of power. Before I encountered the strands of thinking that characterise this book, the sum of my knowledge of power amounted to that old saying 'power corrupts, and absolute power corrupts absolutely.' That's a cute aphorism, but it tends to winnow away power until – once again – it resides only with a handful of people, who are usually those at the top. In other words, power is something only a few extraordinary people possess.

In the pages that follow, however, you will find a radical departure from this somewhat simple conception of power. Instead, power is going to be brought to life in ways that are surprising, and much closer to home. This is really exciting because instead of power being an abstract concept that applies only to the elite, it becomes visible all around us. It runs through things we use every day like words and languages; it is woven into the way we present and think about ourselves (like in our dress, hairstyles, accessories and so on); it filters the way we make sense of the people around us; and it permeates the previously innocuous and taken-for-granted, so things like bank accounts, technological devices, websites (Facebook? The news?), education (like the degree you're currently studying) and even books (including the one in your hands right now!). Every day lines of power flow through our lives and we bump, push, lean on, resist, enact and ignore them constantly.

Although this new picture of power is more complex, it's as rewarding as it is important. For a start it's much more interesting, since it intersects our everyday lives. But more than that, if we are to make any real headway at all with leadership we need to be able to see and engage with power. Any leadership issue you can think of – whether it's climate change, poverty, runaway inequality, corporate corruption, child labour or seemingly intractable lines of war and terrorism – each of these is entrenched in networks of power. But perhaps the most provocative part of all this is that a thorough look at these networks of power will undoubtedly highlight the ways in which even you are implicated. Power is not some possession of distant others: it involves our everyday lives. This is the second reason this other kind of leadership has caught my attention.

That's me though – what does this all mean for you as a reader? Well given that you're about to embark on a journey through a different kind of leadership thinking, I'd like to invite you to make this a different kind of course reading too. Sure you can read through this with the appropriate kind of studying diligence and earn yourself a sweet A+ as your just reward – and so you should. But as the chapters in this book will argue, learning leadership goes well beyond the acquisition of head knowledge. Leadership involves so much more than simply knowing 'about' leadership. Broader knowledge about leadership does help inasmuch as it gives you a repository of lenses on leadership to think through and try out – but there's more to it than this. If you take seriously the ideas in this book, the space of leadership will expand beyond the plush offices of the C-suite and majestic corridors of political power. Instead the space for leadership actually becomes the space you are in right now, regardless of your age, status, experience, employment situation or whatever.

Taking this seriously then, I'd like to invite you simply to 'have a go'. There are opportunities all around you, across the full range of spheres you live in, like university, work, family, church, local community, national community, volunteer groups, protests, Facebook groups, clubs, sports teams, interest groups, hobbies – you name it. The thing about leadership is it takes practice and a willingness to experiment with your 'leadership identity'. Developing your leadership identity is one of the reasons why this book has 'stop and reflect' sections dotted throughout it. As a fellow student, I know that it's tempting to skip over these because they feel maybe a bit soft and fluffy (and they're not likely to have any bearing on whether or not you get that A+!). But because leadership is more than head knowledge, these reflection points are vital for helping you bring yourself into what you are reading. They also help build a practice of reflection that is the lifeblood of leadership. As I heard someone say recently: 'people don't learn from experience – they learn from reflection on experience'. So that's the first part: be reflective and have a go!

Lastly, I want to invite you to be prepared to see the world differently. The chapters in this book will – if you let them – challenge loads of everyday assumptions that we take for granted. Things like gender, diversity, language, power, knowledge, science, charisma, art, and of course what we mean by leadership. Some of the chapters have the potential to bump you right up against the boundaries you hold around the way things are. This is, I think, exactly what students of leadership need right now. The briefest glimpse at a newspaper is as far as you need to go for a sense of the size and scale of the problems we face today in an increasingly globalised world. It's enough to make anyone feel overwhelmed to the brink of apathy, especially if we believe that only a few gifted leaders at the top have the power to do anything. But the truth is these are problems that the self-styled heroic leaders of the world *cause* more often than they solve. What's more, actually no single individual, elected body or leadership position has the power to solve these issues.

What this calls for instead is a growing body of people who think differently. We need people who reject the stale old ideas of leadership and position and power, people who refuse to wait idly by for politicians to do something. We need people who are fluent in the complexity of power, who can call attention to and even disrupt its hidden lines that run through our world. We need people who are engaged in leading everywhere, irrespective of titles and position. This is the context that I invite you to hold in your mind as you read through this book, so that you, my fellow student, might join me in starting to lead differently.

Joshua Firth

Auckland, New Zealand

GUIDED TOUR OF THE BOOK

What this chapter is all about ...

The main idea is that transformational leadership is believed to inspire radical transformation in followers, especially through charisma. This theory of leadership has striking similarities to religious concepts like conversion, in which a follower is transformed from a lower morality to a higher one. It also echoes the concept of redemption, in which people, organizations, business and the world are being redeemed from corruption and made ethical.

What this chapter is all about...
Brief summary of the chapter topic.

The key questions this chapter answers are:

- How do you learn leadership? Why might learning leadership differ from learning other subjects or skills?
- What are the different ways we can think about developing and learning leadership?
- How are learning and development tied up in power?
- How might seeing leadership in relation to learning offer a richer perspective on the nature of leadership?
- Learning doesn't just differ for leadership; it's also integral to it. How and why are leadership, learning and development interconnected?

The key questions this chapter answers are:
Bulleted list of key questions answered or raised in the chapter, to focus your learning as you work through the chapter.

Case study: Natalie Chan

Natalie Chan is a 35-year-old woman of mixed Anglo-Chinese descent who joined the UK-based public sector organization OBP after she graduated from university with a good degree in Economics. She joined the organization's graduate intake scheme, where she was quickly tracked into a 'high flyer' programme. Through that programme she has been placed in a number of different parts of the larger organization in order to develop a broad understanding of its overall activities.

She is particularly recognized for her skills as an analyst and, in fact, she most enjoys this kind of work. Although her technical expertise is very high, she is not particularly confident as a manager. Some of her uncertainties about managing other people began to arise about five years ago when she was promoted to a role that required her to manage a small team. The transition to management was made perhaps even more difficult as she had worked alongside three of the five people who subsequently reported to her.

Although she herself is not sure how she did it, those around her judged her management skills to be very high. As the case study opens, she has just been promoted. This promotion means that along with being responsible for running a department of 60 people, she also reports to the executive team. Both of these duties she finds rather daunting.

(Continued)

Case studies
Leadership case studies have been included in each chapter to help you link theory with practice. Related questions will test your understanding of the issues covered.

The key points in this chapter were ...

- Contingency theories arose out of recognition that leadership traits were not enough to predict good leadership. Rather, a theory was needed that accounted for different contexts. Thus they were one of the earliest moves towards recognizing the relational element of leadership.
- The main contingency theories are:
  - *Fiedler's model* prescribes a relationship between the leader's style and the *favourable-ness* of the situation, which is measured according to the task structures, influence and relationships.
  - *Path–goal* theory categorizes leadership according to two factors: *consideration* (people orientation) and *initiating structure* (task orientation). The optimal combination of these are contingent on the context, such as task ambiguity.
  - *Situational theory* combines much of the above with a new factor: *readiness*. This pertains to the level of followers' willingness and motivation.
  - *Leader participation* is similar to the above, but differs in its focus on decision-making. It suggests that who should make decisions is contingent on context.
- Some of the critiques of contingency theories include:
  - It can be very difficult to get robust data on the context to measure it against things like task structure or influence.
  - They assume leaders are able to read a context objectively, and forget the political or interpretive nature of social reality.
  - They can tend to homogenize organisations and employees. For example, they risk assuming that a goal or task is valued equally in a context.
  - They have been criticized as merely mechanical tools – a situational menu for leadership – which may 'sell' well in management and leadership development programmes, but is actually an over-simplification of the complex social world.
  - Perhaps the most significant critique is that contingency theories are actually a series of strategic tools for 'the leader' to use to exert control of followers and situations.

The key points in this chapter were...
End-of-chapter bulleted summary of main issues covered, ideal for revision.

STOP AND REFLECT 2.2

Researchers creating trait theories of leadership start from the belief that they can't identify what leadership is in itself. Instead, the research they do tries to identify ways that we can identify things that leadership is related to. So, if most people identified as occupying positions of leadership, such as a chief executive officer role, are taller than average, then we have identified something that being or becoming a leader is related to (above average height).

The researchers can then extend this idea in two ways. They could read existing academic theories and make up a list of physical characteristics, personality characteristics or skills that other researchers have identified, then test them on a new group of people. Or, the researchers could observe people in leadership positions (or read auto/biographies) and develop a list of traits in that way, then test them on a group of people.

Trait researchers most often design a long questionnaire that they think establishes whether an individual possesses the traits. Sometimes this can be quite straightforward – for example, someone is either above average height or not. However, most traits are difficult to test for in this way because they are not physically visible – personality characteristics such as initiative or integrity, for example, can be exceptionally difficult to design reliable questions for.

But trait researchers are ingenious and persistent. So they read, think, work and test their questionnaires until they achieve enough reliability and validity to satisfy their academic peers. There are always flaws in research methods – none provide perfect knowledge and all can be critiqued on some basis. The process that trait theorists go through has some very specific and significant flaws, though.

* What's good about the research methods often used in trait-based research?
* What's bad about the methods?

Stop and reflect

These are very specific – when we put one of these boxes into the text, we want to indicate to you that there should be some active thinking going on. Of course, when you read you're already doing something active – understanding, relating to experience, making connections – so these boxes are designed to encourage you to take a moment to do that thinking without going any further in the text itself.

DEFINITION: SOCIAL CONSTRUCTIONISM

'Social constructionism' refers to an ontological stance in which the nature of reality is understood to be 'constructed' by social actors rather than 'given'. In opposition to those who adopt a more 'realist' ontological stance in which reality is seen to be determined prior to the individual's engagement with it (and the point of scientific discovery is to 'uncover its truth'), those who adopt a social constructionist perspective believe that together we create our understanding of how the world works. Thus in some cultures it is polite when eating together to make minimal noise, whereas in others, for instance, to smack one's lips and eat noisily is to demonstrate appreciation to the cook. Neither is an objectively 'right' response, as they are both constructed by the cultures in which these behaviours are enacted.

In Keith Grint's article 'Problems, problems, problems: The social construction of "leadership"' (2005b), he develops the argument that events which catalyse a 'command', 'managerial' or 'leadership' response are themselves 'constructed' rather than predetermined to be one or the other. For instance, in framing the 9/11 attack on the USA as a 'crisis' situation, George W. Bush's response was to 'declare war' on perpetrators of that attack. Had the event been constructed as a 'wicked' problem, however, a different response would have been more appropriate; one in which questions would have been asked before bombs dropped.

The key point of Grint's paper, which is described in more detail below, is that the appropriateness of a given response to an incident is determined by the way in which the incident is constructed, rather than through an objectively determined 'reality' discernment.

Definitions

These are here to explain important academic jargon so that (a) you can understand your module leader better, and (b) communicate with them more effectively when you need to.

 Further thinking

Schyns, B. and Meindl, J. R. (eds) (2005). *Implicit Leadership Theories: Essays and Explorations*. Greenwich, CT: Information Age Publishing.

1 How do implicit leadership theories, which are developed and tacitly held by individuals over the course of their lifespan, challenge contingency-based approaches to understanding leadership? Does engaging with such approaches change how you feel about yourself as a leader or a follower?
2 What are the problems associated with thinking about leadership as something that is implicit? What challenges do such approaches pose to traditional contingency leadership theories?

Tourish, F. (2005). Critical upward communication: Ten commandments for improving strategy and decision making. *Long Range Planning*, 38(5), 485–503.

1 The practice of critical upward communication highlights that personal and cultural barriers often impede leaders' attempts to accurately identify impact factors that are contingent to their followers' situation. What do leaders need to do to overcome these barriers?
2 How can leaders and followers work together to reconfigure their mutual understanding of the contingencies that impact on their organizational situation?

Knights, D. (2009). Power at work in organisations. In M. Alvesson, T. Bridgman and H. Willmott (eds), *The Oxford Handbook of Critical Management Studies* (pp. 144–165). Oxford: Oxford University Press.

1 Critical management theorists reject contingency theories of leadership because they present an over-simplified model of the relationship between leaders and followers. Do contingency theories of leadership have any redeeming factors?
2 Child (1984) suggested that, regardless of the situation, leaders can exercise agency in situations despite the constraints that the external environment places on them. Can you think of a personal example of when you have done this?
3 How can 'agentic strategic choice' be exercised by a contemporary business or political leader currently engaging with a problematic situation?

Further thinking

These sections contain links to journal articles and other resources to encourage further exploration of interesting and important ideas in the book.

 Leadership on screen

Trait theories are not easily represented on screen because we can't see many of them in the same way as we can see, for example, charisma. However, many films, documentaries and television series suggest implicitly or explicitly that traits are the key to understanding leadership, such as:

* *Blade Runner* (1982) – quite old but a classic. The plot centres on whether robots ('replicants') can behave in ways that humans do. It's a fascinating exploration of what it is to be human, how we assess humanity and how we judge others through their personality and behaviour. (If you like the film, you might also enjoy the short story it is based on, 'Do androids dream of electric sheep?', by Philip K. Dick.)
* Recent documentaries about the US corporate world refer frequently to how leaders emerge, are selected and create followers through the use of trait norms, especially *Enron: The Smartest Guys in the Room* (2005), and *The Corporation* (2003). Both are also worth watching for their insights into leadership and leaders more generally.
* A lighter (in some ways) representation of trait theories in action is *Trading Places* (1983) – it's another old movie, but it's still meaningful for thinking through the implications of what researchers call 'heritability', genetics and the 'dark side' of trait theories.

As you watch any of these films, or if you see trait theories of leadership represented anywhere else on screen, you might ask yourself these questions:

* Why are researchers in leadership studies so keen on trait theories when so many fictional films and documentaries seem to be damaging, unhelpful to individuals and organizations and discriminatory?
* If you were identified as a potential leader because of traits that you have inherited or developed, how would you feel about it?

Leadership on screen

This is the part of the book we've had most fun with. Most of us use extracts from film, fiction and documentary, television and other visual materials in our teaching – leadership seems to be especially easy to find materials for because film-makers and television producers are as fascinated by leaders as everyone else. So, we've pulled together a few examples of things we find help us and the students we work with to think through leadership and leading.

Companion website

There's a 'companion website' for this book, as there is for many textbooks. The authors and publisher have worked hard on its design and content, so do visit it – you'll find useful things and videos with everyone who has written the book. Our relatives think they're quite funny; you should also learn something from them – the Editors.

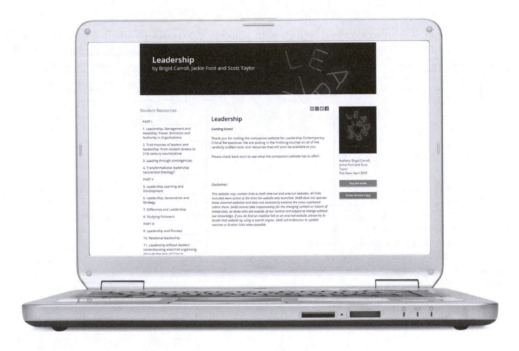

Visit http://study.sagepub.com/carroll for the following teaching and learning resources:
For students:

- Where possible, videos of the book's authors have been made available. These provide an overview of the chapter and discussing issues such as why the topic covered by their chapter is important, how you can apply the ideas discussed in practice, key theories and debates and tips for revision.
- Where possible, journal articles discussed in the book have been placed online allowing you free and fast access to these important papers.
- Links to additional resources highlight useful and original sources of information beyond the book.

For lecturers:

- PowerPoint slides

INTRODUCTION: THE POWERS OF LEADERS

Brigid Carroll, Jackie Ford and Scott Taylor

Welcome to this book. Our intention in it is to go with you into the worlds of leading, leadership, and leadership studies. We are a group of academics who research and teach in this area, to communicate what we know and don't know about it, making the subject as intriguing as possible, and perhaps even entertaining. We're going to start in the classic academic way, exploring and defining key terms with an introduction to the three 'lead-' terms used above, explaining how we think you should approach them. Then we'll introduce the people who have put this book together. But first we think you need to know why this book exists.

As all academic books about leadership tell you in the first few pages, there are (literally) millions of texts by different authors out there in bookshops, on library shelves, in people's offices or houses, in most languages of the world. That means we always have to ask, and answer, the question of 'Why another one?'

Let's start with the specific type of book this is. You know already it's a textbook – textbooks exist for a variety of reasons. The reasons people write them can be negative: perhaps the authors think all existing textbooks in the field are bad, or maybe they think what the research field is *really* about isn't currently represented in published textbooks. Or the reasons might be more positive: because we think we have something really important to say, or a way of saying things that is more interesting, original, or helpful to learning about the topic. Sometimes, you won't be surprised to hear if you've bought this relatively expensive book there are financial reasons, because authors earn royalties from each book sold. Another form of instrumental reason could be careerism, because a really good textbook will help academics get promoted or enhance our standing within the research community. (There's also egotism – academics are people like any others, and sometimes just want to see their names on a book cover.)

Why does *this* textbook exist, then? We're tempted to take the moral high ground and claim it's only for the most noble, positive reasons, because those reasons do apply here. However, this book's existence is more likely to be down to a combination of all of the above, to different degrees of importance, for the people involved. As you know if you've studied organizational behaviour, or worked in an organization, most workplace actions and behaviours are complex in their motives and meanings, and academic work is no different in that. Next, though, we're going to present you here with two key intellectual rationales for writing the book which are based on our understanding of the field of leadership studies after some time teaching and researching within it. As you will see, these rationales are closely linked.

Why leadership? What leadership?

The main rationale is founded on what we understand, and want, the research and educational field of leadership studies to be. There are two aspects to this: we think it's important to locate the ideas and practices associated with the term 'leadership' as a concept through theories that have developed over time, and then to think about how the practices of leading can be understood through theories. We want to present leadership as an act, and people described as leaders, as located in time and space – in other words, to try and understand what leading means for people involved at moments and in places where they live and work. These times and places are always variable, always changing and incredibly important – we think textbooks that claim to present you with eternal, unchanging truths about leadership are, frankly, not helpful. The world is so varied, different moments in time are so distinctive, organizations are so diverse, people are so unpredictable, that theories can only ever be convincing insofar as they are meaningful to people in places at specific times.

This does not mean all theories are equal, or that we are suggesting you take a relativist position. We have preferences; there are theories we think are more convincing and theories we think are less persuasive. We want you to read, think and make a choice that is well informed, critical and clear, so that's why we're presenting as wide a range of options, in as much detail as we can, for you here.

How leading? Who leading?

A British politician died in early 2014. His name was Tony Benn, and he was committed through his life to socialism and democracy. His politics were expressed in lots of different ways through a long and fascinating life; Benn had a particular habit of asking very difficult questions. For example, he encouraged everyone to ask these five questions of leaders:

> What power do you have?
> Where did you get it?
> In whose interests do you exercise it?
> To whom are you accountable?
> How can we get rid of you?

For fun, ask these questions of someone in your life you think of as powerful. Even better, ask them of yourself in relation to whatever power you have. Be creative in this – power takes many different forms, and most of us have or exercise power in some part of life.

We like these questions because they put the leader in the spotlight as a person-among-people. In other words, the leader has to provide an account of how power, and therefore leadership, has actually happened to them. The power of individual people to act (or not act), to speak (or to silence), is questioned by asking about processes and institutions. We're going to ask you to think about power a lot during this book – the power of individual people who we see as leaders, the power of the idea of leadership and the ways that people acquire, or avoid, exercising power in the process of leadership.

As you'll see, these two starting points, time–space location and power, are particular ways of approaching the 'lead-' subject. They also generate a particular way of learning about leadership or developing your own leadership practices, if that's what you want to do in life or at work. This is the second key rationale for writing this book, the pedagogy. We're presenting you with ways of seeing leadership that should then affect how you think about your study of the ideas and practices associated with leadership, leading and leaders. After we've done this in a little more detail, assuming you're reading in the way the book is set out on the pages, we'll introduce ourselves.

Leading, leadership and leadership studies

This section has the potential to unfold as a classic 'academic' exercise, in the sense that academic can mean abstract, unpractical or pointlessly theoretical – detached from a sense of the material world that leading happens in. We don't want that to be a feature of this book. It is an academic book – you know this from the title, the publisher, the authors and the price. But it doesn't need to be academic in that pejorative sense – the research and teaching that happens in business schools can and should be academic in the sense of being informed by theories of social, organizational and individual behaviour, but it always has to be applied, connected to everyday practice and understood by the people we research or teach. That's what we're aiming for.

Leading

So we're starting here with the action, the verb, the *doing* of something – leading. Without this, there can be no idea of leadership, and certainly no academic field called leadership studies. As we've just said, all of what goes on in terms of research and education in business schools is *applied*. To be clear: this means that there should be a relationship to what happens, what people do or what systems and cultures encourage us to do, in workplaces and organizations. It doesn't mean that the research should resemble management consultancy, or always have a relationship to individual and organizational performance, or that it is less worthwhile than 'pure' theory. Rather, it means that we're acknowledging the need for what we do in research and teaching to be applied in the sense of being meaningful.

One way to achieve this is by thinking about the actions, the activities, the people and the processes involved in *doing* leading. This doesn't mean we are doing research *for* leaders, or only concentrating on the people *defined as* leaders by job title. For the people involved in writing this book, for example, the *led* are at least as important as the leaders – as many people have said, it is impossible to lead or be a leader if there are no followers behind or around you. In addition, we are also committed to the idea that leading happens within organizational contexts and cultures that we should critique. In other words, our colleagues in business schools researching organizational behaviour, human resource management, marketing or international management all have an interest in how leading happens – and we have an interest in what they write about their specific fields.

Finally, we'd like to communicate the idea that leading is a process, or series of processes. This is a complex philosophical idea that is explored in more detail later in the book. However, for the moment, we can think of it as simply this – *leading is not a momentary activity, it happens over time, changing continuously depending on place, who is present when leading is happening and the negotiation of authority*. This means that we are not likely to be able to identify an 'essence' of leadership, whether that takes the form of a personality characteristic or trait, a mysterious charismatic gift, an apparent ability to transform people and organizations, or a function of the brain. We do look at all of these various theories of leadership in this book, but always with a healthy scepticism that they are somewhat misguided in their attempts to identify a 'key' to understanding leadership, identifying leaderly activity or developing leaders.

Leadership

Think of the last time you heard someone say, 'What we need here is some good leadership'. Maybe you were in a classroom or lecture theatre; perhaps you were participating in a team sport; you might have been talking about politics or work; or someone might have said it to you to persuade you to stand up and lead. It might even have been you who said the words, expressing your desire for *someone* or *something* to lead you. Invoking the idea of leadership, looking for leadership, is easy. But then you run into the inevitable secondary questions – what, where, why, how, when, how much, do I want to do it …

This is where we start with the idea of identifying leadership, as a series of questions. Where are you likely to find leadership? Can you see, touch, smell or taste it? Is it a thing you'll find lying around like an object? Can you identify it when you see it in a book or film? What sort of clothes does it wear? Does it look like a man or a woman? Does it happen for a set period of time and then stop? How does it feel to be led? Is it dangerous? Can someone teach me to do it, or show me how to be a leader?

Or maybe, as we said when thinking about the idea of *leading*, perhaps *leadership* is also better understood as a process, involving people and therefore fundamentally social, subject to change over time according to where it's happening and why. As every other author of the thousands of books on leadership tells us, the readers, at the beginning of the book, leadership is a term-in-use, a word that many of us fit into sentences every day. Behind or within that usage, we make a series of assumptions – that we understand the term leadership when we use it, that the people who are listening to us share that understanding and that we will be able to identify leadership or make it happen.

As with the idea of leading, we want to get across one key idea when we think about the term leadership – that it's everywhere, all the time, but usually not accompanied with much careful thought. As Brad Jackson and Ken Parry tell us in *A Very Short, Fairly Interesting and Reasonably Cheap Book about Studying Leadership* (2011), we can see leadership in our own attempts to do it, in others' efforts to lead us, we can talk about it and we can read or write about it. Most of the time, however, most of us talk about 'it' in a relatively uninformed way – with authority, often, but without much clarity or reflection, which can be really frustrating. Perhaps this is why you're studying leadership, to become better informed and to be able to think and speak about leadership with more clarity and meaning in life and at work. If you do that, and we hope you will, it will involve challenging myths. As a starter, if anyone ever tries to tell you that leadership is any of the following, we want you to challenge them, using the vocabulary and ideas introduced in this book.

 STOP AND REFLECT

When Scott first started lecturing, he had to speak to a more senior colleague about assessing some undergraduate students' essays. He was unsure whether some of the essays should pass or fail; they weren't very good, he knew that, because they didn't respond to the assessment criteria very well or engage with the ideas in the course he had taught, but he couldn't decide if they were bad enough to force the students into a resit exam, or just good enough to pass. His colleague suggested he think about whether his dad could have written them. In other words, she said, could someone who had never studied in the area have written the essay? If the answer was yes, then he should fail them, because the essays would be little more than a set of assumptions, common sense and assertions. (Of course this doesn't mean that dads, or mums, are lacking intelligence, or unable to write good coursework about leadership. It just means that they haven't been through a formal educational or self-study process that enables them to write about the subject to satisfy an assessment that judges whether they should be trusted as people who know what academic theories can tell us about leadership.)

As well as 'dad-theory', we could also think about the claims these students made in their essays as 'myths'. This isn't a judgement as to their truth or fiction; rather, it's to indicate that the claims should be read as symbolic stories that tell us something about the thing we're storytelling around, and something about ourselves as individuals or within our communities. Thinking about the what, why, where, when and how of leadership helps us to interrogate the many myths surrounding it as an idea and practice. Here are five of our favourite myths to start off with:

When we talk or think about leadership, we're focusing on elites – people at the top of the hierarchy, people who are extraordinary or superhuman, *individuals*. NO WE'RE NOT.

Leadership is rare. NO IT ISN'T.

Leadership is a good thing. NOT ALWAYS, IT ISN'T.

There is such a thing as a typical leader. NO THERE ISN'T.

Leadership exists and can be developed easily. IT MIGHT – BUT IT MIGHT NOT – AND IF IT CAN, WHY DOESN'T EVERYONE DO IT?

These might seem difficult things to question at the moment, at the start of a book or course module on leadership, but it can be fun to think in this way. Take your assumptions and prejudices, hold them up to the light, and see if you still believe them once you've read, thought, reflected, critiqued, engaged with whatever evidence and arguments there are – ground your existing thoughts about leadership in academic research and ideas, in short. Then we can think about leadership academically in a good way – then you'll be able to talk to anyone about leadership, using the grammar and vocabulary of leadership studies, and avoid sounding like someone who is just reproducing a set of unexamined prejudices, assumptions and common sense. (And hopefully you'll also avoid sounding pretentious or full of yourself, but we'll leave that to you.)

This brings us to our third area ...

Leadership studies

You're probably reading this book as a full- or part-time member of a business school community, as someone enrolled on an academic programme that involves thinking about management or organization theory. If you're a full-time business school-based student, you'll know about the bewildering variety of different subjects offered by academics – organization theory, organization studies, marketing of various kinds (consumer, strategic, business-to-business), operations management, supply chain management, public or non-profit management, tourism and leisure management, finance, accounting, all sorts of economics ... it's not an endless list, but it can seem like it.

The curious thing is, many of the theories and concepts that inform analysis of these different aspects of management and organization studies are identical. Take one of the key concepts in leadership studies, the idea of personality traits. You can find this in textbooks about human resource management (in the recruitment and selection chapter), or organizational behaviour (in the chapter on self or identity), or marketing (in the chapter on consumer behaviour) or economics (although economists won't always tell you that they're making assumptions about human behaviour), and of course in this book.

So why have a separate department, specific academics, degree programmes or course modules, and textbooks on leadership studies, if you already know the theory? And how should we think about leadership studies? Is it an academic discipline in its own right, a field of study, or a convenient way for business schools to suggest they're up to date and relevant, speaking to the interests of the most powerful people (in some ways) in organizations?

As with anything connected to higher education and universities, there's an element of organizational politics. Some academics want to lay claim to founding, developing or owning a particular field of study – and one of the best ways to do that is to construct a new one. Leadership studies is currently in the middle of a boom – new peer-reviewed journals (more on this below) have been started, more and more books are being published, programmes of study are appearing around the world and there is an increasing number of academic conferences dedicated to leadership.

The peer-reviewed journals are the most important development. They publish the most prestigious form of academic writing. It involves us writing a relatively short, usually 7000-word, paper or article about a topic, such as transformational leadership, either based on new data or as a review of previously published research. We then submit the paper to a journal, and work with the reviews/comments of three or more anonymous peer reviewers to improve it. Journals that do peer review are crucial to establishing the academic credibility of a research field and individuals. In principle, you can trust what you read in a peer-reviewed journal, because it's been read and approved by the wider research community – perhaps you could think of a journal paper as the direct opposite of a blog, where anyone writes whatever they want without any review. Peer-reviewed journal papers are usually very controlled pieces of writing, in multiple ways. They can also be really hard work to read, because of the language used, the conventions of academic writing and the complexity of the ideas or analysis. But some of them are good to read, and most of them are rewarding to engage with if you're interested in the subject. We want to encourage you to read them, to go beyond the textbook, because we spend a lot of time and energy writing them, and they are the source that this book is based on – so read some of them for yourself and see if you agree with our interpretations of them. Go on – stretch yourself.

However, as Brad Jackson and Ken Parry also argue in their book, leadership is a field of action and research, not a discipline in the way that (for example) psychology or sociology are. This is reflected in how leadership studies academics describe themselves – people working in psychology departments will introduce themselves as psychologists, just as people in sociology departments self-identify as sociologists. The same goes for chemists, physicists, anthropologists, organization theorists – but what of leadership studies? None of us would introduce ourselves at parties or to new friends as 'leaderists' or 'leadershipists'. We usually say we are academics with an interest or specialism in leadership.

So if leadership isn't a specific academic discipline with its own theories, how does it work? Within the broad boundaries of social science, we usually take a psychological or sociological perspective – then we become sociologists or psychologists of leadership. Perhaps in the future, there will be a separate faculty of leaderism, or leaderistry, that is as big and well established as biology or mathematics currently are – perhaps not. What's interesting to us here is that if you examine all of this research and educational activity closely, you won't find much that is distinctive to *leadership*. We research it using methods of data collection that are common in other social or natural science disciplines; we analyse the data by adapting concepts from other parts of the university, such as psychology, sociology, anthropology or sometimes the natural sciences; and we propose theories of leadership and leading that often echo the theories that we've drawn on.

Where does this leave us? And where does it leave you, as a keen student of leadership? After all, you've either bought this book or made the effort to go to a library to borrow it. As you'll see in all of the chapters to come, we think that leadership studies is defined by its focus on the idea of *leadership* and the practice of *leading*, and that those two things are quite specific. There may be a lot of debate as to what leadership is, or isn't, and an equal amount of disagreement about where and when we can say with confidence 'now *that's* leading' or 'she's *definitely* a leader', but we do have to agree to accept that leading and leadership are distinctive, interesting and worth thinking about in detail. That, for us, is leadership studies, and we believe it is important enough to put together a long book about it so that more interesting teaching and learning can happen.

These are our beginnings. Each of these principles inform this entire book, and, we believe, make it different from existing textbooks about leading, leadership or leadership studies.

The power of leaders and leadership studies

As you'll see as you read this book, the most important abstract term that we've used to organize this book is power. We think that the idea and practice of power is a key way to understand leadership as a position, as an act and as an academic subject. It's most obviously present in leader–follower relationships when a leader is persuading or coercing someone to do something they don't want to do, but it is also in the air that surrounds all other relationships (e.g. leader–leader, follower–follower) and actions that we see as leading (e.g. encouraging or legitimizing some personality traits and marginalizing others, shaping individual or organizational identities, trying to be charismatic). Despite this centrality, power is often neglected (perhaps by accident?) or ignored (because it's an uncomfortable subject?) in research and education about leaders, leadership and leading.

If we see leadership as a process of influencing the behaviour of other people – in formal organizational hierarchies for sure, but also across communities and networks where more informal approaches tend to be displayed – power is recognizable as the public and private face of influence and authority. Most academics researching and teaching in the social sciences recognize that although power is a short word we all think we understand, it is also one of the most complex *ideas* we have. Because of this, power can be talked about from a wide range of different perspectives; we each have our preferences based on our reading, thinking and researching, but this book is generally not prescriptive – we want to encourage you to consider what different perspectives can offer in relation to power and its implications for studying leaders and leadership. Overall, though, it'll be helpful to you to be familiar with what we think are the three most significant ways in which power and leadership can be explored, and to start thinking about how these are entwined in studies of leadership in organisations. The three key terms here, which indicate ways of understanding the issue of power, are:

- traditional;
- radical;
- post-structural.

Because you're either an undergraduate or a postgraduate, you're certainly familiar with what the first two terms mean in an academic setting; the third may be new to you. Here's a brief introduction to what they each mean in relation to power.

The earliest studies of leadership, which we are thinking of here when we write about the *traditional* perspective on power, define what they're researching and writing about as the ability of an individual to control or to influence others – most often to get someone to do something that they may not otherwise have done. This doesn't necessarily mean coercion, but it certainly implies persuasion and breaking down some sort of resistance. So, leadership can be defined as a possession, seen in a relationship that happens between leaders and followers (there are lots of examples of this way of thinking in another textbook, Northouse (2013)). In addition, from this perspective, effective leadership is usually said to be one of the best ways to achieve individual, team and organizational success. Over the last 20 years or so, this kind of leadership (and its associated perspective on power) has become more and more exalted, as academics, management consultants, journalists and power-full leaders themselves promote 'it', and sometimes themselves, as the means to cure all organizational ills. (On the other side of this 'leadership as panacea' coin, it can also be used to allocate blame for failures and disasters – so when something goes wrong we look to the leader to take responsibility and resign, even if what has happened was clearly outside their control. This is often referred to as finding the 'bad apple' in the barrel, ignoring the alternative possibilities that perhaps (a) the whole barrel of apples is rotten, or (b) there's a problem with the barrel as well as one or more of the apples.) Whether leaders are positioned as good or bad, there are clear links here between leadership in organizations and the use (or potential abuse) of a thing we call 'power'.

Writers who explore leadership and power in this traditional way usually turn to one of the most renowned academic studies of power in the social sciences, published in 1959 by two American psychologists, John French and Bertram Raven. In this short but incredibly influential piece of writing, they argue for five 'bases' of power: reward, coercive, referent, legitimate and expert. This model pops up in most business school textbooks, even though there has since been an enormous amount of theoretical and empirical debate about power, including specific challenges to French and Raven's ideas (see, just as one example, Podsahoff and Schriesheim's contribution to this debate in 1985). We want to note one thing here from this complex academic literature: use of this model of power is always leader-centric, as it offers legitimacy to the idea that the individual leader and the leadership role are the most significant things in the process of leading. This, as you can guess, in turn means that the needs, actions, thoughts and reactions of other characters in the relationship are mostly ignored, except as 'things to be managed'. (It's also very important to say here that the traditional approach to power is a theory that implies generalizability – in other words, people who believe in the traditional approach think that their theories are correct or true in all social or cultural contexts. We'll come back to this in a moment when we think about post-structural perspectives on power.)

The second perspective is best thought of as *radical*, in that it seeks to explore power as a political and moral issue – in other words, not just as a neutral *thing* people/leaders try to possess to get things done or that is visible in decision-making processes, but as a more multi-dimensional presence in our lives. British sociologist Steven Lukes introduced this term early in the 1970s (Lukes, 1974), and has since returned to it (Lukes, 2005). His key contribution to understanding power is usually described, at least to begin with, by the phrase 'three faces of power'. (Lukes was challenging theories that suggested power had only one or two 'dimensions', or faces.) A radical perspective, then, suggests power has traditionally been thought of in three ways:

as overtly exercised, clearly visible, with the aim of acknowledging and overcoming conflict.

This is, in some ways, the crudest form of traditional power. It is reliant on physical strength and intimidation or material threats such as dismissal, and is designed for one person to win everything and the other to lose everything. Alongside this we find the second dimension, where people think of power:

as covertly exercised, less visible or deliberately excluded from discussion so that potential conflicts are overlooked or ignored.

In organizations and workplaces, this is a very interesting way to think about power; companies that are managed in very political ways, rather than on the basis of merit, are the places where this form of power is most present. Status and success are based on willingness to do things in ways that are acceptable to those with status in the organization, often informally – it can be very frustrating because it's difficult to learn the rules, and some people are excluded simply because of, for example, gender or race. This kind of power is very present in the City of London's financial and banking institutions, as many researchers have argued in recent years. It also produces winners and losers, but usually not quite so clearly.

Lukes' final 'face' or way of thinking about power is:

as embedded within the structure, culture and processes of institutions. (2005)

This is the least visible manifestation of power, and therefore the most difficult to observe or even think about, in its exercise and effects – it's the kind of power we take for granted. Think for example about British society and culture, and the ways in which the British royal family exercise power. Members of that family have no formal position or power in, for example, political debates – and yet the current head of the family has to invite a politician to form a government following elections. If the invite doesn't happen, there is no government. (It always does, and there always is – but the point is that power is being exercised here.) Other members of the royal family occupy positions around the world that enable them to speak and influence countries, organizations and law-making. Finally, it is rare for a week to pass without a 'major news story' involving someone from the royal family or its extended branches in the British aristocracy – all contributing to your understanding of power and how it works if you live in the UK.

Lukes' three faces of power should encourage us to consider the ways in which leaders acquire, maintain and build their positions of leadership. So for example the first face of power, a more hierarchical 'command and control' approach, may be seen operating when leaders focus on the observable behaviours of 'their' teams and try to correct any deviations from the approach they have planned. Thinking about the second face of power, we can focus on non-observable behaviours and the scope for manipulation and other subtle forms of control – such that contentious issues do not even become part of the formal agenda at a meeting, for example. The third face of power involves an even less visible but extremely active shaping of individuals' perceptions, thoughts and preferences such that they are persuaded into believing that they have no alternative reality in which to function. Alternatives are, almost literally, un-thinkable.

So from a traditional perspective of power as a *possession* that an individual can acquire, we come to think of power as a much more complex *process* with multiple faces that is partially hidden by or within cultures or political systems (both of which are of course present in organizations large and small, as well as countries). Our third perspective comes from a more philosophical set of theories usually associated with the French academic Michel Foucault. Foucault worked as a philosopher and historian, mostly in France, but his influence on how we think about societies and organizations is now global. Foucault's writings are usually described as post-structural; his ideas are linked to Lukes' third face of institutionalized power, in which people (leaders) can sustain their dominance through *creating* and *shaping* the realities and norms for subordinates (followers) which reduces subordinates' resistance to these realities, or even denies the possibility of resisting. This perspective also emphasizes that individuals often monitor their own behaviour in a process of 'self-surveillance', as the rules and norms devised and imposed by others are accepted as how things are and must be. From this perspective, people must take a lot of responsibility for their enactment of power through everyday relations.

These ideas will recur throughout this book, sometimes obviously when a chapter is centrally concerned with power and its exercise, sometimes less obviously – but they are always there. However, we are always trying to bring power more consciously into dialogue with leadership to open up a series of thought-paths that rarely feature in either other leadership textbooks or contemporary academic research in the area: we're thinking about things like fairness, equity, justice, resistance, conflict, emancipation, oppression, rationality, politics, globalization, the natural environment and knowledge. The strength and complexity of power as an idea, as a way of thinking, has the capacity to challenge the 'comfort zone' that has been built around leadership through more neutral concepts such as influence, inspiration and values – these ideas are helpful in thinking about leadership, but they both romanticize and simplify leadership-related knowledge and practice. Put simply, bringing power into the leadership equation helps us 'get real' in terms of the interdependent, messy, paradoxical and partial ways that leading and following are practised in and around organizations. If we can understand how power (and, just as importantly, lack of power or powerlessness) operates in the landscape of leadership, we can start to develop insights that have the potential to shape how we develop and practise leadership. This in turn enables us, and you, to pay more attention to the relational and contextual dynamics that leading and following are embedded in and opens up new strategies for learning and for living or working with those who both lead and follow.

But this is taking us into too much detail for an introductory chapter. Let's just say *power is at the centre of leadership* and leave it at that for the moment.

The power of authorship

These ideas also bring us neatly to the question of who we are to write this book – from our position of power, we need to help locate the text you're being presented with. We think this is important in two ways. First, you need to be able to see how and why we come to be in the position of author-ity that we are. This is partly an academic assessment, of us persuading you that we can be trusted as guides to the field of leadership studies. Second, however, it is also so that you can look a little more deeply into our motives – why we are writing this book and what that means for our representation of three aspects of the idea of what it is to lead. So, here we are.

Brigid Carroll completed her first degree in English Literature and History and then went straight into a master's degree programme, also in English. During that she discovered literary theory and became caught up in the ways we can think about thinking. She completed a diploma in Secondary Education and went off to teach 13–17-year-olds English – and loved it. There's something about trying to hook young people into learning that can create a real vitality and Brigid discovered that. Teaching at secondary level involves coaching sport, doing backstage work for school productions, leading outdoor education camps and becoming part of young lives. It's full on.

After a stint of running an English department, Brigid went off to New York to do an MBA. During that MBA a professor passed her an article on literary analysis and organizations. Brigid didn't know you could put the two together; in that moment a PhD was born. On return to New Zealand Brigid embarked on that PhD, focusing on professional work, identity and narrative. Funnily enough leadership isn't in that thesis, although while writing it Brigid started teaching leadership. That's an amazing experience as it connects in multiple ways to who people think they are, what impact they want to make and how they relate to others.

Shortly after completing her PhD the New Zealand Leadership Institute was established at the University of Auckland Business School. She is now an Associate Professor of Organization Studies in the Department of Management and International Business and Director of Research at the New

Zealand Leadership Institute, both at the University of Auckland, and lead facilitates across a number of programmes, especially those that work with professional and knowledge-based organizations. Her research centres on leadership and its development, particularly with reference to practice, identity and discourse. She is part of this book because she believes you have to grapple with leadership, get your hands on it and work it hard, so that it loses what can be a romantic veneer and gets to a real place.

Jackie Ford completed a first degree in Business Studies and French and embarked on her first career in personnel management in the early 1980s. That culminated in the late 1980s as a board-level director position in human resources in a large British National Health Service organization. During this time, Jackie also graduated with a Chartered Institute of Personnel and Development qualification and completed a part-time master's degree in Law and Employment Relations.

Following these studies, the lure of academe in the early 1990s was strong and when the opportunity emerged to direct the first master's programme in leadership in the UK, at the University of Leeds Nuffield Institute for Health, she leapt at the prospect. Her second career started in 1993; her subsequent part-time PhD research explored questions of leadership, gender, power and identity for managers and organizational leaders.

So Jackie's PhD examined new ways of researching, conceptualizing and practising leadership in organizations. These interests continue to inform her research as Professor of Leadership and Organization Studies at the University of Bradford, notably through further development of critical, post-structural and psychosocial research methods and approaches that help to make sense of the experiences of working and organizational lives. She has written and lectured widely on this topic and thinks that this book will enable us collectively to say something new and more critical about the topic.

Scott Taylor did an undergraduate degree at the University of Glasgow in the Faculty of Arts in the 1980s. He left Scotland in 1990 to work in mainland Europe for seven years, then moved to England to study human resource management at the University of Bolton, going from that degree programme to the PhD programme at Manchester Metropolitan University, which he graduated from in 2001. He currently works at the University of Birmingham as a Reader in Leadership and Organization Studies.

That apparently rational process was really a series of accidents and influences. However, it's resulted in doing a job he likes, for a couple of key reasons. First, he wants to understand why the workplaces he's been in for more than 20 years are so strange – odd rules, weird behaviours, apparently rational people doing irrational things. University business schools are the best place to do that. Second, he likes reading, thinking and talking about research evidence and ideas. Universities are the only workplaces he knows of where those things are encouraged.

Leadership studies also happened to him by accident more than design. After working at Open, Birmingham and Essex universities he was offered a job in 2008 at the Centre for Leadership Studies, University of Exeter Business School. He had written and lectured a little about leadership, and thought it would be good to do more of that, maybe to balance his long-standing preference for thinking about the people who are led and managed. That brought him to an emerging approach to researching leadership called 'critical leadership studies', which he's now using to analyse charisma. He's involved in this book because he thinks it's an interesting project and that there is something different to be said about leadership.

We hope you enjoy the rest of the book, and learn with it.

PART I

Classical Theories of Leadership

Contents

I

LEADERSHIP, MANAGEMENT AND HEADSHIP

POWER, EMOTION AND AUTHORITY IN ORGANIZATIONS

Donna Ladkin

A musician and philosopher by background, Donna's research into the aesthetics of leadership and organizations combines these orientations to question and refresh well-worn assumptions within leadership studies. In this chapter she brings philosophical precision to unravelling the dynamics at play within key organizational relations.

What this chapter is all about ...

The main idea is that leadership, management and headship are not necessarily synonyms – they highlight different kinds of influence, authority and power.

The key questions this chapter answers are:

- How are leadership, management and headship different, and why is that important?
- What kinds of power are related to each?
- How is leadership related to hierarchy and authority?

Introduction

The difference between management and leadership has been debated by scholars as well as practitioners over the last 50 years. Indeed, many leadership development courses open with participants reeling off the differences between the two, a list that often looks something like the one shown in Table 1.1. Such a discussion often ends with the flourish of: 'management is about doing things right', whereas 'leadership is about doing the right things'!

Table 1.1   Typically cited differences between 'management' and 'leadership'

Management	Leadership
Planning	Vision
Monitoring	Influencing
Controlling	Inspiring
Co-ordinating	Guiding
Communicating	Being a figurehead
Rational	Emotional
Expertise important	Trust important

Rather than formulating the definitive distinction between these two activities, this chapter enquires into questions lurking beneath the preoccupation with the difference between them, such as:

- Why might it be important to separate them conceptually?
- Does each have a unique purpose?
- Are there times when it is appropriate to lead rather than manage or manage rather than lead?
- How is it possible to decide which activity better suits the context?

There are broader questions to ponder too, such as:

- Where has each arisen within the organizational field more broadly?
- What accounts for the current near obsession with leadership?
- Is it permissible in today's twenty-first-century organizational context to be a mere manager, rather than a 'leader'?

Additionally, the chapter introduces a third concept in order to add further sophistication (or confusion!) to the discussion: that of 'headship'. In brief, 'headship' refers to the situation in which an individual occupies the hierarchical 'head' of their organization, team or group. The chapter will elaborate on this term in more detail in the pages to come, but for now it's fine to know it's waiting in the wings.

Why are these distinctions important?

From the academic viewpoint definitional clarity (that is, being clear about what a term means and how you are using it) is a critical aspect of knowledge. Agreement about what a term means provides precision about how it can be investigated. Scholars working in different contexts can have some sense of surety that they are, indeed, studying the same phenomenon once the academic community agrees on such definitions. This may seem obvious but once you begin to think about concepts critically, you will quickly discover that some of the most important concepts that we take for granted are very difficult to define exactly. For instance, think of concepts such as 'love' or 'justice', or even 'truthfulness' or 'beauty'. Certainly agreeing on definitions for material objects, such as toothpicks or lawn mowers, might be easier but even concrete 'things' can be tricky to define without question (for instance, is a tomato a fruit or a vegetable?). When research is being conducted into a particular phenomenon it is essential that there is a fundamental understanding of what that phenomenon is – or how it is being constructed for the purposes of the research. From a scholarly perspective, then, being clear about the distinctions between concepts such as 'management' and 'leadership' is an essential aspect of theory development.

STOP AND REFLECT 1.1

As a starting activity, reflect on your own experience of being led or being managed in organizations. To what extent have you observed others moving between what you experience as 'management' and what you experience as 'leadership'? In your experience are there contexts in which it is more appropriate to 'manage' rather than to 'lead'? What distinguishes those contexts? In an organization that you have been familiar with, is there more emphasis on 'leading' or 'managing'? Why might that be?

From a practical point of view, when working in organizations it can be helpful to perceive the range of behaviours available within any particular circumstance. Merely understanding that 'managing' and 'leading' can be conceived as different activities is useful when attempting to find effective responses to organizational issues. Adding the concept of 'headship' to the mix affords yet another way of thinking about organizational roles and the expectations that accompany them. From a practitioner's viewpoint, then, an awareness of these three different modes of operating increases the level of choice available in responding to different organizational demands. Of course, having more choices may not always seem like a good thing! However, another aim of this chapter is to reveal some of the underlying dynamics to be considered when trying to discern which activity might be best suited to a specific circumstance. In this way the suitability of either depends upon the particular situation, and indeed the choice to 'lead', 'manage' or 'head' could be seen as 'contingent' on a range of factors, a notion that will be explored in greater depth in Chapter 3, which examines *contingency theory*.

This chapter is set out as follows. First, the historic development of the terms 'management' and 'leadership' will be charted, in order to better understand the purposes each activity was originally intended to fulfil. The next section considers how a number of key scholars have distinguished between the two terms. The concept of 'headship' is introduced, which leads into a discussion of power and how it operates within each of the three concepts. This opens into a broader discussion of the emotional and psychological implications of manager and leader relations with subordinates or followers, respectively. The chapter ends by inviting you to apply what you have learned to the case study of Natalie Chan, a manager within a public sector organization who is grappling with the demands of being promoted from a middle-manager role to that of a senior role in which she is expected to display 'leadership'. Natalie is a fictional character, but the difficulties she faces are a compilation of actual issues that coaching clients with whom I have worked have faced. Her story aims to bring to life the ideas offered by the chapter in a way which will help you relate to them and to your own study and practice of managing and leading.

Before launching into the historic development of the concepts of 'manager' and 'leader', you are invited to take a moment to reflect on your understandings of these terms and where this understanding has come from.

STOP AND REFLECT 1.2

As a starting activity, write your own definitions of 'management' and 'leadership'. Based on the brief description above, you are also invited to put into your own words your starting idea about what 'headship' is.

- My definition of management is:
- My definition of leadership is:
- My definition of headship is:

Perhaps more importantly – can you write something about where your ideas about these concepts come from?

Historic underpinnings

For the purposes of this textbook, management and leadership will be explored as they have been researched and theorized within the larger domain of *organization theory* (OT). It is important to clarify this point because leadership, particularly, has been theorized by a range of subject disciplines including philosophy, history and politics as well as from the OT domain. OT is an umbrella term used for distinguishing the body of research which has been developed in response to the rise of commercially focused organizations, particularly in the aftermath of the Industrial Revolution. Certainly, prior to the Industrial Revolution people had worked together in large organizations – most notably in the military, Churches and government – but in the wake of the Industrial Revolution there were new problems of organizing to be solved.

DEFINITION: ORGANIZATION THEORY

Organization theory (OT) refers to a broad range of different theories concerning organizations and how they have come to be. They include theories about how organizations are structured, how they change and how people work within them, as well as about the very nature of 'organizing' itself and the political, cultural and technical systems which interact with them. There are many 'organization theory' textbooks, but for a thorough account of the history of OT itself, see William Starbuck's chapter in the *Oxford Handbook of Organization Theory* published in 2003.

New organizational forms and the need for managers

Within organizations striving for replicability of quality and efficiency of production new questions arose about how to best structure and coordinate production. Concurrently, the rise of the new social science disciplines of psychology and sociology brought new languages and perspectives about how to meet these challenges. In fact, one of the grandparents of OT, William Starbuck (2003), suggests that it was through the intersection of industrial progress and scholarly interest that the term 'organization' itself was born, as prior to this intersection the activity of people working together in the pursuit of particular purposes was still conceived as the verb 'organizing'.

With the increase in complexity of operations, as well as the growing number of people working within industrial settings, new roles were required. Bureaucratic forms of organizing created the need for an entirely new class of organizational member beyond that of 'owner', 'worker' or 'overseer', namely the 'manager'. The word 'manager' has French and Italian roots, with the Italian *maneggiare* literally coming from the Italian word for 'hand', *manus* (Skeat, 1995, p. 358). A literal rendering thus equates the words 'to manage' and 'to handle' (and in its original sense was used particularly in regard to the handling of horses!). The need for managers of people, rather than horses, arose from the structures predominant in these new organizations. Put most simplistically, with goods no longer produced as 'wholes' but separated and created in component parts, someone was needed to co-ordinate and monitor production activities (see *Fordism* below).

DEFINITION: FORDISM

One of the innovations in production processes central to the success of the Industrial Revolution is known as 'Fordism', for its genesis in the car factories of Henry Ford. Three key elements underpin this approach to manufacturing:

- standardization, with all outputs made by machines rather than being hand-crafted;
- the use of specialized machines to make such standardization possible;
- workers were paid enough so that they could afford the products they were making.

Along with these key aspects, what was particularly special about Henry Ford's factories was that within them complex tasks were broken down into simple ones, thereby bringing high levels of efficiency to the manufacturing process. For more information about Fordism, see Tolliday and Zeitland (1987) or Jessop (1992).

Many of the early studies into what management is or should be identified key aspects of the role. One of the first theorists to focus on these roles was the French engineer Henri Fayol who developed his ideas through working in a French coal mine. He identified six roles managers needed to perform: forecasting, organizing, planning, communicating, co-ordinating and controlling (Fayol, 1949). His 'administrative' approach to managing differed from the 'scientific' approach to management being championed by Frederick Taylor in the United States, which focused primarily on optimizing worker outputs through tight managerial control (Taylor, 1911). Taylor's work spawned a raft of studies which sought to identify and measure variables that would determine the optimal relationships between managers and those they managed. For instance, research was conducted into questions such as:

- What is the optimal 'span of control' of a manager; that is, what is the largest number of direct reports a manager can have and still operate well? (Keren and Levhari, 1979)
- Given an organization's purpose, what is its optimal size? (Williamson, 1971)
- What is the best organizational structure in terms of reporting relationships given an organization's purpose? (Galbraith, 1971)

Scientific management itself fell out of fashion in the 1920s, but many of its precepts still survive today. It was not until Henry Mintzberg's (1973) more qualitative ethnographically based study of managers-in-action that a different view of 'what managers do' began to emerge. In his original PhD study of five male managers working in the USA, Mintzberg discovered that rather than being 'in control of their own destinies' as well as that of their organizations, managers' work was fragmented, iterative and largely a product of happenstance. He identified three areas of their attention – interpersonal, informational and decisional – but these happened in response to environmental factors, rather than being planned.

More recently, the UK-based management theorist Martin Parker has provided an auto-ethnographic account of his process of 'becoming a manager' in taking up the head of department role within his university. In his aptly named article 'Becoming a manager, or: the werewolf looks anxiously in the mirror, checking for unusual facial hair' (2004), Parker echoes Mintzberg's findings by charting a reality which is far removed from the neat 'categories' offered by Fayol's work or the technical precision suggested by Taylor's. In particular, he notes the level of interruption that is endemic to the role, and poignantly likens his handling of issues to that of being both a 'waste bin and King Solomon' (2004, p. 48). Both from Mintzberg's study and Parker's 'insider' account, managing appears not to be the scientifically determined activity many previous studies suggested.

This realization paved the way for an entirely new approach to studying managers and the work that they do within organizations, from looking at managing as an 'improvisational activity' (Weick, 1998) to considering its similarity to 'riding white water' (Vaill, 1991). However, even though the way managing happens varies (either as a linear, agentic activity or a more responsive, iterative one), the purpose of managing is largely the same; enabling the productive aspects of the organization to co-ordinate their functions as effectively as possible, and to monitor outcomes of those processes. Let's leave the story of managing as an organizational activity momentarily and consider the historical development of the concept 'leadership'.

A brief history of leadership as an idea

A common starting place for considering 'leadership' is the work of the Greek philosopher Plato. Plato never uses an equivalent Greek word for 'leader' but in his book *The Republic* he writes about the role and duty of the 'Philosopher King', a figure often seen as analogous to common conceptions of 'leader' (Plato, 1941). The classical origin of leadership theorization points to a critical difference between 'management' and 'leadership' from the very start; as theorized human activities, they have their genesis in different socio-historic requirements. From as long ago as when people first began working together, there seems to have been the recognition of a 'leader' role. They are the men and women to whom others look for direction and guidance or, alternatively, those who sought to dominate others. Interestingly, leaders operate within other non-human communities as well: canines recognize 'pack leaders', herding animals follow 'alpha males or females' and even bees respond to the direction of their Queen. Managers, however, seem absent from other species within the animal kingdom apart from *homo sapiens*.

The purpose that leadership serves, then, can be seen in its very origins: for providing guidance and safety for followers especially in times of uncertainty or change. Leaders are an emblem of social structuring and serve symbolic and emotional purposes that managing does not. The American leadership scholar Eva Kort (2008) characterizes leading as a 'plural action' in which followers give their endorsement to a leader's decisions or direction and follow them from this sense of endorsement. In this way, leading involves an unconscious or conscious contract between individuals who agree, either in the longer term or for the fleeting moment, to be in a particular psychological and emotional bond with one another. These ideas will be explored in more detail later in this chapter.

Management theorists have identified the role 'leading' plays within management. Most notably, Mintzberg (1973) highlights leadership as a key interpersonal role inherent to managing. This inclusion of 'leading' within 'managing' can be seen in much of the academic writing concerning managing right through into the 1980s. Until that time 'managing' was in vogue within the corporate landscape and executives attended 'general management development' programmes to further their careers.

In the late 1980s and moving into the 1990s 'management' as a central activity of those working within organizations went out of fashion. This may have been influenced by the notion that management *per se* was 'disappearing' (Grey, 1999). That is to say those tasks often assumed to be the provenance of managers were increasingly being enacted by people throughout organizations. Aligned with this shift, bookshelves began to be populated by an increasing number of texts with 'leadership' or 'leading' in their titles. One way of explaining this sudden explosion in leadership literature is offered by Gemmil and Oakley (1997) who suggest that it accompanied a cultural move, headed by the United States, into the increasing valorisation of the individual. Rather than recognizing the collective achievement of all of those engaged in organizations, attention was concentrated on the 'hero managerial leader'. People like Jack Welch and Lee Iacocca became celebrity organizational figureheads who were ascribed enormous powers of agency in turning ailing companies around or exploiting new markets.

'Leadership development' as an industry in the USA and the UK in particular burgeoned into a huge market and a recurring mantra underpinning such programmes is the notion that 'anyone can be a leader'. In fact, to solve the many difficulties now facing organizations in the uncertain and often chaotic commercial and societal contexts in which they are embedded, the message conveyed is often that everyone *has* to be a leader. Organizations themselves are required to be 'leader-ful' (Raelin, 2011) and the mere title of 'manager' is no longer fashionable.

The interest in 'leadership' shows little sign of abating. In fact, the fascination with national leaders such as President Barack Obama (and why he can't fix the US economy) or Prime Minister David Cameron (and why he can't fix the UK's ailing National Health Service) or Chancellor Angela Merkel (and why she can't fix the Greek, Spanish and Italian economies) is as healthy as ever. Does this interest say more about our own particular *socio-historic moment* than about the concepts of managing and leading themselves? To consider that question, the next section explores different theoretical constructions of 'management' and 'leadership'.

DEFINITION: SOCIO-HISTORIC MOMENT

The term 'socio-historic moment' refers to the way in which society and its taken-for-granted assumptions about the 'way things are' at a given point in time interweaves with a particular time in history to create a more-or-less socially accepted way of understanding the world. For instance, within the socio-historic moment of the 1800s, the enslavement of Africans for economic prosperity within Western Europe and the Americas was considered acceptable by many governments at that time. However, within our current socio-historic moment, the enslavement of other human beings is considered wrong. The act is still the same, but it is interpreted differently through different socio-historic perspectives.

Theories about the difference between management and leadership

The management scholar Abraham Zaleznik's 1977 *Harvard Business Review* article 'Managers and leaders: Are they different?' serves as the starting point for discussing the theorized differences between 'leaders' and 'managers'. This article provoked a good deal of discussion among management scholars at the time who were primarily concerned with issues of control and efficiency rather than 'vision' and breaking, rather than enforcing rules. Zaleznik's piece disturbed the prevailing orthodoxy by suggesting that an over-reliance on control could even lead to stagnation and organizational decline.

Three aspects of the article are important to note for those interested in leadership from either a practical or theoretical orientation:

- Zaleznik identifies leaders and managers as types of people, rather than as types of activities. According to him, whether one is a 'manager' or a 'leader' results from personality characteristics and may be influenced by social and family factors during childhood and adolescence. There is nothing mentioned about the role context plays in the process.
- Followers are not identified as a key part of how either leadership or management happens.
- An underlying theme of the article concerns how leaders might be developed, particularly given his belief in the role personality plays in determining whether or not one is leader or manager.

Zaleznik first lays out the essential differences between what leaders and managers do, and the attitudes that underlie these differences. For him, managers 'embrace process, seek stability and control, and instinctively try to resolve problems quickly – sometimes before they fully understand a problem's significance' (1977, p. 74). Furthermore, he asserts: 'It takes neither genius nor heroism to be a manager, but rather persistence, tough mindedness, hard work, intelligence, analytical ability, and perhaps most important, tolerance and goodwill' (1977, p. 75).

Leaders, on the other hand, tolerate, if not enjoy, chaos. They prefer a lack of structure and leaving situations open longer in order to understand them fully before acting. They are essentially creative people who do not like being hemmed in by rules. Zaleznik (1977) elaborates on the differences between leaders and managers by considering four key areas in which their attitudes differ. These are summarized below:

Relationship to goals: Zaleznik suggests that managers maintain an impersonal relationship to goals in which they arise from necessity, rather than from their own intrinsic importance. In contrast, leaders engage fully with goals and are personally motivated to achieve them. This attachment to goals is also part of what can help inspire others to work with leaders to achieve those goals.

Conception of work: For managers, work presents the opportunity for people to act together to establish strategies for achieving targets and then deliver on them. Managing is about limiting choices, deciding on the 'right' way forward through rational means and then pursuing that direction in an efficient way. Leaders, on the other hand, see work as an opportunity to expand their desires. They tend to like to take high-risk positions and, rather than reduce options, prefer to multiply them.

Orientation towards others: Managers tend to like to work with others; in fact Zaleznik goes as far as to suggest that managers can sometimes feel anxious when left to their own devices. They like to achieve tasks with the help of others. Leaders, on the other hand, are often most happy in their own company. They prefer to rely on their own resources and tend to be loners.

Life orientation: Zaleznik suggests that individuals are either 'once born' or 'twice born'. Individuals who are 'once born' have led a life of relative safety leading to inner contentment. These people expect to manoeuvre easily through life and happily fall into 'manager' roles. Those who are 'twice born' experience particular moments of knowing, often provoked through hardship, when they realize something essential about themselves and their life's 'mission'. Leaders, Zaleznik argues, are often 'twice born'.

In the wake of Zaleznik's article a number of other scholars explored the question of the differences between managers and leaders. One of the most often cited of these is John Kotter and his *Harvard Business Review* article 'What leaders really do', published in 1990. Kotter's work echoed Zaleznik's ideas in many ways. One of the key differences between the articles is that Kotter focuses rather less on the inherent personality traits of managers and leaders and instead highlights the purpose each serves. Specifically, Kotter argues that managers 'maintain control, while leaders take charge of 'change'. Both are required in order for organizations to flourish' (Kotter, 1990).

The change in orientation from leaders' and managers' personalities to the purpose they serve is also apparent in the work of the next two theoretical perspectives introduced here. The first, offered by the British leadership scholar Keith Grint, takes a *social constructionist* perspective in inquiring into the differences between managing and leading.

DEFINITION: SOCIAL CONSTRUCTIONISM

'Social constructionism' refers to an ontological stance in which the nature of reality is understood to be 'constructed' by social actors rather than 'given'. In opposition to those who adopt a more 'realist' ontological stance in which reality is seen to be determined prior to the individual's engagement with it (and the point of scientific discovery is to 'uncover its truth'), those who adopt a social constructionist perspective believe that together we create our understanding of how the world works. Thus in some cultures it is polite when eating together to make minimal noise, whereas in others, for instance, to smack one's lips and eat noisily is to demonstrate appreciation to the cook. Neither is an objectively 'right' response, as they are both constructed by the cultures in which these behaviours are enacted.

In Keith Grint's article 'Problems, problems, problems: The social construction of "leadership"' (2005b), he develops the argument that events which catalyse a 'command', 'managerial' or 'leadership' response are themselves 'constructed' rather than predetermined to be one or the other. For instance, in framing the 9/11 attack on the USA as a 'crisis' situation, George W. Bush's response was to 'declare war' on perpetrators of that attack. Had the event been constructed as a 'wicked' problem, however, a different response would have been more appropriate; one in which questions would have been asked before bombs dropped.

The key point of Grint's paper, which is described in more detail below, is that the appropriateness of a given response to an incident is determined by the way in which the incident is constructed, rather than through an objectively determined 'reality' discernment.

In his article, 'Problems, problems, problems: The social construction of "leadership"' (2005b), Grint draws from the earlier work of Rittell and Webber (1973) to identify three different kinds of problems faced by individuals in organizational (and indeed other) human contexts. First, there are those problems labelled as 'tame'. These are issues that can be complicated but ultimately they are resolvable. For instance, organizing baggage handling at a large international airport can be difficult – and baggage handlers going on strike can increase this level of complication. However, sorting the growing mountains of luggage is essentially a resolvable issue; a process for dealing with the baggage has to be implemented. In cases like these which are essentially process-driven, management provides an appropriate response.

'Wicked' problems, on the other hand, are complex. They are 'intractable' problems which are multi-layered and not solvable through linear means. More often than not, 'solutions' to wicked problems create other problems. The problem of locating and bringing to justice those responsible for the September 11 attacks in the United States could be classified as a 'wicked problem'. In that case, one of the 'solutions' used – that of detaining potential terrorists on Guantanamo Bay – has proved to create myriad other problems, most notably how to subsequently close down the detainment centre. Grint argues that 'leadership' is the correct response to such wicked problems and the prime activity of leaders in such circumstances is to ask the right questions.

The third type of problem Grint discusses is labelled 'critical'. Situations of crisis in which the needed response is self-evident are considered 'critical'. For instance, if a fire breaks out in a crowded building, the fitting response is to evacuate as quickly as possible. In such cases, it is appropriate to wield the authoritarian power associated with 'command'. Critical problems and their associated requirement for 'command' hint at the term 'headship' which will be discussed in the next section of this chapter. For now, however, the important point to remember is that when in a situation calling for 'command', the prime activity for those taking charge is to provide the right answers.

A central message within the article is that problems can be 'constructed' as 'tame', 'wicked' or 'critical' – that is, situations do not fit into a category in any pre-determined way. However, constructing a problem as one thing or another governs whether the appropriate response is management, leadership or command. In this way, Grint moves beyond characterizing these activities as associated with individual personalities and provides a more sophisticated rendering of the kinds of 'change' associated with each.

Ronald Heifetz and Donald Laurie offer another account of the difference between managing and leading but this time do so from the perspective of leaders' followers or managers' subordinates in their 1997 *Harvard Business Review* article. In common with much of what has previously been covered here, Heifetz and Laurie also regard planning, co-ordinating and monitoring as core managerial activities. Leading, on the other hand, they see as an adaptive process. That is, the work of leadership in their view is to enable organizations to adapt to the requirements of changing contexts.

This alignment of 'leadership' and change echoes the work of John Kotter mentioned previously. However, what is distinctive about Heifetz and Laurie's work is their attention to the needs of followers within the leadership relationship. Coming from a *psychoanalytic* background, they highlight the emotional response in the form of anxiety which often accompanies organizational change initiatives. Because of this, they argue that a prime activity for leaders involves providing a 'containing environment' in which followers can deal with and work through feelings of anxiety and fear as they undergo periods of change. The leader is called to 'take a balcony view' in surveying the changing situation, rather than being single-minded about implementing a chosen 'vision'. They are also urged not to shield followers from the truth of the difficulties associated with a changing landscape but to provide a safe space in which followers can explore their feelings, accept them and then move on with the changes required. In this way then, in Heifetz and Laurie's work, the job of the leader is essentially about relating to followers in a way that enables them to do the work required in a changing and uncertain environment. Their work signals the need for 'emotional intelligence' within the leadership domain, a concept which gained popularity with the work of Eric Goldman in the 1990s (Goldman, 1996).

STOP AND REFLECT 1.3

What are the similarities you notice between these different renditions of 'leading' and 'managing'? What are the ways in which they differ? How do you account for these differences? (You may want to consider the time period in which each theory was written, as well as the backgrounds of the authors in reflecting on this question.)

DEFINITION: PSYCHOANALYTIC APPROACH

The term 'psychoanalytic' refers to the understanding that human behaviour is influenced not only by 'present moment', rational understanding, but is also subject to past interpretations and deep-seated emotional responses to situations which may be interpreted to be similar to those in the here and now. For instance, a follower who has experienced a difficult relationship with their father or other authority figures in their early years may unconsciously expect similar difficulties to arise with other authority figures.

'Anxiety' can often arise through situations that resemble previously disturbing incidents, whether or not a current 'cause' for anxiety exists. This unconscious response can be especially present within leader–follower relations, in which individuals may 'act out' their unresolved (and often hurtful) experiences of being within authority relations. For more information on psychoanalytic approaches within leadership, see the work of Kets de Vries (1998) or more recently Cluley (2012).

This chapter has offered four similar but distinctive 'takes' on the differences between 'managing' and 'leading'. Before the summary of some of the key points below, take a moment to reflect on your own learning so far.

Synopsis of key ideas

It is interesting to note that among the four perspectives covered here there seems to be more consensus around the concept of managing than that of leading. Generally, managing involves those activities necessary for maintaining and monitoring an organization's steady state. When problems arise, it is the manager's job to implement processes that fix them. The nature of the problems for which management is the correct response is that they are 'tame' and have been seen before.

Perhaps one of the reasons for the variances in these authors' take on leadership is that each seems to focus on a different aspect of the 'leadership' dynamic. Zaleznik attends to the personal attributes of leaders and the psychological and developmental factors responsible for these attributes. A sociologist by background, Grint focuses on the role of social construction in the framing of a situation itself and, in this way, points to issues of context that impact on what is considered a situation requiring 'leadership'. Heifetz and Laurie agree that leadership is required in order to adapt to uncertain changing circumstances but suggest that in order to achieve its goal of navigating such territory, the person taking the leader role must provide a certain quality of engagement with their followers. In comparison with this, within Zaleznik's writings followers are not even mentioned!

Absent from all of these accounts, however, is any attention to the structure of the organizations in which either managing or leading is enacted. Those structures, and particularly the way in which they place individuals within certain hierarchical relationships, are implicated in an important dynamic that underpins leader–follower as well as manager–subordinate relationships: power.

The next section explores this dynamic, first by considering the interplay of role and position within organizational hierarchies and what this means for leadership and management. In doing so, it introduces a new term, 'headship' as a further way of describing interactional roles within organizations.

Leadership and 'headship'

So far the discussion of leadership and management has neglected the role organizational structures and hierarchies play in their enactment. Perhaps there is an inherent assumption that 'leaders' are situated at the top of organizational hierarchies but this is certainly not the case. In fact there is a large and growing literature considering how leadership can be shared (Pearce and Conger, 2002), distributed throughout the organization (Gronn, 2000) or emergent (Kickul and Neuman 2000). As an activity that is defined through influence, people can influence one another wherever they are located in organizations (see, for instance, Joe Raelin's (2011) work on 'leader-ful' organizations). However, there is also an assumption about the responsibilities and duties associated with those located at senior levels of an organization's hierarchy.

In order to move forward with this argument, let's take a step back to consider another way of looking at the difference between management and leadership. The American-based leadership scholar Eva Kort uses philosophical logic to determine her definition for leadership (Kort, 2008). The notion of 'plural action' is central to her thinking, which opens out the leadership territory to include not just the proclivities of the leader but the fact that leadership is only apparent through the joint actions of individuals working together. Starting from this assumption, she considers the kinds of purposeful actions undertaken by collections of human beings through which either leadership or management occurs. In particular, she argues that leadership arises from situations calling for 'joint plural action', in which those who take part do so with the intention and desire to co-operate. In such situations, she identifies the 'leader' as the individual who,

> in the course of an ethically neutral or positive cooperative intentional joint plural action or series of actions, makes good decisions and suggestions thereby worthy of endorsement that are endorsed by others and by which, therefore, they are influenced in their doings in the course of the action so that the action is performed (overall) successfully. (Kort, 2008, p. 423)

A number of aspects of her definition are worth reflecting on. First, the type of joint plural action is not one that happens merely through co-ordination. She describes how a building crew who are creating a house may be engaged in 'joint plural action', but the manager who tells the plumber to do her work one day or the joiner to arrive on another is merely co-ordinating, and does not need the endorsement of the workers – they arrive and do their job as part of an original agreement to do so. Their involvement is in the interests of efficiency and receiving their payment in a timely fashion. Leadership, in contrast, requires 'endorsement' from followers in a qualitatively different way from that used when people merely decide to co-operate towards the achievement of a pre-agreed goal. Followers need to actively support and act in accordance with that support for leadership to happen in Kort's terms.

This leads us to the dynamics attendant to those occupying positions of seniority in organizational hierarchies. Kort notices that those who sit in such positions are often called 'leaders' but she challenges the use of this term. She argues that in holding a position of authority, one is (merely) 'well placed or has responsibilities to contribute to plural action in the way that leaders do' (2008, p. 419). However, merely holding a position of authority does not make the position holder automatically a 'leader'. It is more accurate, she suggests, to call such a person the 'head' of the organization, team or group of individuals.

Holding the 'head' position of authority generally bestows power which enables those holding such posts to direct or order others to do things. However, exercising the sort of coercive power associated with being someone's boss, and therefore having the power to fire them or provide them with resources, is not adequate to being a 'leader' in Kort's terms. She cites the extreme examples of prisoners of war and slaves to make her point. Prisoners of war or slaves indeed perform those tasks required of them by those in charge, but do not enter into these actions with the kind of endorsement required in the relationship between leaders and followers 'proper'. It's worth quoting her directly here, because of the sense conveyed by her own words in making this point: 'In both cases (of slaves or prisoners) what is done does not reflect an intention the source of which is an endorsement of the direction given … and cannot be cases of leadership' (2008, p. 419). In other words, followers have to freely endorse the influence leaders assert on them in order for 'proper' leadership relations to occur.

Kort does not dismiss the importance of the co-ordinating roles of managers, and certainly the authority that accompanies certain organizational roles and positions is a vital ingredient to how organizational tasks are achieved. However, she suggests that it is important to distinguish between the authority available to individuals through the organizational positions they hold (let us call this positional authority) and leadership proper, which can occur at any level in the organization.

One of the most important distinguishing features between leadership and headship is that headship is organizationally ordained. That is, decision-makers within the organization authorized to do so choose who will hold particular posts, including who will be at the head of the organization. In that way, the endorsement, to use Kort's terms, comes from the organization, rather than from followers. Any authority to act and influence is held within the organization's bounds. It is also important to note that since power is given to 'heads' by even more senior authorities within it, it is those, more senior people to whom heads are responsible. One implication of this is that an individual can be the 'head' of an organization without being in any way supported or endorsed by the followers. (Heads who find themselves in such a position, however, will have a fairly difficult time!)

'Headship' and 'leadership' are often conceptually amalgamated. However, it can be helpful to disentangle them because there are different roles and expectations associated with each one. Most importantly, headship is organizationally conferred and endorsed, whereas in order to operate, leadership requires the endorsement of followers. The way in which heads influence their subordinates is often through their use of legitimate positional power. Interestingly, Kort suggests that leaders do not use 'power' to gain the endorsement leading requires (2008, p. 420). I will take issue with that assertion in the next section which examines the role power plays within each of these three activities: managing, heading and leading.

Management, leadership and headship: Underlying dynamics of power and emotional engagement

In order to consider how management, leadership and headship work in more depth, it is important to unpick some of the relational dynamics which underpin them. A key dynamic, and one which will be explored throughout this textbook, is that of power. Power is a much theorized concept and it is not my intention to provide a complete rendering of the way this has been done. Instead, this section of the chapter provides an overview of how power has been conceptualized in relation to management, before considering how it operates in relation to the notions of headship and managerial authority. It then explores how power works within leader–follower interactions.

A discussion concerning power in organizations cannot begin without referring to the work of the German sociologist and political philosopher Max Weber. Drawing from Weber's work, Courpasson (2000) suggests that power is 'the instrument of "structures of domination", whose objective is to construct, justify and stabilize the obedience of people' (2000, p. 143). It is important to put this definition into an appropriate context. Weber was primarily concerned with understanding how the new organizations being established in the wake of the Industrial Revolution 'worked'. It was therefore in the context of the earliest factories that Weber developed his ideas about authority and obedience within organizations.

Power and authority are very closely related in his view. Authority is the 'right' one individual has to direct the actions of another. In turn, it is linked to the term 'legitimacy'. Legitimacy is defined as the capacity, at the same time, to justify that some individuals hold the power to govern (which might include coercion and violence) and that others give them consent and submit to authority (Weber, 1947). Notice here that legitimacy is a 'two-way street'. Actions are only legitimate if those affected by those actions accept the legitimacy of the one directing them. In slightly more contemporary times, Marian McNulty, writing about how managerial legitimacy is established, suggests that the acceptance of directors by subordinates involves a perception of the superior's 'right' to give orders, thus creating 'managerial legitimacy' (McNulty, 1975, p. 580).

Weber sees power primarily as a political means of building social order and thereby producing efficiency both for those in power and for their subordinates. In other words, he suggests that the kind of dominating practices that occur in organizations are good for both those who dominate and those subject to domination. Interestingly, to drive that point home, Weber suggests that the 'most solid ground for domination' is not power itself, but the *belief* in the legitimacy of power. A senior manager may hold a hierarchically superior position and through that position be able to direct how work is done. If subordinates do not believe the superior's power to be legitimate, though, they will find ways to disregard the directions given.

An important undercurrent here is that power, especially when linked to the idea of domination, can be regarded in negative terms. However, both Weber and his fellow sociologist Antony Giddens recognized the positive aspects of both domination and the use of power to dominate (Giddens, 1984). Domination, Weber argues, allows for efficiency and this can be good for both managers and those who work under them. Taking a productive view of power, Giddens suggests that power 'is the capacity to achieve outcomes' (1984, p. 257). In this way, power has both constraining and emancipating properties.

Taking a more critical view of power, the French philosopher Michel Foucault encourages us to rethink the way power works (Foucault, 1980a, 1980b). His work particularly questions the assumption that power is exerted from the more powerful to the less powerful. His critique suggests that power is more mutually constituted and that ultimately power is given rather than directed. His critique also notices the way structures, histories and society itself exerts 'power' in the way it frames and names ways of being in the world (particularly in relation to madness and sexual 'deviance').

Interestingly, among the theorists introduced earlier in this chapter writing about management and leadership, scant attention was given to questions of power and authority and how they inform manager–subordinate or leader–follower relations. With the exception of Zaleznik, who suggests that 'leadership inevitably requires using power to influence the thoughts and actions of other people' (1977, p. 74), the rest remain silent on this issue. Indeed, as indicated earlier, Kort goes as far as to purport that leaders do not use power in order to achieve their purposes, almost intimating that the more power and authority that is being used, the less there is leadership.

Perhaps a way of understanding that lack of comment is to return to the origin of these different roles (management, leadership and headship) to consider how they have come to exist within organizations. Generally, managing arises from the need to co-ordinate and monitor disparate activities due to the diffusion of work arrangements. Managers' ability to do their job rests on the expectation of obedience. As Courpasson explains, 'organizations are sustained by an expectation of confidence in the obedience of their members' (2000, p. 142). This has nothing to do with the activity of leading, as leading has been defined here. It has to do with what happens when human beings come together to achieve tasks within organizations, and Weber points out that organizations only exist because 'certain persons will act in such a way as to carry out the order of governing the organization' (Weber, 1978, p. 49). This is not because of unique skills of influence on the part of managers or even on their ability to communicate well but is a result of the very structures of organizing.

The managerial authority that rests with holding 'senior' positions arises primarily through the expectation of authority vested in different levels of management. Again, it is important to recognize that this is not something that exists outside of people's expectations and acquiescence. If the positional authority associated with headship breaks down and is no longer given by subordinates, then work organization also breaks down. This occurs most explicitly when employees resist domination and withdraw their labour by going on strike, or when they decide to 'work to rule', rather than engaging in the non-paid or unrecognized aspects of their jobs which inevitably keep organizations afloat.

This brief explication of the way power works within managing and headship roles indicates the importance of legitimating organizational structures and the propensity for human beings to accept domination when working within such structures. If leadership 'proper', as Kort would put it, operates outside of such structures, what is its relationship to power?

Leadership and power

Kort asserts that 'to be significant for establishing a case of leadership, the influence occurs in the course of performing certain kinds of plural actions, and may well occur in the absence of power' (2008, p. 419). I would argue that, like management or headship, leadership does operate through the expression of power but that power is not necessarily legitimate, organizational power that arises through position within the hierarchy. Instead, leadership often utilizes a different form of power; the kind often associated with characteristics of the individual taking up the leader role himself or herself.

Returning to the work of Weber, he identified three sources of authority within organizations: the rational, the traditional and the charismatic (1947). Rational and traditional sources are present in the structural legitimacy of organizational hierarchies described in the previous section. The third, charisma, is often associated with the kind of power that underpins leader–follower relations. Drawing from Greek sources, for Weber, charisma was genuinely viewed as a 'gift from the gods' described in the following quote:

> The term 'charisma' will be applied to a certain quality of an individual personality by virtue of which he is considered extraordinary and treated as endowed with supernatural, superhuman, or at least specifically exceptional powers or qualities. These are such as are not accessible to the ordinary person, but are regarded as of Divine origin or as exemplary, and on the basis of them the individual concerned is treated as a 'leader'. (1947, p. 241)

Charisma thus originates from a source outside of the individual himself or herself and is associated with 'the Divine'. Charisma and leadership is picked up again in Chapter 4, but the aspect of Weber's fuller account that concerns us here is the part 'followers' play in the assessment of charisma. Weber's writings make it quite clear that leaders are only charismatic if their followers label them as such. In this way, the charismatic relationship echoes the dynamics of legitimacy – both only work by virtue of followers' perceptions and accompanying attributions.

In this way, charisma's power operates through a relational dynamic. In previous work, I have likened charisma with the aesthetic experience of the sublime, in which the experience of attraction is also tinged with a sort of undercurrent of fear or dread (Ladkin, 2006). Followers can be attracted to the seemingly 'charismatic' leader, even if they don't quite trust him or her (or perhaps don't quite trust themselves, in relation to him or her). Critical, however, to the experience of charismatic power is that both leaders and followers 'buy into it'. Charisma can quickly transform into a case of 'the emperor's new clothes' if followers judge the leader to be a buffoon, rather than charismatic. Also, Weber himself notes that unless the charismatic leader achieves goals and wins (battles!), followers will assess that the 'gift from God' has been withdrawn. On a less dramatic scale, however, is the notion of 'referent power' through which leaders influence others. *Referent power* is the power resulting from people identifying with each other in some way (French and Raven, 1959). It is a soft kind of power, associated with high regard or high esteem; however, it can be a potent relational dynamic operating between leaders and their followers. In particular, followers can place unreal expectations on their leaders, wishing them to be 'perfect' and perform the heroic job of 'making everything all right'. Followers' fantasies about what their leaders may be able to accomplish for them is often accompanied by irrational levels of power being given from followers to the leaders. This is at its most extreme in the form of cults (as illustrated, for example, by the case of the mass suicide of members of Jim Jones's Peoples Temple in Guyana in 1978, in which 909 people died). However, even in the everyday workings of organizations leaders are often able to influence followers through emotionally and *psycho-dynamic*-based relational processes.

DEFINITION: REFERENT POWER

A form of personal power based on an individual's ability to influence others because of the respect and admiration they evoke in others. It is also often associated with a high degree of identification between those entering this form of power relations.

DEFINITION: PSYCHO-DYNAMIC

Very close to the notion of 'psychoanalytic', psycho-dynamics refer to the processes informing human relating that operate at below our level of conscious awareness. For instance, when people become anxious they can unconsciously desire leaders to 'save them', and this can result in an unhelpful dependency relationship between leaders and followers.

Emotional and psychological engagement

Management, leadership and headship are each underpinned by certain ways of human beings relating to one another. Within each activity, there is a different type of relational dynamic at play. For instance, it is possible to be a manager of inert resources, such as printing products or widgets or packaging supplies, and not really have very much interaction with other human beings at all. To the extent that managing is primarily concerned with monitoring and co-ordinating, there is potentially little need for human interaction. This is not to say that managers of people can effectively relate to others in the same way they might relate to widgets! However, fulfilling the requirements of the managerial role can rely on minimal co-operation from subordinates. As Kort (2008) explains, working together to achieve goals that are more or less agreed upon (the creation of certain products in exchange for money, for instance) only really requires adequate direction and co-ordination.

Exercising managerial authority through the role of headship, however, introduces a level of relating that extends beyond mere co-ordination. Although a manager may exercise the authority to spend a certain amount of money in their budget, that money doesn't have any emotional attachment to how it is used. However, when an individual assumes the right of 'headship' in which their authority can be wielded in ways that affect others' well-being, a different psychological contract is established. Once again, drawing from a psycho-dynamic perspective individuals can react in unconscious ways to the 'head' role divorced from the person holding it. Individuals can harbour a range of fantasies about the power of the 'head' and can react in myriad ways to these fantasies. Sometimes this emotional reaction is tied to historic patterns that a person has of dealing with authority. Authority can be resisted just by the mere fact that it *is* an authority. It can also be acquiesced to in ways that are not always helpful. For instance, a subordinate may perceive that a particular action will cause damage but refuse to stop acting because 'it's someone else's responsibility'. One of the most startling examples of the power of authority is illustrated by the Milgram experiments, explained below.

The power of authority: The Milgram experiments

The Milgram experiments were conducted in the USA by the psychologist Stanley Milgram in the early 1960s. In the wake of the trial of the Nazi war criminal Eichmann, Milgram set out to understand more about how human beings respond to those they assumed to be occupying positions of authority. Like many at the time, he was seeking to understand whether or not the horrible crimes committed during the Holocaust could be attributed to 'people following orders'.

Research subjects were told to administer electrical shots of increasing voltage to individuals sitting on the other side of a screen when they answered questions on a test incorrectly. Those taking the test were in fact not receiving the shocks, but did scream out with pain in reaction to the shocks that were administered. The experiment (which would be outlawed by any ethically responsible research committee today) demonstrated the willingness of normal people to acquiesce to authority, even when doing so caused pain to others. As many within the psychoanalytic tradition have noted, human beings seem to be hard-wired in some way to obey those they apprehend to hold authority over them.

Leadership 'proper', in Eva Kort's terms, doesn't work like this. In leadership 'proper' followers have endorsed where the leader is taking them. In this way, followers take greater levels of responsibility in going along with the ideas and direction set by the leader. There is more emotional and psychological investment on the part of followers in a leadership 'proper' relationship. *Social identity theory* suggests that key to the cohesion between leaders and followers in 'true' leadership relations is the sense of 'we-ness' established amongst the group (Haslam et al., 2011). This differs from what goes on when managerial authority is exercised, in which individuals may do things but not through a sense of belongingness. Subjects within the Milgram experiments left the room and (in all likelihood) did not want to be associated with what they had done.

DEFINITION: SOCIAL IDENTITY THEORY

Social identity theory suggests that human beings have an innate need to identify with others they see as similar to themselves. This can be on the basis of national culture, gender, sexual orientation, or even allegiance to particular sports clubs. The social identity we 'connect with' at any point in time is dependent on our context, and what is most important to us in terms of our identity at a given point in time.

The power of leadership influence, then, is the power associated with creating a sense of belonging and identity. In his book *The Arts of Leadership* (2001) Keith Grint suggests that, foremost, leaders need to be 'entrepreneurs of identity'. They need to name who 'we' are, together, and, together, what 'we' will do, especially in response to changing and uncertain circumstances. This power of identity-giving is inherent in Barack Obama's initial rallying call during the 2008 presidential election of 'Yes We Can'. Such a general proclamation – not even specific in terms of what 'we' could do – united sufficient numbers of Americans into some kind of understanding of who they could be with Obama as president, so that he successfully won two terms in office.

In summary

Management, leadership and headship are each dependent on different types of human interactions within particular organizational contexts. This chapter has attended specifically to the type of power most frequently associated with each and the quality of emotional engagement inherent to each. Although each can be underpinned by more than one source of power (for instance managers can influence through expert power as well as legitimate power) Table 1.2 suggests the source of power without which management, leadership or headship could not function. Similarly, although the emotional engagement between managers or heads and subordinates, or leaders and their followers can vary, the table highlights a key aspect of their emotional relating. Finally, the table indicates the role that organizational structures play in the enactment of each, from being absolutely critical in the case of headship, to potentially unimportant in the case of leadership.

Table 1.2   Relating management, headship and leadership with power, emotional engagement and the role of organizational structures

	Type of power	**Emotional engagement**	**Role of organization**
Management	Legitimate	Not necessarily important	Key determinate of goals, relationships, and legitimate authority
Headship	Coercive/Reward	In response to authority	Essential
Leadership	Referent/Expert	High	Less important as leadership can arise throughout the organization

Managing, heading and leading organizations: What do they look like in practice?

In the final section of this chapter, you are invited to explore the difference between management, leadership and headship by considering the case study of a young manager working her way through an organization's hierarchy. In particular, you will be asked to suggest what she might do differently, given her recognition of the need for management, leadership or headship as she takes up different organizational roles.

Case study: Natalie Chan

Natalie Chan is a 35-year-old woman of mixed Anglo-Chinese descent who joined the UK-based public sector organization OBP after she graduated from university with a good degree in Economics. She joined the organization's graduate intake scheme, where she was quickly tracked into a 'high flyer' programme. Through that programme she has been placed in a number of different parts of the larger organization in order to develop a broad understanding of its overall activities.

She is particularly recognized for her skills as an analyst and, in fact, she most enjoys this kind of work. Although her technical expertise is very high, she is not particularly confident as a manager. Some of her uncertainties about managing other people began to arise about five years ago when she was promoted to a role that required her to manage a small team. The transition to management was made perhaps even more difficult as she had worked alongside three of the five people who subsequently reported to her.

Although she herself is not sure how she did it, those around her judged her management skills to be very high. As the case study opens, she has just been promoted. This promotion means that along with being responsible for running a department of 60 people, she also reports to the executive team. Both of these duties she finds rather daunting.

(Continued)

(Continued)

In particular she has concerns about:

- How closely does she need to manage those in the department? Most of them knew their areas of work much better than she did – what does it mean to manage a group of experts?
- Her own line manager now talked to her about her need to not just 'manage' her team but to 'lead' them as well. She had never really thought of herself as a 'leader' – what does taking on this role mean?

For the first time in her career she would also be reporting to the executive team. What were the things she needed to pay attention to in interacting with them? What would they be looking for from her in terms of her managing and leading skills?

 1. If you were coaching Natalie, what would you help her to identify as the 'managing' aspects of her new role? How would you go about discerning the level of managerial authority she has? How would you help her think about herself as a 'leader' within the organization and what would be the particular things she would want to attend to as a leader?

Six months into the job, Natalie thinks she is doing well with the exception of two things. First, from a staff point of view, she has to engage the time of a publicist who works not only for her department but for another department as well. The difficulty is, every time she tries to engage this person to work for her department, the person tells her she is already busy and doesn't have time. She understood that indeed the other department had been involved in a big initiative which would have taken this person's time but that project is now finished and she is still getting excuses.

 2. How do you analyse what is going on using the language of 'management', 'managerial authority' and 'leadership'? If she is going to shift this situation, which type of relationship does she need to foster and why?
How should she go about shifting the situation?

The second issue she is having difficulty with concerns her role as leader of her team and how she relates to the executive committee. She is regularly asked to prepare reports for the committee and, as of yet, she feels the reports have not produced the impact she would like them to have. In this way, she is letting her team down she feels, as so far she has been unable to secure them the additional resources they need in order to expand their role further.

 3. What are the issues at stake from a management, leadership and managerial authority perspectives?
What are the different actions Natalie should take, depending on which aspect of her job and the issue you are thinking about?

A year later, Natalie's line manager reassures her in her appraisal that she has been doing well. She has managed to get the publicity person to give her a certain amount of time each week and she feels her profile with the executive team has been successfully raised. In fact, her line manager is suggesting to her that she might think about the possibility of joining the executive team within the next five years. However, what he says to her is that in order to do so, she must focus during the next year on demonstrating her 'leadership' profile. She isn't sure what that means.

4. If you were advising her, what suggestions would you make about how she might go about doing this?

Concluding thoughts

The aim of this chapter has been to demonstrate the benefits of conceptualizing 'managing', 'heading' and 'leading' as distinct activities relying on different types of power and emotional engagement, and arising from specific organizational structures. In current parlance the three are often amalgamated. However, distinguishing between them alerts you to:

- The nature of power associated with each activity (along with the attendant question of whether you have the requisite type of power to achieve your goal – and if not, how can you enhance or alter your power base?).
- The nature of the psychological contract inherent to each relationship. How can you foster the type of engagement central to each activity? How can you signal that you are moving from one mode to the other when you are in a role that requires both?

Managing, heading and leading organizations effectively require sensitivity to the particular context within which you are working as well as to the expectations of those with whom you are working. Even those with high levels of managerial authority can be overthrown by disgruntled followers. Followers or subordinates can sabotage the most carefully laid strategy if they do not 'buy in' to it. A 'great' leader can fail without the operational savvy to co-ordinate organizational operations. As long ago as 1977 Abraham Zaleznik pointed out the downside of too much managerial control, especially within changing competitive contexts. Each of these ways of operating is fine in its own right. The key is in knowing when and how (and whether you have the requisite type of power, quality of emotional engagement and location within your organization's structure) to step into one of these ways of relating.

Finally, this chapter has largely focused on 'managing', 'heading' and 'leading' as *activities*, but lurking behind is a question of *who* is engaged in these activities. Can anyone enact management, headship or leadership? Are some people more suited to a particular type, as we have seen suggested in Zaleznik's work? These questions lead us to the concept of leadership traits, which is the topic of the next chapter.

The key points in this chapter were …

- The main difference between management, leadership and headship is around the organizational purpose they serve and the type of authority and power each relies on.
- Management is about processes that maintain a steady state. Management usually involves a position within an organization, and draws on legitimate power.
- Leadership is more mysterious, but is about working with complex problems and change. Leadership requires endorsement that is given by followers, which involves a psychological contract. It doesn't necessarily mean position! Instead, it draws on referent power.
- Headship is not leadership! It is about the commanding authority that comes from an organizational place of power. It draws on coercion or rewards as its power base.

 # Further thinking

Grint, K. (2005). Problems, problems, problems: The social construction of 'leadership'. *Human Relations*, *58*(11), 1467–1494.

Questions:

1   How does Grint distinguish management, leadership and command? In what ways is this similar to this chapter? How is it different?
2   Grint argues that leadership is needed in the face of intractable, complex problems, and accordingly involves asking questions. How might asking questions affect the psychological contract of leadership articulated in this chapter? Can you think of an experience when a leader asked a lot of questions instead of providing answers? What was it like? How did it affect the relational dynamic between you?
3   Grint makes the point that situations themselves are not 'wicked', 'critical' or 'tame', but that they become constructed as such. Can you identify a current issue that you are dealing with or that has broader interest, such as 'the financial crisis', and depict it as a 'tame', 'wicked' or 'crisis' type problem? How do your responses change depending on how it is constructed?

Kort, E. (2008). What, after all, is leadership? 'Leadership' and plural action. *Leadership Quarterly*, *19*(4), 409–425.

Questions:

1   What is your understanding of Kort's notion of 'joint plural action'? How does it enrich your understanding of how leadership occurs?
2   What do you think of Kort's assertion that 'leadership proper does not involve the use of power'? What assumptions underpin this argument?
3   Can you identify how individuals for whom you have worked have enacted leading, managing and headship? What was the impact of how they took up these roles on your own work?

Zaleznik, A. (1977). Managers and leaders: Are they different? *Harvard Business Review*, May/June, 67–78.

1   What do you think of the distinctions Zaleznik draws between leaders and followers?
2   Are there any problems with this distinction and the way Zaleznik makes his case?
3   What issues remain unresolved by this article?

 # Leadership on screen

Two excellent films that clearly demonstrate the interplay of managing, leading and heading an organization are:

Apollo 13, in which a team of on the ground scientists have to rescue the ill-fated Apollo 13 spacecraft unable to land on the moon due to an on-board explosion;

Margin Call, a fictionalized account of one of a New York City banks' response to the 2008 financial crisis.

2

TRAIT THEORIES OF LEADERS AND LEADERSHIP

FROM ANCIENT GREECE TO TWENTY-FIRST-CENTURY NEUROSCIENCE

Scott Taylor

Scott's been teaching theories of leadership since he started lecturing in 2002, but has resisted researching it until recently. The more research he does in the area, the more interesting it gets …

What this chapter is all about …

The main idea is that trait theories of leadership are one of the oldest ways of thinking about leadership, and these continue to permeate leadership theories today. The idea here is that certain personal characteristics make some people leaders (such as intelligence, height or gender). But we need to question this …

The key questions this chapter answers are:

- How did trait theories come about?
- In what ways are they present today?
- How are trait theories researched?
- What are the main critiques of trait theory?

Introduction: The rise, fall, and rise of trait theories

In most leadership studies textbooks, the chapter on trait theory comes near the beginning. As you can see, this book is no different. Trait theories, or the 'trait approach', are placed in this way because they are usually described as the first systematic way to try to understand how leadership happens and where leaders come from.

This means that trait theories are an important historical artefact – they provide an insight into how researchers and people in organizations thought about leadership in the late nineteenth and early twentieth centuries. After introducing trait theories most textbook stories then tell us that by the mid-twentieth century the approach had been 'challenged' or 'discredited'.

Unlike natural science theories that are challenged, disproven or discredited (think about the theory that all other planets orbited the Earth, or that we could reliably predict behaviour from the shape of someone's head) trait theories have been incredibly resilient. The original theories are still with us in research, and they're also remarkably influential in leadership development practice, as they provide an easily understood framework for consultants, trainers and some business school management education programmes.

In this chapter, we work through the research that trait theories are based on from the beginning. It's important to do this because these ideas are still with us in another very significant way, in the form of neuroscientific approaches to leadership, and we can't understand those unless we understand the roots they have in the earliest trait theory. Neuroscientific approaches are ways of researching leadership and developing leaders that have come to prominence in the last ten years. Although this may seem like a long time period, it is very unusual for an approach to become as established as the neuroscientific perspective has, as quickly as this, so this chapter also asks why that is.

That's the shape of the chapter. We start with what is often thought of as the first academic method of thinking about leaders, leadership and leadership development, then we move through the period when trait theories were being challenged as crude or contradictory. We finish by exploring the brave new world of trait theory as it is expressed in neuroscientific approaches to understanding leadership. It's a long but interesting story, which has significant implications for anyone who wants to do leadership, to be recognized as a leader, or to understand why leadership can sometimes look like an activity that only a very small, very specific group of people are invited into.

Speaking of 'Great Men'

Novelists, playwrights and film-makers have structured many stories around the question of whether people are born to, develop or stumble into 'greatness'. Just as the question of where leaders come from, or how people become leaders, fascinates researchers and educators in business schools, so it is a key theme of stories we tell. The rise and fall of corporate dynasties, the triumph or failure of individual company leaders, provide fascinating human and organizational narratives that take us to the question of whether people are somehow 'suited' for leadership. Biographies and autobiographies always have to deal with the issue of whether a leader was 'born to it', or perhaps better 'bred to it', by dint of possessing a set of personality characteristics that differentiate 'them' from 'us'. The stories are really demonstrations of the 'Great Man' approach to leadership, which works something like this …

 STOP AND REFLECT 2.1

All reviews of leadership theories, and most textbooks, refer to something called 'Great Man' theories. This theory is always presented as the nineteenth-century precursor to the 'proper' psychological trait theories developed in the early twentieth century. However, the reviews and textbooks rarely set out in detail how this way of defining and theorizing leadership actually works in practice. It goes something like this …

First, choose someone who has been generally recognized as an important leader. Preferably someone who is/was globally acknowledged as a leader, and always someone who occupied a position of significant

(Continued)

(Continued)

power (politically, militarily, organizationally, financially, or culturally – we're thinking here about people like Hitler or John F. Kennedy in politics, for example, Napoleon or Wellington in a military context, or Steve Jobs in a corporate context – the kind of person it's difficult to deny had a significant individual effect on societies, large organizations or historical events).

Second, look closely at your chosen person's life history, behaviours (especially at what historians have identified as key moments or potential turning points), and relationships with other people, especially enemies. You should be able to get a sense of behavioural patterns, relationship patterns and significant life event influences on how the leader developed as a person.

This is your data. Now you're in a position to decide what you think makes the person different to non-leaders, all of the non-Hitlers or not-Steve Jobs people. The combination of life history (especially events and relationships in childhood or adolescence), behaviour patterns and how the designated leader dealt with people in everyday life will enable you to say what the specific leaderly personality was. You should identify characteristics of the person such as energy, height, aggression, persistence, tact or intelligence that your leader possessed.

- How does this help you to understand leadership?
- What does this way of understanding leadership neglect, silence or deny?

There are many criticisms of 'Great Man'-based theories of leadership. We'll come to those in a moment, once we've looked in detail at what trait theory is. Before we do, we'd like to try to rescue what we can from the idea of leader biography that 'Great Man' theory works from, because it's not all bad. Here is the critique of the 'Great Man' approach specifically, and a proposal to retain what is valuable in looking at biographies of prominent individual leaders.

The value of biography

Three colleagues based in the Department of Sociology of the Hebrew University of Jerusalem observed recently that the majority of leadership theories still look to personality or character traits and behaviours to explain what leadership is (Shamir et al., 2005). They also note that, even though trait theories have their roots in 'Great Man' theories, very few academic studies of leading take leader auto/biographies seriously. This may be a result of being unsure about the status of the many thousands of books produced about leaders. Most books written by the leaders themselves and those 'ghosted' by people they commission to write their stories must of course be read with some scepticism, for both their content and tone. There are few leaders who either write or commission a critical biography of themselves, or write reflexive critiques of their own practice.

However, these books do have a great significance and value. They provide insight into life, work and leadership practice that cannot be found anywhere else. Most academic researchers find it difficult, or impossible, to gain the kind of access to leaders that some biographers are given. Steve Jobs, for example, apparently provided his official biographer Walter Isaacson with a very high degree of access to his colleagues, family and friends (Isaacson, 2011). Indeed, Jobs told Isaacson that he wanted no control over the published text, claiming he wouldn't even read it. (As it turned out he didn't, because the book was published after his sadly early death in 2011.)

So the stories are important, even if we have to be sceptical about their truth status or accuracy. In their journal paper, Shamir and his colleagues make a series of very practical suggestions about leader biographies and how we can use them to better understand the act of leading and the person. Their key insight is summarized in the idea that auto/biographies perform two functions. First, obviously, they tell us something about how leadership is practised and understood in a particular place at a moment in time. Second, these books contribute towards the construction of leadership. In other words, when we read leader auto/biographies we both look into the leader to understand their leadership practice, and we also contribute towards the continuous construction of what counts as leadership.

To give an example: when we read Steve Jobs's biography, we know we are reading the biography of a significant leader – the book cover tells us this, our colleagues and fellow students tell us this, and we know it from the news media and online sources. As we read the book, however, we also reinforce Jobs's status – as we come to know more about his workplace practice and personality, we talk about it, write about it, perhaps practise it in emulation of the person presented as the great leader. The life story thus becomes part of what we think of as leadership and part of what do when we try to lead or follow. The more powerful the story, the stronger the effect.

As Shamir and his colleagues tell us, it is usual for researchers to read leader biographies only to try to identify the traits and skills that life events and experiences contribute to the development of. Thus we find many leader biographies that emphasize parental divorce, the early death of a parent, an unhappy or disrupted education, poverty or the desire to please an important figure. This, then, is the essence of 'Great Man' theory's contributions to understanding leadership – the identification of personality traits or social skills that important leaders embody or practise. Biographies can be and do much, much more than that, but early theories of leadership used them in a very narrow way – as real, true life stories, mostly of men, that could help us to explain what leadership was and how it developed.

From 'Great Men' to scientific trait theories

Early commentators on 'Great Men' leaders would probably not have described themselves as social scientists creating knowledge or theories. As they described their work, they were trying to achieve:

- insight into how people become leaders who act in the public good;
- insight into how to stop people becoming damaging leaders;
- book sales.

Their general approach, based on the idea that people are born with a set of genetically inherited characteristics that might be further developed through certain life circumstances or experiences, gives us the basis for the approach to leadership studies that we came to call 'trait theory'. The term 'trait' carries a very specific meaning, which is a little more complicated than the standard dictionary definition but also closely related to it. So, the *Oxford English Dictionary* definition of trait as 'a distinguishing quality or characteristic, typically one belonging to a person; a genetically determined characteristic' is the foundation that academic researchers build on, but it is more complex.

Hence there are three key components to the idea of 'leadership traits':

1. Some people have them, some don't (in other words, observation of traits is used to distinguish people from each other).
2. They are a personal possession (in other words, they can't be given to you or taken away from you).
3. They are in place at birth (in other words, they're genetically determined).

For researchers who want to be able to identify what makes individuals in leadership positions leaderly, all of this can be seen as good news. They can write or read biographies as they did in the nineteenth century and work out from interviews, behaviours and events what made those positional leaders different from their followers. Or, as twentieth-century researchers did, they can define physical factors, skills and attributes that they think leaders have (or should have), and then design personality tests to establish whether people in fact do have the traits they should have.

This is, on the face of it, a simple story. Researchers read 'Great Man' theories of leadership and leadership development; through their reading of the stories they identify persistently present physical factors, skills or attributes; then researchers trained in psychological data collection methods reduced the lists found in 'Great Man' theories to what they think are common essentials, and develop ways to measure and test for them.

Although research methods are often seen as somewhat boring, just the tedious detail of how data are collected, they are in fact central to understanding theories in all academic fields. If we don't understand how the data that theories are built on was generated, then we can't assess the credibility of the theory. It is therefore worth spending a few moments looking in depth at the methods trait theories are founded on.

STOP AND REFLECT 2.2

Researchers creating trait theories of leadership start from the belief that they can't identify what leadership is in itself. Instead, the research they do tries to identify ways that we can identify things that leadership is related to. So, if most people identified as occupying positions of leadership, such as a chief executive officer role, are taller than average, then we have identified something that being or becoming a leader is related to (above average height).

The researchers can then extend this idea in two ways. They could read existing academic theories and make up a list of physical characteristics, personality characteristics or skills that other researchers have identified, then test them on a new group of people. Or, the researchers could observe people in leadership positions (or read auto/biographies) and develop a list of traits in that way, then test them on a group of people.

Trait researchers most often design a long questionnaire that they think establishes whether an individual possesses the traits. Sometimes this can be quite straightforward – for example, someone is either above average height or not. However, most traits are difficult to test for in this way because they are not physically visible – personality characteristics such as initiative or integrity, for example, can be exceptionally difficult to design reliable questions for.

But trait researchers are ingenious and persistent. So they read, think, work and test their questionnaires until they achieve enough reliability and validity to satisfy their academic peers. There are always flaws in research methods – none provide perfect knowledge and all can be critiqued on some basis. The process that trait theorists go through has some very specific and significant flaws, though.

- What's good about the research methods often used in trait-based research?
- What's bad about the methods?

To reiterate: trait theories are based in the academic field of psychology, researchers are interested in physical attributes, personality or social characteristics (usually inherited), and sometimes acquired skills. All of these things are collected under the term 'trait'. One of the best reviews of leadership research, written by US-based academic Arthur Jago in the early 1980s, summarized the development of trait theory to that point to resemble something like Table 2.1.

Table 2.1   Trait theories in the early 1980s

Form of trait	Physical	Personality	Social	Skill
Examples	Energy	Aggression	Sensitivity	Intelligence
	Height	Dominance	Prestige	Judgment
	Weight	Enthusiasm	Tact	Knowledge
	Hair	Originality		
	Clothes	Sense of humour		

As always with trait theories, this looks convincing – most of us can think of a leader who embodies one or more of these physical characteristics, or who behaves in ways consistent with the personality characteristics. However, as Jago (1982) also points out, there are some very serious problems with trait theories, some of which are acknowledged by the researchers, some of which are not:

1. The statistical relationships that researchers find between traits and leadership are often weak. In other words, although there may be a correlation between intelligence and propensity to lead, it is not a strong relationship that enables reliable prediction.
2. Traits are never universally or consistently needed to become or be a leader; they vary from research study to research study, as the researchers collect data in different settings. In other words, whether a leader needs to be tall, for example, depends on the organizational context, the market conditions the company operates within, the people they are trying to lead, the cultural conditions that the leader lives within, or one of an infinite number of other issues.
3. Finally, when trait researchers collect their data, they often test both leaders and their followers. Superficially, this sounds like a good idea, but the leaders are the people who are in formal positions of leadership, and the followers are not. This raises the question of how the leader came to be in that position – there is always a selection process of some kind, and in large organizations that process will usually involve a series of psychological tests. In other words, the person in the position of leadership may be there as a result of intelligence as measured in a selection test, rather than an inherent ability to lead. Similarly, after a period of time in a leadership position, a person might become more self-confident (another key trait used to identity leaders), meaning that the trait is not inherent to being a leader, but an outcome of occupying the position.

The problem with trait theories: It's all in the detail

Arthur Jago's review and critique of trait theories builds on one of the most important academic interventions in the development of leadership studies, which came around 40 years before Jago's. In the mid-1940s, Ralph Stodgill joined a group of researchers known as the 'Ohio State Leadership Studies' group. Previously, Stodgill had studied psychology as an undergraduate, master's and PhD student. He was therefore very much an academic insider when he began to think about psychology-based trait theories, with a detailed knowledge of research methods. He had also worked in the US military, in recruitment, selection and classification.

The contribution Stodgill made to leadership studies is immense, and it began with his first piece of published work in the field in 1948. It is sometimes difficult to know what academic research will endure or be influential when first published, but it appears Ralph Stodgill's journal paper 'Personal factors associated with leadership: A survey of the literature' was recognized from the start as important. Although it is now more than 60 years old, it is still worth returning to the original paper, both as an example of the academic work of that period, and as an exemplary critique of a currently dominant approach.

Here is a summary of Stodgill's arguments about trait theories of leadership:

- First, he notes that research methods vary widely. Some researchers use observation, some read biographies, some use ratings. In addition, researchers studied a wide range of social and age groupings.
- Second, he notes (as Jago did many years later) that there are weak relationships between many of the traits studied and leadership.
- Third, he notes the need for researchers to be very clear about their findings (which they often were not). For example, in relation to intelligence, when researchers did find that leaders tend to be 'more intelligent' than their followers, it was clear that the gap between the two groups should only be slight for leaders to work well with followers. Researchers did not always make this clear.

Stodgill's immense labour in reading more than a hundred published studies of leadership and traits is summarized in a series of bullet points towards the end of his 37-page journal paper. His paper is usually represented as a serious challenge to trait theory, a turning point in leadership studies – and this is an accurate representation, to some extent. It can also be read, however, as supporting some aspects of trait theory. As Stodgill writes, he finds a significant number of traits are important presences for people in positions of leadership, across a range of research studies.

However, the key contribution for which Stodgill's work is renowned lies in his observation that, even if traits are important in understanding leader behaviour and leadership effectiveness, context is what determines whether the trait emerges as significant. In other words, the presence or absence of traits in practice depends on the social, cultural or organizational surroundings that the people being researched work in.

The significance of this observation, based on an immense amount of reading and a long training in the research methods used by the researchers whose work he was reading, enable Stodgill to make this strong statement:

> A person does not become a leader by virtue of the possession of some combination of traits, but the pattern of personal characteristics of the leader must bear some relevant relationship to the characteristics, activities, and goals of the followers. (1948, p. 64)

It is difficult to overstate the importance of this when we consider the development of leaderships studies as an academic field. In the sentence, Stodgill sets out both a major intrinsic failing of existing trait theories and a significant absence in all trait theories to that point, the follower.

STOP AND REFLECT 2.3

As all leadership studies textbooks will tell you, Ralph Stodgill was the first and most vocal critic of trait theories. His argument was made considerably stronger by his detailed understanding of the research methods used by trait researchers, and their approach to theory building. Stodgill was trained in psychology and practised clinical psychology before moving into full-time academic work. However, in the best tradition of leadership studies, Stodgill combined this disciplinary background with a long and deep commitment to understanding the practice of leadership and leading, working at Ohio State University for many years. It is intriguing that an obituary written by a colleague notes how Stodgill 'exemplified effective leadership' by being 'quiet and unobtrusive' (Hakel, 1980), suggesting that theory and practice came together for this particular scholar.

- Why do you think Stodgill's colleague wrote that his leadership was exemplary because it was quiet? Have you worked with a quiet leader? If you have, what was it like? If you haven't, would you like to?

What you've just read might seem to indicate that trait theories, and personality theories in general, are unhelpful when we're trying to understand leadership, leading and the development of people in positions of power. This is, of course, not the case. Trait theories were the first attempt to bring the study of leadership into the social sciences, building on the 'gentleman amateur' approach that early 'Great Man' explorations of leadership involved. We cannot simply dismiss more than a hundred years of careful, thoughtful, empirical research because the approach has flaws. For this reason, it is worth looking in more detail at recent studies of leadership and leading in which the researchers take a trait approach, both explicitly and implicitly. The next two sections encourage you to read and think about two very important recent studies of leadership: the first is a classic, sophisticated exploration of trait theory, focusing on a very obvious trait, sex; the second is a more controversial way of thinking about leadership and leadership development, focused on the brain and the potential of neurological research to identify and develop leaders.

Contemporary trait theory: Why are there so few women CEOs?

As fourth-wave feminism has gathered momentum in recent years, the lack of women in obvious positions of leadership has become a pressing concern for journalists, researchers, politicians, and above all for women. If you imagine that women have achieved equality in reaching or occupying positions of leadership, you should read about the career of Julia Gillard, (first ever woman) prime minister of Australia from 2010 to 2013. Gillard was subject to quite extraordinary abuse from political colleagues and news media, often focusing on the fact that she is a woman. Gillard and many of her female colleagues decided to confront what they experienced as sexism and misogyny, most famously when Gillard spoke with great anger, passion and eloquence in the Australian parliament (we will discuss this speech again in Chapter 7, 'Difference and leadership', and you can also find a link to it at the end of this chapter).

In a British corporate context, at the moment of writing, Angela Ahrendts, the chief executive of UK-based clothing company Burberry, has just resigned to join Apple as head of the global retail division. Embedded within this 'business' story, some journalists noted that Ahrendts' resignation reduced the number of women CEOs in the FTSE 100 list of the UK's largest corporations by a third (e.g. Butler et al., 2013). It's worth saying that again in a different way – when one woman CEO resigns in the UK, it means that the proportion of the country's largest companies led by men rise from 97 per cent to 98 per cent, and the number of women CEOs reduces by a third.

This is, to say the least, puzzling, for men and women. Are there so few good women leaders? Is it so difficult for women specifically to reach the peak of a large organization? Is this a peculiarly British thing? Asking a group of around a hundred final-year undergraduates, mostly women, taking a Leadership Development module at the University of Birmingham in 2013 why they thought the FTSE 100 companies are like this, there was a great range of thoughtful responses: women are expected to take time off to give birth to and act as primary carer for children, thereby interrupting their careers; there is a social stigma attached to being a woman executive; women want this kind of career less than men, perhaps because of education or family background; sexism and patriarchy. (The solutions this group produced to the problem were also fantastic, ranging from an idea to develop an 'external womb' so that women's careers wouldn't be hindered physically by child-carrying, to re-education for men who displayed sexist behaviours or attitudes. The first solution is sort of possible at the moment, the second would be a truly excellent thing if it happened.)

I especially liked the responses because they acknowledge the social contexts of work, organization and leadership. I also like them because none of them say anything like 'because women are naturally less suited to being CEO than men'. There are still traces of sex, or sexist, determinism in many discussions of leadership. The term 'determinism' is often used in academic debates about psychologically based approaches to research, and also in research that takes sex as a characteristic to be researched. Determinism is not complicated to understand – essentially its academic usage is somewhat negative. If we call a piece of research 'determinist' it means that the researchers are assuming that something a person has or is, usually a biological feature (such as sex, height or ethnicity), affects behaviour in ways that the person struggles to control. Every time, for everyone, no matter what the situation or the person. You can see the problems with this quite easily. Determinism suggests that we are all prisoners of our physical, genetic or cultural inheritance. It suggests that we are less able to exercise agency in our working lives, as we are mostly dependent on our biology or inherited character traits.

Many researchers are not satisfied with existing explanations of 'gender disparity in the C-suite', and one group in Queensland is especially unsatisfied with what they read as deterministic explanations. Despite the global profile that a very small number of women chief executives and chief officers achieve (for example, most recently, Cheryl Sandberg at Facebook) the overall picture remains incredibly depressing in terms of equality. Autobiographies such as Sandberg's, or biographies written by journalists for prominent women leaders, can be useful and helpful, especially as inspiration or to share 'war stories'. However, they explain very little in a more general sense. For that, we have to turn to more detailed, careful, peer-reviewed research – such as that conducted by Fitzsimmons and his colleagues at Queensland (Fizsimmons et al., 2014).

If you read Fitzsimmons and colleagues' paper, and you should, you'll find they do something very interesting. They present an argument that is based on qualitative data – in other words, data which does not involve statistical analysis and enables discussion of the research questions in a different way. The researchers want to achieve theory development, but based on their arguments and the meaning of the data they've collected and analysed, rather than making an argument based on the size of their dataset, the reliability of the statistical tests they've done, or the generalizability of their analysis. It's very different to most trait theory-based studies of leadership.

The researchers conducted in-depth interviews with a carefully constructed matched sample of women and men, which then enabled them to put together life narratives that can be compared. This in turn allows the identification of differences in how women and men accrue the kind of experience, or achieve entry into the kind of educational institution, or develop the kind of identity and meet the kind of mentors, that will in the future enable entry into the very small, mostly male, club of chief executives and chief officers in large corporate organizations.

The conclusions are, in some ways, unremarkable – the researchers tell us that life outside the work-place is extremely significant in both enabling and constraining the achievement of positions of power such as chief executive. This isn't surprising – if a person's education has been disrupted, if a person has caring responsibilities for others, if a person doesn't have good contacts in an industry that values social networks, then it seems obvious that success (as measured by arrival in an executive position) should be elusive. What makes this research fascinating, however, is the way it weaves extremely sophisticated qualitative data collection and analysis, complex theories of society and leadership, and policy implications, with a surprisingly narrow perspective on how we think of the sex we each embody.

We can think of being a man or being a woman as a trait – a physical characteristic that we can do little or nothing about. Clothes, hair, shoes and material artefacts such as glasses can all be more or less sex-specific – men with long hair, women wearing trousers, may upset what some think of as normal, but doesn't usually fundamentally affect how we see the person in front of us, whether we think of them as 'woman' or 'man'.

However, this way of thinking about sex in leadership research takes little or no account of social, organizational or cultural context in shaping expectations of leaders/leadership, or in the behaviours that are observed to build the theory. Organizational researchers have been telling us for some time that the sex we inhabit is better understood as *gender*. This term is quite different, as it involves the idea that who or what we are in relation to being woman or man is socially constructed – in other words, what and who we are in relation to the sexual orientations, identities and performances available to us is not fixed or determined by our genitals or chromosomes. Instead, gender can be understood as something we perform, an achievement we make happen every day – sometimes through relatively straightforward things such as clothes, hair, which toilet door we go through, but also through more complex things such as how we behave, how we speak, what we say and the roles we choose to occupy in social situations. Each of these choices in miniature will have a singular and cumulative effect on both us as people, people we work with, lead or follow, and the social context we work within.

If we try to understand sex in this way, as gender, we re-orient the issue from being one that we can research through trait research to a set of complex interlocking issues that start from a very different position. This 'anti-determinist' way of thinking, and being, challenges one of the foundations of trait theory, essentialism. Essentialism suggests that there are irreducible differences between women and men. That's it. Stated like that, it seems very straightforward and not at all complicated – and perhaps also very, very obviously true and correct. However, if we introduce the possibility that sex is a biological category and gender is a set of socially constructed distinctions, then we can see instantly that there are two potential threads of analysis and controversy here. In relation to the research described here, on the experiences of women and men leaders in Australia, we are clearly reading a study of 'leadership and sex' – in other words, a trait-based theory of how women and men do leadership. If we introduce the idea of gender, meaning the patterns we are brought up with as 'male' or 'female', the behaviours we are taught to expect of biological women and biological men, then we could conduct an entirely different piece of research, with different conclusions.

To make this clearer through an example from the research conducted by Fitzsimmons and his colleagues: towards the end of their analysis the authors suggest a series of ways to overcome the disparity in the number of women and men in leadership positions in their sample. They argue that leadership development should be offered to women to provide understanding of the experiences men have that make them leaders, and for more opportunities to be offered to women to, for example, network more effectively and thereby be invited into the men's clubs that apparently control entry to senior leadership positions. The biological traits possessed by each group would stay the same, but women might learn to behave more like men, performing a masculinity that would open doors hitherto closed because of a lack of a Y chromosome.

What you make of this will depend on how you feel, or what you think, about a range of complicated things. If you think that characteristics such as sex, ethnicity, sexuality or nationality are fixed and determine who we are, how we behave, then you will tend towards an essentialist, perhaps determinist, perspective on debates such as this one. You might find yourself saying something like, 'I think that women are made differently to men and therefore don't reach positions of leadership for those reasons'. On the other side you'll find people who take an anti-essentialist perspective, articulating the belief that our identities are constructed, performed, in social contexts. If you're in this group you might say, for example, that that women are under-represented in 'the C-suite' because men, and the masculinities associated with men, are largely in control of entry to 'their' leadership groups and they prefer to maintain a homogeneous group that they can rely on to be wholly committed to work and better predict the behaviours of. It's a complex and controversial debate, based on complicated and controversial workplace practices, that provides a fascinating contemporary window on to trait theories of leadership and their problems.

From observation of traits to brain scans: The introduction of neuroscience to leadership studies

The most significant recent development in trait theories of leadership is the 'union' of leadership theory with cognitive neuroscience, as part of a fashion called the 'new biology of leadership'. A series of research studies published in prestigious peer-reviewed journals, the Neuro-Leadership Institute (http://www.neuroleadership.org), and management consultancy activity in the area all suggest this is a growing community of academics and practitioners. The best place to start in understanding this new field of research and organizational interventions is with the introduction to a special themed issue of the foremost journal in the field of leadership studies, *The Leadership Quarterly*. There, three UK-based academics outline the field and what its research means (Lee et al., 2012).

First, Lee and his colleagues tell us that they have no wish to be associated with the term 'neuro-leadership'. They prefer to think of what they do as part of a much wider new biological approach to understanding issues related to leading. This could be read as an attempt to legitimize their research through association with a well-established and ostensibly neutral academic discipline, while simultaneously distancing their theories from more popular accounts of how we can explain all human experience through measuring brain patterns and activity, which can be a disturbing idea for some people.

Thus, it seems we should think of neuro-approaches to understanding leadership as just one specific way of doing research into explaining how and why leadership happens, or doesn't happen, based on human biology. It is easy to see the links to early trait theory where this chapter started, even if the research methods are quite different. This is extremely significant, and again worth exploring in detail.

Brain-work and leadership: Collecting data

The idea of biology and neuroscience as a way of exploring leadership conjures up some intriguing images – scientists in white coats, perhaps, experiments that require things to be attached to your head, maybe even brain scans using enormous expensive machines in hospitals, all as ways of developing new theories of leadership. These images are, to some extent, accurate. Researchers in this area are often based in departments of life science or biology in universities, working together with scholars based in business schools. The data are collected through experiments that are more commonly conducted for medical research or in experimental psychology research – some of the data collection monitors and measures neural activity inside the brain through magnetic resonance imaging, for example when people are asked questions about leadership experiences (Boyatzis et al., 2012); other research explores the individual's genetic map looking for variance to explain achievement of leadership positions (Chaturvedi et al., 2012); others test how people react to images of faces when asked to analyse a situation that suggests a particular approach to leadership (Spisak et al., 2012).

It is intriguing to talk to students about this rapidly expanding field of research and the methods used. Some react with interest and enthusiasm; some show a great deal of discomfort. The difference appears to be rooted in whether we believe that this kind of data can contribute to the development of meaningful leadership theory, or explain the development of leaders. The research is certainly presented in a convincing way in journal articles by the researchers. They make claims such as '[k]nowing the neurological responses behind both a leader's behaviour and his or her followers' responses may allow for improved pedagogy and training, thus helping leaders to form more effective relationships' (Boyatzis et al., 2012, p. 270); or: '… 40% of the variance [in 'leadership emergence' – in other words, explaining who becomes a leader and who doesn't] being attributable to genetics' (Chaturvedi et al., 2012, p. 228). This is extremely seductive, especially if you have to write an essay or sit an exam on where leaders come from.

It is more difficult to articulate exactly what creates the discomfort some people feel when confronted with this research. Perhaps there is something socially uncomfortable about the idea that we can explain, or predict, which people will become leaders through something as mechanical as genetic testing. (This could, of course, happen at a very early age, or perhaps even pre-birth. If sex selection of babies happens, then perhaps prospective parents might be tempted to choose whether to have a child or not based on genetic prediction of leadership capability.) Maybe we want to think we have more control over ourselves and our working environments than this research suggests? Or could we be worried that we would find out we are in the 'not-leader' category and therefore destined to follow?

Fortunately, two academics based at the University of Liverpool Management School have thought about this new version of trait theory from a critical, especially ethical, standpoint, and written a series of journal articles to explain why they think we should all be uncomfortable with this biological turn in leadership studies (Lindebaum, 2013; Lindebaum and Zundel, 2013).

Creating a pathology, not a biology, of leadership

Dirk Lindebaum and Mike Zundel share disquiets about the wider research field of organizational neuroscience, which covers all areas of management and organization such as marketing or employee behaviour. They are specifically concerned about neuroscience-based leadership research, however, because of the ethical implications it carries. The first worry they have is that such research *dehumanizes* people, especially if the research published in journals like *The Leadership Quarterly* results in neurological modification of people at work. In other words, Lindebaum and Zundel are unhappy about the prospect of workplace training interventions that are based on reshaping how we think or respond to complex working situations. This possibility is based on the theory that how we think, the neural pathways that we develop, can be changed in specific ways, to enable us to be better leaders or followers. While some people may be happy to experience this degree of personal change for the sake of work, others may not – and if neuro-interventions are seen as a reliable means of developing leaders then people will come under pressure to submit to them.

The second ethical concern relates to selection processes. As many undergraduate students in business schools discover, large organizations invest huge amounts of time and money in complex selection processes for new graduates, to identify those most likely to either work most effectively or fit in best. To date, selection processes have mostly involved psychological or social psychological tests, such as the almost-universal psychometric testing and generic personality testing. Biology, however, offers a new, more attractive, way of selecting people for jobs based on brain scans for patterns relating to, for example, leadership capability, or even genetic testing for propensity towards desirable (or, of course, undesirable) behaviours. The difficulties with this approach to selection are clear even to researchers committed to a biology of leadership – they will include and exclude on the basis of *likelihood* and propensities. In addition, the research on which such selection process are based would be open to challenge, as the psychometric research is.

Third, Lindebaum and Zundel suggest we (researchers, leaders and management consultants) should think very hard about what this research means for how we think about organizational life. Work and the workplace are, whether we like it or not, an activity and place where actions have ethical bases and consequences. Ethics, however, are not something that are amenable to natural scientific research methods and ways of thinking. Instead, thinking and behaving ethically remain stubbornly social, cultural and human – simultaneously inside the brain and hence partly biological in the sense that all human action or thought might be classed as such, but stubbornly resistant to reduction to a neurological image or genetic code.

Reducing leadership

This term, 'reduction' brings us to the final challenge to this way of thinking about leadership and leaders. It is raised and worked through by Lindebaum and Zundel at length when they assess the claims and methods of both organizational neuroscience and specific studies of leadership from that perspective. It is a complex argument, but well worth engaging with because it has broader implications for how we think about leadership studies as a research field.

In short, Lindebaum and Zundel suggest that biological, especially neuroscientific, approaches to complex social phenomena such as leadership are being reduced, or simplified in an explanatory way, by being broken down into parts which are then brought back together to look for causal links.

In relation to leadership, this might work as follows: imagine we want to understand why some leaders appear to be more popular or successful than others. First, we need to break down what we mean by 'leader' and 'leadership'. We probably do this be looking at previous studies and picking out the behaviours that researchers generally agree enable us to identify a leader. Second, we'll have to think about what popularity or success mean, most likely through some kind of measurement – this is relatively straightforward for success in a shareholder-owned corporation where most of us look to profit or return on investment or company size. For popularity, perhaps we'd use an established leadership research tool such as the Leader–Member Exchange questionnaire.

Once we've done that, we collect our data. Then we try to establish links, or correlations, between specific variables. We might then perform statistical tests, most likely probability tests or significance tests, to make claims about causality – in other words, to suggest that one thing causes another.

These processes are well established in natural science research, and often used in parts of the social sciences. Journals such as *The Leadership Quarterly* often publish research of this kind. However, other journals, such as *Leadership*, tend to publish work which is either critical of or ignores reductionist positivist research. This critique or rejection can take many forms: some researchers believe that reductionist research is impossible because it applies a natural science model to social processes and dynamics that involve surprisingly irrational or a-rational people; others argue that all research is conducted by people and therefore both politicized and personalized; yet others argue in a more conciliatory way that biological, neuroscientific or trait-based theories should be understood as only one way among many to understand leadership. Above all, critiques of this way of thinking about leadership emphasize that leaders and followers are people – thinking, feeling, emotional, unpredictable, irreducible people, rather than simply mechanical systems of interlocking and interrelating neurons and cells.

Trait theories of leadership: A never-ending quest

This chapter has a number of aims, summarized at the start and also in this sentence: trait theories have been with us a long time in leadership studies and need to be taken seriously, but also approached critically.

This chapter describes trait theory's relatively qualitative historical roots in philosophical and literary descriptions of leaders' practices and personalities. Since then, as the final section above emphasizes, trait theories have taken a series of increasingly natural scientific turns, culminating in a new biology of leadership. However, there is also a critical community analysing this development, asking whether it is appropriate, what it means, and what its effects on the research and practice communities might be (especially if it is unchallenged).

The chapter should also leave you with a clear sense of the value of trait theories. Attempting to define traits is, and always will be, one of the foundations of leadership studies. The numerous critical analyses of it, based on either 'internal' critiques (such as the low reliability and validity of this approach outside experimental laboratory-based studies), or 'external' critiques that challenge the plausibility of achieving a behavioural understanding of and leadership through cognitive research and individual level data, challenge but do not destroy it.

Hence we understand trait theories generally, and biological studies in particular, as reductionist, neglecting human constants such as culture, social context and process. However, trait theories will continue to have both a high degree of relevance and immensely seductive properties as social and cultural phenomena as much as for empirical or theoretical insight. It is important to recognize their rhetorical power to persuade and their suggestion that they can make sense of irritatingly complex questions such as 'Where do leaders come from?' Perhaps most importantly, though, it is always important to remember that trait theories are as prone to changes in fashion as any other theory, despite their presentation as eternal truth. This means that the people that trait theories exclude as 'non-leaders' one day may become exactly the same people that another trait theory tells us are ideal leaders. Which brings us to the case study that completes this chapter.

 # Case study: The secret of becoming a leader: (Dame) Stella Rimington

The book this case study is based on, *Open Secret: The Autobiography of the Former Director-General of MI5* (2001), is remarkable in many ways. First, it is a detailed account of working at a high level in the British intelligence services – in other words, how it was to be a spy for the British state. Books such as this did not exist at all before the mid-1990s, despite the long history of spying. Second, it is written by a woman, unusual in itself for such a masculine profession. Third, as the sub-title tells you, this particular woman became the Director-General of the organization she worked for – the first, of two so far, in a little over a hundred years, and also the first to write a book about her work. Finally, it is dedicated to her daughters, suggesting that it is a book about being a woman as much as a book about intelligence gathering, spying or leadership.

Rimington's story is also remarkable because it is tells us about a woman achieving a position of authority and leadership by breaking through a series of barriers and taboos that, once broken, can never be completely reconstructed. She was born in the UK in 1935, when women were still usually required to leave British government service on marriage. The proportion of women working was relatively low compared with 2014; women were mostly confined to specific types of work or organization, and usually expected to become a full-time homemaker, mother or wife before the age of 30. These cultural expectations and organizational norms would change, but only slowly, and not completely until the introduction of sex discrimination legislation in 1975.

Aged 57, however, Rimington became, as she says in the introduction, a 'sort of female James Bond' – or perhaps a better description would be a 'sort of real-life "M"', as she would have been James Bond's boss, telling him what to do. (The makers of the James Bond films had Rimington in mind when they made 'M' a woman for the first time in 1995.) In becoming the positional leader of her employing organization Rimington quietly challenged a string of trait- and biology-based assumptions, norms, conventions, prejudices and practices that dissuaded many women from thinking of themselves as potential or actual leaders. Her story goes something like this …

Joining

It soon became clear to me [on joining in 1969] that a strict sex discrimination policy was in place in MI5 and women were treated quite differently to men. They had only recently abandoned the dauntingly entitled post of The Lady Superintendent, whose job it was to supervise the welfare of all the female staff and to ensure that the proprieties were observed. No doubt this position dated from the days when only girls from 'good families' were employed, and their mothers and fathers were promised that they would be properly looked after. (p. 90)

Rimington's story emphasizes that it is a very quirky organization, employing some very idiosyncratic people to do unique jobs. However, it is also a mundane organizational story, of (as she says) sex discrimination. Women were only employed as 'assistant officers', never full officers, and a separate (very short) career ladder was available. MI5 was different from other British Civil Service departments, where women were then able to rise to positions of leadership, but practices reflected a very common attitude in 1960s England – that there were men's jobs and women's jobs. This way of thinking about people clearly has its roots in the trait approach, as women are defined as 'different' simply because of biology and, by extension, personality and behaviour.

The MI5 organizational culture that these managerial norms produced was particularly masculine. However, as in many organizations during the mid-twentieth century, there was slow change happening, in part because MI5 needed clever hard-working people, and labour markets were such that women had to be considered as well as men. Higher education in the UK was also changing rapidly; many more women were attending university and graduating. Second-wave feminism appears in the background as well, with women arguing for equality across social contexts, including workplaces. As Rimington says:

> This [sexist] attitude to women seems incredible now, looked at from the standpoint of the 21st century. So much has changed in women's employment expectations since those days. But I don't think it ever occurred to my male colleagues that they were discriminating against us and in those days it was not really questioned inside the Service [MI5]. And to be fair to them, even I, coming in from the outside, did not question it at first. (p. 103)

This is a fascinating reflection, because it makes clear two aspects of assessing people through traits. First, it suggests that judging a group of people by the traits we expect them to have simply because they belong to a category such as 'woman' can become so normalized in an organization that it is invisible – in other words, the trait theory becomes an unquestioned aspect of the culture. Second, it also implies that even the members of the trait group don't see the assumptions being made about them, or are not able to question them.

Questioning

Rimington did come to question the idea that, as a woman, she should not expect to aspire to certain jobs or organizational positions, such as leadership posts. The culture was maintained in part by the recruitment process, which was founded on the 'tap on the shoulder' (p. 120) method – friends of friends, people (men) that organizational members could be confident were 'one of us'. (Of course, this could go spectacularly wrong – the British Secret Service was also notorious in the 1960s for recruiting and promoting people through this method who went on to spy for other governments from positions of safety precisely because no one could believe they would. John le Carré's wonderful novels, recommended by Rimington as an accurate portrayal of the organization she joined, tell us a lot about these assumptions and how difficult they are to challenge.)

Rimington began to protest about this relatively quickly. She had been working for MI5 for only a few years when she noticed younger, less competent men being promoted to more senior posts. Initially, she took the bureaucratic approach – she asked the personnel officer in her annual appraisal interview what she would have to do to be promoted. The scene must have been amusing in some ways:

> The poor man was completely taken aback. I felt rather like Oliver Twist when he asked for more … I do not think it had ever occurred to him that a woman might want to become an officer … After all, no doubt the women he knew stayed at home and did the flowers, so why was this woman, who had already broken all known conventions by returning to work with a baby, now demand to be treated as if she were a man? He muttered about all the things one could not do as a woman, which made one less than wholly useful. (p. 121)

(Continued)

(Continued)

The interview description provides a series of insights into how trait theories can be mobilized to define 'outsiders' as lacking, only suited for specific work, positioned to stay where they 'belong'. Rimington's protest quickly extended and she won the support of some men in the organization to achieve promotion, a significant pay rise and more interesting work. Her success was not followed by, as she puts it, an 'opening of the floodgates' (p. 124) such that all women were considered as equal colleagues. Change happened for a more mundane reason – the introduction of legislation by the British government making sex discrimination illegal. The organizational culture and its unique legal status meant that it would have been a very brave woman, or group of women, that explored discrimination in the courts, but it turned out that wasn't necessary. A letter signed by a group of women outlining their unhappiness at how they were managed provoked change in the organizational rules; however, as Rimington notes, the cultural 'taboos' on what women were considered able to do took a lot longer to disappear, if they ever have.

The traits needed for intelligence work

Rimington puzzles at length throughout her book as to why she was so successful in her profession. She discusses education, culture, and many different traits such as self-confidence or persistence. However, she dismisses the argument that specific traits are needed for the work she did, putting her success down to determination, energy and an ability to 'get things done'. These qualities, or practices, were present throughout Rimington's working life so that in 1992, she was appointed Director-General – interestingly, the selection process was entirely opaque:

> one day, shortly before Christmas, I was asked to stay behind and he [the retiring Director-General] said 'Congratulations. You are to be the next Director-General.' By then, it did not come as a great surprise to me, but thinking about it now, it is, to say the least, rather strange that no-one had thought to ask me if I wanted the job. Whatever process had brought us to the point of my being told that I'd got it, this certainly was not open competition … What would have happened if it that late stage I had said I did not want it, I don't know. But I did not say that, though it soon became clear that what I was being offered was something of a poisoned chalice. (p. 241)

There is an irony in the fact that Rimington was promoted partly on the basis of being the 'right kind of person', an insider, after spending so many years fighting against exactly that attitude. However, more importantly, her appointment also marked the moment when MI5 would change for ever – she discovered she was to be the first leader to be named publicly. That decision, made by politicians and civil servants, would frame her time as the organization's leader – the one wholly good thing about it, as Rimington notes, is that it also resulted in the wonderful book she wrote after she retired.

Rimington, S. (2001) *Open Secret: The Autobiography of the Former Director-General of MI5*. London: Hutchinson.

1. Why do you think Stella Rimington was so persistent in her working life? In other words, why did she not do as so many women of her generation did, and leave?
2. What do you think was necessary to becoming the Director-General of MI5 in the time that she worked there? Are any of the things you identify traits?
3. If you were in her position, how would you develop yourself as a leader?

The key points in this chapter were ...

I hope there are three themes that you have in your head as you leave this chapter for the next one, on contingency theories of leadership. First, the staying power of trait theories of leadership – this should suggest to you that trait theories are academically important, culturally significant and likely to stay with us for as long as we research and practice leadership. Second, related to this, that theories of leadership do not get 'disproved' or dismissed – there are fashions as in all aspects of management and organization theory, but theories are rarely entirely discredited or shown to be completely wrong. Third, similar to the previous chapter and the next one, this chapter should also help you to think of leadership studies as a research field in which there is a range of perspectives, competing for your attention and trust.

- Trait theories are one of the earliest ways of thinking about and researching leadership. They grew out of Great Man theories.
- They continue to be important today, especially through gender and neuroscience perspectives on leadership.
- Biographies and psychological surveys are some of the main ways leadership traits are researched.
- Trait theories have been heavily critiqued. In particular, early theories had a lack of real world research support. Yet even their most recent forms continue to reduce leadership down to minimal traits (like sex or neurons) in a way that risks ignoring the importance of context.

 # Further thinking

If you want to understand trait theories, then you need to read at least one of the extended reviews of them as an approach – there are three important ones, in order of publication:

Stodgill, R. (1948). Personal factors associated with leadership: A survey of the literature. *The Journal of Psychology, 25*(1), 35–71.

Jago, A. (1982). Leadership: Perspectives in theory and research. *Management Science, 28*(3), 315–336.

Judge, T., Piccolo, R. and Kosalka, T. (2009). The bright and dark side of traits: A review and theoretical extension of the leader trait paradigm. *The Leadership Quarterly, 20*, 855–875.

If you're interested in neuro- or biological approaches, it's best to start with the internet, here:

www.neuroleadership.org

but you must then move on to the peer-reviewed academic research – you'll find references at the end of this book.

Julia Gillard's speech:

Sydney Morning Herald, 10 October 2012, www.smh.com.au/federal-politics/political-news/transcript-of-julia-gillards-speech-20121010-27c36.html (accessed 30 January 2014).

As you read through these articles, reflect on them in light of the critique offered in this chapter. Consider the following questions:

1   Do you think trait theory is worthwhile as an approach to researching and teaching leadership?
2   If you were offered a neurological test to find out if you think like a leader by a research team in a university, would you accept the offer and do it? Why/why not?
3   Imagine that you were forced to take a neurological or genetic test by your employer, and you have been called into a meeting with your supervisor. They explain to you that you have tested negative for leadership traits. How would you feel about this? Would you believe it? How might this affect your future employment? How might it affect the way you think about yourself?

Leadership on screen

Trait theories are not easily represented on screen because we can't see many of them in the same way as we can see, for example, charisma. However, many films, documentaries and television series suggest implicitly or explicitly that traits are the key to understanding leadership, such as:

- *Blade Runner* (1982) – quite old but a classic. The plot centres on whether robots ('replicants') can behave in ways that humans do. It's a fascinating exploration of what it is to be human, how we assess humanity and how we judge others through their personality and behaviour. (If you like the film, you might also enjoy the short story it is based on, 'Do androids dream of electric sheep?', by Philip K. Dick.)
- Recent documentaries about the US corporate world refer frequently to how leaders emerge, are selected and create followers through the use of trait norms, especially *Enron: The Smartest Guys in the Room* (2005), and *The Corporation* (2003). Both are also worth watching for their insights into leadership and leaders more generally.
- A lighter (in some ways) representation of trait theories in action is *Trading Places* (1983) – it's another old movie, but it's still meaningful for thinking through the implications of what researchers call 'heritability', genetics and the 'dark side' of trait theories.

As you watch any of these films, or if you see trait theories of leadership represented anywhere else on screen, you might ask yourself these questions:

- Why are researchers in leadership studies so keen on trait theories when so many fictional films and documentaries suggest they are damaging, unhelpful to individuals and organizations and discriminatory?
- If you were identified as a potential leader because of traits that you have inherited or developed, how would you feel about it?

3

LEADING THROUGH CONTINGENCIES

John Cullen

John believes that thinking seriously about leadership can transform any situation. He is always on the look-out for contexts that challenge received beliefs about who leaders are or what they do.

What this chapter is all about …

The main idea is that contingency theories of leadership focus on the effect of different leadership styles on followers in different contexts. These were some of the earliest theories of leadership that encourage us to look beyond the individual leader and see the importance of others and contexts.

The key questions this chapter answers are:

- How is leadership affected by context?
- Why did contingency theories become popular?
- What are the main contingency theories?
- What are the critiques of contingency theories?

Introduction

When I teach a course on leadership theory, I usually begin by asking students to write down their definition of 'leadership'. Next, I ask them to reflect on who the worst boss they ever had was, and the reasons why they have attained this benighted position. Finally, I ask them to think of the person that they would most like to have as their leader at work, or in some other important part of their lives.

This brief exercise serves as a type of 'Rorschach test' where class participants begin to think about how they have experienced leadership in their own lives. Although the three questions are not designed to elicit answers in a way that could be considered valid in terms of research, they serve the purpose of eliciting certain responses. The answers to the first request ('Write down your definition of leadership') inevitably produces responses that contain the phrases 'getting things done through people', 'motivating people to do things that they would not otherwise do' and 'doing the right thing rather than doing things right'. The responses demonstrate that over time people unconsciously 'pick up' definitions of what *other people* think leadership is. The second question ('Who was the worst boss you have ever had and why?') is usually answered swiftly and without hesitation. The person is unimportant, but identifying the *reasons* for why this person was problematic can tell an individual a huge amount about the type of behaviours they expect from potential leaders. Answers to the final question ('Who would you most like to have as your leader?') can go a long way to helping an individual identify the type of behaviours they most clearly associate with leadership. The exercise can thus assist students to identify how other people's understanding of leadership has influenced their own, but more importantly can help them clarify what they understand leadership to *be*, and what it isn't. Although many researchers and theorists have developed definitions and understandings of leadership, it is important to recognize that we all hold our own *implicit leadership theory*.

DEFINITION: IMPLICIT LEADERSHIP THEORIES (ILTs)

Loosely based on implicit personality theories, **implicit leadership theories** (or ILTs) are concerned with the internally (and often unknowingly) held beliefs that individuals have developed about what constitutes a leader or leadership. A significant amount of research work has been undertaken on ILTs since the mid-1970s. For an excellent summary and overview of ILTs, see Schyns and Meindl (2005).

Implicit leadership theories are theories about leadership that individuals have developed over their life, tacitly hold and use to make sense of the actions and activities of leaders. Because implicit leadership theories are tacit (we don't know that we have them) they have the potential to exert considerable influence on the decisions we make and how we live our lives. ILTs are powerful indicators of how we understand and *do* leadership.

STOP AND REFLECT 3.1

Let's take a moment to explore your own implicit leadership theory. Reflect on the following questions:

- How would you define leadership?
- Who was the worst leader you've ever experienced in person? Why?
- Who would you like to have as a boss or leader at work? Why?

Teaching leadership often involves discussing significant historical or contemporary figures in business and politics, which is probably a demonstration of the continuing influence of the traits approach to studying leadership discussed in the previous chapter. Almost inevitably, when teaching leadership to classes in the Irish context, students often mention Ryanair boss Michael O'Leary as someone who they would love or hate to have as a boss. Granted, such opinions are often based on appraisals of O'Leary's persona when engaging with the media or controversial Ryanair decisions or practices, rather than on personal experiences of working with the man himself. Students who don't like the idea of O'Leary being their leader often claim that they believe his manner might be abrasive or abusive; students who think he is an exemplary leader focus on the manner in which he not only changed a small loss-making airline into one of the largest and most successful in the world. Those who dislike him often say that he has made the experience of air travel unpleasant; those who don't dislike him laud the way in which he has not only changed a single company, but has also transformed an entire industry. What is interesting about these reasons for loving and hating the idea of Ryanair's Michael O'Leary as a leader is that they are actually quite similar. Students often say that they imagine that O'Leary would permit no questioning of decisions after he has made them. Some students hate this, but others like the decisiveness of his character. So what, then, is the real answer to the question, 'Is Michael O'Leary a good leader?'

The failure of the classical traits approach to studying leadership to answer questions like this goes a long way to explaining why contingency-based approaches became popular in the aftermath of the Second World War. Studying leadership traits is possible in stable situations. Many theories of economics are based on a similar perception of what the world *should* look like if everything was kept on an even keel. The problem is that stable social and economic situations no longer, if they ever did, exist. This meant that the *situation* or circumstances in which leadership was done were understood to have an enormous bearing on the way that leaders should conduct themselves, and the type of leadership that followers required. Even if the leader was successful in their endeavours, it meant that the situation in turn would change, which would require the leader to change yet again. Research that studied the interaction of the leader and the circumstances in which leadership was undertaken became known as *contingency* theories. There are many different theoretical contributions to consider, but it is worth bearing in mind that 'good' leadership can change a situation, but when that situation changes, what happens to leadership then? One final example of how leadership is contingent on the context in which it is practised was provided by Charlie Clifton, a former steward at Ryanair who worked his way up the ranks to a management position under Michael O'Leary. Clifton was asked by Tony Ryan, co-founder of Ryanair, to assist in the creation of an Asian low-cost airline, Tiger Airways, in late 2003. The Asian aviation market was similar to that in Europe when Ryanair was beginning its ascent, but Clifton commented that, due to cultural differences, replicating the style of leadership that had driven Ryanair's growth at that point was not an option for the then nascent Tiger Airways.

We would be delighted if we got somebody of the calibre of Michael O'Leary. Michael has got a very personal way of doing business that might work down here or people might be highly insulted by it. I don't know. We will do what we feel is the best thing locally and adapt it. If a potential candidate comes in cursing, roaring and shouting, that doesn't mean that they will get the job. (Creaton, 2003, p. 60)

Case study: *Gang Leader for a Day* (1)

Ethnographic studies of urban criminal gangs are surprisingly common. Those of us who live in cities and their suburbs in the 'developed world' often hear about the results of gang feud-related violence in daily news bulletins, and some of us have been directly affected by it. Although many police procedural dramas continue to depict that forces of law and government as the 'good guys' working against the Machiavellian strategies of drugs barons and their evil-spirited minions, the academic tradition of urban ethnography attempts to get inside the world of the gang members to understand them, and the situations in which they live (and often

(Continued)

(Continued)

cannot escape from). From Piri Thomas's *Down These Mean Streets* (1967) to Philippe Bourjois's *In Search of Respect* (2003) ethnographers have steadily worked to understand the lives of those who are not counted among the beneficiaries of pro-capital policies. Contemporary mainstream media rarely produces shows that fairly present people who have been born into positions of disadvantage. It is not surprising that the shows that actually manage to present a more balanced perspective, such as HBO's *The Wire*, are based on accounts that are largely ethnographic.

Sudhir Venkatesh's (2008) ethnography of his experiences with Chicago's Black Kings gang is not unique because it is the account of an academic social scientist studying an urban gang on its own terms, but because it is specifically focused on how *leadership* is done within such contexts. In the main it focuses on the Venkatesh's relationship with up-and-coming Black Kings gang leader 'JT' who, after a stand-off with the middle-class and naïve doctoral student, quickly takes him under his wing. The bleak social situation in which JT attempts to rise higher through the ranks of the Black Kings permeates the context in which leadership is done in a desperately poor inner-city housing project. Readers of *Gang Leader for a Day* are left with no sense of 'judgement' directed towards the various gang members or other residents of the notorious Roger Taylor Homes housing project, but rather are left wondering if they would have behaved differently if born into a similar situation. In the largely under-resourced and under-policed public housing complex, leadership was practised in a way where results mattered and second chances were rare. However, it also became apparent to Venkatesh over the decade that he spent with the gang that, even though they operated a form of 'outlaw capitalism' (p. 37) in the underground economy, the Black Kings structured themselves, interacted with competitors, conducted promotions and demotions, and sought to stabilize external conditions as if they were a legitimate business. The 'hustlers' clearly wanted to identify themselves as business people. This concern with being taken 'seriously' as business people led many to disclose specific details about their economic activities. The data collected by Venkatesh informed one of the chapters, 'Why Do Drug Dealers Still Live with Their Moms', in Levitt and Dubner's bestselling *Freakonomics* (2005).

Gang Leader for a Day is very much the study of one leader working in a very difficult and ethically dubious space. Because of Venkatesh's relationship with JT, he also gained access to several other parts of the Roger Taylor community and saw how leadership was undertaken among people who were homeless and addicted to various substances, by community workers and by mothers who were heading up single-parent households. The various ways in which leadership can be done is explored throughout the text, but not just with reference to the titular 'gang leader'. It is an apt context to discuss how leadership is contingent to the situation in which leaders and followers find themselves given that the situation often involved events (and responses to events) that would be considered 'extreme' in a mainstream business leadership text. An influential community leader instructed Venkatesh: 'But don't make us the victim ... We'll take responsibility for what we can control. It's just that not everything is in our hands' (p. 148). One of the major events facing everyone in the text, which would fundamentally change the situation in which all of the participants in the ethnography lived, was the looming demolition of the Roger Taylor Homes.

1. What are some of the ethical issues that might arise in studying leadership in illegal gangs?
2. What can we learn about business leadership from ethnographies of socially deprived areas?

The story of contingency approaches to studying leadership

Many textbooks present the evolution of leadership theory in a linear fashion. First came trait theory, then behavioural or style-based leadership, then contingency and context-specific approaches, then charismatic leadership, which is followed by transformational and ethical leadership. Although this is, broadly speaking, the case for how leadership theories and approaches have developed over time, this text makes the point that it is never really the case that when new findings are made that one approach replaces another and the previous set of findings are dismissed as irrelevant and stored in the archives of academic curiosities from a bygone age. Rather, formerly fashionable approaches remain somewhere in the background of new theoretical developments and are often re-discovered and re-packaged for new audiences. Take, for example, this quote from a contemporary leadership text that introduces contingency approaches to a student readership:

> The failure to find universal leader traits or behaviours that would always determine effective leadership led researchers in a new direction. Although leadership behaviour was still examined, the central focus of the new research was the situation in which leadership occurred. (Daft, 2011, p. 58)

The idea that trait theory was a failure and had to be replaced by contingency approaches is a very common perspective in leadership studies, and one which is deserving of scrutiny. As the previous chapter has shown, traits remain an enduring perspective in *positivistic* leadership studies and mainstream leadership guidebooks.

DEFINITION: POSITIVISM

Positivism is a philosophical paradigm which prioritizes the scientific observation of phenomena. It is a highly contentious term among social scientists as positivists often assume that many social events and psychological processes can be measured in an impartial and objective way in the same way that, say, coastal erosion or temperature rises can be recorded. As Raymond Williams wrote, positivism 'neglects the position of the observer, who is also a fact and not merely an instrument' (1976, p. 389).

Type in 'traits' and 'leaders' into any good academic research database and you'll quickly see that the search for the ideal leadership trait is far from being abandoned! A similar search on the highly regarded *Social Science Citation Index* demonstrates that 71 pieces of peer-reviewed research with 'leadership' and 'traits' in the title have been published over the past 20 years, with the greatest number of items being published in 2012. Over the same time period, only 17 items have been published with the words 'contingency' and 'leadership' in the article title. In research terms, trait approaches appear to have survived the test of time, with contingency theories becoming something of an appendix in the history of leadership theory.

This is probably one of the reasons why excellent texts on leadership such as Brad Jackson and Ken Parry's *A Very Short, Fairly Interesting and Reasonably Cheap Book about Studying Leadership* (2011) do not delve into contingency leadership in a huge amount of detail. However, the contingency approach to studying leadership has actually changed its form in ways that have informed the development of transformational and ethical forms of leadership. Classical definitions of contingency approaches to studying leadership recognize that organizations and their external environments undergo constant change. Leaders, thus, are compelled to change their leadership style and behaviours in accordance with these changes. Variables that influence the style that the leader chooses include task structure, the quality of existing relationships between the leader and other members of the organisation, and the level of discretion or authority available to the leader and their followers to make necessary changes. The biggest shift from the trait approach to the contingency approach to studying leadership is a challenge to the assumption that leaders alone dictate success. The success of leaders is dependent on the characteristics of followers and the nature of the actual situation in which it is undertaken. In the 70 or so years since the end of the Second World War 'more than 65 classification systems have been developed to define the dimensions of leadership, and more than 15,000 books and articles have been written about the elements that contribute to leadership effectiveness' (Manning and Curtis, 2009, p. 25). Perhaps another of the central reasons why contingency theories have become less *noticeable* is because they are, in their contemporary forms, ubiquitous in management theory.

One final reason why contingency theories appear to have been superseded by transformational and ethical/anti-charismatic forms of leadership in recent years is the *diversity* and *heterogeneity* of the contingency approach. Several of the main models developed in relation to contingency-based conceptualizations of leadership were developed in isolation from each other and soon afterwards were grouped together under the 'contingency' label. This gives the impression of a contingency *movement* which simply did not exist. There are some marked similarities between some of the best-known contingency-based approaches and these are discussed in relation to the four best-known models of contingency-centred understandings of leadership below.

Contingency approach 1: Fiedler's contingency model

Contemporary contingency approaches to studying leadership emerged around the same time as the rise of organizational contingency theory in the 1960s. Organizational contingency theory was very much a reaction to the ongoing dominance of normative models of organizing. The related, but distinct, disciplines of organizational behaviour and management studies had largely taken on board the findings of the Hawthorne studies and attempted to inform the 'humanization' of workplaces. Classical and scientific models of organizing, however, persisted in the field of organizational design theory and continued in their attempts to find 'one best way' of organizing. Organizational contingency theorists challenged this as something of a wild-goose chase and instead proposed that each organization could find its own best way of working by determining how their desired performance was contingent on factors such as people, technological sophistication and what was happening in their external market. Influenced by this approach, Fred Fiedler began theorizing how organizations and managers could determine what their best form of *local* leadership could be. Fiedler went on to develop one of the first and most influential contingency theories of leadership which was published in the late 1960s.

Fiedler's (1967) theory of leadership effectiveness is anchored in an individual's leadership style and the degree to which the situation in which they find themselves enables their ability to exert influence

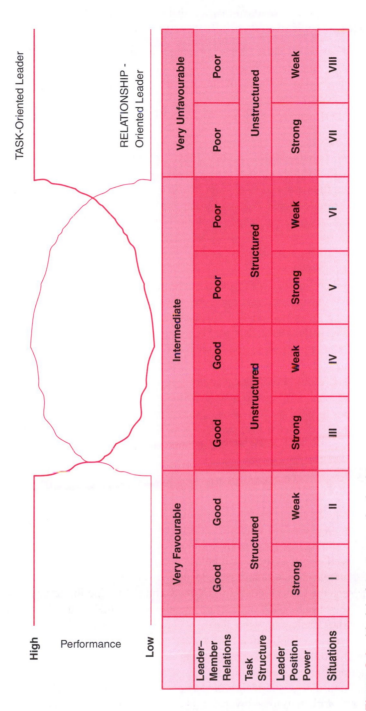

Figure 3.1 Model of contingency leadership

over a group of followers. The *favourableness* of the situation (which is how Fiedler referred to the extent to which a leader could exert their influence) depends on three basic situational variables:

- the quality of personal relationships that leaders have with members of their group (otherwise known as *leader–member relations*);
- the level of clarity that exists about the work that the group have to do (or the degree to which *task structure* is unambiguous);
- the power and influence that a leader has over their 'subordinates' (or the *position power of the leader*).

When the situation was analysed, leaders could then decide on the type of leadership style they should adopt. For example, if the three variables above were either very favourable or very unfavourable in all three respects then the leader should adopt an *authoritarian* style of leadership. However if leader–member relations were intermediate (as might happen when, say, leader–member relations were good, but the task was unstructured and leader position power was weak) then the leader should adopt a *relationship-oriented* (or *democratic-considerate*) style of leadership. If leader–member relations and leader position power are high, but the task is unstructured, leaders should adopt a task-oriented (results-oriented) style (see Figure 3.1).

There have been several critiques of Fiedler's model, not least of which has been a concern that, despite its claims to address universalistic normative approaches to studying leadership, it actually still proposes a menu of leadership styles which are supposed to be applicable in most situations. Additionally, some of the key variables are very difficult to gather robust data on. For example, leaders may be led to believe that they have high levels of respect and strong position power on the basis of their previous dealings with followers. However, as Tourish (2005) has pointed out, many leaders tend to uncritically accept positive feedback on their actions and initiatives as an endorsement of their capabilities from their followers. In doing so, they forget that these followers often communicate like this to their leaders because they wish to ingratiate themselves with them for a variety of reasons (promotion, job security, etc.). Findings like these make two of the key variables on which Fiedler's model stands open to critique. That said, Fiedler did much to move theory away from the idea that leadership is a monolithic entity that can be deployed in the same fashion in all locations.

Contingency approach 2: Path–goal theory

Another significant contribution to contingency-based approaches to studying leadership is found in *path–goal*-based approaches. This approach addressed a concern that had arisen with previous understandings of leadership behavioural styles. Many of these approaches discussed grouping leaders according to how well they can be considered autocratic, democratic leaders or 'hands-off' leaders. Others, in a very general sense, tended to rate leadership on two central components.

The first of these is the leaders' concern for how well the 'production orientation' of the organization functions. That is, they are focused on how efficiently the organization achieves its goals. The second is their concern for the people who work for them. The higher the individual leader performs according to both of these criteria is an indication for how effective they can be considered as a leader. One such study was that which would later become known as the 'Ohio State Studies', which organized leadership behaviour across a dual axis based on high or low levels of *consideration* (the extent to which a leader cares and respects subordinates) and *initiating structure* (the extent to which a leader is task oriented and directs subordinates' work activities towards goal achievement). Subsequent empirical research on this model found a number of exceptions to the initial finding that the most effective leaders scored highly on both consideration and initiating structure. The emergence of the path–goal theory of leadership emerged from research that focused on analysing these 'high/high' circumstances (Figure 3.2).

The discipline of organizational behaviour might recognize path–goal theory as a motivational model. Based on Yale University professor Victor Vroom's core concept of *expectancy* (or the belief that

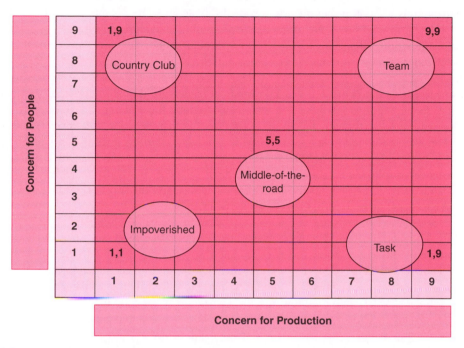

Figure 3.2   The Managerial Grid

a certain level of effort will be followed by a particular level of performance), path–goal theory simply states that the key role of leadership is directly related to their ability to clarify a follower's path to what they desire to achieve at work. The leader's role then becomes one of clarifying important and attainable objectives and goals for followers. Leadership, according to this approach, is about helping followers or subordinates find their path to a particular goal.

Although this appears very straightforward, the empirical work undertaken to develop path–goal theory demonstrated that if the follower perceives the route to their goal as being clear, any additional information provided by the leader will be seen as superfluous. If this happens, satisfaction with the leader will diminish amongst the group of followers. For this reason the 'high consideration' mode is most important (and leads to greater follower satisfaction with leaders) when individuals work in routine or highly structured tasks. Additionally higher levels of the 'initiating structure' style become most important in situations where tasks are ambiguous.

Alongside inconsistent research results on the effectiveness of path–goal theory, research on motivation in the workplace has also demonstrated a number of problems with this approach. These include a lack of understanding of how an individual is motivated in the context of their participation in organized work, the fact that individuals *value* goals differently and the changing nature of the complexities of tasks in the postmodern, networked workplace.

Contingency approach 3: Hersey and Blanchard's situational theory

Hersey and Blanchard's theory of situational leadership is one of the most recent and perhaps best-known contributions to contingency theory. A part of the model's fame is due to one of its originators being Ken Blanchard, who owns one of the most successful leadership and management development companies in the world. Blanchard became famous through authoring short management fables such as *The One Minute Manager* (which itself was co-authored with Spencer Johnson of *Who Moved My Cheese?*). The main reason for the success of Hersey and Blanchard's situational leadership theory is it attempts to integrate much of what was known about leadership into a comprehensive model. Their situational leadership approach is based on three basic factors: the amount of task-oriented behaviour that a leader demonstrates (through the guidance and direction that they give to followers); the amount of relationship-oriented behaviour that a leader provides; and the *readiness* level that organizational members exhibit in performing a specific task, function or objective. Hersey and Blanchard pointed out that the readiness level of followers is constituted by the degree they are motivated to achieve set goals, their willingness and ability to assume responsibility for outcomes, and the level of training and experience that they have to assist them to fulfil the task set for them.

As an accumulation of existing contingency leadership theory, the situational leadership model shares many elements with existing approaches. For example, like the Ohio State model, it includes the extent to which the leader listens to, cares for and respects subordinates. In the Ohio State model, this was known as *consideration*; in Hersey and Blanchard's situational leadership model it is named *relationship* (or supportive) behaviours. Similarly, the extent to which a leader is task oriented and directs subordinates' work activities towards the achievement of particular goals, which is named *initiating structure* in the Ohio State model, is referred to as *task* behaviours in the Hersey and Blanchard situational leadership model. When the task and relationship behaviours are analysed together, they aim to propose an appropriate leadership style for the situation in which the leader finds themselves. If the situation involves low levels of task and relationship (where followers are willing and confident), the model recommends that the leader should adopt a *delegating* style, and turn over responsibilities for making and implementing decisions to followers. If relationships are strong, but the situation is low on the task element (where followers are able, but may be unwilling and feel insecure), Hersey and Blanchard recommend that the leader *participate* by sharing ideas and facilitating discussions among followers that will lead to firm decisions. If the situation is high on both relationship and task, the leader's style should become one of *selling*, where they explain and clarify decisions. Finally, if the situation is high on task, but low on relationship, the most appropriate leadership style is one of *telling*, where specific instructions are given to subordinates and their subsequent performance is closely supervised.

 ## Case study: *Gang Leader for a Day* (2)

Everyone wants to kill the leader, so you got to get to them first. (Venkatesh, 2008, p. 71)

Although Venkatesh often reports the level of compassion and tenderness that the residents of the Roger Taylor Homes demonstrated for each other, he is also careful not to romanticize or gloss over the harsh realities of living in a neglected area or participating in gang activities. JT often meted out violent physical punishments to members of his gang, and to others who challenged his position of formal authority within the hierarchy. The leader of a group of squatters, the likeable C-Note, was mercilessly beaten by JT and his lieutenants for refusing to clear vehicles he was working on from an area where the gang wanted to play basketball. It was later explained that this wasn't done from an innate need to be violent, but in the unregulated environment that the gangs operate in, any lack of deference to his position could ultimately have led to de-stabilizing his position as leader. Gang leaders constantly had to reinforce an understanding that they were to be feared by their own members to prevent a coup d'état. This may seem like the leaders must ensure that leader–member relations are very unfavourable (in Fiedler's terms), but the harsh logic of working in an environment like this perhaps dictates otherwise.

In one memorable sequence, Venkatesh travelled with JT and some of his most trusted aides to visit the sales teams of the various Black Kings drug-dealing operations that he was responsible for overseeing. Rather than taking reports from the 'sales directors' of these teams, JT virtually interrogated them about new developments on their patch and tried to trick them into admitting that they had been retaining profits from their drug deals for themselves. On one occasion he used violence to mediate a dispute between two members of a dealing team who argued about stealing profits. However, in another case a gang member diluted the crack cocaine he had been dealing so much that his customers complained. The idea that the Black Kings might become known for selling inferior 'product' was one of JT's strongest worries, as it would mean that they would lose business to other gangs. However, rather than beating the gang member who admitted to 'stretching' the product he was supposed to sell, JT merely fined the culprit so as not to send a message that entrepreneurial thinking was forbidden, only that certain tactics (stealing, over-diluting product) were. This could perhaps be taken as an example of 'path–goal' leadership where certain types of activities are discouraged, and others are supported. Various other leaders in the Roger Taylor Homes community also provided Venkatesh with advice on how he was to proceed on his path to reaching his goal of really understanding how the community worked. Several, from the homeless C-Note, to JT and even the police advised him to speak with the elected building president of the Local Advisory Council and long-time Roger Taylor Homes resident Ms Bailey.

As JT rose through the ranks of the Black Kings hierarchy he was responsible for over 20 Black Kings sales teams outside his own territory. This meant that he was the de facto leader of groups of often very young men, many of whom grew up in impoverished circumstances and did not come from stable family backgrounds. Most did not have high levels of educational attainment. These men also worked in perhaps the most dangerous part of the illegal, underground economy, where violence and fatalities were common (Levitt and Dubner (2005) report that members of JT's gang stood a one in four chance of being killed at work). These were the circumstances over which JT had to ensure that he provided a form of leadership that ensured his operations remained profitable. Street units were closely scrutinized and their directors regularly grilled to ensure profitability. According to the Hersey–Blanchard model of situational leadership, these circumstances call for a 'telling' leadership style (high task behaviour, low relationship behaviour). However, realizing that such a style wasn't sustainable over long periods of time, JT frequently called large-scale gang meetings, ostensibly to inform and instruct on practical matters, but really to motivate his gang by discussing concepts such as courage, community and loyalty. Such meetings were really about promoting gang solidarity so all members could be clear on the reasons for tactical changes and the values of the groups. In Hersey–Blanchard terms this is a 'selling' leadership style (high task behaviour, high relationship behaviour). Throughout the book, we learn that JT kept his 'officer' group very small, usually consisting of gang members that he had known for a long time, because there were very few that he trusted to carry out his actions. Rather than suggesting that JT did not value delegating, the opposite is more likely to be the

(Continued)

(Continued)

case. Given that the 'organization' he had to run was diverse, fragmented and under constant threat from surveillance and competition, there were very few members who did not require strong levels of guidance and support (low task and support behaviours).

1. What other leadership models could be applied to the incident where JT fined the gang member who 'stretched' his product?
2. Describe JT's leadership style.
3. How are contingency theories useful in making sense of this story?
4. Where are there weaknesses? What is missed or inconsistent?

Contingency approach 4: Leader-participation style model

It is perhaps not surprising to see motivational theorists sharing significant conceptual space with many leadership researchers. Motivating followers, after all, is often seen as constituting a core element of what leaders actually do. Victor Vroom's work has already been mentioned in relation to path–goal theory above, but he has also exerted significant influence with another contingency leadership model, that which has been variously known as 'the leadership-participation style model' or the 'Vroom–Jago contingency model' as he first developed it with Phillip Yetton, and later Arthur Jago (Vroom and Yetton, 1973; Vroom and Jago, 1988). Much of Vroom's work focuses on leadership in the context of team situations, and the leadership-participation style model does this in relation to how groups and their leaders solve problems. It shares a lot of similarities with other contingency theories, so it is important to highlight the ways in which it differs.

The leadership-participation style model focuses on decision-making, with specific emphasis on solving a specific, identified problem, and is concerned with finding an answer to the question: who should solve the problem? The model recognizes that there are varying degrees of participative leadership and tries to delineate a 'rational' method for deciding on the amount of participation that leaders should *bring* to the effective solving of problems. The leader who has to make this decision first applies a self-assessment tool to assess the situation. This tool attempts to ascertain: how important the decision is to the organization; how important is the commitment of the team members to successful implementation of the decision (especially if it was made by the team leader without consulting the rest of the group); how much expertise and competence does the group and leader have in solving similar problems; and the degree to which the team supports the organization's goals and objectives.

When analysis of the situation has been completed the leader then decides on the appropriate leadership-participation style that they will apply. Briefly, there are five basic leadership approaches that can be decided on, which are broadly based on the amount of influence that a leader can exert on the group, and the opposing amount of freedom that a group believes it can bring to making a decision to solve the identified problem. Beginning with the highest area of leadership influence, and moving to the situation where groups can exert most influence on the decision, these basic leadership styles are:

- Autocratic 1: The leader alone makes the decision, and then either announces or 'sells' it to the group.
- Autocratic 2: The leader presents the problem to group members as individuals, collects their suggestions and makes a decision.
- Consultative 1: The leader gathers the members of the group together, collects their input and then makes a decision.
- Consultative 2: The leaders gathers the members of the group together, but rather than collecting information on a problem as they have defined it, explains the problem and the parameters it exists within. The objective is to get agreement from a group on the best decision that can be made. Throughout this process, the leader must be careful not to show that their ideas are given greater weight simply because of their position or power.
- Group based: The group is permitted to make the decision about how the problem will be solved within prescribed limits. The group identifies and diagnoses the problem, decides on solutions and develops procedures for implementing these. The leader's role becomes one of supporting, resourcing and encouraging the group. The leader plays no direct role in the group's work of solving the problem unless directly asked.

Case study: *Gang Leader for a Day (3)*

Although *Gang Leader for a Day* provides lots of micro-examples of how leadership is done in difficult situations, it is also provides strong examples of when leadership is required in a specific situation. The Vroom–Jago contingency model of leadership focuses on how leaders chose to adopt various styles based on problems that their group faces. One such example was provided one summer afternoon when Venkatesh was talking with a middle-aged resident in front of one of the Roger Taylor Homes building. The resident noticed a young white man driving slowly in front of the building. The resident, believing that the young man was seeking out a woman working as a prostitute, warned him to go away. The young man remained in his car and ignored the resident, which aroused the suspicions of the Black Kings gang. They approached the man's car and began intimidating him in the hope that he would leave the area. However, while distracted, another gang conducted a 'drive-by' shooting, terrifying the residents of the building and injuring Price, the senior officer of the gang responsible for security.

Despite representations in the popular media, drive-by shootings are not a daily occurrence in illegal gang activities. Shootings attract unwanted attention from police departments. Additionally, public and political outcries in the aftermath of such incidents lead to additional resources being provided to police, who then become better resourced to disrupt gang activities. As with more legitimate sectors, gang businesses require stable environments to operate in. Because of this, the drive-by shooting incident described in *Gang Leader for a Day*, although not unprecedented, was certainly unusual. In the immediate aftermath of the shooting, the

(Continued)

(Continued)

residents and the gang members sequestered themselves in a building and attention quickly turned to JT who had to demonstrate leadership in the midst of a highly unstructured, problematic situation.

Many of the young gang members wanted to retaliate immediately for the shooting, without knowing who the perpetrators were. It soon transpired that the shooting had been conducted by a very small group of men 'with no business sense' (p. 225) who had decided to try to intimidate the gang by force. However, JT commandeered a vacant apartment to act as a war room and consulted with several of his gang members individually and as small groups, demonstrating a mixture between 'lighter' authoritative styles and consultative styles. At the outset of the crisis he made a number of authoritative decisions about smaller matters (buying food for the families sequestered in the building, commandeering Venkatesh's car and ordering Price to be taken to hospital). These doubtlessly gave the impression that he was taking direct action, but he was hesitant to engage in any activities that might impact on future long-term relationships with other gangs or criminal organisations. The attackers were later dispossessed of their weapons and money by the Black Kings; they were beaten up as punishment for the attack.

In an unstructured situation like this, acting hastily or without full information can have further detrimental consequences down the line. Recognizing that the group he led were overly emotional in the wake of the drive-by shooting, JT demonstrated a calm unemotional front, but made some tactical decisions that would settle the situation down and make his followers feel more secure. The reasons why the more consultative styles weren't chosen perhaps stem from this mind-set. If JT attempted to facilitate a discussion about how the group would respond to this direct assault on its own territory, questions would later be raised about his appropriateness to lead the gang. Additionally, he needed to demonstrate solidarity with his gang members, rather than being a resource for them, so he participated directly in the punitive beating that was meted out to Price's assailants.

1. What other style(s) of contingency leadership theory best describe JT's response to the desire of the younger gang members to seek an immediate reprisal to the attack?
2. Are contingency theories of leadership more suited to crises or unanticipated emergencies? Why/why not?

Contingency theories in practice

If you look at the portion of any mainstream leadership textbook which treats contingency leadership theories, you'll notice that they often do not take up very much space. As mentioned above, although they are often considered as an important phase in the development of leadership theory, there is a sense that they have been surpassed by more recent iterations. As a necessary bridge stage, one could be forgiven for assuming that contingency theories are somewhat passé. The reality, however, is a little different.

Because contingency theories were largely developed on a *positivistic* grounding that de-emphasized larger socio-cultural contexts, it meant that they are easily *teachable* and *testable* in practice. This means that they have immediate utility to the management development industry, where human resource development professionals can apply their associated tools in practice with the aim of developing greater understandings of leadership as part of organizational training and development. Given that it has been estimated that the size of the leadership development market ten years ago was worth up to 60 million US dollars annually (Burgoyne, 2004), it is perhaps a little hasty to suggest that they are no longer used in practice. Many of the tools have associated questionnaires which can be used by managers and leaders to self-diagnose situational contingencies such as the leaders' preferred style, the characteristics of their group members and the work environment in which they must lead. Hersey and Blanchard's situational leadership model, which is one of the best-known self-assessment tools known to the management development community (Dalton, 2010), has often been compared to the earlier Blake and Mouton leadership grid which remains a highly used assessment tool in management and organizational development.

However, research and theorization on contingency-based leadership tools appears to have greatly decreased since the field's hey-day in the 1970s. The Social Sciences Citation Index (hereafter SSCI), which indexes and rates citations of research published in peer-reviewed periodical publications, has, according to Wang et al. (2012), 'become a synonym of quality for all social science journals' (p. 509). This index demonstrates that most of the work published over the last 50 years that contained the search terms 'leadership' and 'continge*' (to capture various forms of words related to *contingency*) in peer-reviewed article titles spiked in the mid-1970s and gradually decreased until quite recently (Figure 3.3).

However, when these results are compared to a similar search on 'leadership' combined with 'trans*' (to capture various forms of words associated with the related terms of *transactional* and *transformational* leadership), a clearer picture of how contingency leadership models have been superseded by work in other leadership research fields emerges (Figure 3.4).

The figures speak largely for themselves. Almost ten times more peer-reviewed theory and research has been published on transactional/transformational leadership, and the volume of work on the later area continues to grow, while work on contingency-based understandings of leadership continues to appear in something of a piecemeal manner. Part of the reason for this lies in the nature of more expressive forms of leadership that have become fashionable since the 1980s, and part in an apparent lack of engagement by researchers with some of the more glaring flaws that exist in relation to contingency theories.

First, as will be discussed in a later chapter, transformational leadership and its promises of being about changing leaders, organizations and followers for the better of all has its roots in the large-scale 'spiritualization' of the workplace that began to take place in the 1980s (Heelas, 1996; Ackers and Preston, 1997). As such, it surfed the rising wave of searches for meaningfulness and authenticity in work that became prevalent in many management development programmes (Bell and Taylor, 2004) at that time, which made the more mechanistic offerings from leadership contingency theory appear dry and 'soulless'. Second, a number of critiques of contingency leadership approaches had either been left unaddressed, or had not been adequately engaged with. The fact that such tools are easily accessible and usable by human resource development and management development professionals may be good news for the training sector, but this has meant that they have often been perceived as being based on simplistic formulae that are easy to sell and apply. From the four leading examples of contingency theory discussed in the sections above, the reader will quickly see that they are all the products of business school-based academics in the United States. They have been developed within an uncritical psychologistic paradigm which does not always travel easily outside its own context. The scientistic, managerialist

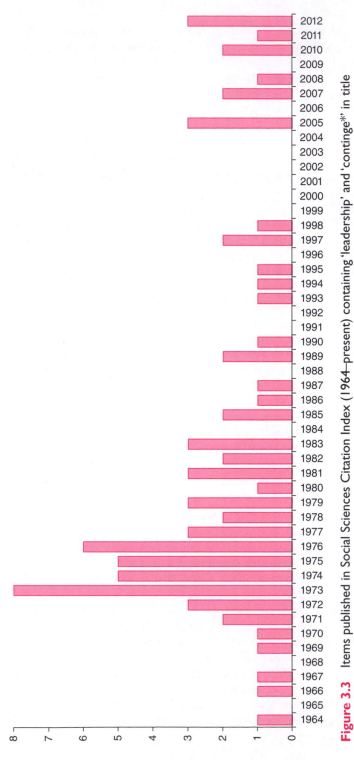

Figure 3.3 Items published in Social Sciences Citation Index (1964–present) containing 'leadership' and 'continge*' in title

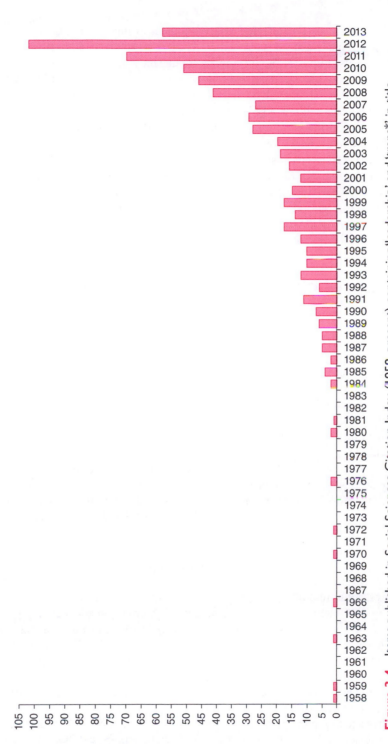

Figure 3.4 Items published in Social Sciences Citation Index (1958–present) containing 'leadership' and 'trans*' in title

This material is reproduced under a license from Thomson Reuters. You may not copy or re-distribute this material in whole or in part without the prior written consent of Thomson Reuters approach suggested by many contingency leadership theories implies that in all situations a menu for actions can be used to make decisions: a position that many experienced managers know simply not to be the case. Despite its origins in organisational contingency theory, leadership contingency theories appear to suggest that one person can control followers and environments. Many contingency leadership theories are based on an assumption that leaders work in stable, un-dynamic environments that they can easily control, a belief that will quickly be challenged by the experiences of most managers or leaders. If contingency leadership theory promises would-be leaders that they will be effective if they follow its prescripts, the outcomes may often disappoint. When the stated outcomes of adopting a particular approach based on a leader's analysis of a contingent situation does not materialize, it will doubtless lead to frustration on behalf of the leader who had been led to believe that the approach would offer a different result. In such situations, perhaps leading without attempting to control followers and a changing environment might prove to be a more effective way of dealing with contingencies. As one of the tenant leaders in *Gang Leader for a Day* offered, 'Things never go as planned ... because we're dealing with poor people' (p. 265).

Critical approaches to contingency theories of leadership

The point made by the tenant leader at the end of the previous section of this chapter highlights a major aspect of contingency theories of leadership: they are part of the mainstream of the traditional leadership 'canon'. They emerge from, and are designed for, conservative organizational scenarios. Among the key contingency leadership theorists discussed in this chapter are management consultants, Ivy League business-school professors and industrial psychologists. Michel Foucault pointed out that understanding any claims to knowledge from a critical perspective should involve uncovering the 'truth games' that influential elites play in order to reinforce their social position. Groups and individuals who attempt to exist at the margins of society are very aware of the context in which they find themselves and must resist any attempt to influence or persuade them in order to avoid further marginalization. Contingency theories are replete with language that attempts to de-politicize the self-determination of 'follower' groups: in what other branch of theory could the words 'autocratic' come to represent anything other than an unacceptable attempt to wield power in a negative way? Why do contingency leadership theorists often discuss the malleability of an organizational population using positive terms such as 'readiness'?

Knights (2009) highlights that critical management theorists generally found contingency theories to be problematic due to their highly positivistic and deterministic nature. Mainstream theorists assumed power to be an essential resource that it was the responsibility of managers to understand and use in a deterministic way to interact with the changing external environment. Few adopted a *Foucauldian* perspective which saw power as something that could be deployed in an organizational setting with productive and positive results for the people it was projected onto. Knights, however, sees the potential of the work of John Child (1984) who incorporated the concept of agentic strategic choice into the study of organizations and how they were managed. Although the choices available to leaders (agents) were constrained by the vagaries of the external environment, 'strategic choices' were still available to them in *how* they chose to react to these changes.

The questions asked by more critical management theorists about contingency theories can help us develop a deeper understanding of the ideas and models that are proposed. It has already been mentioned that contingency theories hinge on a recognition that all organizations and their external environments change constantly. Thinking critically about contingency leadership leads us to ask: what is it that these theories want organizations and their employees to change into? The fundamental nature of change is also a constant of Marxist theory where it is proposed that through cycles of change, power and resources will gradually become more evenly distributed. Contingency theories, on the other hand, can be accused of recognizing that change occurs, but provides models and tactics for the powerful to maintain control of 'their' workers and followers, prolonging their exploitation through reinforcing their dependence on the owners of the means of production. Contingency leadership theories, despite having context at their core, are still very much theories for the leader to use to exert control over followers and situations. Such approaches serve to bolster the idea of a 'reified' leader, whose concerns and interests must be prioritized over those they lead.

Do contingency theories of leadership have a future?

Despite the territory of contingency leadership theories appearing neglected and abused, especially when compared with some of the newer and shinier leadership theories, it is important to ask whether it is worthwhile consigning them to the rubbish tip of leadership theory. Clearly, mainstream leadership textbooks appear keen to continue to include them, and leadership and organizational development specialists seem to find them useful in their work with managers and executives. At some time in every manager's career, they will find themselves in the position of being a newly appointed manager and having to deal with a situation that requires leadership. The apparent utility of applying a contingency-based approach to working through a problem with a unit may be a simple first step to experimenting with leadership identity. We are seldom prepared for these challenges, and when thrust into a leadership position often have to use the most accessible and understandable tool, and many contingency approaches provide this as an *entrée* into the world of leadership.

If this chapter had been written ten years ago in 2004, it would have likely concluded that contingency theories of leadership were beginning to wind down in terms of theoretical relevance to the rest of the oeuvre of leadership studies. From Figure 3.3 it can be plainly seen that there had been no articles published in journals indexed by the SSCI for almost six years at that point. In the same timeframe almost 100 articles relating to transformational leadership had been published. However, in the latter half of the 2000s, peer-reviewed research work referring to contingency theories of leadership began to emerge again. The articles that have been published more recently have opened up some interesting new vistas for how we examine the relationship between leadership and contingencies. Some of these look at 'morals' or ethics as being a key contingency that impacts on leadership style (ethics and leadership is discussed in more detail in a later chapter), but others consider 'culture' as an important contingency. This is interesting given that, after leadership, culture probably is the most written about and researched topic in management and organizational studies. Culture and leadership have often been written about together, but national, social and organizational culture have rarely been discussed as *contingencies in* leadership studies.

No organization and no leader exists in a vacuum, and the global economic crisis has demonstrated that leaders in one sector cannot treat broader socio-cultural contingencies as if they are externalities. Contingency theory may undergo a new resurgence if it can be developed to address new forms of working (particularly the opportunities provided by 'virtual' work spaces), but even more so as a way of developing new forms of critical reflexivity among leaders. If contingency approaches to studying leadership peaked 40 years ago, it is well worth considering the changes that the world has undergone since then, such as increased neoliberalism in economic policy, accelerated globalization, and new forms of cultural or political imperialism. Perhaps the reason for the abeyance of contingency leadership approaches is not that the approach became irrelevant, but a more pressing set of contingencies emerged that the existing models could not accommodate due to their ideological biases.

When they were first introduced contingency approaches to studying leadership involved something of a first step to acknowledging the *relational* role of leaders, and the importance of followers and followership. This role appeared to be have been appropriated (within mainstream leadership studies) by transformational leadership (through approaches such as Leader Member eXchange theory (LMX), etc.). Knights and Wilmott (2007) have pointed out that although mainstream management theories appear to favour open and participative approaches by leaders, elements which are at the core of contingency theory, these often reinforce inequalities that are embedded in hierarchical systems.

One of the first 'Stop and Reflect' boxes in this chapter asks you to consider the ethics of using a drug-dealing gang as a case study. The violence used to reinforce the hegemony of the leader and the subordination of individual gang members concerns is explicit throughout *Gang Leader for a Day*. However, as Knights and Wilmott point out, although contemporary democracies are built upon the idea of civil equality between all citizens, that this is rarely the case in the organizations that we work in. Although followers are valued and given much consideration in contingency leadership theories, they do not have the same value or status as their leaders.

> In short, mainstream thinking implicitly endorses and legitimizes the values of the status quo, and the distribution of material and symbolic (e.g. status) goods that flow from it. It plays upon, rather than addresses the roots of the insecurities that are engendered by patterns of domination. (Knights and Wilmott, 2007, p. 290)

If we consider contingency theories to be the group of theories that gave greater consideration to relationships between leaders and followers, however, there is potential to change the dominant belief that they are an outdated footnote in the development of contemporary leadership theory. Instead we can see them as part of the spirit of capitalism of the 1960s and 1970s which depicted organizations as providers of meaning and stability to individuals who worked for them (Whyte, 1960; Boltanski and Chiapello, 2005). Although contingency leadership theories do not challenge established orders of organizational power, they remain the area of leadership studies which are most concerned which the position of followers. Because leadership contingency theories move the spotlight away from the figure of the leader, they might be thought of as a *pre-critical* stage in leadership studies away from person-centred, trait-based approaches. New opportunities to address previous limitations of the contingency approach can critically accommodate issues not previously 'admitted' into leadership studies.

 ## Case study: *Gang Leader for a Day* (4)

JT's position as gang leader, as represented in Venkatesh's *Gang Leader for a Day*, is difficult to appraise from the context of leadership contingency theory. JT's decisions appear sensible in hindsight, the result of spending the most significant part of his upbringing in the context within which the Black Kings gang operated.

However, the very way that he understood leadership and the decisions he makes as an up-and-coming leader across the broader Black Kings organization was highly contingent on a number of socio-cultural factors outside his control. Even Venkatesh's entrée into the research field was contingent on his race (Indian-American) being misinterpreted by the gang members as Mexican. He naïvely wandered into the Roger Taylor Homes development with the expectation that residents would answer his questions about how it feels to be poor and black in contemporary America. The gang members grew immediately suspicious of his goals (even calling him by a Latino name), and held him hostage until he was appraised by the gang leader, JT, who was interested in having his life documented. Being granted legitimacy by a character with such strong social capital meant that he was gradually granted increasing levels of access to the community and the gang.

JT's leadership, however, was not just contingent on his relationship with his followers in the gang; it was contingent on the gang's relationship with the community. The Black Kings had developed from the radical socialist movement the Black Panther Party, which was founded in the 1960s and became a centre for social and community activity. With the gradual decline of the Black Panthers, some members became involved in gang-related activity, but continued to fund community activities with the proceeds of illegal activities. Although older residents complained that contemporary gangs had become more commercial than social, the Black Kings had a strong corporate social responsibility (CSR) programme which involved policing many of the drug addicts and drifters who congregated in the Roger Taylor Homes buildings and surroundings, funding activities for children, organizing basketball tournaments and organizing community 'clean-up' days. At one stage, during a strike in Chicago's city schools, JT even organized classes (albeit unsuccessfully) for teenage gang members. However, this 'Robin Hood'-type activity does not explain the full impact of this cultural contingency on JT's leadership.

From the outset of his research, several participants informed Venkatesh that they did not see the Black Kings as a gang entity that preyed on their community; rather they saw the Black Kings as an integral *part* of the community. Venkatesh is also clear that 'community' also meant something very different in the Roger Taylor Homes than it did in the middle-class environment he grew up in where detachment from one's neighbours was very much the norm. In the Roger Taylor Homes, people lived *for* each other in a much more salient way than Venkatesh appreciated at the outset of his fieldwork. With minimal resources at their disposal, the community survived by watching out for each other and supporting one another at times of crisis. The Black Kings were part of this system, and JT was as central to its administration as any official from the Chicago Housing Association. As one of the few sources of cash flow in a community devastated by long-term structural poverty, although many of the residents feared the gang, it is not unfeasible that others clearly considered them to be a resource that could be drawn on in times of absolute necessity.

Both the gang and the residents formed part of an intricate economic and cultural system. One of the residents told Venkatesh: 'The gang and the building ... are the same' (p. 89). It is important to point out, however, that this did not result in an urban pastoral. The system of exchanges was appropriated by unscrupulous building representatives who ensured that anyone who benefited from their favours were simultaneously compromised by them. Although the residents and the gang benefited from their membership of the community, this was at a price that often drew them deeper into the sphere of influence of other parties.

The implications of this important cultural contingency for a figure like JT was enormous. His decisions did not solely depend on the relationship he had with his followers; they also had to take into account how they would benefit members of the broader community that his gang was intertwined with. If the decision

(Continued)

(Continued)

benefited them too much, he had to consider how this would impact on his relationship with the upper echelons of the broader Black Kings hierarchy (known as the 'Board of Management'). How exactly can one address the task structure of the organization, when it has also to take into account the structure of community that it is embedded in? What happens when official policy decides that it is time to literally tear down the buildings which provide the physical structure to how life has been lived for decades?

Contingency theories of leadership focus on how effective leadership changes in line with fluid events, environments and circumstances, and assists followers find stability in challenging motivational environments. *Gang Leader for a Day* demonstrates that the contingencies that leaders deal with are far broader and more dynamic that classical contingency leadership theorists imagined.

The key points in this chapter were ...

- Contingency theories arose out of recognition that leadership traits were not enough to predict good leadership. Rather, a theory was needed that accounted for different contexts. Thus they were one of the earliest moves towards recognizing the relational element of leadership.
- The main contingency theories are:

  o *Fiedler's model* prescribes a relationship between the leader's style and the *favourable-ness* of the situation, which is measured according to the task structures, influence and relationships.
  o *Path–goal* theory categorizes leadership according to two factors: *consideration* (people orientation) and *initiating structure* (task orientation). The optimal combination of these are contingent on the context, such as task ambiguity.
  o *Situational theory* combines much of the above with a new factor: *readiness*. This pertains to the level of followers' willingness and motivation.
  o *Leader participation* is similar to the above, but differs in its focus on decision-making. It suggests that who should make decisions is contingent on context.

- Some of the critiques of contingency theories include:

  o It can be very difficult to get robust data on the context to measure it against things like task structure or influence.
  o They assume leaders are able to read a context objectively, and forget the political or interpretive nature of social reality.
  o They can tend to homogenize organisations and employees. For example, they risk assuming that a goal or task is valued equally in a context.
  o They have been criticized as merely mechanical tools – a situational menu for leadership – which may 'sell' well in management and leadership development programmes, but is actually an over-simplification of the complex social world.
  o Perhaps the most significant critique is that contingency theories are actually a series of strategic tools for 'the leader' to use to exert control of followers and situations.

Further thinking

Schyns, B. and Meindl, J. R. (eds) (2005). *Implicit Leadership Theories: Essays and Explorations*. Greenwich, CT: Information Age Publishing.

1 How do implicit leadership theories, which are developed and tacitly held by individuals over the course of their lifespan, challenge contingency-based approaches to understanding leadership? Does engaging with such approaches change how you feel about yourself as a leader or a follower?
2 What are the problems associated with thinking about leadership as something that is implicit? What challenges do such approaches pose to traditional contingency leadership theories?

Tourish, F. (2005). Critical upward communication: Ten commandments for improving strategy and decision making. *Long Range Planning, 38*(5), 485–503.

1 The practice of critical upward communication highlights that personal and cultural barriers often impede leaders' attempts to accurately identify impact factors that are contingent to their followers' situation. What do leaders need to do to overcome these barriers?
2 How can leaders and followers work together to reconfigure their mutual understanding of the contingencies that impact on their organizational situation?

Knights, D. (2009). Power at work in organisations. In M. Alvesson, T. Bridgman and H. Wilmott (eds), *The Oxford Handbook of Critical Management Studies* (pp. 144–165). Oxford: Oxford University Press.

1 Critical management theorists reject contingency theories of leadership because they present an over-simplified model of the relationship between leaders and followers. Do contingency theories of leadership have any redeeming factors?
2 Child (1984) suggested that, regardless of the situation, leaders can exercise agency in situations despite the constraints that the external environment places on them. Can you think of a personal example of when you have done this?
3 How can 'agentic strategic choice' be exercised by a contemporary business or political leader currently engaging with a problematic situation?

Leadership on screen

After Johnathan Demme's 1991 film of Thomas Harris' novel the *Silence of the Lambs* was released it became something of a cultural phenomenon. Both commercially successful and critically acclaimed it introduced a unique character in the form of a deranged serial killer who was highly intelligent, exquisitely 'cultured' and extensively educated. Anthony Hopkins' portrayal of Dr Hannibal 'The Cannibal' Lecter became the focus for much of the commentary on this film, but we want you think about another central character in the film and her relationship with the organisation for which she works and the various managers she encounters: trainee FBI agent Clarice Starling (played by Jodie Foster).

The character of Agent Starling is the central protagonist of the *Silence of the Lambs*, and the complexity of her relationship with the psychopathic Lecter is often mirrored in the relationship she has with the organisation she is attempting to gain membership of: the Federal Bureau of Investigation. Lecter toys with Starling's aspirations and the ambitions of her mentor in the Bureau's Behavioural Science Division, Jack Crawford. One of the most interesting elements of Starling's character is her ability to read situations, and adopt a style of leadership which is *contingent* on her ability to influence the behaviours of the people around her. Starling often finds herself as the most disadvantaged and technically disempowered in many situations in which she finds herself placed. The reasons for this are contingent on her position as a junior member at the fringes of the organisation, her age and gender.

We want you to think about Starling's interactions with the following throughout the film, particularly in relation to how she interacts with contingencies, in order to practice leadership:

1. Her 'official' manager and mentor, Jack Crawford, in the FBI's Behavioural Science Unit. In particular, pay attention to Starling's interaction with Crawford following the autopsy scene.
2. Dr Frederick Chilton, the director of the fictional hospital for the criminally insane, who interferes with Starling's questioning of Lecter for his own gain.
3. Dr Hannibal Lecter. How does Starling gain his trust and deflect his attempts to manipulate her?
4. The FBI as an organization. We hear throughout the film that the organization expects Starling to successfully complete all her admission tests successfully if she is to be admitted as a full member (Agent). Note the various physical, intellectual and behavioural cues about the culture of the FBI that the viewer receives throughout the film. How does Starling interact and engage with these cues, and how are these demonstrative of contingency approaches to leadership?

TRANSFORMATIONAL LEADERSHIP

SECULARIZED THEOLOGY?

Helen Delaney and Sverre Spoelstra

Helen Delaney is a research fellow at Lund University and lecturer at the University of Auckland. Her research and teaching focuses primarily on the sociology of work and critical perspectives towards leadership.

Sverre Spoelstra is an associate professor at Lund University, Sweden. His research interests include leadership and organizational philosophy.

What this chapter is all about ...

The main idea is that transformational leadership is believed to inspire radical transformation in followers, especially through charisma. This theory of leadership has striking similarities to religious concepts like conversion, in which a follower is transformed from a lower morality to a higher one. It also echoes the concept of redemption, in which people, organizations, business and the world are being redeemed from corruption and made ethical.

The key questions this chapter answers are:

- What kind of transformation happens and how?
- Why is this desirable?
- How can we measure transformational leadership?
- How is it linked to charisma?
- How is it related to religious ideas such as conversion and redemption?

Introduction

In the past 30 years, transformational leadership has been the most popular leadership concept among leadership academics by far. The concept was first developed in the late 1970s by the political theorist James McGregor Burns (1978), and soon found its way in the world of business. Today the literature on transformational leadership is still steadily growing and an increasing number of business schools and consultancy firms offer programmes on how to become a transformational leader. In its most basic form, transformational leadership refers to an alignment of goals between leaders and followers for the good of the organization or society. It is the virtue of the transformational leader to establish this alignment through, for example, charisma, inspiration, individual consideration and intellectual stimulation (Bass, 1985).

In this chapter we focus on this notion of 'transformation', which seems to be strangely under-explored in leadership studies. We raise a number of questions, such as: What kind of transformation happens in transformational leadership? Who is transformed and why? How does it happen? Why is it seen to be desirable? How is it measured and constructed? How is it related to charisma? What strikes us as particularly interesting are the religious undercurrents in some of the literature; therefore we turn to a discussion about how religious ideas like conversion and redemption can help us better understand this concept. We use the case of Steve Jobs, the co-founder and previous Chief Executive Officer (CEO) of Apple, who is celebrated for his transformative powers, to illustrate the intricacy of these ideas. We finish with some concluding thoughts about the possibilities and limits of thinking about leadership in terms of transformation.

What does transformation mean?

One of the first questions to consider is what kind of transformation is implied in transformational leadership? This is indeed a fundamental question to ask, and it is the main focus of this section. In order to explore some of the underlying assumptions in the leadership literature, let's start with a basic dictionary definition of what 'transform' means. Here's a selection:

- to alter or be altered radically in form, function, etc.;
- to change in form, appearance, or structure; metamorphose;
- to change in condition, nature, or character; convert.

What we notice first of all is this word 'radically'. To transform, or be transformed, is not about making minor changes; rather the changes are fundamental, complete and extreme. What's more, these radical alterations are made to both superficial and deep aspects of the object. So if we apply this to leaders and followers, it implies that the leader will fundamentally change the followers' appearance or form, as well as their character or nature. It's no wonder, then, that 'transform' also carries a variety of connotations ranging from the more benign (alter, renew, develop) to the more severe (mould, mutate, doctor). This is something to keep in mind as we explore how leadership scholars have interpreted who and what should be transformed.

Transformational leadership scholars distinguish between transformational leadership and transactional leadership. Transactional leaders, as the name suggests, get things done through exchange relations with their subordinates. They spell out what work should be done, and how. As long as the followers meet these expectations, the leader rewards them with pay increases, promotions, recognition, and so on. According to transformational leadership scholars the best leaders demonstrate both transformational and transactional behaviour. They also emphasize, however, that organizations tend to be overly populated by transactional leaders (Avolio and Bass, 1995).

So, what is 'transformed' in transformational leadership? Burns's (1978) early book on transformational leadership (to be precise, he spoke of transforming leadership) provides a partial answer to this question. According to Burns, transformational leadership consists of a 'transformation of values' where followers are raised up to a 'higher morality', where they have higher ethical aspirations. In other words, transformational leaders would ensure that their followers become more moral as a consequence of their leadership. Burns does not provide a detailed account of how this may work in practice, nor does he clarify what values, morals or morality is at stake. However, we do learn from his book that transformational leadership has something to do with morality (existing beliefs on what constitutes good behaviour) and ethics (a theory or philosophy of goodness).

This is a helpful starting point, but we must immediately acknowledge that it is contested. As soon as the concept was introduced in a business context, the meaning ascribed to transformational leadership changed quite drastically. When Bernard Bass, the most influential theorist on the topic of transformational leadership for business, introduced the concept to an audience of business students and scholars he argued that transformational leadership does not need to involve morality (Bass, 1985). Instead, the transformation that Bass had in mind was one where followers give up their personal goals for the goals of the organization, and will perform beyond what is expected. In other words, under a transformational leader followers are said to transcend their self-interests by putting the aims and values of the organization first. In the late 1990s, Bass changed his position on this point by siding with Burns: transformational leaders are only 'truly' transformational when they transform their followers into more moral persons who also have a collective commitment to a higher moral cause (Bass and Steidlmeier, 1999). These leaders have formulated certain values, goals and a world-view that they then try to 'convert' followers to (Bryman, 1992, p. 101). Like Burns, however, Bass is not very clear on the question of what or whose values and morality transformational leaders are supposed to work with. We can also ask to what extent this is even possible within a complex organizational context.

So far we have learned one thing: for most scholars, transformational leadership has something to do with morality and ethics. The transformation that transformational leadership refers to is one where followers transform from a situation in which they are not so ethical (they follow their self-interests, and don't care much about others in or outside the organizations) to a situation where they behave more ethically.

How does transformation happen?

The majority of research has looked at the behaviours and capacities of the transformational leader to initiate this moral transformation in people. A variety of different answers have been suggested, but the most influential and enduring comes from Bass and his colleagues: a transformational leader transforms followers through charisma, inspiration, personal consideration and intellectual stimulation (Bass, 1985). Over the years, Bass and colleagues went on to develop these features into the 'four I's'. We briefly explain these below. As you're reading them, try to think of any limitations, inconsistencies or contradictions in and between the concepts.

Much has been written about charisma and leadership ('charismatic leadership' is a separate, if overlapping, field of research that we discuss in a later section). At the most basic level, a leader with charisma has some kind of special power and influence over their followers. This is the first 'I': 'idealized influence' is how the leader arouses strong emotional responses and bonds in followers. If a follower sees their leader as charismatic, they may strongly identify with and emulate them, and ultimately work harder and longer (Bass, 1985). Similar to the trait approach to leadership presented in Chapter 2, many writers have tried to nail down the traits and behaviours that are more likely to create a sense of charisma, including being visionary, self-confident, ambitious, dominant, persuasive, trustworthy and enthusiastic (to name but a few).

Transformational leaders also need to inspire (the 'second I', 'inspirational motivation'). They make followers feel extremely alive, excited, passionate and motivated. This 'arousal process' (Bass, 1985, p. 66) involves the leader appealing to the followers' emotions (rather than intellect) in a way that stimulates and invigorates the followers to believe in the leader's vision and to go above and beyond their own expectations to achieve it. An example that may come to mind is a sports coach delivering a hearty half-time speech to his/her downtrodden team that tugs at their fears (of failure, shame, etc.) and hopes (of glory, pride, success, etc.) to inspire exceptional performance and ultimately secure their win, like Al Pacino in the movie *Any Given Sunday* (1999) or Samuel Jackson in *Coach Carter* (2005).

As well as emotionally energizing the follower, transformational leaders also 'intellectually stimulate' and challenge their followers in order to generate extra effort and performance (Bass, 1985). In order to do this, the leader needs to be intellectually 'superior in ability' compared with their followers – but not too much in case they alienate their followers (Bass, 1985, p. 104). Transformational leaders are seen as more creative, novel, radical and innovative in their thinking, and as a result stimulate followers through these transformative ideas. The image that comes to mind is of a maverick CEO striding around the board room, 'tossing out the rule book' and imagining ideas, products or concepts above and beyond the status quo – and challenging the followers to do the same (like Robin Williams's character did in the prep school of the 1989 movie *Dead Poets Society*).

Finally, leaders aspiring to be transformational need to give personal attention to their followers ('individualized consideration'). Doing so means that the leader can develop familiarity with their followers (who may in turn feel unique and valued), they can understand their followers' needs (and use these to motivate), and they can communicate their expectations (as well as give feedback, delegate, set goals, etc.). An example that comes to mind is the heroic villain 'Gru' from *Despicable Me* who greets his scores of minions by their first names, asks how their families are and appears to love, and be loved, by his devoted followers.

At this point we may also ask a critical question: why these four characteristics and not four other ones (for example, integrity, courage, responsibility and care)? Did Burns, Bass and other transformational leadership scholars discover the existence of transformational leaders (who happen to demonstrate the four 'I's') or did they define transformational leadership prior to any empirical observations? The answer to this question is not clear, and it is one of the reasons why studies of transformational leadership are sometimes criticized (e.g. Van Knippenberg and Sitkin, 2013).

 ## STOP AND REFLECT 4.1

What are the four traits of a transformational leader proposed by Bass? Note these down. Now imagine you met a leader who embodies these traits: how do they look, act, talk? With this image in mind, how do these four traits rule in – and rule out – certain ways of being a leader?

Now imagine that transformational leadership is characterized by an entirely different set of traits, such as empathy, presence, shyness, reliability, doubtfulness, or any others that strike you as unconventional.

How would transformational leadership look and feel different if it focused on these traits? What would it mean for leaders, followers and the interaction between the two?

Why do you think these traits have been excluded from the traditional definitions of transformational leadership?

It is also important to understand what transformational leadership is meant to achieve or create. The title of Bass's seminal work, *Leadership and Performance Beyond Expectations*, gives us some clues. It's not enough for leaders to entice followers to perform what is expected in their work; rather, transformational leaders will inspire their followers to perform 'beyond the ordinary limits' (Bass, 1985a, p. xiii), and to display 'extraordinary effort' in their work (p. xiv). The worker will be transformed from one 'merely' meeting the requirements and expectations of their job to one who goes above and beyond the call of duty. Transformational leadership therefore is seen as 'true leadership' as it 'entices' workers to 'transcend everyday routine' and their self-interested goals, and to imagine worlds 'beyond the here-and-now' (Bryman, 1992, p. 97). The transformational leader appeals to the workers' higher-order needs (think of Maslow's hierarchy and self-actualization) while at the same time the workers' aims and aspirations align with the leader's. Workers feel committed and loyal to their leader, and somehow this increases the performance of the organization. Perhaps this is because a 'true' leader is able to delegate more and more work to their followers, get them to take on greater responsibilities, and become 'self-actualisers, self-regulators, and self-controllers' (Bass, 1985, p. 16). To sum up, then, advocates believe that transformational leaders will get followers to work harder, smarter and faster, as their goals are aligned with the leader/organization, and for which they will be rewarded with a sense of self-actualization and satisfaction, rather than material rewards.

Is transformational leadership desirable?

So far you may have noticed that the literature suggests that transformational leadership is invariably a good thing: it creates more satisfied workers, and more productive and effective workplaces. You may also be thinking about leaders in your own world who seem transformational, leaders who are figures of inspiration or admiration for you, who make you feel like you want to become more than you are. Certainly popular culture and media tends to repeat such a message: think of Facebook Chief Operating Officer (COO) Sheryl Sandberg's book *Lean In* encouraging woman to get rid of internal barriers holding them back from achieving career success; or Obama's 2008 speech calling for a 'more perfect union' to overcome racial divides and discrimination in the USA; Pope Francis urging us not to be ruled by money or consumer trappings; any number of 'change your life' TV programmes like *Oprah* or *Dr. Phil*; or religious programming on television. Set against this backdrop, transformational leadership is portrayed as necessary and desirable for creating a better world. However, some scholars have recently questioned exactly this assumption. Are transformational leaders inherently as good as we're led to believe? Could transformational leaders also be harmful, manipulative, unethical and oppressive? May they indeed play a part in creating corrupt, overly compliant and destructive organizations? Are they really the 'Great Men' that scholars purport them to be?

We have seen the notion of the 'Great Man' in Chapter 2. This idea infuses the majority of transformational leadership theorizing but is a highly problematic image – one that leadership scholars rarely acknowledge. The most obvious problem is that the leader is cast as an adventurous risk-taking man, thus excluding (or at least diminishing) females, femininity or less macho forms of leadership thinking or practice. He is seen as the powerful almighty leader responsible for both success and failure, and the paternal, protective leader who saves followers from their anxieties and vulnerabilities (Gemmill and Oakley, 1992; Spoelstra and ten Bos, 2011). Casting transformational leaders in the image of a Great Man is thus dangerous because of the fundamentally unequal power relationship between the leader and the follower, which makes us question what (and whose) interest this power serves.

In answer to this question, Dennis Tourish (2013) uses case studies of corporate and religious cults to explore the 'dark side of transformational leadership'. Tourish's research offers a significant warning about how transformational leaders may actually create authoritarian organizations marked by cultures of conformity where followers feel little power or safety to resist or disagree with the leader's immoral, unethical or damaging practices or beliefs. He argues that the key elements of transformational leadership (the 'four I's' we summarized previously) bear a striking similarity to the defining features of cults. He believes leadership scholars tend to grant transformational leaders too much agency and influence – the powerful leader inspires followers to adopt the leader's vision, and if they don't the leader has the power to punish, manipulate or coerce the follower. The follower may also endow their leader with the power to lead, change and shape their reality – they place their faith in their leader. By using cases like Enron, the culture of investment banking and the Jonestown massacre (among others), Tourish highlights the significant 'potential for abuse' that may result if we unreflexively follow the model of transformational leadership that scholars like Bass advocate. He argues for a dismantling of the 'Great Man' image of leadership, displacing the powerful leader from his central podium, and instead for creating more participatory, equal and democratic forms of leading, following and organizing.

You may be starting to tire of this hardened distinction between the leader and their followers, and the seeming obsession with focusing on the leader. Some writers raise this concern about what is lost or ignored by a myopic focus on the great transformational leader. Some have highlighted how marginal social groups are neglected in order to 'hoist up' the leader (Calas, 1993), how the actions of policymakers (not leaders) are actually what transforms organizations (Currie and Lockett, 2007), or even how fictitious company mascots may be the source of transformational leadership (see the case of Ronald McDonald, in Boje and Rhodes, 2006, and below). If you think about other business/management courses you may have taken, what other features or functions are responsible for creating productive and efficient organizations? Marketers may point to the company's branding strategy; economists may point to pricing strategies or the nature of the market; and accountants to strategies for cost reductions. It is therefore quite striking how the leadership literature tends to completely ignore other significant players, influences and forces (especially those outside of the leader's sphere of control) in order to emphasize how desirable and necessary the 'great' transformational leader is to organizations.

STOP AND REFLECT 4.2

Why it is that when we think of leaders, we think of 'real life' people? Perhaps transformational leadership can also be done by fictional characters. This is the argument explored by Boje and Rhodes (2006) who argue that the transformation of McDonald's from an unhealthy, fatty fast-food provider to a healthy, 'green' option was facilitated through the voice, representation and, hence, leadership of Ronald McDonald. The authors analysed a selection of animated children's films (produced on behalf of McDonald's) starring Ronald McDonald as a slimmed-down super-hero clown embarking on a number of other-worldly feats. They argue that fictional characters may even have more latitude for dissent than real-life transformational leaders. Considering this study, what do you make of the argument that transformational leadership transcends real-life humans?

What other unconventional figures could be classed as transformational leaders? It could be a fictional character, or another non-human figure/object. How may transformational leadership function differently through these characters compared to real-life humans?

How is transformational leadership found or constructed?

We can also ask critical questions about how transformational leadership tends to be researched. Many leadership researchers have dedicated significant attention and energy to trying to capture, measure and pin down transformational leadership 'in the flesh'. Much of this research uses quantitative research methods (i.e. surveys and questionnaires) where either leaders rate themselves against a number of the transformational qualities, or peers, subordinates and superiors are asked to rate their leaders. The most popular of these questionnaires is the so-called Multifactor Leadership Questionnaire (MLQ), which was developed by Bernard Bass and associates in the 1980s.

Questionnaires like the MLQ decide who is transformational and who is not. Put simply: it is not the researcher who makes the judgement about who is legitimately considered to be a transformational leader, but the people who fill out the questionnaire. In that sense, the method of deciding who is transformational is 'objective', in the sense that the personal judgement (or 'bias') of the researcher is not allowed to enter the picture. However, measuring leadership by means of questionnaires brings its own problems. This is obvious when one considers a leader's self-assessment; the situation where a 'leader' fills out a questionnaire about themselves. There are good reasons to be sceptical of the outcomes of such a test, for the simple reason that many people may not have a picture of themselves that accurately aligns with reality. Arguably more reliable are the perceptions of others, and this is also how most studies of transformational leadership proceed: a 'leader' (or not) is rated by followers/subordinates. If subordinates rate their manager as charismatic, for instance, then that person is considered to be charismatic.

How reliable is such a conclusion? This is by no means a straightforward question, and raises the question to what extent leadership is 'real' to begin with. Some leadership scholars argue that leadership is not something that is found within the 'real world', but something *constructed* by human beings. Charisma, for instance, would not be something that a leader has, but something that followers attribute to someone. The religious origin of the term 'charisma' as a 'gift of grace' (which we shall return to later) is of relevance here: a charismatic person is *considered* to have some kind of special gift, but does not necessarily *have* a special gift. From such a perspective, one may even suggest that leadership attributions substantiate leadership (leadership becomes real by means of attributions).

Transformational leadership researchers typically do not share the view that charisma, or other elements of transformational leadership, are attributed rather than real. For them, transformational leadership is very real. Measures of transformational leadership, they argue, may not be reliable in every single case, but overall they give a good indication of who is truly transformational and who is not. To put it simply, transformational scholars tend to have faith in the attributions of followers: if followers believe that someone is charismatic, this person probably is charismatic.

We will not pick sides in the debate about whether (transformational) leadership is something real or constructed. However, we would like to alert you to the possibility that questionnaires to identify transformational leadership may measure fantasies of leadership rather than leadership itself.

Measuring transformational leadership through the Multifactor Leadership Questionnaire

The most popular measure of transformational leadership is the MLQ, which Bass initially developed. Essentially, Bass 'operationalized' the term by itemizing the 'four I's' we covered above and the traits associated with them (and contrasted it with transactional and laissez-faire leadership). Along with his colleague Bruce Avolio, he refined the model and eventually constructed a way of trying to measure these traits using a 'scientific' tool – the MLQ. (Lowe et al., 1996, provide an account of the history and purpose of the MLQ.) This instrument claims to investigate if/how transformational leadership correlates with, for example, organizational/worker performance and satisfaction. It can be used to profile and diagnose a leader in regards to how 'transformational' they are – or aren't – in comparison with an 'optimal profile' and therefore how they can be trained and developed. This questionnaire has undergone several iterations in its time, and many studies have tried to validate how accurate and reliable it is for measuring transformational leadership.

So, how is transformational leadership made visible by means of the MLQ? The MLQ contains 73 items in total, some of which measure transformational leadership, and others that measure transactional and laissez-faire leadership. How did these 73 items come to exist? Bass and Avolio initially designed 142 items by reviewing the trait theory literature, and by surveying 70 executives for the traits they associate with transformational and transactional leaders. This number was then whittled down by what is called 'factor analysis', which claims to select the items that most 'reliably' predict a given trait (Lowe et al., 1996). One of the sales pitches for the MLQ is that it only takes 15 minutes to determine if you're a 'truly exceptional' or 'marginal' leader (www.mindgarden.com).

As we said before, the MLQ asks respondents to rate on a scale of 0 to 4 (where 0 = not, and 4 = frequently) the leader/themselves on a number of items – these items then measure dimensions of leadership. Here is a selection of the questions. As you read them, imagine you are answering them about yourself or your leader.

- 'I go beyond self-interest for the good of the group' (claims to measure idealized influence).
- 'I consider the moral and ethical consequences of decisions' (claims to measure idealized influence).
- 'I talk optimistically about the future' (claims to measure inspirational motivation).
- 'I re-examine critical assumptions to question whether they are appropriate' (claims to measure intellectual stimulation).
- 'I help others to develop their strengths' (claims to measure individualized consideration).

What do you notice about these items and your answers to them? You might notice that with each question you were thinking 'well, it depends on ...' or 'sometimes' or 'I'd like to think so'. Imagine filling out 73 of these items in a short time-frame. The wording is seductive: by phrasing each question to personally appeal to you (through the use of 'I') they almost induce you to own each statement as yours, thus potentially creating a higher rating for yourself.

The authors of the MLQ seem aware of some of the problems of asking leaders to rate themselves, which is why they encourage other people to rate the leader. Therefore, the MLQ strongly rests on the assumption that leadership is in 'the eye of the beholder' (www.mindgarden.com). That is, when the leader rates themselves, we get access to their perceptions of their leadership, but when someone else (a subordinate, peer, etc.) rates this leader, this is the real measure of leadership. The MLQ – its authors/users – seems to faithfully believe that real leadership is found when followers attribute it to a given person.

One of the things we find interesting about the MLQ is how some researchers have a vested interest in protecting, promoting and profiting from it. In order to use the MLQ for research purposes, a researcher has to apply to the company that owns it and gain permission to use it – and possibly pay a fee. To use it for organizational consulting/development one also needs to pay for the right to do so. It is therefore important to note that tools of science, and the knowledge produced in their name, are here shaped by broader political and economic forces.

Charisma and transformational leadership

We have already noted the link between transformational leadership and charisma, the latter being one of the dimensions of transformational leadership. But there is more to say about this link. Alongside research on transformational leadership, many studies appeared in the 1980s that focused on charismatic leadership. Together they have been labelled as 'new leadership' (Bryman, 1992) or as a new 'paradigm' within leadership studies (Bass, 1996), as they supposedly marked a new way of doing leadership research. What has not been highlighted much, however, are the religious connotations that both of these notions of leadership share. One might even argue that the turn to 'new leadership' is in fact a rediscovery of the religious dimension of everyday connotations of leadership, which distinguishes leadership from management (Spoelstra, 2013). We discuss the religious dimension of transformational leadership in the next section; in this section we give you a brief background on the notion of charisma, and the way it has entered leadership studies.

The history of the term 'charisma' goes back approximately two thousand years. The term first appeared in writing in the epistles of Saint Paul (Potts, 2009), which he wrote in the period AD 50–62. The original meaning of the term was 'gift of grace' or 'spiritual gift', that is to say a gift bestowed by God to specific individuals. However, our use of the term today, with its link to leadership, has been marked significantly by the sociologist Max Weber. In the early twentieth century, Weber famously defined charisma as

> a certain quality of an individual personality by virtue of which he is considered extraordinary and treated as endowed with supernatural, superhuman, or at least specifically exceptional power qualities. These are such as are not accessible to the ordinary person, but are regarded as of divine origin or as exemplary, and on the basis of them the individual concerned is treated as a 'leader'. (1978, p. 241)

There are two things that are important to note in this definition. The first is that Weber does not understand charisma as a quality that leaders actually receive (from God, or some other higher power): the crucial point is that charismatic people are treated *as if* they possess supernatural qualities, irrespective of the question if they actually have these qualities. According to Weber, charisma is a social phenomenon in the sense that a charismatic leader requires what he calls a 'charismatic community' (1992, p. 243), that is a group of people or followers who attribute these extraordinary qualities to a person. The second thing to note is that charisma in Weber's account is 'value-free', which is to say that it can be something positive or negative. We may say that in Weber's terms Hitler and Mandela are equally charismatic in the sense that they both had a large community of followers who attributed special qualities to them.

Weber's work on charismatic leadership has had a profound impact on leadership studies from the 1970s onwards (half a century after Weber's seminal work!). However, as Beyer (1999) has shown, the concept of charisma in leadership studies also differs significantly from Weber's original outline. Within leadership studies, charisma is predominantly seen as a trait of an extraordinary individual (like the original notion of charisma as a 'gift of grace'), rather than a sociological phenomenon established by a charismatic community. The other important modification is that charisma is now almost exclusively seen as a positive thing, partly due to the numerous studies that tried to establish a link between charisma and various positive performance indicators (such as organizational performance, employee motivation, job satisfaction and ethical climate). Well into the 1990s, some leadership scholars painted one-sided celebratory accounts of charismatic leaders, ignoring, or even denying, the charisma of leaders like Hitler.

As Shamir et al. (1993, p. 582) write, 'awareness of these risks [of charisma] is missing from most of the current literature on organizational charismatic or transformational leadership', though they unwittingly contribute to this state of affairs by only mentioning these dangers in a footnote of an otherwise suspiciously positive account of the corporate benefits of charisma.

Beyer (1999) aptly calls the transformation of the concept of charisma in leadership studies a 'taming', in the sense that charisma, in contrast to Weber's idea, now appears to be a harmless phenomenon. In a direct response to Beyer, Bass (2000, p. 549) tries to modify this picture somewhat by claiming that charismatic leaders 'are more like lions than pussy cats'; his work implies we should conclude that they are friendly lions, similar to Simba and his father, Mufasa, in the movie *The Lion King* (rather than Scar, the 'evil' lion).

STOP AND REFLECT 4.3

Think about a leader you would describe as 'charismatic'. To what extent are you reproducing a 'tamed' version of charisma? For example, do you see charisma as a trait this leader possesses? Are you associating charisma with positive and extraordinary qualities? Then consider what may be obscured or blurred in your vision of this leader as a result? How would your perspective of leadership (and followership) alter if you saw yourself as part of a 'charismatic community' who constructs and attributes charisma to a leader?

But there is more to say on the transformations that the term 'charisma' has undergone. Where Beyer focuses on the way leadership studies has 'tamed' the notion of charisma in Weber, the American sociologist Philip Rieff (2007) has argued that it was in fact Max Weber who 'corrupted' the notion of charisma, with bad consequences for Western culture. Rieff argues that Weber altered the notion of charisma as it can be found in the epistles of St Paul. According to Rieff, the original notion of charisma was used to refer to people who follow God's law, which is how they receive the 'gift of grace'. For Weber, however, charisma is attributed to people who break or transcend the law. If we translate this idea to an organizational context, the charismatic leader is somebody who is considered bigger than the organization. For that reason, they are not only allowed but even expected to break the rules of the organization: the charismatic leader dispenses with 'business as usual'. This may sound attractive if a radically new course is needed, but it is hardly a surprise that many of these corporate charismatics turn out to be rather dangerous, disruptive or problematic for organizations, as they change things at will, against cultural or established wisdom.

In his 2002 book *Searching for a Corporate Savior*, Rakesh Khurana shows how American corporations, and many ordinary people, have suffered from what he calls an 'irrational' love-affair with charismatic CEOs. The problem with many of the (grossly overpaid) charismatic CEOs, he argues, is that they are new to the organization and therefore know little about the organizational culture, its people and its problems. Instead, they are appointed for their charisma, which is seen as necessary to save the company from its crisis. Khurana shows, however, that the problems tend to get worse as crucial management skills are 'discounted as pedestrian and boring, or simply ignored as irrelevant' (Khurana, 2002, p. xi).

A case in point is Enron's Jeff Skilling, once a celebrated charismatic CEO, who quickly appeared to be a great danger to the company, its customers and ultimately the world economy. On a cultural level, this is also Rieff's critique. According to Rieff, our Western culture has internalized Weber's concept of charisma, to the extent that we have come to put too much of our faith in charismatics, in business but also in other spheres such as politics and popular culture.

Now that we have discussed the religious connotations of one of the elements of transformational leadership, charisma, it is time to go back to the concept of transformational leadership, and discuss to what extent it may also be interpreted as a religious concept.

The religious dimension of transformational leadership

When reading the academic literature on transformational leadership, one gets the impression that we are dealing with a very serious academic theory. Typically, journal papers in the field either propose hypotheses that can be tested, measures that facilitate the testing of hypotheses or conduct testing of hypotheses. A typical example would be something like 'Is transformational leadership related to job satisfaction?' (the answer is apparently 'yes'). This type of research is rooted in a research tradition known as positivism (see Chapter 3). This research tradition is based on the idea that religion can be overcome by means of scientific studies of social phenomena, using methods similar to those used in the natural sciences. The ideal is that the subjectivity of the researcher is blocked out of the research process to avoid any 'bias'. Positivistic research is designed in such a way that anyone could get the same results, as long as the appropriate, and highly standardized, method is followed. We have already seen how this plays out in leadership studies: leadership concepts such as transformational leadership come with a particular questionnaire (such as the MLQ) that determines the score of a particular person on various leadership dimensions. These data are then correlated to a different measure, such as a measure of job satisfaction or financial performance. Given that this is the predominant form of research in leadership studies, one could justifiably assume that transformational leadership research is 'pure science' and far removed from any religious beliefs.

However, we suggest that this is a false conclusion, as much thinking about transformational leadership is driven by a (pseudo-)religious faith which often goes unacknowledged. This leads us back to the question of what is meant by 'transformation' in transformational leadership. To us, 'transformation' has close links to a religious (mostly Christian) way of thinking: it bears a strong resemblance to religious concepts such as 'conversion' and 'redemption'. This is perhaps not such a surprise, given that many concepts used in texts and talk about leadership are of religious origin: apart from charismatic leadership, you can think of 'servant leadership' (a Christian connotation is to lead life as Jesus did, exemplifying love, humility and service, also with links to Taoism and Islam), 'self-sacrificial leadership' (to sacrifice means etymologically to 'make sacred') and spiritual leadership (leadership infused by the Holy Spirit).

What else makes us say that also transformational leadership should be seen in a religious light? Consider the case of St Paul, and his conversion on the road to Damascus. According to Paul's own account (which you can read in the Christian New Testament), Paul was on his way to Damascus to arrest followers of Jesus, but on his way he was overwhelmed by a blinding light, upon which God spoke to him. From that moment, Paul embraced the higher order of God – which, from a Christian perspective is the most substantial transformation a human being could ever experience in life.

A far-fetched comparison, you may think. Maybe so, but consider the basic movement that is captured in the story, namely the movement from a lower sphere to a higher sphere (or, in the case of St Paul, from an earthly sphere to a divine sphere). Does that sound familiar? We have already seen versions of this in Burns's (1978) classic understanding of transforming leadership, which, he argued, consists of 'lifting people up' from a lower morality (grounded in self-interest) to a higher morality (of common purpose). Similarly, Bass (with Steidlmeier, 1999) has argued that transformational leaders are grounded in a 'morality' or 'ethics' (they do not specify which one), and that they are capable of transferring this morality to others in their organizations.

The figure of St Paul is not only of interest because of the story of his conversion. Interestingly, as Potts (2009) shows, Paul popularized and (re)invented the term 'charisma' long before its more recent revival in the twentieth century. For Paul, '[charisma] is the act of God in the present, a transforming power that is experienced by the believer' (Potts, 2009, p. 34). No wonder that charisma is one of the main components of transformational leadership – it is Paul's term for the transforming power as such!

In the versions of Burns and Bass, the transformational leader is perhaps best understood in analogy to God: he (or He) is already part of a higher order and is therefore capable of realizing a transformation in others by means of charisma (that is, by means of bestowing gifts on people). This may also be linked to the popular distinction between management and leadership: management is typically thought of as 'earthly' (i.e. part of mundane organizational life), whereas leadership tends to be seen as something extraordinary. The decisive difference between the two, says Bass (1985, p. 34), fully in line with St Paul, is to be found in charisma: 'Charisma is one of the elements separating the ordinary manager from the true leader in organizational settings.'

Furthermore, in more recent texts on transformational leadership, the term 'transformation' not only refers to the transformation process observed in followers (or subordinates). Of equal importance is the transformation process of the leader himself or herself. So, for instance, Hacker and Roberts (2003) explain that transformational leadership encompasses the 'leader's personal transformation', 'relational transformation' and 'enterprise transformation'. In other words, the self-transformation process of the leader is considered to be as important as the transformation process of the followers and the transformation process of the organization. Such a perspective chimes well with more recent approaches towards leadership that emphasize the importance of so-called 'self-leadership', the idea that good leadership starts with a transformation process within oneself. Pearson (2012, p. 2) puts this as follows: 'as leaders are transformed, so is their work and those with whom they work'. In this understanding, it is only through self-transformation that transformational leaders get access to a higher sphere, which in turns provides them with the capacity to help others to make the same transformation.

We started this section by suggesting that there is a link between transformational leadership and the religious terms conversion and redemption. Up until now we have only focused on the link between transformational leadership and religious conversion, so where does redemption come in? Redemption is a central concept in many of the world religions (not just Christianity, Islam and Buddhism also). If we stick to the Christian tradition, redemption may be understood as a 'deliverance from sin'. How does this relate to transformational leadership in organizations, you may wonder? We would like to suggest that there is a pretty strong link.

To illustrate this point we may go back again to St Paul's conversion. We noted that his conversion on the road to Damascus is, within Christianity, as substantial as transformations could possibly be. What we haven't mentioned yet, however, is that something much more than a personal transformation is said to have happened. According to Paul, his conversion was a 'calling'. Paul was called to become part of something much bigger than himself; he became part of God's mission (*Missio Dei*) to redeem the world.[1]

---

1   We would like to thank Joshua Firth for suggesting this link to us, and for other helpful suggestions on this chapter.

We suggest that something similar is true for transformational leadership. Just as the world is in need of redemption in Christianity, many feel that the business world is in need of redemption today (Sørensen and Spoelstra, 2013). The reason for this is that many people have lost their faith in business and capitalism, following the corporate scandals of the 1990s and 2000s, the current ecological crisis and the 2008 financial crisis. As a consequence, business needs a helping hand, 'from above', to be redeemed from its 'evil' (instrumental, profit-seeking) character. Transformational leadership is one of the concepts that has been brought forward to bridge the 'sinful' world of business with the higher order to which the transformational leader is thought to belong. Other leadership concepts that function in similar ways are 'authentic leadership', 'responsible leadership', 'ethical leadership' and 'spiritual leadership': all of these concepts point towards a figure who stands outside of business in the sense that they are not motivated solely by profit but by a higher calling, just like St Paul (Spoelstra, 2013). By virtue of standing outside of business, they are able to lift the organization up to higher ground, and – indeed – offer some form of redemption in troubled times for capitalism.

Case study: Steve Jobs as a transformational leader

Steve Jobs is an example of a leader who is often associated with transformational leadership, in particular when it comes to his charismatic and inspirational qualities (e.g. Bryant, 2003; Bass and Riggio, 2005). A simple internet search on his name heralds a raft of articles describing him as 'iconic', 'visionary', 'genius', 'brilliant', 'mythic', 'magical', 'charismatic', or 'authentic'. The New York Times argued that he 'led a cultural transformation in the way music, movies and mobile communications were experienced in the digital age' (Madoff, 2011). Or as another newspaper says, 'our lives are different and much more interesting with this man leading us to the land of what's next' ('A design, a dream', 2010). Jobs himself was driven to transform the world, as captured in this mantra: 'I want to put a ding in the universe' (Isaacson, 2011). Academics also attributed transformational powers to Jobs. Victor Vroom, a prominent professor at the Yale School of Management, said in 2010 that '[Jobs] is the supreme example of the transformational leader who stands for higher order values ... he has caused people to do things they might never have done before' ('A design, a dream', 2010). Religious language is often used when describing Jobs, some calling him a 'saviour' (Mishkin, 2009), or as one writer says, 'Jobs himself has been labeled a saint, a sinner, and now a saint again' ('A design, a dream', 2010).

After Jobs's death in 2011, the Board of Directors of Apple issued a statement saying that 'The world is immeasurably better because of Steve', which may indeed be seen as 'leadership beyond expectations' (Bass, 1985). This was echoed in the media and the numerous blog posts that eulogised Steve's impact. US President Barack Obama said, 'Steve was among the greatest of American innovators – brave enough to think differently, bold enough to believe he could change the world, and talented enough to do it'. He goes on, 'Steve was fond of saying that he lived every day like it was his last. Because he did, he transformed our lives, redefined entire industries, and achieved one of the rarest feats in human history: he changed the way each of us sees the world' (Gardner and Thornhill, 2011).

Let's start with some of the language used in these quotes. The use of religious metaphors (the saviour, sinner, saint) illustrates our previous discussion about the strong religious dimension of transformational leadership

(Continued)

(Continued)

that is rarely admitted by the scholars who research this concept. Yet Jobs is a perfect example of a corporate leader who was inspired by and fascinated with the charisma of cult leaders and spiritual gurus (he was a devoted follower of Zen Buddhism) and 'borrowed' charismatic traits from these leaders (Isaacson, 2011, p. 38).

We notice the totalizing nature of the language and sentiments – Steve single-handedly changed not only several industries, but the universe (a bit like God?) and every person in it. Whilst we could debate the likelihood of whether 'every person' has been changed by Jobs's hand, nevertheless the hyperbolic nature of this writing ('entire', 'greatest', 'immeasurably') conveys how journalists, politicians, CEOs, writers and the general public construct him as a 'Great Man', a supreme leader 'leading us to the land of what's next'.

This highly romanticized image of Jobs (which perhaps says more about the needs, desires and anxieties of those constructing this image than Jobs himself) has recently been called into question. While some may celebrate Jobs's ability to make people 'do things they might never have done before', this cannot solely be read in a positive light. Jobs was known for his 'reality distortion field' or, in other words, he had a tendency to wilfully deny reality, to completely ignore certain truths or facts. He then used this to 'con people into believing his vision' as one colleague says (Isaacson, 2011, p. 118). He 'hypnotized' people to do 'the impossible because you didn't realise it was impossible' (p. 119). He transformed 'reality' and 'truth' to get people to perform beyond their expectations.

Jobs's case therefore also links to our previous discussion about the dysfunctional or destructive side of charismatic leadership. Workers describe how they worked beyond their expectations out of fear. Jobs was known to have moments where he was aggressive and belittling in his treatment of peers, superiors and subordinates (Isaacson, 2011). As a senior colleague says, 'He had the uncanny capacity to . . . make you feel small . . . it's a common trait in people who are charismatic and know how to manipulate people. Knowing that he can crush you makes you feel weakened and eager for his approval, so then he can elevate you and put you on a pedestal and own you' (Isaacson, 2011, p. 120). One colleague describes Jobs's leadership as 'management by character assassination' (p. 196). Another senior colleague at one point said, 'we should expose him for the fraud that he is so that people here stop regarding him as a messiah' (p. 214). Such stories therefore pointedly question the problematic assumption in transformational leadership literature that the transformational leader is inherently benign and good. And yet many of those who felt the wrath of Jobs's aggression and bullying also counted themselves 'the absolute luckiest person in the world to have worked with him' (p. 124). This hardly sounds like the individualized consideration or stimulation that the transformational leadership literature prizes, so is the MLQ really a 'relevant' or 'accurate' measure of the complex reality of how transformational leaders indeed get people to work harder?

But it's easy to place far too much emphasis on Jobs's personality and influence. Indeed, there is a lot more going on in a complex, high-tech, entrepreneurial and competitive company like Apple that contributes to the workers' and organization's performance and productivity than just one man. For example, the team who created the first Macintosh computer seemed highly dedicated not only to each other, but also to the product and the competition between the Macintosh product/team and the Apple II product/group. However, these powerful 'transformational' influences invariably become ignored in a contemporary society that worships the idea of a heroic 'saviour' leader.

Finally, the transformational leadership literature rarely (if ever) considers in a broader sense whether the outcomes of this 'transformation' are as beneficial as assumed. In other words, is the new world that Jobs apparently created really as good as it's assumed to be? Has his inventions led to a higher quality of life like many claim? One could argue that the lives of the Foxconn factory workers who produce thousands of Apple products a day in alienating conditions for very low pay have been transformed, but not for the better (see any of David Barboza's investigative journalism pieces published in the *New York Times* for accounts of the working conditions). One could also question the extreme working conditions of Apple's senior executives, engineers, technicians and others many of whom who work long hours in stressful and competitive conditions – is performing 'beyond expectations' (like Bass celebrates) a sustainable, meaningful way of living 'the good life'? We don't doubt that Apple products have benefited certain groups – this chapter has been written on our MacBooks – but what we are concerned with is the imbalanced nature of discussions about Apple and Jobs that tend to over-celebrate the positive way these products have changed our lives. So, what are some of the harmful consequences of the infusion of technology in our lives, created by products like the iPhone? At a macro level, we may ask how technology is being used by governments (or their intelligence agencies) to facilitate more invasive means of monitoring citizens – and how technology companies are co-operating with these ethically questionable initiatives. At a micro level, we may ask how technological devices (like the iPhone and iPad, and their raft of 'apps') are having negative impacts on our identities, relationships, and communities.

1. Why do you think so much attention has been placed on Steve Jobs as an individual over Apple as a collective? Do you agree/disagree with these attributions of single-handedly 'saving' Apple, or personally 'dinging' the universe? Why?
2. What did Steve Jobs transform? How was it transformed?
3. How and why did people think Steve Jobs was charismatic?
4. What parallels can you see in this case study between Steve Jobs and a religious leader? What do you make of those? How might this be helpful? How might it be harmful?
5. Where can you see redemption in this case study?

Concluding thoughts

In this chapter we have focused on the concept of 'transformation'. We started by showing how the definition of transformation refers to undergoing significant and fundamental changes. Not all changes in behaviour deserve to be labelled transformational: something substantial must be happening, such as a transition from a low morality to a higher morality. This interest in the nature of transformation led us to discuss the links between transformational leadership and charisma, as well as religious concepts that denote similarly radical change processes, such as 'conversion' and 'redemption'. On the basis of this we have drawn the conclusion that transformational leadership literature is heavily indebted to religious traditions (foremost Christianity), even though it may not show much awareness of this fact.

The religious underpinnings of the academic literature on transformational leaders are somewhat surprising. On the face of it, the literature seems to be simply and objectively measuring the effects of transformational leaders on various performance indicators such as job satisfaction, follower morality and organizational performance. We think, however, that there is more at stake than meets the eye. First of all, the decision to decide who is transformational (and who isn't) by using a questionnaire like the MLQ is problematic. We have suggested that what questionnaires measures may not be 'real' transformational leadership, but a fantasy of some great (larger-than-life, 'sacred') person. These fantasies, as some researchers have suggested, can be more dangerous than desirable. The concept of transformational leadership, then, may produce fantasies and practices that could result in the 'cult' status of the leader, and dangerous worshipping from the followers, as Dennis Tourish's work shows.

However, we do not go as far as suggesting that transformational leadership is inherently dangerous. The links that we have made to religion are not meant as a warning about the dangers that may come with some forms of religious belief (such as cult-formation). In fact, contrary to the tradition of (neo-)positivism on which most transformational leadership research is based (which adamantly cleaves a distance between science and religion), we do not see religious elements in theorizing as a danger for research/science. Instead, there is much to learn from theological concepts and they can, at times, be used to challenge our thinking or to invent new practices. It is important to recognize this religious dimension of transformational leadership, which is lacking in the literature, so that we can start to ask a number of critical questions (Sørensen et al., 2012).

The case of Steve Jobs provides an example of where such critical questioning may take us. If one simply accepts Jobs as an example of a transformational leader, one will only see the positives of Jobs and the 'new world' that he has (allegedly) created. However, if we focus on a question like 'How does a (pseudo-)religious faith in Jobs as a leader influence the way we see and experience Apple?' we begin to see a different picture. For example, we may start to pay attention to other elements that are usually ignored, such as the many other workers who have contributed to the success of Apple, the bullying, coercive and nasty side of Jobs, the exploitative working conditions in Chinese factories that have contributed to this 'success', or the harmful effects of Apple products on the way people communicate and relate to one another. From this perspective, transformational leadership is perhaps not so much a leadership practice that offers redemption as much as it is a way of seeing the world that hides its less beautiful sides.

But none of this takes away the possibility of a 'truly' transformational leader, who realizes everything that the literature suggests (and more). We all know somebody who we find inspiring and who motivates us to bring the best out of ourselves. In some cases that impression lasts; in other cases we look back later and wonder why we were so naïve to be infatuated with that person (which is not necessarily a more developed or 'mature' perspective, mind you). What we want to draw attention to is the impossibility of making an objective or unbiased assessment when it comes to transformational leadership; transformational leadership is always a matter of faith. Faith, as the religious traditions show us, can be a wonderful, comforting and uplifting thing but, as history shows us, it can also give rise to beliefs and practices that are diminishing, harmful and worrying.

The key points in this chapter were ...

- Transformational leadership has been one of the most popular leadership concepts over the last 40 years. It focuses on a leader's ability to inspire change within their followers in such a powerful way that they are 'transformed' into more effective, engaged or even more moral people.

- Transformational leadership is often measured against a scale. One of the most popular of these is the Multifactor Leadership Questionnaire, which measures the four 'I's of transformational leadership: idealized influence; inspirational motivation; intellectual stimulation; individualized consideration.
- Transformational leadership is closely linked to the idea of charisma, which has historical roots in the writings of the New Testament. In particular, it carries the notion that a charismatic person is endowed (by God?) with special qualities which designate them as above ordinary followers.
- Transformational leadership is driven by a (pseudo-)religious faith which often goes unacknowledged, such as its significant parallels with religious ideas of conversion and redemption. It paints a picture of followers being transformed (i.e. converted) into higher moral beings by charismatic leaders, who then go out and redeem their organizations (or even the world).

 # Further thinking

Bass, B. M. (1985b). Leadership: Good, better, best. *Organizational Dynamics*, *13*, 26–40.

1 Bass does not draw explicitly on religion in his presentation of transformational leadership, but he does use quite a few religious metaphors. Can you find some?
2 Bass concludes his article with the conclusion that 'organizations need to draw more on the resources of charismatic leaders'. Do you agree?
3 The article was published 30 years ago: do you feel it is still relevant? Why, or why not? Find a recent article on transformational leadership and compare it to Bass's article: do you see any important differences?

Kelly, S. (2014). Horses for courses: Exploring the limits of leadership development through equine-assisted learning. *Journal of Management Education*, *38*(2), 216–233.

1 Though Kelly doesn't explicitly focus on transformational leadership, how does the leadership development programme he studied draw on similar language and beliefs evident in transformational leadership?
2 What do you think about the validity of developing one's leadership through a horse-whispering activity?
3 Thinking about Kelly's experience on the programme, how could religious ideas like conversion, redemption, faith and shame be helpful in understanding what happens on leadership development programmes?

If you would like to learn more about the relation between leadership and the sacred, you could read the following papers:

Grint, K. (2010). The sacred in leadership: Separation, sacrifice and silence. *Organization Studies*, *31*(1), 89–107.

Śliwa, M., Spoelstra, S., Sørensen, B. M. and Land, C. (2013). Profaning the sacred in leadership studies: A reading of Murakami's *A Wild Sheep Chase*. *Organization*, *20*(6), 860–880.

1   If you are asked to lead a team, will you try to live up to the ideals articulated in the idea of transformational leadership? Why, or why not?

2   Think about a time when you've felt inspired, motivated or energized in an interaction with a leader. Are there valuable aspects of transformational leadership that could be held on to in the face of this critique?

 # Leadership on screen

Watch the scene 'Mufasa's Ghost' from the 1994 film *The Lion King* (scene 21, available on YouTube).

Interpret the scene as a representation of transformational leadership and complete the following tasks:

- Explain who is exercising transformational leadership and why (the most obvious candidates are Simba, Mufasa and Rafiki).
- Describe the religious dimension to the scene, and explain how this may be linked to the religious aspects of transformational and charismatic leadership.

PART II

Leading in Context

Contents

5

LEADERSHIP LEARNING AND DEVELOPMENT

Brigid Carroll

Brigid has a lot of learning about leadership still to do. That's why she both researches and develops it with/ in others. She like mysteries and questions and wonders what leadership could achieve if it could pursue and unlock things we don't know yet as organizsations, communities and societies.

What this chapter is all about …

The main idea is that learning and development are related, different and integral to leadership. And not only are they connected, but both learning knowledge about, and the development of, leadership are invested with power.

The key questions this chapter answers are:

- How do you learn leadership? Why might learning leadership differ from learning other subjects or skills?
- What are the different ways we can think about developing and learning leadership?
- How are learning and development tied up in power?
- How might seeing leadership in relation to learning offer a richer perspective on the nature of leadership?
- Learning doesn't just differ for leadership; it's also integral to it. How and why are leadership, learning and development interconnected?

Introduction

If you are even reading this chapter then our presumption is you are some way through a formal course on leadership where you are endeavouring to learn leadership. We'd be putting thoughts in your head at this stage but you may even be asking the question of why there is a chapter on leadership learning and development. After all you have learnt a great deal of things in your life already and are probably envisaging learning a great many more so why would learning leadership be any different from learning to read or developing a swimming stroke or learning calculus, gourmet cooking or contemporary dance?

Learning, we would assume, is something you do willingly or unwillingly, energetically or otherwise, effectively or not. If there is something like that in your head then that's a great starting place for a number of reasons.

It's a great starting place because we are going to make a case that there's something about leadership that brings it into relationship with learning and development differently to learning calculus or cooking or developing mathematical and food technology skill. You will probably all have learnt to make a cake (successfully or otherwise). In order to do that you might have observed or helped someone who has cake baking as a skill, watched a demo or cooking show on screen, attended a baking course or just followed a recipe. That form of learning involves a defined goal or outcome, specific learning resources and opportunities, the repetition of experiences and the building of mastery. You can learn to bake a cake without greatly impacting on any other aspect of yourself, relationships and work/life. Not so with leadership learning and development.

First, we argue that leadership and learning/development are more intimately connected than something like baking and learning. So while we need to learn or develop our capacity to lead, the reverse is also true – that leading involves challenging others' and indeed whole organizations' learning. We suspect that hasn't always been so strongly the case but by now, assuming you have read other chapters in this book, you'll understand that the leadership landscape has changed a lot recently and is still changing markedly from what it used to look like. If the myth of leaders as 'superheroic' individuals, already pre-packaged with the answers that will change the trajectories of whole organizations, communities and societies, is busted (and we think it is) then all there is left is the capacity of people from all walks of life to learn how to face leadership possibilities and challenges between them. What builds that capacity above everything else is the capacity to learn and develop as individuals and collectives.

You will also have read that leadership tends to pursue change, possibility, innovation, novelty or alternatives. We would tend to call it administration or management if it was orientated at keeping things ticking over. So there's something about leadership that associates it with moving beyond what is known or in existence at any time (Grint, 2005b). We have to learn and develop ways of not just doing things differently but also doing different things (Kotter, 2001), hence leadership/learning development is core to that. That should feel different to the old 'being in charge' notions of leadership but even so don't equate leadership to something like teaching. There are all sorts of ways of enabling or sparking learning and development that go way beyond teaching.

Finally, we are going to propose that, through exploring leadership *in relationship to* learning and development, you will get further real and relevant insight into the nature of leadership, leadership work and the potential of leadership to impact lives, relationships and world. So don't see this chapter as about learning to lead; see this chapter as about the interrelationships, interplay and intersections of leadership, learning and development. To do this, we are going to write this chapter for you directly. We are going to assume you have learnt a lot about leadership already, not only in whatever course this book is associated with, but through being part of dynamics of leading and following at many points in your life. We are assuming that you want to learn how to be part of leadership – how to both lead and follow, in other words – to make your contribution in the collectives that matter to you in the future. That will mean some theoretical and conceptual material (head stuff) but it will also mean developing your capacity to understand leadership (we could call that developing a leadership mindset), seeing yourself in leadership (we could call that developing a leadership identity) and acquiring the capacity to do that work (we could call this developing a leadership practice). If you are up for that challenge then that is how we want you to respond and read this chapter.

Figure 5.1

Delineating learning and development

We have been writing about learning and development as if they are more or less one and the same thing. We've got to stop doing that as they are very different and if we want you to do both – learn about leadership and develop leadership – then we have to help you be clear about what is required to achieve both. Let's go to the dictionary to put up a strawman that begins to do this.

DEFINITION: LEARNING

- knowledge acquired by systematic study in any field of scholarly application;
- the act or process of acquiring knowledge or skill.

We figure you'll readily identify with these definitions of learning. In fact you are probably experts at these. So you'll see 'knowledge' appears to be the key word in both of these. You 'acquire' knowledge in these definitions and the 'acquire' is linked to fairly intentional 'systematic study' in one definition and something called an 'act or process' in the other. So we have institutions where you acquire knowledge which tends to look like attending courses and classes and doing reading and learning tasks usually with extensive systems of assessment thrown in. Knowledge in a learning frame looks to be something that you seek to possess or have and has a rather solid feel to it as if it can be quantified or measured or converted into something else. One of the things this chapter will ask you to do is think hard about this idea of knowledge. It sounds so neutral and objective and unproblematically useful in definitions like this, but there's some really interesting thinking that argues the opposite and that knowledge in fact is highly political, subjective and controlled/controlling.

DEFINITION: DEVELOPMENT

- to come or bring to a later or more advanced or expanded stage; grow or cause to grow gradually;
- to elaborate or work out in detail;
- to disclose or unfold gradually or to be gradually disclosed or unfolded;
- to come or bring into existence; generate or be generated.

We're hoping you are struck immediately by the difference in this dictionary definition of development. It doesn't even talk about knowledge, for instance, but something akin to growing or creating. Notice how often 'gradually' is mentioned as if development follows a slow, evolutionary, partial kind of trajectory. There's no particular tangible outcome like 'application' or 'acquisition' as there was in the learning definition but qualifiers like 'later', 'advanced', 'expanded' and 'in detail'. Notice too that sometimes development is something that someone does ('to elaborate' or 'to bring into existence') or sometimes something that appears done to one ('be gradually disclosed' or 'be generated'). Development feels a very different kind of experience to learning, doesn't it, in these words? We are going to suggest that these definitions point to development, not as something one has like knowledge, but as becoming or being something other or more than what one has been.

At this point it might be worth drawing your attention to a distinction made by a philosopher called Erich Fromm several decades ago (1976). He argued that there were two basic orientations: one he called 'having' and the other 'being'. A 'having' orientation is about acquiring, possessing and consuming, while a 'being' orientation is about exploring, relating and becoming. For instance one can *have* love, friends or children or *be* in love, a friend and a parent. Fromm was critical of the dominance of the having orientation in the world as he thought it would encourage the growth of static, passive and transactional relationship to people or things. For him the being orientation was a way of being alive, fluid and dynamic with people and things. You can possibly see from this that one can have knowledge or be engaged in knowing. We wouldn't be as pessimistic about the having orientation as Fromm; however, we do wonder if his distinction is a useful way of understanding the distinction between learning and development. It would seem you and indeed organizations need to have knowledge and the process of acquiring such knowledge is learning. At the same time you and organizations need to be growing and creating new capacities and we could call that development.

DEFINITION: ERICH FROMM

Erich Fromm (1900–1980) was a German social psychologist, psychoanalyst, sociologist, humanistic philosopher and democratic socialist. He was associated with what became known as the Frankfurt School of critical theory. He wrote such books such as *Escape from Freedom* (1941) and *The Art of Loving* (1956), and argued that while we desire freedom, at the same time we fear it and end up escaping from it.

Obviously the two can't be separated out from each other entirely. As one develops then one learns and should have new knowledge as a result. If there is such a relationship then those involved in leadership will need to be integral to that developing/learning cycle that both builds the capacity and realizes the potential of individuals and organizations. That's the real promise of this chapter we propose.

We are sure that you have had experiences of being in development but they may be harder to pinpoint than the more formalized learning processes you've been through, so we are also going to start the chapter by helping you locate some of the moments that have this development quality.

Experiential learning

We are going to start with experience. Arguably, however, this is where you have tried leading and following for yourself. You have all *had* experience and presumably have *had* some learnings out of those but have you *been* developing as a result? If you know anything about learning and development then you could guess that experience is going to be pretty central to those (Kolb, 1984). There are those who claim this is *the* pivotal dimension of learning and development associated with leadership. You are in a good position to assess that given you are likely halfway through a course on leadership, but also because you have a significant store of experience. So we're going to give these questions to you now and ask you to formulate answers as we go.

STOP AND REFLECT 5.1

What is the importance of experience in learning and developing leadership?
What are the ways that experience can enter the learning and development of leadership?

Big experiential moments

A significant stream of research in this experiential terrain associated with leadership and its development focuses on *big*, important moments and experiences that are deemed to stand out from the myriad less significant moments and experiences. Thus some experiences are deemed more formative on your leadership than others, and therefore more valuable to reflect on and learn from. One of the most popular and widely read articles in the whole leadership canon is an article called 'Crucibles of leadership', which terms some experiences 'crucibles' in that they are unexpected and unsolicited, usually linked to adversity and often traumatic, and have the potential to be transformative (Bennis and Thomas, 2002). Crucibles are often described as a test or turning point in your beliefs or value structures and spur you to rethink who you are, what matters to you and where you are going. They are likened to a crucible because out of the turmoil and deep questioning can come new direction, insight and energy. They can forge a new you in identity terms but only if you accept them as a test, front up to the learning they contain, go to a place of deep reflection and weave them into an ongoing story in which you are part.

STOP AND REFLECT 5.2

Your interest should be piqued at this point so let's invite you to identify a crucible experience for you. Think back over your broader experience to something that has seemed to make a big impact on you and your leadership. While you may not have recognized it at the time, you may be able to recognize it looking back because your mind has gone back to this moment at times, because it has stuck in your mind and you took something from it that has shaped who you are and how you respond to things. The feel of the impact might be like an anchor or non-negotiable that you rely on when you need to make a decision or come to a point of judgement. Think through this crucible now particularly in the context of leadership and your relationship with leadership.

The academics who wrote the 'crucible' article, Bennis and Thomas, also argue that there are four skills that get you through crucible moments and those happen to be the four skills that we often see in great leaders. The first one is the ability to engage others in shared meaning or, put differently, relate powerfully with others involved in the context of that moment or beyond. The second is developing a powerful sense of voice or the ability to put things into words. The third is a sense of integrity or living by foundational principles or beliefs. The fourth, and most important, is what they call 'adaptive capacity' or 'applied creativity', which one grows by having to front up to a demanding context and find a way through when times get tough. They are arguing, in essence, that leadership is forged in these kinds of experiences which makes these crucibles vital to the whole enterprise of learning and developing leadership.

We imagine that much of this might resonate. That most of us have experiences that, whether wanted or not at the time, have left a real mark on us. But some of you may be sitting there looking over a life of a great many experiences but none that really seem to fit the description of adversity, trauma and transformation. Some of you find also be experiencing a little bit of unrest at some of the assumptions that are sitting underneath this thinking. Crucible moments seem to have a touch of the heroic about them, as if they might forge larger than life or superhero-type figures. You'll have read enough of this book to question whether leadership is only the province of what are often represented as exceptional figures who most of us can't compete with. There are other ways of identifying and working very differently with experience so let's go to one as a form of contrast.

Little experiential moments

There's another stream of writing that is interested in the everydayness of experience and how we connect to the multitude of things that we are involved in over the course of our days, weeks and lives. While some of those experiences might be stand-outs, the huge majority of them are mundane, routine, small and partial but, it could be argued, they shape us at least as much as, or even more so, than big one-off experiences. Sitting underneath this stream of thought is the thought that being in leadership is really being in a set of ongoing and connected relationships and interactions, and hence being able to learn from those, even as they are unfolding, is vital to the ongoing development of our leadership. This ability to learn from the unfolding stream of experiences in profound ways that provide the context for our leadership is called critical reflexivity.

We need to note here that academics use all sorts of terms involving reflection and reflexivity, but we don't think there's a need to run you through all the various permutations of those — except we have used one already in discussing crucible experiences, *self-reflection*, so let's use that as a point of contrast to this new term we have introduced. We are going to draw on one of the world's key thinkers in the area of critical reflexivity, Ann Cunliffe (2009), to draw this distinction. She calls self-reflection, the crucible practice, a form of 'dialogue-with-self' where we ask ourselves questions about our own responses to others and interpretation of events. It's a form of trying to figure out why we have thought and acted in the ways we chose to, and it can feel like an internal conversation going on in our head. Critical reflexivity goes a whole lot further, however, and involves unsettling not just our own assumptions about ourselves but broader assumptions about the nature of this world we live in and how phenomena such as leadership are both *constructed* by us and for us. One way to describe it would be to say that it is thinking about our thinking and seeking to uncover our assumptions, limits and blind-spots in our ordinary reflection in relation to the politics, ethics and structures and the larger realities of our organizations, communities and societies.

STOP AND REFLECT 5.3

Let's lead you through how you might actually do some critical reflexivity. Remember first that it is everyday experience that provides the catalyst. Given all we know about you is that you are likely to be a student of some sort then let's ask you to think about this week. There will be myriad moments when you chose either to act or not act that might offer a small but significant insight not just to you but to the wider system leadership is a part of. Select a moment, not because it seems large and important, but maybe because it puzzles you a little for some reason. Approach this moment existentially by asking questions like, 'Was I the person I think I am or want to be?', or, then relationally ('What are the clues here about how I relate to others and the world?'), and also ethically ('How have I interpreted the realities that inform this experience?').

Now those questions have hopefully opened up more complex ways of thinking about yourself, others and the world, but if you are alert then you may be thinking that you are still in your own head and exploring experience from your own perspective and no amount of clever questions will get you out of that place. You'd be right in thinking that, so there's a further dimension to this. What say you asked these questions about you and others and what you were doing out loud *while* you were engaged in that activity? Obviously this would create some interesting social exchanges, but it would also mean you would get different perspectives from others about the same experience *as you go* and you'd have to learn and develop ways of being and acting differently together. Another scholar, Joe Raelin, calls this being in a 'reflective community' (2007) rather like playing in an orchestra where you rehearse and work on being critically reflexive with each other in terms of what you are doing together. You will still learn about yourself but what you are really doing is developing a collective capacity to approach your organization, community or society differently.

So let's put all of this together in leadership terms. Neither of our perspectives on experience doubt that experience shapes your leadership. One focuses on big, signature and crucible experiences and argues you learn the lessons of leadership through those moments and become stronger as a leader as a result. The second focuses on small, everyday experiences and argues you catch yourselves in ways that reflect you in relation to others and broader structures and, if you can voice those beyond yourself, you can catalyse potential and capacity in the collectives you are part of. We are going to assert that they tap into different ways of being in leadership. The former might build resilience and a sense of individual robustness while the latter seems to build attentiveness and collaboration. So it would seem that how we learn from experience and what we develop from it reflect wider truths we hold about leadership.

The larger learning/development terrain

From following this chapter so far you might well have the impression that both learning and development happen internally to an individual, and even that individuals seem well in control of their own leadership learning and development. If we pause for a moment, however, you'll readily sense that learning and development doesn't happen in a social or cultural vacuum, and that there are larger structural, economic, cultural and societal pressures or forces in learning and development – very strongly so in terms of the field of leadership. So let's rebalance an inside-out view of learning with an outside-in view and build a more complex terrain around the ideas of learning and development. After all you are unlikely to be sitting reading this book from unfettered choice, if you think about it. This book is likely to be a prescribed or recommended one for you, which means a staff member has chosen it out of literally thousands of options for a course, most likely inside a tertiary or higher education institution structure which in turn sets boundaries around about what is valuable for students to learn. Your tertiary institution sits in a contested education environment where questions of what kinds of knowledge and learning are desirable and relevant are being vigorously debated by all sorts of stakeholders (you as students, we as researchers/teachers and those in the community/world looking to action such learning). Long before you internally work through any kind of learning and development then you can see a whole lot of decisions and choices have been already made about what leadership is and how it should be taught and approached.

What you will be aware of is that leadership is a widely talked about construct and that daily you are bombarded with messages, brands, ads, media and talk that evoke 'it'. Have a look at the box below. It's a tiny snapshot of the headlines and evocations of leadership that were reported during one hour of the writing of this chapter. Even from these few examples you can see clear patterns in when and how leadership is characterized at the present time. Given you have worked through much of this book already you'll be noting that leadership seems most commonly associated with high-profile individuals (still more often men than women) who are at the pinnacle of careers, organizations, groups and projects and who are strongly credited with decision-making, strategic vision and authority over others. Although it is possible you'll have had other experiences of leading that differ from these patterns, it is highly likely that such dominant patterns have shaped your learning and developing of leadership without you fully being aware of it. Without getting too Orwellian on you, you have already been shaped and developed in terms of leadership without your having had to formally learn or develop anything.

LEADERSHIP HEADLINES

- High-profile battle on for Cantor's leadership post (CNN)
- Bergdahl prison letters cite lack of leadership, bad conditions in his Afghanistan unit (RT Network)
- GOP leadership scramble: Six lawmakers to watch (*Wall Street Journal*)
- Change of leadership in Infosys has cheered investors (*Economic Times*)
- Rep. Marlin Stutzman seeks House leadership post (*Indianapolis Star*)
- To become a better leader, be aware (*Businessweek*)
- 5 signs you're not leadership material (*Entrepreneur*)
- Theresa May loses her passport to Tory leadership (*Guardian*)
- Strong leadership needed in battle against bad food (New Zealand Doctor Online)
- The surprising countries with more women in corporate leadership than the U.S. – or even Scandinavia (*Time*)
- Negligent leaders are sucking Nigeria dry (*Deutsche Welle*)
- Socialist Party leadership elections agreed for late September (*Portugal News*)

To think this through we are going to introduce you to a philosopher/thinker who can help explain the wider societal/cultural/political forces at work shaping your views of leadership. His name is Michel Foucault and he argued essentially that knowledge is not a neutral thing.[1] Instead, he argued that it is invariably embedded in power relations or socially constructed 'truths', and that such power or 'truths' exert a form of control over what he called subjects (that is, you, I, everyone). As a way of showing this he introduced the compound term *power/knowledge* (read that as one word) to indicate that any knowledge we might acquire or have is shot through with power and control which acts as a form of discipline – disciplining us to think and act in certain ways. If we translate this to the leadership field then what we find we (think we) know about leadership has come about through the influence of *power/knowledge* acting on us. Now, in a further twist, Foucault also argued that all *power/knowledge* is very contextual and historical, which means that it is shaped by the society we are in and the 'truths' which are held in place by the educational, media and economic institutions we are in at that moment and in that place. Most of the time it's important and indeed vital for us to see ourselves as proactive and agentic (choosing) selves, but just for a second try and imagine yourself as a site or outline at the nexus of all these power-full knowledge-producing forces (Foucault calls them discourses) that are at work shaping you. If you can do that, then what feels internal to you (what you think and believe) can actually be understood as something external to you, folded into your identity but not within your control. You've incorporated what is circulating as leadership 'truths' external to you, in other words.

DEFINITION: MICHEL FOUCAULT

Michel Foucault (pronounced 'fuko') (1926–1984) was a French philosopher, historian of ideas, social theorist, philologist and literary critic. His theories addressed the relationship between power and knowledge, and how they are used as a form of social control through societal institutions.

Such a way of thinking has been applied specifically to the leadership development field in an article called 'Identity undoing and power relations in leadership development'. In that article the authors argue that contemporary leadership development shapes a certain kind of self, called an enterprising self (Du Gay, 1996), which is strongly individualistic, entrepreneurial and self-improving, and happens to be most congruent with the world of work today. Leadership development uses a number of what Foucault called 'technologies of the self' in constructing those leadership selves, including one we have talked about (self-reflection), but also others you may be aware of such as psychometric testing and certain feedback formats. Individuals submit themselves to such leadership development and their associated technologies of the self because they have a particular currency for organizations at the present time, and represent institutionally and organizationally desired identities and behaviour. Important decisions such as recruitment, promotion or retention depend on them. While individuals may feel they have choice *inside* these parameters, they may have little choice *about* them. It may be difficult to be recognized in leadership if you want to behave counter to this kind of identity or behaviour. In this way, then, what is

---

1   Foucault wrote a lot and we aren't going to pretend he's easy to read but if you are interested in this line of thinking then try John Gaventa (2003), *Power after Lukes: A Review of the Literatures,* to start with.

offered as leadership learning and development shapes or constructs the emergent or aspirant leadership that is likely to result.

We hope that doesn't sound too sinister or depressing. Foucault thought understanding the ability of *power/knowledge* to produce or construct 'truths' was actually positive. With such an awareness you can challenge or resist these truths that are in circulation in the world and, with others, shape other and even new truths. In fact, in a small way, we'd like to think this is partly what this textbook is about: giving you the awareness, language and practices to think through what is being offered as leadership 'truths', to understand your own role in confirming or subverting these, and to give you a larger repertoire of leadership identities to choose from.

Leadership development interventions

We have called this section 'Leadership development interventions' to keep the usage of development here separate from the learning (having)/development (being) distinction that we are exploring over the chapter. In this section, then, we are using Development (let's keep designating it with a capital letter) to signify the host of Development-type interventions that largely, although not exclusively, sit outside formal educational qualifications. You may well have been involved in some of these, such as corporate in-house organizational leadership workshops or retreats, student or community programmes, or online development/learning platforms. If not, the chances are you will be in the foreseeable future at just about any stage of your life and career. These are attracting widespread interest at the moment because this is a huge and growing business – some call it an 'industry' and are highly critical of 'the countless leadership centers, institutes, programs, courses, seminars, workshops, experiences, trainers, books, blogs, articles, websites, webinars, videos, conferences, consultants, and coaches claiming to teach people – usually for money – how to lead' (Kellerman, 2012, p. xiii). Despite its name, it would be wrong to see Development as necessarily likely to possess a less 'having' orientation than education since, although there are not normally grades or qualifications, there is often retention, promotion, visibility, status, special projects and senior management goodwill at stake. We are not, however, going to focus on the 'industry' aspect of this steadily increasing body of Development opportunities, even though the propensity of our contemporary world to spend considerable amounts of money pursuing leadership is certainly worthy of much more scrutiny. Instead we are going to seize the opportunity to look through different theoretical discourses (research perspectives) at what it means to develop leadership in the belief that in pitting different ways of seeing a topic or process against each other, we can drill deeper and probe the very assumptions that sit under development. So there's a change of orientation you'll need in reading through this section. This section is going to give you some learning in order for you to be able to bring an analytic set of frames to any discussion, reading or experience of leadership development.

We are going to draw on Christopher Mabey's (2013) 'discourse framework' to do this pitting of theoretical perspectives. An assumption we need you to make is that leadership development isn't like a chair or a table in the sense that it has an undeniable, 'objective' form that people recognize easily. We are going to term leadership development a 'constructed reality', which reveals as much about how the person/people are looking as it does about what is being looked at. Mabey describes four different ways of talking or writing about leadership development; he calls these discourses (but they could also be referred to as frames or research perspectives). Depending which discourse you are using will determine what you see and what you prioritize when you think about or do leadership development. It's important you can identify these discourses not just because everything (including this chapter) that is written about leadership development is written through one (or sometimes more) of them, but also because those seeking or offering leadership development will draw on assumptions from one or more of these as to what they see as the value of leadership development. Understanding the discourses will make you a much better informed and critical consumer. Let's take you through each discourse in turn.

Functionalist leadership development discourse

We will start with the functionalist discourse because most of what you read or experience in the way of leadership development will be driven from this research perspective. This discourse is distinctive for two central preoccupations: the first is an individual- or leader-centric focus and the second is a performance emphasis. This discourse is primarily focused on how individuals build leader capability through a raft of formal techniques such as competency frameworks, psychometric and 360-degree type instruments and coaching/mentoring type programmes. It is assumed that 'developed' individuals will lift their own and others' performance in line with organizational priorities. The feel of such development often aspires to be scientific, where leadership is approached rationally as primarily a matter of 'knowledge-gain, skills-acquisition and attitude shift' (Mabey, 2013, p. 363). It is also assumed that superiorly performing individuals will deliver enhanced organizational performance. Perhaps not surprisingly the predominant focus of this kind of discourse is on ROI (return on investment), impact and outcome although these are notoriously difficult to evaluate with any tangibility. In short, what drives much of this discourse is discovering whether particular leadership development works, in a very specific sense, and what might make it work even better.

Given the increasing global expenditure on leadership development and the contemporary desire to develop people in line with organizational strategic direction then it does seem sensible to pursue an evidential line with regards to the claims made for the efficacy of leadership development. However, there are assumptions in this discourse that seem to require greater scrutiny at the same time. We need to ask some serious questions here. For instance: What is the relationship between individual development and organizational performance given the unlikelihood of being able to credit any individual with success or failure at a collective, macro level? What is the relationship of performance (and leadership for that matter) to less technical and rational phenomena such as power, control, relationship and conflict? Functional discourses are often charged with being overly instrumental (preoccupied with the 'ends' or outcomes of what they are researching), and not with the myriad processes and phenomena that actually constitute or make them up.

Interpretive leadership development discourse

While it's a distant second to the dominance of the functionalist discourse, interpretive studies of leadership development are a small but consistently occurring part of this field. Radically different assumptions drive an interpretive approach from a functionalist one (remember often writers or providers don't know they are using a discourse (or don't reveal they are directly) so think of yourself as changing discourses and trying to see leadership development from each one of these as we introduce them here). An interpretive discourse assumes that leadership, as opposed to being an unproblematic, objective, fixed reality, is in fact a highly variable, relational and contextual phenomenon that people construct differently depending on who they are and how they interact in their context. There are a number of implications for understanding leadership development that arise from this. The first is that leadership looks somewhat different for every group of people and in every context/situation, so the focus of research and development is strongly on exploring how people are defining and characterizing the leadership they think they have or need. The second is that leadership is never the property of any individual and research needs to follow how leadership is attributed and performed across a collective over time. We term this kind of leadership inter-subjective or relational as leadership seems to be move between a number of people and indeed it can be difficult to pinpoint actual leaders, although it is still useful to talk of people being in leadership together.

Leadership development from such a research perspective focuses on dimensions such as meaning, language, symbols, artefacts and interactions as core in how leadership is created (or not) by a group of people. While development can be formal it is much more likely to be focused on the in-the-moment work. Driving this discourse is the assumption that collectives can learn to be in leadership more effectively if their language, dynamics and assumptions become visible enough to them to enable patterns of talking, working and interacting to be changed and experimented with. This discourse thus brings a strong focus on process or how change might happen, which seems valuable, although the sheer timeframe, complexities and intangibility of collectives of people learning to do things differently can seem daunting and demanding.

Dialogic leadership development discourse

'Dialogic' might not be a word you have met before, although you have probably met the words that are often used in association with it – *postmodernism* and *post-structuralism*. Full descriptions of any of these are out of the scope of this chapter so we'll take a direct line on dialogic. At its simplest, it means 'to be in dialogue with'. A dialogic perspective signifies that anything we want to consider as leading happens in dialogue or connected with other modes of being. This should make intuitive sense to you. No one has the luxury of being purely leading: we lead, manage, administrate and do the technical/professional/occupational aspects of what we do, as well as being a friend, parent, peer/colleague and subordinate at the same time too. Many of those things we do concurrently. 'Dialogic' goes further than just proposing leading is part of a multiple repertoire, however, in that it suggests that consistency or holism is impossible and we need to admit that, despite the allure of a strong, connected self-trajectory, the reality we have to contend with is fragmented, disconnected, incohesive and even contradictory as we make continuous attempts to be and do what we think we need and want to. So we need to stop thinking about leadership as static, fixed and unproblematic and accept it signifies a fluid, changeable, dynamic set of processes.

The focus of this dialogue is on how people struggle to be in leadership which is necessarily a messy, often paradoxical and conflictual endeavour. Core to this discourse is the notion of identity, or how one understands and articulates who one is given the multiple possibilities in any one moment. If you think back to earlier in the chapter then you'll remember there are *inside-out* and *outside-in* ways of exploring dimensions such as identity. Identity-orientated research is interested in how we go about the process of constructing ourselves in leadership (sometimes termed *identity construction*) but also how our leadership identities are shaped and disciplined (sometimes termed *identity regulation*). *Constructionist* research assumes we make choices in our leadership and construct our leadership as an ongoing kind of project or accomplishment. *Regulation* research assumes that, while we might have the illusion of choices, we are in fact heavily shaped to be the kind of leader our organizations or communities prioritize. Many researchers have given the processes (often called technologies, following Foucault's ideas which we saw above) particular scrutiny and have noted that organizations and providers have a sophisticated array of instruments, activities, language and interventions that create a formidable array of expectations as to the leadership that those in leadership development need to display. They also note that participants ignore or resist these at their peril. Thus leadership development needs to be seen as holding both problems and possibilities for participants and organizations that are not pre-determined going into it.

Critical leadership development discourse

While there is overlap or similarity between the dialogic and the critical, this last one is strongly focused on the idea and practice of power. In this discourse leadership development is assumed to be an ideological enterprise which privileges particular realities, states, parties and outcomes over others. This invariably means that development marginalizes, oppresses, excludes and dominates others. In short leadership development is a political enterprise. A critical perspective points out that leadership development is usually status quo confirming. In other words most organizations don't appear to radically transform as a result of leadership development. Researchers point to the asymmetrical and gendered nature of much leadership development where 'high potential' too often means male, executive in style and aligned/acquiescent to what the organization already is. This is coupled by a lack of emancipatory outcomes or aims, with leadership development not seeming to be influential in creating new pathways for justice, ethics and diversity/difference, to name just a few of the socially desirable phenomena that critical researchers pay attention to.

It's important to unpack what bringing power and ideology into the terrain draws our attention to, for undoubtedly those two things can make people feel very uncomfortable indeed. Most potently they invite us to ask different questions about leadership development such as: What is the purpose of leadership development? Who needs to be developed? (And by association not developed?) Who gets to design, shape, lead or control the development experience? Who gets to decide what kind of leadership should be developed? These simple but dangerous questions alert us to the wider organizational context, history and power/relational dynamics that development invariably sits in. Most important, critical approaches stretch us beyond the vacuum in which much research on leadership development seems to happen. It is important to note too that this discourse is also important in supporting the emergence of actual leadership development interventions that are avowedly critical in purpose and pursuing emancipatory, liberating and alternative directions for those in organizations (Carroll and Nicholson, 2014).

Working with different discourses

In representing these four discourses and inviting you to reflect and try on alternative ways of understanding and thinking about leadership development, we are certainly bringing some complexity to a topic that is too often presented as simply a question of 'how to make more (effective) leaders'. We think it's a complexity that is important for you to grapple with. We know we are dispelling a myth, if you still have it, that what you read can be neutral and perspective-less. These discourses should help you identify the assumptions that underlie anything you read about leadership development (including of course this chapter) and any experience you have or will have as a provider, participant or contributor to leadership development. These four discourses point to tensions in leadership development between performance, relevance, power, means, outcomes, individuals and collectives, to name but a few issues represented here. Your ability to negotiate and talk to these tensions will help bring a productive robustness to what is a growing and contested dimension of contemporary organizational life. While you will probably find that one or more of these discourses seemed to appeal to you over others, the capacity to identify what kind of research perspective is in operation in a piece of work means you can ask questions and form opinions at a deep level.

Leading learning and development

If we are giving the impression that one needs to sign up to, or be sent into, a development programme or intervention in order to learn or develop leadership then you would be utterly right if that felt a much too narrow focus. People learn *at* work and *in* their organization and develop *throughout* the day-to-day routines and special events of their lives. The previous section about learning from experience tried to give you a sense of the different ways one can learn while one moves through one's life and engages with what one meets. This section is going to introduce you to another important kind of learning that is increasingly being associated with leadership, something called 'sensemaking' (and its corollary 'sensegiving'). This is work associated with a key North American organizational scholar called Karl Weick (2005); it represents a new paradigm of not just thinking about learning and leadership, but how organizing (and organization) happens at all. In the paradigm of sensemaking, those in leadership need to learn consciously alongside and with others in the organization to integrate together in an ongoing way all the bits and pieces of awareness, instinct, interpretation and knowledge that different people have but don't necessarily share as part of their collective action. With sensemaking, learning is core to leadership and leadership is core to learning.

You'll notice that the word 'sensemaking' has two words in it that you immediately understand, and if we invert them then we get 'making sense'. In fact, Weick argues that 'Sensemaking is what it says it is, namely, making something sensible' (1995, p. 15). To make something sensible we have to articulate something, clarify it, test our assumptions of it, check others' interpretations and perspectives, ask questions of it and reach some shared sense of what it is together we know and don't know about the 'something'. That explanation runs the risk of seeming too sensible and rational and Weick warns us making it so. In fact what we see (or don't see) is heavily influenced by who we think we are (identity), what we are used to (history or experience), and what we expect or even need to see (blind-spots and prejudices), presumptions about patterns (confirmation bias), and justifications (influence of power norms and structures). Sensemaking as a way of seeing is trying to get groups and organisations to refresh how they see and operate, shake out existing rigidities, incorporate the perspectives of many and be able to keep learning, particularly in the face of uncertainty, unpredictability, ambiguity and complexity. You might be beginning to see that much of this will resonate with contemporary understandings of leadership as collective, attuned to complexity and orientated at possibility and newness.

Sensemaking makes an association between leadership and learning that proposes the two are interdependent (Pye, 2005). There are two key components to this. Firstly leadership needs to elicit all the parts of the puzzle held by people who sometimes don't even know they have something to contribute; and second, in what some call sensegiving, leadership puts out an interpretation or meaning acts as a reference point or point of calibration for others to contest or confirm that interpretation and meaning. The larger story here is that learning has become a continual, unfolding, piece-by-piece process in organizations and one that needs a leadership sensibility to give it shape, permission, momentum and impact.

Conclusion

There is a story or narrative underlying this chapter – in fact there are probably a number and you may even have built one for yourself – but we'll try and round out ours here. Many textbooks don't have chapters on leadership, learning and development and, where they do, it tends to be a more direct 'how to' develop leadership than this one presents. What we have tried to do is assume you will one day be a sponsor, researcher, facilitator, participant, decision-maker or evaluator of leadership development and to equip you to be that through the different sections of this chapter.

The first part of our story is to pose the relationship between a form of leadership and an approach to development. So, we used experiential learning to associate crucible moments with more heroic types of leadership, and critical reflexivity with a more relational, emergent practice of leading. We would argue that in the future leadership development should be better able to differentiate itself in terms of development pedagogies and practices depending on its underlying assumptions about the leadership it is trying to develop.

The second part is to support you to be critical researchers, providers and consumers of leadership development through being able to recognize and talk to the different assumptions that are brought to development and the tensions that underpin those. So the point isn't being able to just classify functionalist, interpretive, dialogic and critical discourses of leadership development, but to understand the impact of privileging dimensions such as performance, meaning, identity and power when organizing, participating or measuring the impact of leadership development.

Finally, we have proposed that the three terms in this chapter title – leadership, learning and development – are becoming more intimately linked as organizations seeking to navigate differently through contexts and scenarios that require people with shared work to keep learning together in order to recalibrate with changing contexts and patterns. In doing this we have tried to go beyond the proposition that leadership learning and development is solely about learning to lead and increasingly about leading learning.

In ending we would like to go back to the having/being distinction we used to separate out learning and development. We hope you have *acquired* knowledge about leadership development. For instance, you should be able to talk knowledgeably about crucible moments and critical reflexivity, the four different discourses that drive leadership development and a couple of the scholars we have used like Fromm and Foucault. In addition we hope you have been developing your sense of yourself in leadership as you have read through this chapter. Maybe you have set off a train of reflection on the moments when you have led or followed and have begun to be conscious about how you are shaping a leadership identity. Maybe you hear the word leader or leadership and you start to probe underneath it for assumptions about performance, relationships and power. This won't feel so much like knowledge you have acquired but more like capacities and skills you are trying to develop. We hope this chapter has given you a language, experience and confidence with both modes and that you take this into your own growth and experience with leadership.

We're conscious, though, that many of you will not have consciously tracked with a learning or development process around leadership so we would like to introduce you to someone who has. This person is just a few years older than you, is a health professional, and put himself forward for an 18-month cross-sectoral leadership development programme that required him to develop alongside 30-odd others as well as support others to learn with them back in their work context. The following excerpts come verbatim from their reflective journals and written on-line tasks. We offer this as a case study to help the story of this chapter come alive.

Case study: Developing leadership

Leadership to me is about recognizing your own strengths and weaknesses, understanding your own personality and what makes you successful and able to draw the best out of the team you work with to make your joint ventures successful; as well as recognizing the areas you need to find help or guidance in. It is about having a sense of purpose, a moral compass and an understanding of why you are taking a course of action.

I think this course has taught me that leadership is and can be part of how I go about the work I do rather than a role I take on in certain times or places. It is a way of choosing to participate in an interaction to draw together, colleagues, groups and communities to stimulate, provoke and articulate the nature of change within that collective. It involves the exchange of ideas between peoples, communities, and the formation of partnerships. Leadership rather than something that is in you or me, it is something that is between you and me, it involves a tension between the people leading and following, it involves the sharing of ideas and the action and interaction of the collective.

1. The above descriptions of leadership were written at different stages of the leadership development programme by our case study participant. Read each of them and identify:

   - What is similar in his perception about leadership across all three definitions?
   - What has changed about his perception about leadership from the first to the last definition?

Now read how this participant describes what has changed.

It is quite interesting that my response has shifted quite markedly from looking at the personal characteristics of a leader to looking rather at the nature of the relationship between leadership and the collective of other leaders and followers. I have focused now much more on the development of skills that drive relationship rather than purely personal development. I have recognized that it is a way of interacting moment by moment – not solely when a 'leadership crisis' comes along. I think this is very important as it can be in small interactions that significant growth and change can occur. [Across all] that it is for doing good and that there is a personal ethos and sense of responsibility that drives it.

Reflecting on experience

I think both the highlight and lowlight of my leadership experiences was the first cardiac arrest I was called to. It was the early hours of the morning and I was called to the ward to see a woman who was gravely ill – an emergency call was sent out but for what seemed like the longest few minutes of my life it was myself and one nurse resuscitating Mrs A. This was not the chaos and drama of a medical TV show. It was quiet, and collected, the patient was ventilated, CPR was started and drugs administered, we worked as a team and help arrived. It is with hindsight and careful reflection on what has happened that we are able to learn from experiences such as these and think what could have been done differently. I wonder if anything could have been done to detect Mrs A's deterioration so that assistance could have been called earlier. I am thankful for the development in our hospital of a system to detect patients who are unwell – an early warning scoring system that is used by our nurses to assist them to call for help earlier which should lead to improved patient outcomes. I feel that part of what I can do differently is to ensure better systems are in place within our hospital and thus participate in the ongoing audit of these systems. It made me realize two very important things, firstly that I could do it, that I could manage this event and what it was like to be the leader in something that influenced life and death. Secondly it reminded me why I do what I do. As I, close to tears myself, talked to her family about what had happened, I realized that my sadness was because of the value I have for human life and my hope to help my patients. I felt when I talked to her family afterward that despite our minutes of solitary CPR in a dark cold ward, we could say truly that we did 'everything we could'.

2.   What does this participant learn about leadership in this reflection?

Discourse work

Over the course of this year I have been involved in setting up a forum at a hospital. I came into it with the realization that for this to be a sustainable venture, and for it to continue to work into the future, there had to be investment from the other doctors who were planning on being there longer term after I would have moved on with my training programme. That led me to a realization that 'taking over', organizing and planning and taking all the responsibility myself was not going to lead to a sustainable solution. The question I had to ask myself was 'who do I need to be' in this scenario to help others make it happen. One of the constructs I found really useful was the identity work we had been doing. When this was first presented I struggled a little with this idea, was it like putting on a costume, or playing a game, was it all artificial? One of the things I realized as I put this into practice in the scenario is that for me it was really about choosing aspects of 'me' that were right for the situation I was in. We are all multifaceted and have different ways of being in different situations. One of the things that I really learned during this was to be braver and try things out. I was able to remain genuine in terms of my vision and what I wanted to achieve but to still try different identities out and see what worked. For me one of the roles I tried was to move from my usual 'take action, fixit' approach to take more of a facilitator role. For me this was me learning to translate skills and ways of being that I had already, but to use them in a scenario where my tried and true, all out approach would probably not have been a successful longer term approach.

3.   In the chapter we talked about four core discourses of leadership development (functionalist, interpretive, dialogic and critical). Identify which discourse(s) this seems to be an example of and comment on what this discourse privileges (emphasizes) and what it leaves out or excludes?

(Continued)

(Continued)

Learning leading and leading learning

I have a belief that there is no point complaining about something if you are not prepared to make it better. I work in a large organization that has multiple complex functions and which is part of a wider network of health centres that must work together. I constantly see questions, possibilities, frustrations, and solutions, adaptations and energy in my work setting. I often see patients, colleagues, community groups who feel disenfranchised and unable to input to the complex situations within health they find themselves in. Sometimes I feel this way myself! I feel I am already a passionate voice within my work, for my patients and the aspects of healthcare that affect them, for my colleagues in education and workforce issues. The larger frame of my leadership story is my question of how to make this bigger than me, to be part of a larger story of leadership within health?

4. This is the last entry this participant wrote for the course. Assume you are in a position to comment or guide this participant into the future. The participant asks 'how to make this bigger than me'. How could you answer given what you have read in terms of leadership, learning and development?

The key points in this chapter were …

- Learning and developing are quite different, though both related to leadership. The difference is similar to the distinction between *having* knowledge and *being* in leadership.
- Experience is an important part of learning leadership. Some scholars have highlighted the importance of 'crucible moments', which are big important moments that stand out in life. These moments can offer sudden insight that shapes us as leaders.
- Other scholars point to the small ongoing experiences in life. The ability to learn from this unfolding stream of experiences is called critical reflexivity.
- Even the idea of leadership as 'objective' knowledge needs to be held critically, for knowledge can be seen as a form of power, shaping the way we think. This affects what we learn about leadership and what it means to do leadership development.
- Leadership development is thus shaped by up of four different perspectives:

  - functionalist – skills orientation for leader performance;
  - interpretive – focused on meaning and context of leadership;
  - dialogic – leadership as messy and ongoing, related to identities;
  - critical – leadership development as a technology of power.

- Learning and leadership are interconnected in that leadership is integral to organisational sensemaking and sensegiving. This link is especially important as organizations seek to navigate through uncertainty.

Further thinking

Day, D. (2001). Leadership development: A review in context. *The Leadership Quarterly*, 11(4), 581–613.

Questions:

1. How is leader and leadership development defined in this article? What kinds of processes, technologies and learning formats support each?
2. Think of your own development or education (maybe the one you are reading this chapter for). Is it leader or leadership orientated? What tells you this? How might you redesign the experience to re-orientate it?
3. Think of an organization, community or social group you are in or have an awareness of. What kind of human and/or social capital does it need in the future? How does it link to the leadership you think it needs? How does this article help you with how to go about growing these different types of capital?

Grint, K. (2007). Learning to lead: Can Aristotle help us find the road to wisdom? *Leadership*, 3, 231–245.

Questions:

1. Does the author think that leadership can be taught? Argue your answer.
2. What's the difference between techne, episteme and phronesis? Can you give examples from your own broad learning experience of the three?
3. If you had the opportunity to design a learning course for the leaders prominent in your own community/ society that acknowledges their current strengths but further develops them then what would you emphasize (techne, epistem or phronesis)? Why? For what purpose?

Gagnon, S. and Collinson, D. (2014). Rethinking global leadership development programmes: The interrelated significance of power, context and identity. *Human Relations*, 35(5), 645–670.

Questions:

1. Which discourse(s) (functionalist, interpretive, dialogic, critical) are driving the viewpoint of the authors and their approach to the development programmes they analyse in this article? How does this influence what they focus on in this article and what do they not engage with?
2. What is an 'idealized leader identity'? How was this similar and different across the two programmes discussed in this article? What aspects of leaders and leadership discussed in this book seem present and absent in these idealized leader identities? What is it about our organizations and societies that reinforce or challenge these idealized leader identities?
3. After reading this article and the account of these two leadership development programmes what tensions do you see as important for those who sponsor, design, provide and participate in leadership development? What, after reading this chapter and these further thinking articles, might help engage with such tensions constructively?

Leadership on screen

We want you to watch the New Zealand film *Whale Rider* (2002). This film is about a small Maori (New Zealand's indigenous people) community on the coast of New Zealand. There's a consciousness portrayed throughout the film that this community needs to find and grow its next generation of leadership. In doing so the film plays out the legacies and traditions of learning in this community, the encroachment of more modern and contemporary notions of leadership, the conflict between established and emergent leadership, and the different ways that leadership is developed by different characters. Neither leadership nor development is a neutral process in this film and instead is deeply cultural, anchored in a historical and political context, and intimately related to the identity stories of its main characters.

After watching the film answer the following clusters of questions:

1. What kinds of understandings of leadership are held by those in this film and how does this shape their attitudes to leadership learning and development? What big crucible and small routine life moments are key in these for the main characters?
2. What supports the leadership learning and development of characters? (Think of knowledge, skills, relationships, rituals, identity work, stories and artefacts (objects).)
3. Try and play the film through your four discourse lenses – functionalist, interpretive, dialogic and critical. What kinds of debates/tensions on performance or effectiveness, relationships and meaning, identity and complexity, power and voice come through for you?
4. Be reflective about your own community, history and traditions. How have these shaped your understandings of leadership? How have these developed you in terms of leading/following? Have you come into contact with other approaches to leadership that have challenged these and what has resulted from that?

6

LEADERSHIP, GOVERNANCE AND STRATEGY

Annie Pye

Annie pye's enduring fascination and research focuses on 'how small groups of people "run" organizations' – how they interact, organize and take action. This chapter draws attention to some particular ways to help us make sense of this by bringing together the concepts of leadership, strategy and governance.

What this chapter is all about …

The main idea is that strategy, governance and leadership are interrelated practices in organizations. They are generally taken to refer to the activities of those designated leaders at the very top of organizations; however, this is a reductionist perspective that overlooks the considerable influence of micro practices that occur throughout all levels of the organization.

The key questions this chapter answers are:

- What do we mean by strategy in organizations?
- What do we mean by governance in organizations?
- How do strategy, governance and leadership intersect?

Introduction

This chapter brings together three concepts that are key to understanding how collectives of people called organizations work. Put very simply, the assumption is that there are people who lead (usually assumed to be at the helm or top of the organization). These leaders are presumed to have a strategy that helps set or at least outline the direction of travel for which they're aiming. There are governance rules and regulations which provide some means of control of what these leaders and organizations do.

As you'll have learned through previous chapters, there's a vast amount of research literature that considers leaders and leadership and offers many different definitions, dimensions, perspectives, approaches, understandings, observations, insights and so forth. Likewise, there's much research into strategy and governance as well as ample debate and variance as to how to define and theorize each.

So this chapter covers a very broad field of academic interest that can be integrated and understood as being part of what leaders do. Interestingly, in doing this, leaders have a powerful influence and effect on shaping the governance of their organizations, which in turn impacts strongly on the effectiveness of their strategic endeavours.

This chapter will integrate core conceptual elements of each of these three fields of research, and will also illustrate practical implications by using a case study throughout. The first section will provide some definitions and a brief introduction to each of these concepts and show how and why these tend to come together in research amongst the 'upper echelons', 'top management teams' and 'boards'. While this might sound as if governance and strategy only have relevance to 'top leaders', they also relate to leadership and organizing at all levels of organization. So the chapter will then explore some theoretical dimensions of each of the concepts through the lens of leaders and leadership. Peppered throughout this chapter, we'll use a case study of a company that I researched that illustrates the setting in which such concepts may (or may not) be seen at work as well (Pye, 2002). The final section will then consider how these can be woven together as leadership, strategy and governance don't actually work as separate elements of organization: they are woven together in the 'daily doings' of people in organizations. So this will bring these dimensions together to help us make sense of leadership, governance and strategy for leaders at all 'levels' of organizations.

 ## Case study: Williams and Wright plc (1)

Williams and Wright plc are a large global manufacturer and retail distributor of FMCG. Their original family heritage began to dissipate in the 'noughties' following the sale of one of the core founding brands and subsequent resignation of the final family member of the board. Amidst the economic turbulence of the early 2000s, the company's results had been 'in decline' and the board were aware of the need for significant change. However, once the major shareholders began to press hard for change, the board decided to accelerate the appointment of a new chief executive officer (CEO). This person had already been identified as being the likely internal candidate, and was in the midst of a development programme that had been devised in their succession planning. Hence he came into the post with the full backing from the board and an agenda for change.

The new CEO felt great need for action both to keep the business running and performing well, and also to start raising performance levels to a much higher level of achievement through undertaking a strategic change initiative. In order to do this, he already had internal knowledge of the organization but decided that to help maximize the chance of achieving the best outcome, he'd gather data and talk to people, in order to shape up and fine tune a plan.

An introduction to strategy

The notion of strategy is a concept in organization studies which has many different definitions and dimensions. Indeed, if you ask Google, there are over one billion answers to the question of 'what is strategy'! In brief, it was originally rooted in what was known as business policy and planning. It almost goes without saying that to plan something requires you to have some intention of what you're trying to achieve. That is, what are your goals or objectives? Even if this eludes close specification, you can usually identify an aim – an overall direction or target you're trying to get to. As the saying goes, 'If you don't know where you're going, any road will get you there' (often attributed to Lewis Carroll in *Alice in Wonderland*). So the assumption is that organizations have strategies that reflect the objectives they're trying to achieve, that is the overall direction in which they're aiming to go.

If you think about the scale and speed of change in technology, markets, economics, political upheavals and so on, this may seem slightly idealistic although it remains a common expectation and practice of most organizations. For example, many corporate websites have a page, even if only in their Annual Report and Accounts, that states their strategy. This may also be complemented by statements of their vision, their mission, their business model and their values. These are effectively banners under which organizations present themselves and can often be found represented on walls or windows around the buildings to remind employees of these corporate messages.

STOP AND REFLECT 6.1

What do you think this says about the nature of the senior leadership in an organization which works in this way?

Non-private sector organizations are similar in how they talk about and represent their future intentions too. For example, most organizations aim to be the best in their field, and perhaps express ambition to spread their 'best' practice to other fields of interest, that is expand and grow their revenues and wealth creation, or their impact and effects. However, strategy researchers dig much deeper than these (largely superficial) representations to explore more closely the practices and processes of people engaged in organizations and their endeavours to shape the future direction in which the organization is heading.

An introduction of governance

Governance is a word that originates in both Greek and Latin, and has evolved into an all-encompassing idea which for most people can be summed up as everything to do with making sure an organization runs well. One problem with this statement is that it involves a value judgement – that is, to run something 'well' as opposed to averagely or badly. For example, if you ask Google 'what is governance?', you find within 0.2 seconds that there are 217 million web links that might help you answer that question, and roughly half of those (114 million) will tell you 'what is "good" governance'! What they don't necessarily tell you is what the criteria are for judging 'good'ness. So to identify something as being run 'well' means you have to have an idea of what factors comprise an organization that is being not run well.

Another challenge about understanding what is meant by governance is locating what it's referring to; that is, what is it that is being governed? Is it a nation-state, a company, a non-governmental organization (NGO), a school or a charity? The alternatives are multiple. It is relatively easy to see how the verb 'to govern' can be derived from the word 'government' although quite what and how governments do this is not quite so easy to see. However, as you begin to tease away at this and explore how organizations work, so this draws attention to the systems and processes through which it operates.

Then once you start digging deeper this begins to open up other angles as you have to remember that organizations don't operate in a vacuum. They are embedded in socio-ecological systems, that is complex interwoven networks of people and ecologies which are knotted and nested together in what might resemble a wriggly mass of spaghetti rather than more common-place organization charts – a neat map of boxes with connecting lines drawn between each.

Not surprisingly, most organizational research looks at single organizations as entities rather than as part of deeply embedded socio-economic systems. So the first part of this chapter will start at an organizational level by looking at strategy, and then gradually widen the perspective as there are many other people and levels of engagement with, and interest in, the governance of organizations. This may also be from both from a country and cultural point of view as well as from a global-international level. For example, across the world, there are almost as many different governance models as there are nations (Organisation for Economic Co-operation and Development – OECD); and most democratic nations have their own corporate governance code (or equivalent). From the point of view of multinational companies that are registered and listed in one nation-state, yet operate in many different parts of the world, this represents an interesting challenge in the extent to which national codes may or may not impact on what they do and how they do it. Similarly, while the recent financial crisis caused by the 'debt crisis' and the collapse of Western banking organizations was often attributed to 'poor governance', there is no global agreement or governance regulator that might have helped ensure all banking organizations operated to the same set of governance principles and achieved global 'goodness'. Should this be a role for the World Bank or the OECD to undertake? And what are the implications for corporate leaders and their organization's strategies in this deeply interwoven, global, socio-ecological system?

Introducing leadership to the mix

Bringing leaders and leadership into the picture, strategic leadership is about mapping how to achieve the organization's objectives, and recognizes that the direction of travel may need to adjust from time to time to take advantage of changing circumstances. Clearly, however, this may also need to be tweaked and tuned to adjust to the systems and processes of governance, and/or these systems and processes may need to be adjusted to accommodate the changing circumstances along the road to achieving strategic aims. These are the finer judgements of leaders and leadership, which have moral and ethical implications that underpin organizing and organizations; this gets us back to the very core of how collectives of people, that is organizations, work.

Many people, including the media, business analysts, academics and organizational employees assume that the people 'at the top' of an organization make a difference: that they are 'in charge' and have overall control and responsibility for what happens in their organizations. Indeed, as the saying goes: if the people at the top of the organization aren't in charge, then who is?! But who do you think is actually 'in charge'? For some people, this responsibility and accountability lies with the board; others see this as firmly resting with the top management team. Either way, these two groups and their responsibilities comprise what became known as the 'upper echelons' of organization (Hambrick and Mason, 1984; Hambrick, 2007).

As can be seen from these brief introductory sections, all three concepts – leadership, strategy and governance – are elusive and have multiple definitions, perspectives, models and theories. Not surprisingly, the challenge of weaving them together is rarely addressed in theory although this comprises the daily practice of senior leaders in organizations. The next two sections will briefly keep them separate for now, so we can understand some more of what comprises different ways of thinking about strategy and governance from an academic research point of view. We will also keep the case illustration running throughout and use the lens of leadership to make sense of how theory and practice effectively bring these concepts to life through leaders in and of organizations.

Strategy

The concept of strategy grew out of its original 1960s identity in the corporate planning function which had meant it was associated with portfolio planning and diversification. Management and organization studies and theorizing at that time were largely based on rationalistic assumptions – that is, assumed that people were rational beings whose behaviour could be explained and hypothesised in terms of cause-and-effect relationships. Hence as far as directing organizations was concerned, this was a matter to be planned and delivered.

The early days of strategy theorizing were characterised by debate about whether or not strategy followed structure or should structure follow strategy: that is, did the organization need to structure itself to deliver on its strategy or vice versa (Chandler, 1962)? There is undoubtedly a relationship between strategy and structure, and to an extent, the debate continues (Harris and Ruefli, 2000). Gradually, this field of research began to develop more people-oriented and less quantitatively based approaches to analysing and understanding organizations and strategy. Consequently, the field has become more complex and contested as different approaches and viewpoints have become established.

For example, do companies have a strategy or does strategy 'emerge'? That is, do people decide on 'a strategy' and then take action to make it happen? Or do things happen in an organization that then steer it towards a line of action which becomes its strategy? This debate has persisted in strategy research and remains an open question (Mintzberg and Waters, 1985; Morrison and Salipante, 2007). It also has implications for how you see the role of senior managers and leaders: are they choosing a strategy or are they leaving themselves and their organizations to being battered about by contingency factors and, in effect, led by whichever way the wind blows?

 Case study: Williams and Wright plc (2)

The board's chosen strategy for Williams and Wright was to be 'an outstanding global organization with leading brands'.

What does this say about Williams and Wright's senior leadership?

This was the strategy strapline that could easily be recited as a reminder to employees about the vision of the company and strategic ambition. So the senior leaders were seen to have demonstrated their leadership ability by selecting a clear strategic direction for the company and communicating it to all employees, shareholders and other stakeholders.

(Continued)

(Continued)

However, clearly there is much more that has to lie beneath this phrasing, which elaborates what defines an organization as being an 'outstanding global' one and what defines something as being a brand leader. Early strategy researchers would see this as illustrating the difference between strategy and tactics: strategy being the overall aim and tactics being the means by which you get to those ends. For the directors of Williams and Wright, they were performing their governance responsibility for setting the strategic direction while also leaving it for the executive directors to use their operational expertise to work out how to achieve this strategic intention. In so doing, the non-executive directors were performing what is sometimes known as NIFO – noses in, fingers out; that is, they were sufficiently sensitive to sniff out what really was going on and where the company needed to go, but suitably detached to keep their hands off the machinery to get them there.

Building on work by Miles and Snow (1978) and Porter (1980), the predominant focus in strategy research in the 1980s was on strategy content. Porter's (1979) Five Forces Model provided a framework that brought together the five key drivers of competitive advantage, which was assumed to be the purpose of corporate strategy: bargaining power of suppliers; bargaining power of buyers; threat of new entrants; threat of substitute products or services; and rivalry among existing competitors. The assumption underpinning this model is that by understanding the competitive forces and their underlying causes, you will be able to identify the roots of profitability and develop the means for anticipating and influencing competitive advantage and future profitability. Although originally associated more with firm strategic positioning within an industry, Porter's model has persisted (see also Porter, 2008) and remains one of the most commonly used strategy frameworks in strategy consulting, and is usually the core model taught in many strategy courses.

Building on this work in the 1990s, the study of organizational capabilities as the enduring source of competitive advantage became a particular area of strategy research interest (Teece et al., 1997). For example, working with the resources and competence that a firm has, what are its dynamic capabilities? What is the minimum threshold or the distinctive capabilities a firm would need to undertake a new strategic ambition? This burgeoning area of interest was also complemented by the growing focus on strategy process research (Pettigrew, 1992). That is, regardless of how well crafted any strategy might be, the key to its success is strategic decision-making and implementation. In most managers' experience the decision-making process and process of implementation have a significant effect on outcome, such that 'the devil is in the detail'. To this end, researchers began to study more closely the strategy process and management.

A model of this era that, like Porter's, remains widely and persistently used in organizations is Kaplan and Norton's (1996) Balanced Scorecard of Strategic Management. Their proposition was that there are four different perspectives that underpin achieving vision and strategy: finance, internal organizational process, customer, and learning and development. By separating the analysis of vision and strategy from each of these perspectives, they would help link together today's actions with tomorrow's goals in terms of achieving strategic objectives. In so doing, this aimed to balance the inevitable focus on short-term financial performance with longer-term operational requirements and changes needed to achieve the strategy.

Case study: Williams and Wright plc (3)

Williams and Wright plc used management consultants to facilitate their board's Annual 'Strategy Away Day' (two days) to help them develop their strategy and also articulate the criteria for achievement. During this time, they were identifying the means by which they would achieve their strategic ambition and, in effect, were creating a balanced scorecard indicating the measures by which that achievement could be identified and evaluated.

The most common way to encourage strategic thinking in an organization and to develop its strategy is to organize a Strategy Away Day. This is usually held off-site to help managers and leaders step out of their usual operational routines and ways of thinking to develop a more strategic view of their organization. Usually facilitated by management consultants, such events serve a variety of functions. In part, there's an opportunity to reflect collectively on progress to date against previous strategic ambitions, and to share information, views, reports and projections as to future strategic prospects, possibilities and options. It is also an opportunity in which to spend time (both work and socially oriented) with peers and colleagues, building networks of relationships that may be of value to achieving the next steps.

Management consultants may have a 'model' that they are effectively selling to the client as their framework to guide strategy development. However, it is often said that the role of management consultants proves to be more about telling managers what they already knew about their organization and its need for strategic change (Jackson, 2010). From the point of view of strategy research, however, although this was known to be an important step in an organization's strategy process, little was known about what this process actually entailed or how strategy was developed (Jarzabkowski et al., 2007). That is, practitioners talked about strategy tools and techniques but there was little academic research into the area of how managers go about 'doing' strategy.

This gave birth to the next stream of strategy research, known as strategy-as-practice,[1] defined as 'a concern with what people do in relation to strategy and how this is influenced by and influences their organizational and institutional context" (Johnson et al., 2007). This approach has helped to bring the focus back to micro-level details about developing and delivering strategy in organizations. For example, in addition to exploring tools and techniques such as the role of management consultants (Bürgi et al., 2005) and strategy workshops and away-days (Hodgkinson and Wright, 2002), researchers also highlight the role of middle managers as well as executive directors in the micro-processes of shaping and communicating of strategy (Balogun and Johnson, 2004).

There are many other matters to take into account in consideration of the notion of strategy and the role this plays in organizations and the role that an organization's leadership and culture can play in the development of strategy. In grappling with some of the many different aspects of strategy that have been identified in this section, leaders must also pay attention to the nature of governance as this also impacts on and is affected by the nature of strategic leadership in an organization.

1   There is a community of strategy-as-practice researchers who have set up and maintain a website of resources accessible to anyone who has an interest in this field of research. This includes a bibliography of core reading materials as well as other research and teaching discussions, which can be accessed by registering on the site: www.s-as-p.org.

Governance

Academic research into what comprises governance is developed on the basis of different assumptions and perspectives, which means they each see different factors as being key to defining and understanding it.

The majority of research into governance has been generated under the banner of 'corporate governance' which tends to be based on the agency approach. This assumes that managers act as self-interested agents rather than doing what's best for the principals (the organization's owners/shareholders), that is creating shareholder value (Daily et al., 2003). With this way of thinking, executive directors (i.e. the corporate leaders) are seen as the most powerful and self-interested managers as their pay and rewards are most often predominantly based on evaluation of the organization's financial performance against criteria set by the board. As the phrase 'corporate governance' implies, this work is primarily related to business and commercial organizations although the ideas and principles of corporate governance apply and are applied to most other kinds of organizations, be they public sector, non-governmental, health, charity or co-operative enterprises.

Much of corporate governance research is quantitative in nature, for example counting, correlating and ratio analyses of indicators such as number of directors on a board, gender or ethnicity of directors, type of direct, number of sub-committees, meetings per year, in an endeavour to prove a link between governance and organizational performance (Durisin and Puzone, 2009). However, this link remains unproven for two simple reasons. One is that such indicators of governance are elements that can be counted whereas much else is to do with processes and people; the second is that there are many other factors that affect organizational performance.

This is where the role of the top management team or board leading the organization becomes more difficult to evaluate. On the one hand, these kinds of people are assumed to be 'in charge' but, on the other hand, they may well be so far removed from the day-to-day business of whatever the organization does that their leadership influence is barely felt. So is it reasonable for them to receive generous remuneration and reward packages for their leadership in achieving the company's performance?

Boards are the governing body that provide leadership, set direction and ensure appropriate standards of governance to deliver the purpose of the organization. In so doing, the assumption is that they create a leadership group that balances out self-interested managers (chief executive/leaders and top management team executives) with independent/non-executive directors who represent shareholder interests and contribute views and experience from outside the company.

 Case study: Williams and Wright plc (4)

The board of Williams and Wright had taken a strategic view of where the organization was and, in particular, were concerned to regain good support from investors in the City of London, not least to help improve the share price as this was lower than was characteristic of the firm, indicating it was viewed as under-performing. To this end, they'd helped the current CEO effectively to take 'early retirement', and appointed a new CEO with the mandate to bring about 'global change', as the board were clear that the scale of change had to be radical to lift the company out of 'the doldrums'.

In their management oversight role, boards are responsible for evaluating the CEO performance and appointing him/her. Hence, from a formal governance point of view, the board in this case were adequately performing their monitoring role of 'overseeing the management' and their strategic role of 'setting direction'.

Looking more closely at the case details, the current CEO effectively took what is known as a 'golden parachute' and the incoming CEO was offered a 'golden handshake' to compensate respectively for their accelerated retirement and promotion. Remuneration is also a board decision which will be addressed later in this section. For now, please just consider:

STOP AND REFLECT 6.2

If promotion to a challenging senior leadership role is accelerated with lack of appropriate developmental experience and/or due care and support, this might ensure you're being promoted to failure. Yet this is the job which you've always wanted and comes with a very attractive compensation package.

- Would you accept the promotion, and if so, are there any conditions that you'd ask for?
- Would your decision be different depending on the country in which you're working?

The key elements of corporate governance practice are defined by law in the USA and in the UK by principles laid down in government regulations. The rules-based approach to regulation is prevalent throughout the USA and while corporate law varies from state to state, the majority of corporations register their companies in the state of Delaware as corporate law is considered to be most favourable.

In the UK, Australia, Canada and some European countries, regulation is principles based, which requires companies to 'comply or explain' their aims to ensure any variance from the principles is fully accounted for and remains open to challenge. This principle was first established by the Cadbury Review (Cadbury, 1992) and continues to underpin all UK corporate governance regulation.[2] That is, companies are expected to 'comply' with the principles but should compliance be either detrimental to or unachievable by the company, it can then 'explain' their reasoning for this to shareholders and regulators.

The most common examples in the UK for 'explanation' relate to combining the chair/CEO roles and remuneration packages. In the USA, the chairman and CEO roles can be, and are usually encouraged to be, combined and performed by one person. This allows an extraordinary concentration of power in the hands

2   The Cadbury Review (1992) was initiated by the Institute of Chartered Accountants for England and Wales in order to review accounting and auditing practices of UK companies (Spira and Slinn, 2013). This coincided with several corporate scandals that were happening in the UK at that time (e.g. the Maxwell Pension Fund, Barings Bank and Polly Peck scandals). The review Chairman, Sir Adrian Cadbury, had been Chairman of Cadbury Ltd and was very well experienced in the processes and practices of running a large company.

The outcome of the Cadbury Review led to three more being set up by government: the Greenbury Report (1995), which was prompted by concern about increasing levels of executive remuneration; the Hampel Report (1998), which reviewed the progress of companies' responses to Cadbury; and the Turnbull Report (1999), which, in effect, tightened up the implications of the Cadbury Review by addressing the particularly important issue of how to implement the best practice systems of internal control. Together, these were integrated into the Combined Code of Practice (1998, 2003, 2006), which effectively laid out a set of principles against which UK companies had to 'comply or explain' their conduct in order to retain their listing on the UK Stock Exchange.

of one person. In the UK and also in Germany, government regulation requires that these roles must be split and only rarely will shareholders and the regulator in the UK (Financial Reporting Council) accept an explanation.

The regulatory approach and legal framework of each country clearly has a strong influence on board practice and process in every jurisdiction and would require several volumes in which to collate them all, only to find that this would probably then need updating as regulations continue to change. For this reason, it will be more fruitful for you to search the web if you're interested in learning more about the history and detail of key governance regimes systems. Almost every country has some form of corporate governance requirement, and the (UK-based) Institute of Directors has shared its UK model of best practice widely around the world. Some useful corporate governance sites are listed at the end of this chapter to help get you started on your travels.

Multinationals operate globally although register their company listing in one country only, hence abide only by that country (or state)'s regulations. Consequently, rules and principles of governance are not universal to all corporates, even if they are global or multinational, and neither are they uniformly practised by all organizations. For an example, see below.

Case study: Williams and Wright plc (5)

The board of Williams and Wright plc complied with the UK Combined Code (2006) and had the appropriate board sub-committees, that is the Audit Committee and Remuneration and Nomination Committee.

By way of case explanation, the board of Williams and Wright plc comprised nine people: five non-executive and four executive directors. One of the non-executives was female and two others were non-UK passport holders. The chairman (who was British) spent two-thirds of every month in the USA as he had substantial business interests there and was also an independent director of a US company. However, he stayed in touch with people at Williams and Wright via regular email and phone conversations, occasional Skype meetings and by returning to the UK for board meetings, which were held approximately eight times per year. These were usually also scheduled to follow a board sub-committee meeting such that they took either a whole day or, occasionally, an overnight stay for those involved in the sub-committee as well. The only exception to this was the annual 'Strategy Away Day', which involved management consultants and took place off-site over two days.

What kinds of leadership and followship relationships and effects does this board example illustrate?

In the UK, the Combined Code has been updated and now comprises the UK Corporate Governance Code (2010).[3] This latest code was in part prompted by the financial collapse of Western economies following the 2007 banking crisis, and provides stronger and clearer direction to board directors about their

3   At the time of writing (2014), the FRC is currently consulting on potential revisions to the UK Corporate Governance Code (2010).

role requirements, board structures and processes. During the 2000s, company adherence to increasing amounts of regulation in both the UK and USA had become a 'tick-box' exercise. For example, following the dot.com crash in the early 2000s, there was another serious of corporate collapses and scandals, including WorldCom, Enron, Marconi, Arthur Andersen, Parmalat, Ahold and others. In the UK, this led to the Higgs Review (2003) of the role of the non-executive director and the Smith Review (2004) of Audit Committees.

In the USA, this led to the Sarbanes–Oxley Act (2002), which quickly became a highly influential and internationally significant piece of US Federal law (aka SOX). This was because not only do all public corporations listed in the USA have to comply with it but this also includes companies such as UK-based ones that have dual-listing. In addition, it gave rise to other countries – as far apart as Japan, France, Australia, South Africa and Israel – implementing their own versions of SOX. Apart from the fact that in its endeavour to heighten transparency and accountability, SOX requires an extraordinary amount of financial detail but also compliance is critical. In requiring finance directors literally to sign off their organization's accounts, this subsequently led to finance directors requiring every level of accountability below them also to sign off their accounts in the corporate accounting process.

STOP AND REFLECT 6.3

Imagine yourself in the role of leading the finance team at mid-level in the divisional hierarchy of an international company, how would you feel about having to do this on behalf of the accounts you're overseeing from the operations of the 200 people who work 'below' you?

Together with the increasing numbers and tightening up of national corporate governance codes at this time, the consequence was to encourage a 'tick-box' culture to achieve compliance. That is, each regulatory code was met to the extent that board directors, executives, corporate lawyers and all else involved in accounting for their organization could tick the box such that they'd not have to account further either to shareholders, regulators or the law courts.

This was spotlighted in the Preface to the recent UK Corporate Governance Code (2010), where Sir Christopher Hogg noted that one aim of this revision to UK regulation was to ensure that boards adhered to 'the spirit of the governance code rather than the letter' (précised from the Corporate Governance Code (Financial Reporting Council, 2010, p. 2)). As he goes on to say, 'Absolutely key to this endeavour are the leadership of the chairman of the board, the support given to and by the CEO, and the frankness and openness of mind with which issues are discussed and tackled by all directors' (p. 2). Furthermore, in the Main Principles of the Code, Section A is now entitled 'Leadership' and explicitly states that 'The chairman is responsible for leadership of the board and ensuring its effectiveness on all aspects of its role' (p. 6).

So while we started this section with the classic quantitative research driven, self-interested agent view of corporate governance, we conclude with a view that is distinctively qualitative and very much geared to trying to ensure that chairmen, as board leaders, take responsibility for creating healthy environments in which their organizations can thrive and be successful.

STOP AND REFLECT 6.4

Do you think it's reasonable and/or feasible to place this much responsibility and accountability in one person's hands?

Is your answer affected by the size or the nature of the organization you're imagining or does your view on this apply to any organization of any size, anywhere in the world?

Making sense of leadership, strategy and governance

So far, we've covered some introductory ground to two complex topics that run through all organizations and are effectively held together by the notion of leadership to the extent that leaders are expected to make strategy and to govern organizations (Colville and Murphy, 2006). We have also only looked at this through the eyes of 'top leaders'. So this means we've been thinking of organizations as having hierarchical layers, with a board of directors at the top having ultimate responsibility for the organization – most easily summed up as its purpose, its practice and its performance. And then everything else, that is people and work responsibilities, is neatly structured into layers that get wider and wider as you progress down through 'middle management' towards the bottom, often called 'the front line'.

So what does that mean for people in the organization? Do they leave leadership, strategy and governance to 'them up there' or do other employees have any part in this? There are no easy answers to these questions. It is clearly the case that the chief executive and chairman are the ones who are seen as *the* leaders of the organization and stand in the spotlight as far as outside interest is concerned, and also often from an employee's view too. This is particularly the case when things go wrong and, in essence, they are called to account by the media, their shareholders or the regulators for poor performance or non-compliance with regulation, and so on. But if you think of a recent case of bad practice – for instance, one of the banks that have recently collapsed – can you remember the names of anyone other involved than the chief executive or perhaps the chairman?

Undoubtedly the CEO and chairman have figurehead roles – they are seen as the leaders and, in the UK, the chairman now has regulatory responsibility for leadership of the organization. But they are not the only people who have a hand in the purpose, practice and performance of the organization: clearly everyone else plays a part in this and in theory, this is not least because this picture of top leaders 'doing leadership' implies that everyone else must be 'followers'. This is not entirely the case because leadership happens throughout the whole organization but, in principle, the top leaders are at the top of this pyramid and everyone else reports to someone 'above' them, so they hold ultimate responsibility for the organization and its performance.

This raises some important questions to ask which give a very clear indication as to why leadership is so hard to analyse (Schein, 1980). For example, *who is 'the' leader*? Is there actually only one leader involved in this? And what does the 'this' refer to – that is, *what actually is the leader's task*? What's the nature of the place in which they are trying to do 'this' – for example, *what's the cultural context* like? Is it an organization that routinely has to perform to the highest possible safety standards (e.g. a nuclear power plant) or is it a small advertising design agency? Or is it the Accident and Emergency unit of a large hospital in a poor area of a big multiracial city?

In each of these examples, just give some thought to another important question about its top leadership which is, *how far does their influence reach* through the organization? And amidst that, who gets involved in influencing strategy and governance? Some authors talk of leadership alignment (O'Reilly et al., 2009; Ernst and Chrobot-Mason, 2010), but to what extent is that possible and is it necessarily a bonus, as sometimes it's helpful to have some counter-viewpoints to ensure appropriate action is taken.

As ever with analysis of behaviour, it doesn't happen in neatly labelled boxes so it's pretty much impossible to come up with an answer that everyone else will agree with. So I make some suggestions here for you to consider, and hope that this will help alert you to some of the important factors to be aware of in whatever you do as an employee of an organization and to whatever level you go in your career. We will then return to our case example and see how things worked out for them.

Imagine the advertising design agency situation – a small business of about 50 people, set up by an innovative entrepreneur who saw a niche market opportunity and persuaded three others friends to put up some money and join him in getting this enterprise off the ground. In its first five years, it has now grown to be a highly successful, creative and technologically advanced agency with some big clients in a fast-growing market. So who does leadership, strategy and governance in this kind of organization and how? The CEO is still the original business founder, and has had five years' experience of working with a top team of people who've been with him/her since the start.

This means that in terms of *the 'developmental stage'* between them, they all know each other and the business very well, and they probably work on almost a peer-group basis as they all have a financial stake in the business and all want it to perform well. Ultimately the CEO will be responsible for this and for accounting for performance to the external world. However, they all have a close hand in it and recognize their responsibility too for the success of the enterprise. In terms of governance, certain principles will be set by the business regulator and during the five years they will have created their own systems and processes by which the business runs effectively and also meets these external governance criteria. They will also have had to do this to get financial support from banks and investors, which will have been essential to help develop the company.

With regards to other employees, it's likely that they are also employed to be proactive contributors to this lively small business as it's a place where energy and engagement as well as expertise are all important capabilities – even among those in more administrative roles such as finance or technical support. So the business premises are probably open plan, with space for socializing and making good coffee as well!

In this kind of cultural context, leadership and followership might seem to be shared by everyone as they all have a part in delivering a good product, from the person who first engages with the client through to everyone else involved in fulfilling this contract and ensuring the client relationship remains positive in the longer term too. The person seen to be 'in charge' of this product (i.e. creative process and performance) will be the account manager – note these roles are rarely called account leader. However, this person is likely to expect, encourage and ensure that everyone plays an active part in this process and voices any concerns they may have should something problematic arise or be anticipated.

In this kind of example, the top team may have a clear sense of the strategy but everyone has a part to play in implementing and delivering on it. They may also have a part to play in shaping how it might change. For instance, the front-line sales force and client managers may be beginning to pick up signs that the market is changing. Or the founder and top team may anticipate the future and see need to get ahead of the competition by developing a new form or focus to their creative outputs. Or it may be through a combination of all these different influences that the top team and board conclude it's time for change. It is also likely that the company is at a strategic turning point at this time in its evolution, so insight from across the business will be particularly valuable.

Similarly with regards to their systems and processes for controlling operations, transparency and integrity will continue to be the core governance principles. However, there may be a need to change some of the financial reporting governance systems and processes as the business is getting bigger and adding a new market to its growing income stream.

Contrast this example with the Accident and Emergency department of a hospital. Is there *a* leader? If so, who is that person and, if not, is there any leadership going on? It may sometimes feel pretty chaotic in an A&E department but, at the very least, you can't help but hope that *someone* is 'in charge'! The hospital will have a CEO but that person and their leadership influence may feel and may actually be very remote from the frontline of A&E. There are also likely to be many people in leadership roles in the unit at any time in its 24/7 operations. For example, the clinical director (i.e. the most senior medical person) and the clinical manager (i.e. the most senior administrative person) often in effect 'share' the top leadership role for that unit, but they will each have different perspectives, priorities and areas of particular responsibility and must co-ordinate well in order for the unit to run well.

In terms of doing A&E business, it's very varied and responsive, has a high volume of patients requiring attention, is highly regulated (e.g. in the UK it has a four-hour throughput target set by the government) and needs very skilful, professionally qualified staff to work long hours, in flexible teams and often in under-resourced environments in which doing their jobs to the highest standards is an extremely difficult and emotionally charged challenge.

So what about strategy and governance? In terms of governance, there has been a great deal of attention given to clinical governance in recent years and it echoes many of the same principles as underpin corporate governance. For example, transparency and integrity lie at the core and underpin the expectation that the structures, systems and processes of the organization will ensure high quality standards of health care, full accountability of all staff and effective management of the organization in delivering its health service. To this extent, everyone has a part to play in ensuring good governance practices are upheld throughout the organization.

However, the hospital board hold ultimate responsibility for ensuring this takes place and their provision of investment and resources to do so is key to this. It also affects their strategic role as in the case of state-funded hospitals, government reform of health-care systems may mean hospitals have to become more strategic in their delivery of high-quality health care. For example, this may mean becoming more specialized in a particular field or outsourcing some element of health care to a treatment centre run by a private company.

Unpacking the case

So how does leadership, strategy and governance happen in a large, multinational enterprise (MNE)? There's no single or simple answer to that question as MNEs are all different although some of the patterns of behaviour are similar across many large companies. In the case of Williams and Wright, remember that they had a new CEO who'd had his promotion from within the company accelerated to solve what was seen to have been a lack of leadership shown by his predecessor. This meant that even though he knew most of the top team, he was now promoted above them to lead them and the company. There was also a felt need that he should 'show' leadership.

From his point of view, there were two sides to doing this: one was to keep the business running and ensure it performed well, and the other was to develop a new strategy to raise performance levels to a higher level which would satisfy shareholders and media commentators, as well as strengthen its competitive position and future success. As far as corporate governance was concerned, the company was being run well – it had a good board of executives and non-executive directors and complied with all the governance regulation. The directors had a variety of skills and capabilities, and worked well together in sub-committees and as a main board with the aim of achieving the long-term success of the company. It was for this reason that they'd decided to appoint a new CEO, Vaughan (pseudonym), before they'd reached the date sketched out in the succession plan.

The company had an annual turnover of approx. £3,000 million, profits of approx. £350 million, it employed roughly 18,500 people and sold over 8 million products every day of the year. Vaughan set about tackling both sides of his new role with his usual high energy and optimism. The daily operational details had to be tackled immediately and there was much for him to learn about the business from this overall position of responsibility. So he spent much of his time meeting people, talking and listening not just amidst the senior executive cadre but in as many of the different parts of the business as he could reasonably reach. This meant a great deal of global travel, not least as the company had operations in every continent of the world, and at least 30 different countries. In effect, he was 'walking the talk' and being seen to be 'doing' leadership by meeting senior managers in as many different operational units and departments as possible.

Importantly for him, as he explained, he was using this opportunity not only to perform his leadership role and literally 'be seen' as the company's leader, but also meeting and building relationships with key people across the company across the globe as these would create the networks through which communication, engagement and, effectively, leadership would happen. So he was using these opportunities to listen and learn about what was going on in the company from their point of view. In so doing, he was effectively gathering information, insight and advice from key people as to what did and didn't work well in the company, and also learning where and how they saw change could and should be made.

He already felt he knew from his previous role that there were areas of the organization that could be strengthened. So drawing the information and ideas he'd gathered from across the company together with his own insight and experience, he began to design a strategic change initiative that he could tailor to address the corporate change agenda he'd be given by the board. He developed and discussed this with his senior executive group (top management team) and fairly swiftly had a strategy in shape to present to the board.

There was unanimous support for this from both executive and non-executive directors, and the strategy implementation process began to roll out across the company. In this way, Vaughan was being seen to be performing all that had been asked of him to a high standard and achieving leadership impact and effects throughout the company. He'd forged strong relationships with key executives across the globe and was known and was apparently well respected in every part of the company.

This way you can see how it is not just overt acts such as announcing a new strategy or declaring the annual profit margin that symbolize leadership. In Vaughan's case, he was performing leadership acts and having leadership effects through almost everything that he did, from literally the way in which he walked through the door onwards. How did he meet and greet people? How did he look? Did he listen and did he actually hear what was being said? Was he respectful of others' views and, if so, how did he show that? Was he encouraging? Did he recognize people's hard work and achievements? And so on. These are all small acts which cost nothing to do but their effect for leaders and leadership can be very valuable.

There are many such questions that can be asked about Vaughan, each of which gives an indication of how he was enacting leadership in literally everything he did and even if he wasn't aware of that, others were so they'd be making evaluations of him as their leader all the time. The same is true of anyone in a leader role at any level of an organization. Everyone else with whom you interact will be quietly absorbing impressions of what you're like as a leader, so that leadership can be said to be 'invisible' (Mintzberg, 1998). Are you a self-opinionated, egocentric know-it-all who really only needs followers who act like sheep (Kelley, 1988) or are you the kind of leader who knows you can't and don't have all the answers to the organization's problems? If the latter, you'll 'lead quietly', encouraging people to step forward to help share that responsibility, facilitating people who can and will ask constructive, critical questions and will be active in playing a part in achieving the collective outcomes (Badaracco, 2002).

Vaughan felt he was more the latter type of leader and began to feel disappointed when progress with the new strategy implementation plan seemed to be happening at a snail's pace and there were no apparent obstacles or reasons as to why this should be the case. It was then by chance during a factory visit that he overheard a middle manager say, 'Oh, that's Vaughan's vision'. On reflection, he then realized that while the strategy was very logical and well considered, and was fully supported by the directors and the senior executives, it lacked the 'hearts and minds' of most employees.

The governance structure of this company sought to achieve transparency and engagement throughout by delegating considerable power, authority and responsibility to the divisional level, which meant that the head of a local business unit level could potentially undermine a centrally driven strategic initiative through: obstruction – we can only do that at an unacceptable cost to the centre; obfuscation – well, we'd like to do that but we need time to work out quite how we could do it and either we don't have time or resource to do it right now, so just leave it with us; or oversight – we choose to ignore that for as long as we can because we think it's going to undermine the future of this unit, so we won't do it.

Each of these practices is commonplace to all leadership situations where the leader of one group is trying to get another group 'on board' with a new plan that requires them to make changes to what they do and how they do it (Kotter, 2012). As seen in this case too, it also has knock-on consequences for the group or division's identity and purpose.

 STOP AND REFLECT 6.5

Do you recognize this kind of obstructive group behaviour in your own group experience?

    What were the causes and effects of this?

    If both leaders and followers 'dig their heels in' and refuse to accept the others' influence, what needs to change to unblock this situation?

    From what you know about leadership, strategy and governance, what action would you take in order to lead effective change in this situation?

These examples raise many questions of leadership, strategy and governance. It is often said that people resist change, but it's more usually the fact that people resist change being 'done to' them (Senge, 2006). In Vaughan's case, he realized that although he'd talked with people, they didn't feel as if they'd had any part in shaping the strategy, so he went back to the drawing board and started again. This time, he arranged an off-site, three-day strategy review gathering with the top 30 executives (leaders). He also engaged outside consultants to help organize and facilitate the three days so that, through a mixture of working together and in smaller groups, they worked out a vision of what they should be. The ultimate outcome of this was a set of words that articulated the company's core strategic ambition and that had unanimous support from all the group members. This was also made public through them each putting their signature on the document.

Surprisingly in this example of leadership, some of those signing the document were effectively and knowingly signing their own redundancy as they'd agreed that restructuring would be necessary to achieve this new strategic direction for the company. For example, one of the consequences of their new global strategy was the need to reorganize marketing from a regional to a global basis which meant fewer marketing directors would be needed. However, in terms of implementing this new strategic initiative, these overt signatures showed that the hearts and minds of senior executives were all in tune with this strategic initiative and sent a powerful leadership message to all parts and people in the company. It also gave a good indication to shareholders that there was now strong, decisive and clear-sighted strategic leadership taking place amidst the top management layer (approx. 150 people) which would redress the previous era which lacked leadership and strategic direction.

The problem of any such case study is that it will only offer a very small, partial snapshot of what is going on in an organization. In Williams and Wright, there were many other issues and problems, challenges and changes to be dealt with in trying to implement their new global strategy. The tool they used to help map the territory and manage their performance was their adaptation of the Balanced Scorecard. This neatly illustrates how strategy and governance come together through leadership which endeavours to keep the organization on the right track.

Inevitably, though, with this kind of major strategic initiative, the implementation programme can also lead to 'unintended consequences'. So, for example, to achieve support for the newly appointed worldwide marketing director who would lead the new strategic aim to achieve global brands, they needed to harmonize the selling, marketing and advertising programmes across the world.

While an MNE may aim for a global strategy, people live in countries where there are particular cultural customs and practices, local languages, preferences and tastes and so on, which require attention and consideration. This also highlights another realm of questions which relate to multicultural dynamics and developments of behaviour and the diverse expectations people have of leaders, followers and leadership in different parts of the globe.

Some lessons for leaders and leadership

In conclusion, this chapter has shown how leadership, governance and strategy go hand in hand through the core of any organization. Governance is an umbrella term for the systems and processes that provide the operating infrastructure of the organization. Strategy is a term used to describe the sense or statement of the organization's aim for the future. Leadership is the term that embraces the impacts and effects of individuals and groups in shaping their future, and leaders are the people who are identified as having particular responsibility and accountability for elements of achieving this purpose.

Strategy and governance are usually assumed to be the responsibility of employees near the top of organizations. While senior leaders may be seen in this way, their ability to do this depends on the contributions of everyone else in the organization. So to that extent, everyone has a part to play in strategy and governance. It is also the case that everyone has a part to play in leadership, even if as 'followers', because as the William and Wright case showed, even the most well-crafted strategy and governance systems may not be effective if 'followers' desist from joining in.

This can be a problem for leaders at any level of an organization but is particularly notable as you go up the ladder, as the governance and strategy stakes get higher. If we go back to the introductory sections, strategy is about identifying an angle or a competitive edge to your organization that will sustain its longer-term future. The organization in this statement can just as easily be a department or a project group as it can be a division or a whole company. And the 'you' relates to the leader who effectively holds responsibility and accountability for what the group does and how they do it, that is the group's purpose, practice and performance.

As we saw in Vaughan's case, not only did the people within his group/organization have expectations of him as he took up the role of CEO, but there were also many people external to the company with some very big expectations of his ability to steer the company in a new direction and deliver high returns. While the stakes may not be so high, the principle is just the same at any level of leadership appointment within an organization: there will be people within the group who expect to be led and there will be people 'outside' the group watching to see if there's 'any leadership happening' – that is, keeping an eye on the actions and outcomes of the leader and group and so evaluating and making judgements of 'leadership' in this context.

This is where skilful leaders endeavour to steer a steady course between past, present and future, and between inside and outside. Vaughan showed us how the history of a group/organization has an important effect in creating the climate and conduct of the present, which has implications for its future strategic direction. Similarly the systems and processes by which it has operated and continue to do so are also likely to need amending as, without that, the same behaviours will continue to keep happening and this may not be what's needed next.

In doing this as we saw in the case study, every little bit counts: from the grand gestures and statements, the signatures on the strategy document, and the multiple meetings and engagements across the globe, and so also to all the micro-gestures and statements – the encouragements, the recognition and saying thank you, for example. These are all behaviours of leaders and they all have an impact and effect on 'followers' and essentially on the leader–follower relationship through which things are 'made to happen' and strategy is developed and brought about (Kouzes and Posner, 2012).

This is where governance comes to the fore as it effectively describes the framework through which strategic leadership can be exercised. But don't forget, it is also the framework that has been decided upon by leaders, even if they were your predecessors or they are working at a higher level in the organization and setting the framework for you. Similarly, leadership and strategy are often seen to be two sides of the same coin, to the extent that the choice of strategy says something about the leaders and their leadership, while what leaders do has effect on their strategic choices and outcomes.

For all leaders at all levels of organization, there's a need to keep their eyes on both these aspects as the governance dimension provides the operational scaffolding around which organization and strategy develop, and it is leaders and (their) leadership that embody these. Hierarchical level might make a difference to the extent to which there's a greater or lesser emphasis on the strategic rather than operational or governance elements of the role, but the one thing that is essential to their achievement and runs through every level of organization is the code of values on which these behaviours and choices are based.

Everyone has a set of values and even if you can't describe them, these are still the basis on which you evaluate other people's behaviour and also make choices of your own. Sometimes called a moral compass, it is this guidance system which provides strong influence and direction. They also act as a powerful guide to behaviour and choices you might make, be that about governance, about strategy, or about leading your group, regardless of whatever kind of organization you're working for or leadership role you might have.

The key points in this chapter were ...

- Strategy is hugely varied in practice but generally refers to the setting of goals or objectives as well as the plans to achieve these. Although there is a tendency to focus on the planning that takes place away from the day-to-day activities, recent research has highlighted the role of middle managers as well as executive directors in the micro-processes of shaping and communicating of strategy.
- Governance is an umbrella term for the systems and processes that provide the operating infrastructure of the organization.
- The dominant perspective behind corporate governance is agency theory, in which senior managers are held accountable by the board to maximize shareholder value.
- Governance practices are defined and regulated by law, which varies across different countries and states. This is especially interesting in the case of multinational enterprises, which abide only by the regulations of the country in which they are registered.
- An interesting shift in thinking around the board is a move from a quantitative box-ticking approach to that which sees chairmen as board leaders who take responsibility for creating healthy environments in which their organizations can thrive and be successful.
- Both strategy and governance are held together by the notion of leadership to the extent that leaders are expected to make and implement strategy, and to govern organizations.
- However, this combination tends to view the organization as a pyramid, which portrays leadership as coming from the top and everyone else as followers. This is a reductionist view of leadership in organizations which overlooks the significant influence those at 'lower' levels to affect strategy and leadership, even despite governance.

Further thinking

As shown through each of the chapters in this book, leadership is infused with many other concepts that help us to understand behaviour in organizations and the processes of organizing. In this chapter, we have added strategy and governance to the leadership melting pot. To help highlight some additional qualities that these concepts add to understanding leadership and leading, read the following and consider the questions identified below. Both will remind you that leadership and change go hand-in-hand to the extent that to lead implies 'movement from here to there'. Likewise, strategies always need updating and sometimes need radical change too to accommodate shifts in market, technology, resources, competitive advantage, and so on. Governance systems and processes may also need changing but tend to be a more enduring aspect of organizing, related to and embedded in the organization's culture.

Narayan, V. K. and Fahey, L. (2013). Seven management follies that threaten strategic success. *Strategy & Leadership, 41*(4): 24–29.

Although described as 'management follies', these are also problems for leaders and leadership.

1   As a leader, what would you do to tackle each of these follies/problems?
2   If you were successful in addressing each of them, do you think you'd be able to achieve successful implementation of your strategic initiative, or is there more than this to achieving successful implementation of strategy?
3   How and in what ways does each folly have implications for an organization's systems and processes of corporate governance?
4   What else might you need to take into account as leader to achieve successful change?
5   What could you do as leader to help to ensure others have the capabilities, interest and motivation to engage effectively in the changes you're seeking to bring about?

Osborn, R. N. and Marion, R. (2009). Contextual leadership, transformational leadership and the performance of international innovation-seeking alliances. *Leadership Quarterly*, 20: 191–206.

It goes without saying that behaviour gains meaning in context; for example, does that hand in the distance waving mean that someone is saying hello to you or calling for help because they're drowning? This paper moves the attention on from a typical organization situation and context to consider leadership in international innovation-seeking alliances in a sample of Japanese and US research and development (R&D) firms. This brings together leadership, strategy and governance and also offers lessons for similar international interest groups, ranging from student project groups and organizational teams made up of people of different ethnicity, through to any organization seeking to bridge boundaries with external partners.

1   While you might assume that innovation alliances need transformational leadership to enhance the motivation, morale and performance of people who are working outside their usual organizational environments, the researchers actually found 'Greater transformational leadership by either sponsoring executive was dysfunctional for innovation' (p. 202). Why is this the case and what needs to happen to overcome this obstacle to leading innovation in this alliance context?
2   Differentiate between the actions you've listed in question 1 and list them under the headings of leadership actions, governance actions and strategic actions. Do any of these actions qualify as being on all three lists? If so, what does that say about the nature of leadership, strategy and governance in organizations?
3   The researchers conclude on p. 203 that they have actually been focusing on managers not leaders. Do you think the sponsoring executives and the alliance head are managers, or are they leaders who also do managing, or managers who also do leading?
4   Reflecting on the findings of this research and your answers to the above questions, can you see any parallels with a student project group to which you belong in which members come from a variety of different national backgrounds? What lessons you can take from this which might help everyone in the group contribute to improving the process and outcomes of working together in your creative project alliance?

Leadership on screen

A great example of the multi-faceted nature of leadership is captured in the film *Take the Lead* (2006), with its tagline 'Never follow'. It is not set in a corporation and is also funny and full of great music and dancing, so please watch it and reflect on what's happening for individuals and the different groupings, with the concepts of leadership, governance and strategy in mind. The subtitle 'never follow' might make it sound like leadership mayhem, but it's not. It simply reflects an essential theme of leadership – we all do it for ourselves and for others too, and we all sometimes play the role of 'follower' to another's leader. The extent and ways in which we do this 'depends' on many other factors at any particular time. This film gives a very fine-grained and deeply personal account of people in a deeply divided situation, bringing about change in ways that challenge the governance (e.g. structures and systems) and strategy of the institution as a whole and of individuals too.

After watching the film, give thought to and answer the following:

1. This film is full of leaders. Pick out the three who stand out most clearly in your mind: who are they, what personal qualities to they bring to their role and how do they 'do' leadership?
2. This film is also full of follower moments. Pick out three that stand out most clearly in your mind: who's involved, what personal qualities do they bring to their role and how do they 'do' followership?
3. What are the key differences (if any) in your answers to questions 1 and 2?
4. Choose two of the leaders you've identified and reflect on how their behaviour demonstrated strategy in action; that is, working towards the achievement of particular goals and ambitions. What were the obstacles to them achieving these outcomes and how did they work with overcome them? What were the enablers – factors that helped them – to implementing and achieving their strategies?
5. Of these two leaders, what were the systems of governance within which they each worked? How did this help or hinder them in achieving their strategy? How did their leadership effect and/or challenge and change these systems? If you're stuck for an example, reflect on the situation where Mr Temple, a rule-bound, self-interested agent, demands that the Principal (Augustine James) calls Pierre Dulaine (the unconventional detention class teacher) before the Parent Teachers' Association to account for his behaviour.

Appendix: Useful governance websites

- FRC, UK regulator: www.frc.org.uk
- US Securities and Exchange Commission: www.sec.gov
- Australian Securities Exchange (now known as ASXGroup): www.asxgroup.com.au
- Johannesburg Stock Exchange review of governance principles and regulation for South African listed companies, now into its third iteration, the King Report III (2009): www.ecgi.org/codes/documents/king3.pdf
- Organization for Economic Co-operation and Development: www.oecd.org
- World Bank: www.worldbank.org
- European Corporate Governance Institute: www.ecgi.org/codes

7

DIFFERENCE AND LEADERSHIP

Amanda Sinclair and Michelle Evans

Amanda Sinclair is an academic who is also a yoga and meditation teacher. She has been a long-term advocate for putting 'leadership' and 'difference' together and for 'doing leadership differently'.

Michelle Evans is an Aboriginal woman and a theatre-maker by background. She is interested in the intersection of cultural identity and leadership and the collective dimensions of identity and leadership.

What this chapter is all about …

The main idea is that leadership and diversity are usually combined in ways that collapse the multiplicity of differences. However, these ideas need to be unpacked from a critical perspective that calls attention to the power dynamics behind the construction of difference.

The key questions this chapter answers are:

- What does it mean to take a critical perspective on difference and diversity?
- How are difference and diversity significant for leadership?
- How has the idea of diversity evolved in organizations, and what does this mean for notions of 'managing' diversity?
- What does leadership look like when it celebrates diversity?

Introduction

Amanda: So, Michelle, we've got this book chapter to write about leadership and difference. In the spirit of writing about this area, I suggest we do it differently: as a dialogue between two different voices on the question of difference, each with our own histories, experiences and interests.

STOP AND REFLECT 7.1

Before we go any further, we also want to invite you to pause and reflect on your own experiences of difference and leadership and reflect on the following questions:

- Under what circumstances have you felt 'different' and what was your experience?
- What kinds of pressures (if any) did you come under to 'fit in', to modify what you said or to conform to norms?
- Has it been important to you to speak up or stand out on a particular issue against the views of the majority and, if so, what happened?
- Have you had experiences of seeking to introduce new and different perspectives into group discussions and, if so, what unfolded? Were you heard? Did what you said change things?

Michelle: OK, Amanda, I'd like to give it a go. It's important to say at the outset that not only are we are adopting a very 'different' style of writing about difference, we want to highlight that in this chapter we are not opting to assert one 'truth' about difference. Instead we are choosing to lay out the perspectives and tensions in constructing and experiencing difference, and how these experiences relate to leadership.

Amanda: Throughout this textbook, including in the editors' Introduction, are discussions of what it means to take a critical perspective. For us, taking a critical perspective means that we are interested in interrogating leadership as a set of ideas, rather than doing what leadership gurus tell us we need to do, to 'be' leaders. We will ask questions like:

- How have terms like 'difference' and 'diversity' come to be connected to leadership?
- How have they acquired particular meanings and imperatives such as the need to 'manage diversity'?

Michelle: So what might be some of the takeaways from reading this chapter on difference and leadership? We hope it provides you, the reader, with an example of a critical engagement with leadership literature and theories on difference; and that we provide a framework for you to consider your own experiences of difference and leadership; for example, how your own narratives and life experiences have shaped your understandings of leadership, and are a resource for you to draw upon as you study, and do, leadership.

Where are we speaking from about difference and leadership?

Amanda: Difference is not an objectively allocated marker, like skin colour, but an experience that results from many social interactions and socially mediated designations – in people's histories, their lives and careers. There is no one 'truth' about difference and leadership, but many. Accordingly, for you as readers to interpret and assess what we say here about difference, you need to know about us and about where we are speaking from.

Michelle: I was born in Newcastle, Australia and raised in Cessnock in the Hunter Valley of New South Wales in a working-class family living in the housing commissions. My experiences about being 'different' began early as we moved from public school into the Catholic school system when I was seven. My early experiences of class difference and being poor had a major influence on me. My father is also a strong unionist and we discussed politics often at the dinner table (later fighting about politics as I grew into my own voice). I was 12 when Mum and Dad told my sisters and I that we were Aboriginal. I remember, far from being surprised, I felt like something was affirmed within me. Embraced by the Aboriginal community in the Newcastle region, I began to actively contribute to the community by becoming a community radio broadcaster, a student politician, and then moving into community based arts, management and now academia.

Amanda: I was born in Melbourne, Australia into a struggling but stable lower-middle-class family. As a young white woman I had little exposure to other cultures until my brother became good friends with an Indigenous boy who had arrived at our high school from the Torres Strait. He and I later had a 'bit of a thing' for each other, which my father was horrified about. I remember him standing in the kitchen and saying to my mother 'He's black!' as if this self-evidently determined the future of our relationship. My experiences of 'being different' as a woman didn't really kick in until later, when I started work and found myself in almost exclusively male environments in government and consulting. Those early experiences of starting to notice power dynamics and my own relative powerlessness and marginalization later became the fuel for a lot of my subsequent research of women's experiences in leadership.

Defining difference and diversity

Amanda: There is a whole history about the ideology and power of these terms, how their meanings have been employed in organization behaviour and leadership scholarship to achieve certain things. These terms of difference and especially 'diversity' are often used as if they are objectively measurable phenomena, not a complex product of language, power and ideology.

Michelle: Can I just unpack that last sentence, Amanda? Often, the way 'difference' is employed in the writing of leadership (and management) is as a divergence from general understandings about leadership. In journals, for example, there are articles about 'cross-cultural leadership' or 'African' leadership or 'women's' leadership. All of these are marked as divergent to the mainstream concepts and theories, comprehensible as 'special categories' of leadership and often grouped together under one abstract concept like 'diversity'.

Amanda: I'd probably put it more bluntly. It's inappropriate to create a category that corrals together experiences of, for example, race and gender, treating them as in some way equivalent, all just 'difference' or 'diversity'. My view is that this process often occurs for political or management reasons. It enables managers to design one programme that supposedly accommodates women, Indigenous people, gays, transsexuals, people with disabilities and everyone else, without recognizing the difference issues and forms of prejudice that members of each group are dealing with.

STOP AND REFLECT 7.2

Michelle: An example of allocating and grouping together non-equivalent differences is the UK government-funded leadership development programme for Black, Asian and Minority Ethnic Leaders (BAME). Although it looked like a promising initiative, those categorized brought a range of different and sometimes, irreconcilable, issues and obstacles they were confronting in leadership. A category like BAME is a construct with multiple and divergent histories and brings with it certain intents. Ask yourself:

- Who benefits from this allocation and categorization of differences like BAME?
- Why do such categorizations of difference occur?
- What might be some of the consequences, positive and negative?

So now let us highlight some key points and ask you to consider and reflect upon as you read this chapter:

- First, we need to be aware that there is a history behind the use of the terms diversity and difference that fall outside the literature of leadership and management, yet impact keenly on our shared thinking of these ideas.
- Second, we want to critically engage in understanding who is designating 'difference' and 'diversity', and we are asking to what ends are these categorizations put to use?
- Third, we are asking readers to consider the genealogy of privilege we see reinforced in contemporary society through social constructs like 'leadership'.

Ideologies and discourses of difference and diversity

Amanda: Part of taking a critical perspective is seeing the historical and political context around the emergence of terms, such as 'leadership' and 'difference'. French philosopher Michel Foucault reminds us that words do not benignly pop up into usage because they objectively capture a phenomenon. Rather, terms, bundles of words and ways talking (which some define as 'discourses') are a product of power and they reinforce particular interests and purposes (Foucault, 1972). For example, even the phrase 'managing diversity' contains the idea that diversity is something that needs to be managed (presumably by those who are somehow outside this designation of different). The phrase itself creates diversity as a problem, imposing a managerial solution.

Building on this perspective, it's possible to discern at least three major discourses of difference and diversity that have influenced management and leadership studies, including justifications for why difference and diversity are important for leadership and, if so, what should be done about them! We have called these: the business discourse on diversity; the social psychological discourse; and critical perspectives on difference.

Each of these discourses are situated within, and are reinforced by, broader social ideologies or philosophies. The first two discourses we discuss are located within a rational instrumental ideology which assumes that the point of knowledge production is to use it as a means to advance economic and other ends. In contrast, a critical perspective is more likely to be informed by the idea that the revealing of social and political processes is of value because those revelations may reduce oppression and promote more equitable societies.

The business discourse on diversity

Amanda: In much of the business literature, difference and diversity are used interchangeably and are defined as dimensions of overt or less visible difference including cultural, racial, ability, sexual orientation and gender heterogeneity. Businesses are encouraged to take a proactive approach to diversity and advocates for diversity are advised to develop a strong 'business case for diversity', that is to spell out all the rational economic and instrumental reasons why diversity will advance 'the bottom line'.

Cross-cultural differences

Michelle: The best known of the studies into the impact of culture and geography on leadership has been the work of Geert Hofstede (1980, 1991) and the subsequent international GLOBE (Global Leadership and Organizational Behaviour Effectiveness) project founded by Robert House in 1993. These two researchers (and House's significant research team) employed psychometric measures and surveys to understand and assess the role cultural/geographic difference makes to leadership. Hofstede used anthropological, historical, psychological and sociological sources to develop a theoretical model from a 're-analysis of an existing database of employee attitude scores assembled by one single multinational: the IBM corporation, from its subsidiaries in 72 countries, between 1967 and 1973' (Hofstede, 2006, p. 883). House and his team (2004) built upon Hofstede's five dimensions (which include high and low power distance; individualism vs. collectivism; masculinity vs. femininity; uncertainty avoidance; and long-term orientation), adding a further four dimensions that show the cultural practices and values of 62 societies from around the globe (humane orientation; performance orientation; institutional collectivism vs. in-group collectivism; and assertiveness vs. gender egalitarianism).

These two studies aim to demonstrate the impact cultural diversity has on the work of leadership. The GLOBE study explicitly asks if there are 'cultural universals' when it comes to leadership and answers this question with their nine dimensions. It analysed '17,370 middle managers from 951 organizations in three industries' (House et al., 2004, p. 96).

 STOP AND REFLECT 7.3

Taking a critical perspective on this highly influential area of research into difference and leadership we need to ask some questions, such as:

- To what ends was the research conducted? Why was a comparison of cultures being sought?
- Who is this research useful for? Who stands to benefit from the measurement and codification of cultural differences?
- What contextual considerations might influence both the intent and results of the research?
- At a more specific level, what are the relationships between the researcher and the field site companies and how does this influence the study?

Hofstede (2001) has subsequently addressed some of the criticisms made of his research, such as whether surveys are the best way to measure cultural difference or if using 'nation' as a unit of analysis is a valid approach. What's useful for our purposes about the debate between cultural difference theorists such as Hofstede, House et al. and their critics is its highlighting of how research allows for knowledge claims to be made and how theorists can then construct systems of cultural classification as a truth.

Amanda: Michelle you seem to be concerned here about the relationship between researchers to this research? Are you suggesting that in the very construction of research, with variables and hypotheses, already assumptions have been made about difference, who is different and who is the norm?

Michelle: Yes, researchers are meant to be transparent about their assumptions and these are supposed to be stated as limitations to what knowledge they produce. The reality is that when this research data gets translated into leadership training programmes, those assumptions get lost and material gets presented as if it is truth.

The social psychological discourse on diversity

Amanda: Well said, and what you've argued there also applies to the social psychological discourse on diversity. This research focuses on difference and diversity as a measurable feature of individuals and teams. The research typically also attributes the problems and the remedies for dysfunctional diversity outcomes at the individual and team level. In their critique of this kind of diversity research, Ahonen et al. (2013) argue that the very research technologies and taxonomies 'commodifies', obscures and neutralizes the fluidity and multiplicity of diversity. Researchers that create and measure diversity as a category negate the specificity of experiences of difference, rather supplanting a 'representation of bodies', 'an optimal mix of talent' that serves positive organizational outcomes.

Tackling the obstacles to women in leadership

The 'women in leadership' field provides many examples of individualized remedies for what is more likely to be a system-wide or structurally based problem. Predominantly, many of the solutions have focused on helping women change themselves so they don't 'look' so different, for example, getting the right experience, dressing inconspicuously, negotiating in not too aggressive ways. As more research has revealed that overcoming the obstacles to women requires a change in the mindset of men, new solutions have focused on helping men recognize their 'unconscious bias' and using strategies to avoid such stereotypes in their selection and hiring decisions. More about this later …

The critical discourse of difference and diversity

Amanda: Third, we introduce the critical discourse on difference and diversity. But the first thing to note is that it is not one view! There are many writers who engage critically with notions of difference and diversity. They come from divergent fields such as cultural studies, anthropology and international relations, and there are many areas of disagreement. In some respects, this whole chapter draws on and exemplifies a critical discourse on difference. But by way of introduction …

Through the mid- to late twentieth century, philosophers and linguists such as Jacques Derrida and Luce Irigaray explored the semiotic roots and construction of meaning in terms 'difference'. Focusing on how power and language intersect, they show that it is power-holders with privilege who designate certain individuals and groups as 'other' or 'different'. The designation is a political act using language. Building on these and other insights, post-colonial theorizing emerged through the later twentieth century from writers concerned about the lasting impacts of colonization in many parts of the world, but also the new forms of colonization that occur in globalized environments. Post-colonialism brought with it a focus on the impact of the colonizer in the construction of who and what was deemed different, and these perspectives made their way into critical analysis of diversity and diversity management.

Prefacing leadership with a different classification

Michelle: When 'different' leadership is studied it inevitably evokes use of a prefix like 'Indigenous' leadership or 'Queer' leadership. This grammatical alteration signals difference but it also alerts us to a standard with which this different leadership is being compared. My own work also falls into this problematized space through my use of the prefix 'Indigenous'. I choose to use the word Indigenous because it speaks to the breadth of Indigenous peoples across the world who share the experience of colonization and the struggle to reclaim land, language and culture. Yet, despite my intentional use of this word 'Indigenous', it can create tension for me as a researcher. This tension is not necessarily a bad thing; it signals the importance of language to participants, critics and readers and the way I, and more broadly, we use the word Indigenous and what we might mean and hope to engage through its use.

Using a prefix both claims space for difference and implies that there are perceived norms in leadership. In the English language when words like 'white' are spoken it invisibly also implies black; male evokes female; insider also speaks to outsider. These bounded pairs are examples of the operationalization of durable inequality (Tilly, 1998).

Summarizing some key points, we have suggested that the dominance of the business discourse can lead to oversimplified and impoverished notions of leadership and difference. In contrast, a critical perspective insists on making visible:

1   the power relations occurring when one group manages the 'diversity' that has been designated and labelled on 'others', with the privilege, biases and interests of the dominant group usually remaining out of sight;
2   the purposes and dangers of bundling together a range of organizational 'minorities' (even though they may be numerical majorities) under a common category of 'diversity' when they have different experiences and needs;
3   the causes and remedies of discrimination as underlying and group-based structural inequities and power differentials in society, rather than individual weaknesses;
4   that valuing difference is important ethically to the health of society, organizations and individuals, not just because or when it delivers benefits for the 'bottom line'.

And how can leadership scholars emphasize difference in a positive but also critical way? We will say more about this as the chapter unfolds but as a starting point Nkomo (2011) suggests that working towards a decolonizing or anticolonial agenda we:

1   avoid binary language;
2   challenge cultural essentializing, both within conventional and non-conventional writings about leadership;
3   consider the impacts of globalisation on leaders.

Leadership and difference

Amanda: We've spent a lot of time focusing on difference, but since this is a book primarily about leadership, we should introduce leadership and its connection to difference, shouldn't we?

Much of what we have suggested above about difference can also be applied to leadership. In taking a critical perspective, we are endeavouring to see how 'leadership' has come to be constructed as an 'answer' to problems – in societies and organizations – and it typically brings with it a set of culture-centric frameworks that are products of, not outside, broader societal relations of power and ideology.

Scholars have long drawn our attention to some of the biases and self-serving perspectives that are widespread in leadership literature. For example, early American sociologists such as Alvin Gouldner (in the 1950s) and Loren Baritz (in 1960) provided warnings about the consequences of an American-dominated leadership industry, an elite conglomeration of business, the military and academics who looked to narratives about leadership to retrieve political and economic dominance. Contemporary leadership scholar Barbara Kellerman observes: 'The contemporary leadership field is an American product, planted in American soil and harvested by American scholars, educators and consultants' (2004, p. 10).

Michelle: From my experience, studying leadership with groups and individuals who have experienced historical inequality brings up very different responses to leadership – what is generally framed as a positive phenomenon. When I ask Indigenous participants to tell me about leadership, there is a fundamental push back on the idea. Very frequently the responses I hear are that leadership is about power; it's about individuals asserting themselves over others, it's coercive. These personal theories of leadership that we carry around are important but they can get in the way of understanding leadership as a phenomenon that occurs in all communities and groups. Understanding how leadership is enacted in community-based settings may also give us other ideas about leadership, especially when we listen to how leadership is understood from the perspective of those who experience persistent social inequality.

Amanda: What this means, in the study of leadership and difference, is that there is a 'hegemonic' or dominant view of what leadership looks like and how leadership should be understood and studied. When alternative views on or different experiences of, leadership begin to be expressed they get relegated, as we have discussed above, under the headings of 'different': categories like 'women's leadership'; 'cross-cultural leadership'; 'Asian', 'minority' and 'indigenous leadership'.

Michelle: Hence, the onus is placed on the reader of leadership texts to critically engage with what is presented as assumed and reinforcing norms of leadership. We need to remind ourselves that concepts like leadership and difference are constructed through social and group relations; that is, the leader and follower constitute each other through a relational process (Uhl-Bien and Ospina, 2012). Durable social inequities are thus reproduced in leadership, while we argue that leadership interested in difference should be aiming to remedy these inequities, or at the very least question them.

Approaches to doing leadership in ways that honour and sponsor difference

Our conclusion is that leadership that aims to work respectfully with difference needs to avoid some of the traps we have discussed. Initiatives that operationalize difference as an individual attribute and that fail to properly acknowledge the diversity in difference will, we have argued, fail to deliver leadership. In this section we describe some leadership work that, in contrast, recognizes and works explicitly with issues of power and context. In these examples we are also interested in justifications for honouring difference that go beyond 'good business', invoking ethical arguments to treat people without discrimination and enable them to enjoy opportunities to fulfil their potential.

Cultural identity work and leadership

> Our approach is one which argues that context, individual biographies and idioms of the self…
> cannot be ignored as leadership, indeed work in general, involves interpersonal relationships. We
> bring our selves, our psyches, our histories, our idiosyncrasies, our ways of talking and thinking
> and acting, to these workplace relationships. (Ford et al., 2008, p. 175)

Michelle: I have come to studying leadership sometime into my career after working in theatre, community-based cultural development, community radio, Indigenous arts and teaching in higher education. These diverse and rich experiences are a blessing when it comes to applying my experiential knowledge to the area of leadership studies. I also come to leadership studies with a specific political agenda – to study leadership in spaces that are not conventionally selected as sites to learn about leadership, like my recent study of Indigenous artists and arts managers in both Australia and the USA. The editors suggest in the Introduction to this book that leadership is 'a process, involving people and therefore fundamentally social, subject to change over time and according to where it's happening', while I consider the phenomenon of leadership is something open and exciting to investigate.

Leadership involves dynamic processes of navigating who we are and what we bring to leadership, which may involve performing or conforming to expected ideas and narratives of who we are as well as resistance to and disruption of stereotyped ideas of who we are. Some of the richest and most interesting accounts of leadership come from critical research of leaders working against gender, racial and cultural stereotypes (see, for example, Ford and Harding, 2007; Ospina and Foldy, 2009; Nkomo, 2011; Kirton and Healy, 2012). Because leadership has historically been 'a white male idea' (Sinclair, 2007), leaders who are neither white nor male encounter challenges such as being rated less 'leader-like' (Eagly, 2011).

The work individuals do within themselves to perform 'leadership' is of great interest in the leadership field. What aspects of their thoughts, emotions and embodied experiences do they actively work to contain within themselves when doing the work of leadership? And what aspects of themselves do they bring forward, making available to others around them new ways of seeing and understanding? In my work into Indigenous leadership I investigated this internalized and embodied work individuals do, in order to provide leadership on behalf of themselves, others and sometimes communities. What I found was that individuals have these territories inside of their bodies; these spaces of tension that they need to navigate in order to do the work of leadership (Evans, 2012).

One territory that Indigenous leaders navigate is around authorization and voice. As an Indigenous person speaking out:

- Do I need cultural authorization to say and do the work of leadership?
- Do I need the community or group's authorization to do the work of leadership?
- Or do I find it within my own self this authorization of voice to speak and act out in ways that may be framed as the work of leadership?

These three considerations – personal, communal and cultural authorization – speak strongly beyond the experience of Indigenous leaders.

Amanda: Hang on, Michelle, I think there are many questions that you are posing here. You talk about how Indigenous cultures and groups mandate, affirm and attribute leadership differently to say a Western idea of self-selected leadership. And further, that these leaders then need to navigate the work of leadership differently from a more individualized approach to leadership.

Michelle: Thanks, Amanda, yes, exploring this way of thinking about leadership raises a few key ideas. First, that leadership is a process that happens both within individuals and between individuals and both of these processes are important to the work of leadership; that is, that individuals can find within themselves a voice and purpose to engage as much as they need to find that voice and purpose in group relationships. Second, that if the individual and social environments are important, then context to is important to the work of leadership. Taking a systemic rather than purely individual perspective to thinking about leadership is important. And third, the responsibility rests upon us to be cognizant to the operationalization of difference when engaged in the work of leadership.

Gender, women and leadership

Amanda: I'd like now to explore the category of difference focused on gender (which includes both men and women) and provide a critical reading of how research on gender and leadership has unfolded.

Leadership as a concept has been consistently construed in highly masculine terms. Yet much of mainstream leadership research has ignored that leadership is already gendered, that is it assumes and reinforces a set of masculine norms. Starting around the 1990s researchers started to explore the way in which leadership cultures were often dominated by masculine norms, such as valuing heroism and stoicism, rejecting weakness and vulnerability. Yet the vast bulk of leadership research continues to treat leadership as an unproblematized norm, towards which men and women alike should aspire. Within the literature on women and leadership, three roughly chronological approaches can be identified, which I'll briefly summarize.

'Add women and stir'

Women managers and the challenges they faced entering the 'foreign country' of male management constituted the focus of early studies. In this approach, women were advised on how to perform against pre-existing criteria of leadership: for example, they needed to gain line-management experience. Once these hurdles had been surmounted and women were 'in the pipeline' in sufficient numbers, they would bubble up into management and leadership positions, or so the argument went.

Also through this time, individual, psychological perspectives became dominant, with a focus on measurement of individual abilities for management and leadership that perpetuate assumptions that women just need to be the right 'fit' in order to be considered for leadership. Research, such as the 'sex differences' approach explored the qualities women needed in management and whether there were enduring sex differences that meant that women and men led and managed differently. While meta studies concluded that there was little difference due to sex in achievement, motivation, risk taking, task persistence and other managerial skills, the legacy of this research is an enduring focus on understanding the 'problem' of women's absence from leadership in terms of women's individual qualities and skills for leadership, or a lack of them.

'Women's ways of leading'

By the late 1980s and early 1990s, a new interest specifically focused on women and leadership was emerging, and, again, much of the early work came from American business-oriented researchers. Judy Rosener, writing in *Harvard Business Review* in 1990, argued that there was now a 'second wave' of women leaders who no longer had to mimic the 'command and control' male model of organizational leadership. Further, they were 'succeeding because of – not in spite of – certain characteristics generally considered to be "feminine" and inappropriate in leaders, such as encouraging participation, sharing power and information, enhancing other people's self-worth, and getting others excited about their work'.

The argument that women lead differently from men has continued, and continued to elicit controversy. Researchers have explored some of the consequences of identifying a female style of leading, such as creating new stereotypes such as women as more naturally nurturing and relational and holding all women to higher standards. Scholar of women's leadership Alice Eagly notes the tensions in research on women leaders. They are identified as having a 'female advantage': showing up as consistently demonstrating dimensions of transformational leadership such as 'individualized consideration', 'inspirational motivation' and 'intellectual stimulation'. However, women leaders are simultaneously disadvantaged by stereotypes of leadership that generally resemble stereotypes of men, that is agentic, confident, aggressive and self-determined. Eagly concludes: 'men can seem usual or natural in most leadership roles … people more easily credit men with leadership ability and more readily accept them as leaders' (2011, p. 257).

Equally importantly, the two approaches described above keep the focus on the individual and the individual woman, rather than looking at analyses of systemic power and how it is distributed, to explain what Australian scholar Joan Eveline (1994) described as 'the politics of men's advantage' in leadership.

Critical perspectives on women and leadership

Simultaneously from the late 1970s saw the emergence of pioneering work by gender scholars and feminists deconstructing organizational and leadership life. Instead of focusing on women as the 'other' who needed to learn how to do leadership, researchers began documenting how organizations and leadership were set up to maintain a gender order where masculinities were privileged. Administrative logic and 'merit-based' principles and practices are not neutral but designed, in the words of Australian scholar Clare Burton (1989), to 'mobilize masculine bias'. In *The Feminist Case Against Bureaucracy* (1984), Ferguson notes the power of supposedly neutral 'bureaucratic discourse' to 'manipulate, twist, and damage human possibility' in pursuit of capitalist goals (p. xii). Similarly, Acker (1990) argues that gender assumptions that devalue women are deeply embedded in organizational processes, language and metaphors.

Efforts to re-insert women's experiences into leadership and to re-make leadership from a critical and feminist perspective come from several places. For example, feminist standpoint theory has advanced the idea that the perspectives of the marginalized and disempowered are a source of leadership.

Indigenous and post-colonial scholars have offered powerful critiques of the dominance of elites and institutions such as the World Bank and the mechanisms by which oppression is perpetuated through neo-colonial structures. These scholars have consistently shown that leadership is often done in resistance and refusal from the bottom or the margins of society, rather than from formal positions at the top.

Other authors and activists have been interested in organizations created along feminist lines. Guided by values of devolution and inclusivity, some of these organizational forms reject leadership, preferring instead to enact rotated, consultative forms of governing.

Although the theories and perspectives described above share many differences (!), they can be understood to provide critical perspectives on leadership in the following ways:

1   They argue for a focus on underlying assumptions and distributions of power in systems, to understand how the status quo gets perpetuated and to understand the exclusion (not just absence) of women from senior roles. There is a recognition that power structures and institutions are gendered in both overt and more deeply embedded ways.
2   An interest in how leadership is exercised from below and within, as well as against, appointed leadership, which may be oppressive and hierarchical, gendered and racist.

3   An acknowledgement of diversity in women's experiences and voices. Following second-wave feminism and a critique of many white women's tendency to act as if they spoke for all women, there is now wide acknowledgement that it is important to avoid universalizing and essentializing women.

4   A rejection of what is seen to be individualistic, heroic, out-front notions of leadership in favour of more distributed and context-determined leadership exemplified in processes of consultation, devolved decision-making, development and empowerment of other women.

5   Promotion and integration into leadership and organizations of what are understood as feminine or women's values and ethics, such as putting a value on care and nurturance, especially of the weak, on maternal strength and resilience, and on community and relationships.

6   An emphasis on practice and seeing that 'the personal' is political and also often provides leadership. Reflective practice and consciousness raising are important tools, personal experience is valued.

'Making a difference' in leadership and difference

In the preceding section, we've provided overviews of two areas of research where critical perspectives have been incorporated in the way the leadership and difference have been conceptualized and theorized. From here on, we'd like to focus more on practices of leadership that actively engage with, and validate, difference.

STOP AND REFLECT 7.4

- Have you come across individual leaders or acts of leadership that seemed open and inviting of difference? What occurred and what were the consequences?
- How would you characterize or describe leadership that is open and sensitive to exploring issues of difference?
- What are the institutional, political or social supports that enable that kind of leadership and what kinds of obstacles are likely to block or undermine it?

Amanda: Below we will describe some examples of leadership practices that we suggest impact positively on understandings about difference. We suggest that each of these processes can be framed and viewed as examples of leadership; that is, they:

- shape or have the potential to shape public discourse on difference and diversity;
- address underlying assumptions and power-arrangements;
- create space for different experiences to be valued (Sinclair and Wilson, 2002).

Outsiders learn and adapt to dominant culture

This category of leadership practice occurs where people who have strong experiences of being 'outside' the dominant culture use these experiences to create a new place within the dominant culture. Far from being about assimilation, this leadership practice demonstrates the adaptive nature of 'outsiders', and how their success and work resonates with and ultimately changes the mainstream.

Case study: Noel Tovey, author/director/performer/choreographer

Michelle: I interviewed Noel Tovey, one of the fathers of Indigenous performing arts in Australia, for my study on Indigenous artists and leadership. Noel's career spans over 60 years in Australia, Europe and the USA where he has worked as a performer, dancer, choreographer, director, writer and teacher. Noel describes how, during the fifties at the beginning of his career, he was designated as the other, as not belonging or fitting in:

> I was really persona non grata when I was in *Paint Your Wagon*. I'll tell you why. Eight of the boys, the chorus boys, went up to the English choreographer and told him that I was notorious, that I'd been in gaol, that I was Aboriginal, that they didn't want to work with me.

Noel, having had already experienced much violence and neglect throughout his childhood, did not let the jibes and games of these chorus boys hurt his ambition to realize his dreams of dancing, directing and acting on main stages across the world. Noel led in the main-stage performance sector for Aboriginal people, treading the boards without (m)any other Aboriginal performers around him. Noel went on to explore these early experiences of being the outsider and how he constructed a strong inner narrative as a way to deal with this rejection within himself. I suggested, 'You have a really strong sense of self it seems to me.'

> It wasn't a strong sense of self. How can I put it? In a way it was but you see I was always, I had this terrible inferiority complex as well ... I'd walk on stage and I'd judge myself. Before I'd go on I'd say you're no good. That came from being Aboriginal and a good little black bastard and being taken away from my family and being in gaol at 17 and trying to commit suicide and you know all of those things all impinged on my ... but at the same time there was a determination to succeed ... It didn't stop me no. You see I could have fallen by the wayside but I didn't ... No, no and I never really became negative in front of other people. In fact I sometimes used to become the opposite and people used to think I was too grand but that covered up really huge negative ... You know, I'd walk in to a room and I'd be nine feet tall. That was only because I was nervous. Instead of going in bent over ...

Noel's determination to succeed meant that he became the best dancer, actor, singer, choreographer and director. Noel describes inverting his fear and projecting a 'nine feet tall' persona. That internal drive coupled with a suppression of his Aboriginal cultural identity drove Tovey to London and great critical success as an actor and choreographer. Adapting to the dominant culture ensured commercial success for Tovey; however, on his return to Australia in the 1990s Tovey invested in his own cultural identity, strengthening as well as setting up spaces for Indigenous young people to learn about theatre in a cultural safe space.

Reflect on Tovey's 'containment' of his Aboriginal cultural identity.

1. How does this sit with you? Why was it important in this story?
2. How did being 'outside' impact Tovey's leadership?
3. Have you ever experienced the need to suppress an identity? If so, how did it feel?

Speaking out about one's own difference

This category of leadership practice occurs where people with influence own up to their own difference, not denying it or going into camouflage in order to look like one of the dominant majority.

Case study: Christine Nixon, former Police Chief Commissioner, Victoria

Amanda: A central part of how Christine Nixon went about her leadership roles, as a senior and rare female officer in the New South Wales police force, then from 2001 to 2009 as Chief Commissioner of Victoria Police, and from 2009 to 2011 as head of the Bushfire Reconstruction and Recovery Authority, was about bringing herself to the job, including her values of treating people decently and with dignity. She also emphasized and practised care and the value of mothering, which she argued the leadership literature 'resisted recognising' (Nixon and Chandler, 2011, p. 222). As an example, one of her early actions in the Victoria police was to properly recognize those police who had died on duty and to support their families.

In her swearing-in speech as Police Commissioner, she began 'First, I am a woman' and then went on to outline the role of caring and compassionate values in good policing (p. 126). She also warned the audience not to confuse these values with 'softness' – which inevitably some stakeholders did. Nixon came under great pressure to play the 'hard cop' and she admitted her life would be much easier if she did. However, she continued to 'work hard to be authentic'. By this, she meant to speak truthfully and of her feelings and to uphold values that others might regard narrowly as too feminine (and therefore 'too soft'). Eventually in her later years in policing she observes that she had 'invested so many years in authentic behaviour', she wasn't frightened of risks to her reputation.

In reflecting on women and leadership and the extra scrutiny that they get she writes:

I know I can do the job, and that I can do it as a woman should – not as a bloke might, and not as someone else might, just as me. I know some women adopt the model of looking like the blokes, but I don't think that's the way for women to progress and so, as a role model, I try to just be me – unashamedly, honestly me. (p. 221)

Christine Nixon's approach is quite different to Noel Tovey's above. In this story, Nixon emphasizes her 'authentic behaviour' and doesn't shy away from her point of difference.

1. What do you think of Nixon's explicit recognition that she would do the leadership job as a woman?
2. What was gained from this leadership approach in contrast to Tovey's? And what's at stake in both of these examples?
3. What were the risks in claiming her difference?

Working bi-culturally: Moving across, within and outside boundaries

In this practice we are interested in people who navigate the boundaries between cultures and cultural identities. Individuals who use their bi-cultural and multi-cultural identities to operate across borders without exclusively residing in one or the other, but influencing in both spaces and using both spaces as a source of inspiration and tension in their work.

Case study: Stephen Page, Artistic Director of Bangarra Dance Theatre

Michelle: For 20 years, Stephen Page has been the Artistic Director of Bangarra Dance Theatre, Australia's pre-eminent Indigenous performing arts company. In this position he spans traditional/contemporary Indigenous cultural spaces as well as operating as one of the most successful Indigenous arts companies in Australia playing to audiences across the world each year. Moving between cultural spaces is integral to the work Stephen produces. In the following excerpt Stephen describes the complexity of working between Aboriginal and Western systems:

> I look at all my brothers and sisters that are in all their different cults of expertise and I think we spend a lot of time trying to work out the Western system which really I think exhausts a lot of the true cultural power within one. And I think we've got to stop getting in that road of wanting to understand the [Western] system – there's not too much to understand. I think we have to accept our own complexities and the more that we're black on black and the more that we can confront and find new ways to communicate in our leadership and the sharing of stories in our leadership way without having that Western barrier.

Stephen demonstrates how Indigenous people battle with the fatigue and inevitability of having to navigate the Western system. Having to negotiate these different worldviews and make decisions and choices daily about what to prioritize in any given moment is the work of those of us that span bi/multi-cultural worlds. Exerting influence, working with persuasion and doing leadership work despite and/or because of these challenging realities hones bi-cultural mastery. Stephen describes how he deals with these pressures in his work:

> Look there's no way we can escape the Western system but I think we've got to not be afraid of it and I think we've got to try not to let our egos to get absorbed in it, I think it needs to be enriched in a different way and that will probably help our focus a lot better.

Developing a multi-worldview fluency is important to the work of leadership. Being different brings strength to leadership because individuals develop a quality of observation and innovation in their worldviews and enact this through their work. Yet the individual also has to navigate and contain a lot of the pressures and tensions they encounter in the work of moving between cultural worldviews. This embodied work is discussed further in the following section.

Stephen Page's story illustrates how different worldviews can bring into focus things that are otherwise unseen. How might bringing different worldviews impact on leadership? A key purpose in leadership is often said to be about bringing unity (e.g. of purpose and as a group). How does the idea of unity sit with the 'pressures and tensions' in Page's story?

Leadership that places emphasis back on the dominant system/context but also preserves individual agency

In this practice we are interested in people who use their leadership and authority to name discriminatory conditions, to go to the root of how those who are labelled different in some way or another are not treated equally.

Case study: Julia Gillard's speech to the Australian parliament

Amanda: On 10 October 2012, Australia's then Prime Minister, Julia Gillard, addressed the Australian parliament, in response to a motion put by the opposition leader, Tony Abbott. While the motion concerned the future of the Speaker, Gillard's speech was an impassioned and galvanizing effort to draw attention to a concerted campaign of misogynistic, sexist attacks from the opposition and some of their associates, not just towards herself but towards Australian women in general.

The speech came after concerns expressed by prominent feminists about the escalating sexism in public commentary about the Prime Minister. For example, Ann Summers argued that a new and contagious level of misogyny has been given voice via social media sites, evidencing a level of discrimination and bullying that would be treated as illegal were it to occur in a company.

What is notable about this speech that drew international support is Gillard's insistence on facing squarely several things. First, it demanded we pay attention to the sustained, yet routinized way in which women are demeaned, discriminated against and subordinated because of their sex. Second, it showed why the special category of women with power (leaders) may attract particularly vicious and brutal efforts to drive women into silence or submission. Third, Gillard's speech invited listeners to notice the insidious ways sexism continues to work against women, and to see how public platforms of leadership are often used, consciously and unconsciously, to advance this agenda. Women's efforts towards leadership take place against the backdrop of women's subordination. For example, women's bodies are scrutinized and routinely measured against sex stereotypes, making them viewed as less leader-like. Though some may argue that instances of outright discrimination have reduced, there is plenty of evidence of emerging forms of media where women are routinely derogated or treated as sex objects. This backdrop shapes how women are seen, and their experiences in public life, in turn affecting their appetite for leadership.

The reasons why this leadership speech was particularly remarkable and influential have been widely discussed, and we have already seen a glimpse of these in Chapter 2. For our purposes here, the example shows how a leader can use their formal authority to name systemic experiences that have been rendered – by language or convention – unnameable. There was a determination not to lose the point and the power in careful phrases or policy obfuscation.

Julia Gillard was in a rare situation in terms of positional authority, from which she was able to draw attention to systemic discrimination. Why do you think it happens so rarely that high-profile leaders take a stand on a difference issue? How might you lead in drawing attention to discrimination without being in a similar position? This story shows how discrimination and domination can be systemic and yet remain unnamed and unnoticed. What other forms of discrimination or domination have you seen or experienced in today's organizations and communities?

The section above with its four categories of leadership practice was aimed at giving you, the student, a sense of the diversity of practices in leadership and difference that are possible. We've provided these examples that we have encountered and observed because we think they are inspiring and courageous. It also seems, though, that more modest, 'micro' practices of leadership often 'make a difference' to how difference is felt and experienced by others.

STOP AND REFLECT 7.5

Can you identify other examples – from your own context or the public arena – of leadership practices with significant positive impacts on appreciation of difference?

Making a difference to difference: Our own practices in leadership and difference

Amanda: At the start of this chapter, Michelle and I introduced ourselves, partially to help you understand where our interests in leadership and difference come from and how to 'read' what we say, given these interests. As we approach the end of the chapter we thought it might be helpful for you to know a bit more about how we've sought to 'make a difference' in the leadership and difference work we do. Our experiences and our advice to you are different. But they are both aimed at encouraging you to ask:

- How have my history and the narratives I've absorbed about who I am influenced my understanding and readiness to appreciate difference? How might this experience base be expanded?
- How has, and can, my leadership support the expression and celebration of difference?
- How might small leadership acts on my part, make a difference to the difference others experience?

Michelle: I'll begin. I wonder whether leadership and difference are irreconcilable paradigms, unable to sit comfortably together because of the different histories, assumptions and power contestations dwelling within each 'idea'. Conceptually, leadership is mostly an iconic, aspirational and positive identity many people strive to become, to own and to be. So what is the 'leadership and difference' space?

How do we conceive truly different ideas about leadership and how can we operate with difference without automatically being labelled as relevant only to those 'different' people we research? My own research has often been labelled culturally relativist. My work is generally of curious interest, yet colleagues can't readily work out ways to make the links between what they know, understand and think about as leadership from the literature and the way that I am presenting Indigenous narratives about how leadership is perceived and works in a variety of contexts, most importantly in a community framework. I approach leadership as primarily a process of building community, building spaces for community to gather, focusing more on the relational and social aspects of what individuals can do when they come together. I am also interested in creating platforms for community members and individuals to have a voice.

Amanda: Certainly I spent the first half of my career with a very ambivalent attitude to leadership. I had spent my professional and academic life in male-dominated organizations feeling like the 'odd one out', the one who did things differently, argued for different values and looked different. It was often a pretty debilitating and disempowering place to be – both placing myself and being routinely placed by others on the margin. Yet as I found my voice and started to speak up, initially about issues for women and the problems with executive culture that they encountered, it became clear that I was providing leadership. I was drawing attention to important discriminatory dynamics and I was working to change norms and practices.

Far from difference taking me away from leadership, I have found that in being different and voicing those experiences, I have sometimes provided leadership. For me then, difference and leadership go hand in hand. Rather than suppress my interests and experiences to 'look like a leader', leadership depends on me being attuned to difference – in myself and others.[1] A lot of my leadership work in the classroom with students and managers is about supporting individuals to understand how their different histories and narratives have shaped them. Part of this process is supporting people to value and voice their own experiences as leadership: to free them up from unhelpful narratives about themselves, and about how they should conform to be leaders. For me, the greatest satisfaction comes from seeing people allow their different experiences to feature in their leadership.

Conclusions

In this chapter we have highlighted that difference, diversity and leadership are all historically constructed concepts. They cannot be just studied as phenomena without appreciating their context: how they have arisen as ideas and gained momentum, and whose interests they have served. We have concluded that often those who are deemed different are not necessarily empowered by traditional processes of managing and leading difference and diversity, even those initiatives ostensibly aimed at 'inclusion'.

However, we believe that leadership can be an agent for the expression of the value and multiplicity of differences. The examples given show the range of ways that leaders can advocate for difference with or without formal authority. The chapter has echoed Ospina and Foldy's (2009) call for further study of difference as a particularly productive space for leadership research because we need to have a fuller understanding of the complexity and limitations of current formulations of leadership.

The key points in this chapter were ...

- Difference is tightly interwoven with dynamics of power. Even though things like 'managing diversity' appear to be working towards inclusion, they can reinforce privilege.
- Leadership is by no means exempt from this critique. It has a long history of being constructed in ways which privilege and empower some people over others. For example, it is often imbued with ideals of masculinity and Western individualism.
- Critical perspectives on leadership and diversity seek to engage more reflexively with power and privilege. Sometimes enacting diverse identities that challenge hegemonic or stereotypical ideas of difference can itself be a form of leadership.

---

1   For those who may be interested, the work of feminist Luce Irigaray similarly argues that acknowledging and working with difference, not 'merit' or 'equality' as defined by patriarchy, is a central philosophical challenge.

Further thinking

Ospina, S and Su, C. (2009). Weaving color lines: Race, ethnicity, and the work of leadership in social change organizations. *Leadership*, 5(2): 131–170.

- Describe some of the different relationships between race-ethnicity and leadership explored in Ospina and Su's article. How did the article extend your understanding of leadership?
- Ospina and Su propose that race-ethnicity is a building block that social change activists draw upon to mobilize leadership – can you describe an example 'on screen' of this way of doing leadership?

Warner, L.S. and Grint, K. (2006). American Indian ways of leading and knowing. *Leadership*, 2(2): 225–244.

- What do Warner and Grint believe are the benefits of deeply studying difference and leadership, in this case American Indian leadership?
- Why is understanding context important to the study of leadership?
- What are the benefits and the risks of presenting a model of American Indian leadership?

Leadership and difference on screen

Many films and especially Hollywood blockbusters like *Master and Commander* provide stereotypical views of leaders. We suggest screen alternatives here that challenge conventional notions of what leadership is, of who and how it is exercised. One first example is the film *Rabbit Proof Fence* (2002), based on a book by Doris Pilkington Garimara about the story of her mother being taken away from her Indigenous community and home as a three-year-old and taken to Moore River Mission. The film portrays the nineteenth- and twentieth-century Australian government practice of seizing Aboriginal children from their families and communities and placing them away from Indigenous influence. As well as being a very moving portrayal of the impact of these policies, the film is also about leadership. Those in conventional positions of authority in the film do not demonstrate leadership, but instead are agents of brutal and misguided government policy. Leadership, rather, is shown by the Aboriginal children, and particularly Molly, the oldest girl, who escape the Mission, and then for nine weeks and 1500 miles, evade the authorities to return to their homelands, following the rabbit-proof fence that ran north through Western Australia.

While *Rabbit Proof Fence* is a film based on real historical events, the TV series *Redfern Now* (2012, 2013: Blackfella Films) also provides examples of Indigenous leadership being done in community and family-centred ways. Largely written by, directed and starring Indigenous people, the series challenges stereotypes of Aboriginal people and their families, forcing viewers to get out of their comfort zone and bring new understanding of the obstacles that those seeking to exercise leadership in different ways encounter. For example, in the first episode of the first season 'Family', the main protagonist Grace demonstrates the tensions inherent in Indigenous leadership as she chooses to look after her niece and nephew when their mother is taken to hospital, rather than go on a planned family holiday with her immediate family. This episode surfaces tensions between Grace's own middle-class family and her sister's family who continue to struggle all sorts of disadvantage. Grace is a leader in the wider family, forced to make constant trade-offs while keeping a sense of the bigger picture of what's at stake. The two sets of children in this episode enact class differences and the episode highlights through the character of Grace, differences in cultural values and understandings of what family leadership often entails.

Our third example is the Danish TV series *Borgen* (2010, 2011, 2013). It portrays the coming to power of Birgitte Nyborg, a woman prime minister, who is initially head of a relatively minor moderate party. In contrast to many other TV series such as *Suits*, women in leadership in Borgen are portrayed in complex but embodied ways. They are not sexualized, or treated as supports to the main action, but are given agency to challenge traditional conventions of politics and leading. It is argued that Borgen is a case of life imitating art. Not long after the series aired in Denmark a woman prime minister was elected and some argued that the TV series increased public openness to, and sympathy for, having a woman in a top political leadership role.

STOP AND REFLECT 7.6

Think about the films you've seen and been influenced by, from *Star Wars* on. How have leaders been portrayed? Leadership scholars sometimes talk about 'distributed leadership'. By that they mean that the leadership work is distributed across different members of a group or team, who offer particular capabilities and strengths to suit changing circumstances. In the films you've seen, is there a pattern to the way leadership roles are distributed? Is the hero often a white male with supporting or 'side kick' roles played by black Americans, Asians or women? Even if the lead character is, as in *Hunger Games*, a young woman, is she portrayed as offering a different kind of leadership? More broadly, how influential do you think popular culture, such as films and TV series, are on our appetite for people doing leadership differently? Do they make it more possible for non-stereotypical leaders to disrupt conventional expectations?

8

STUDYING FOLLOWERS

Nancy Harding

Nancy is Professor of Organization Studies at Bradford School of Management. She was the first person in her family to go to university, and gets frustrated by the elitism she sees in much leadership theory.

What this chapter is all about …

The main idea is that followers are a typically neglected, and consequently often imagined, part of leadership studies. In contrast this chapter critically explores the way followers are constructed in the assumptions that underpin many leadership theories.

The key questions this chapter answers are:

- How can we undertake an in-depth analysis of a text (a transferable skill)?
- How can we think about followers and followers critically?
- What can we learn about leadership theories by thinking about followers?

Introduction

By definition, to be a leader one has to have followers. However, leadership theory has until recently had curiously little to say explicitly about followers. Followers feature in much of the vast body of research into leadership, if they appear at all, only in the passive role of rating leaders against lists of pre-defined characteristics (charisma, traits, competences, and so on). That is, followers are included in research studies largely as indicators of leader influence and effectiveness (Ford and Collinson, 2011; Bligh and Kohles, 2008; Jackson and Parry, 2011).

On the other hand, every leadership theory has an implicit theory about followers. In this chapter I will explore what leadership theory has to say about followers, and introduce you to ways of undertaking an in-depth analysis of what you read so that you can understand authors' implicit assumptions and decide whether or not you agree with them. This is another way of verifying the credibility of the theories you study in your undergraduate or postgraduate programme.

But first, let's carry out some research.

STOP AND REFLECT 8.1

Before you read any further, carry out a small piece of research

Ask three or four of your friends, colleagues or relatives the following questions:

- Can you think of someone you know as a leader, who you think you have willingly followed?
- Did you realize you were a follower at the time?
- What did it feel like?

Next: explore what they said

- What do they say about leaders?
- What do they say about followers?
- What do they say about themselves as followers?
- Have they thought about their relationships with people as 'leader/follower' relations?
- Is there any evidence that people are putting the labels of 'leader' and 'follower' onto concepts they previously

What have you found out about leaders and followers as a result of asking these questions?

Context

A person cannot, by definition, be a leader unless s/he has followers. Given the vast amount of research that has been carried out into leadership, you would expect that there would have been a great deal of research into followers – but you would be mistaken. Followers are noticeable in their absence from much leadership research. However, they are there in all leadership theories – they appear as the people who will be seduced by the charisma of the Great Leader, or who will fall in behind the leader's vision. But who is this person, the follower who is seduced or eager to set about achieving the vision? Why do they follow their leaders, what do they do as they go through the processes of following them and how are they personally affected by the leader? We have few answers to these questions, because very little research has been undertaken that answers them. The follower who appears in many theories of leadership is therefore imaginary.

STOP AND REFLECT 8.2

Can we have a good understanding of leadership if we know very little about followers?

My own answer to this question is: no, we cannot. We need to be able to understand such issues as staff attitudes to the people who are called 'leaders', whether or not they feel motivated to follow them, their experiences of working with leaders (good and bad), what we can learn from those experiences, and so on. By understanding what people called 'followers' think about people called 'leaders' we should have much richer theories of leadership, theories that could improve how people work together.

But we also need to know what people think about the identity of 'the follower'. Is it one that is welcomed and worked on, or is it one that is rejected because it says one person is superior and the other inferior? There are some hints that no one wants to be known as a follower (Jackson and Parry, 2011), and also some hints that very few people have ever worked with someone they would describe as an influential leader. One manager in a study I carried out with Jackie Ford and others said he imagined that if he visited an organization famous for its leadership he would

> simply wander around like on another planet going 'shit', you know, 'this is far out'. There is something about the quality of the light and what those people are doing over there. … What's this thing about the quality of the light in the place why does it seem brighter? – what is it? – are you nearer the sun on this bit of the planet? – what is it about?

> (Harding et al., 2011, p. 935)

He lamented that he had never worked with a person who could make the office light up in such a way. People often have difficulty in identifying people (including people with whom they have worked, teachers, members of sports teams, etc.) who they would regard as good leaders. Can you? How have the leaders you have known made you feel about yourself as a follower?

 ## STOP AND REFLECT 8.3

Complete the following table, considering:

- a list of the people you have met who you would describe as poor leaders, those you would describe as good leaders and those you would describe as great leaders. What is it that makes them poor, good or great?
- Now, thinking of these people, what was their impact on *you*? How did they make you feel?

Poor leaders' names	Their effect on you
Good leaders' names	Their effect on you
Great leaders' names	Their effect on you

What does your experience tell you about leadership and followers?

Given that we know so little about followers, a chapter in this textbook could be a very short one! But that would be to ignore how important it is to find out what the imaginary follower in various leadership theories looks like. When we know that, we can discuss the influence this imaginary figure has on the theory itself, because the theory may be influencing what people do when they are at work. If someone sets themselves up as a leader using theories that have not been tested in practice, they may do all sorts of damage to the people over whom they have power.

Structure of the chapter

First, I will summarize some of the comparatively sparse literature on followers. Second, I will encourage you to go and watch an all-action film to see how leaders and followers are depicted in them – what does this tell us about people's attitudes to being followers? Third, I will introduce a way of finding out about the imaginary followers in various leadership theories. Finally, I will suggest you choose a theory of leadership you like, and explore what it implies about 'the follower'.

Thinking and writing on followers/ship

Background

The majority of the vast literature on leadership focuses on identifying ways in which leaders can encourage better performance from followers. Much theoretical and empirical (largely quantitative) research has explored leaders and leadership, and especially the forms that leadership should take if followers are to be encouraged to give of their best to their employing organizations. There has been much less emphasis on followership, although there is currently a surge in interest in followers and followership. Indeed, by 2008 there were sufficient discussions of followers to allow Bligh and Kohles (2008) to review the literature and report that articles on followers fall into three broad categories: (i) follower attributes that are pertinent to the leadership process, including such constructs as perceptions, identity, affect, motivations and values; (ii) leader–follower relations including the active role played by followers on the leadership dynamic; and (iii) follower outcomes of leadership behaviour, including performance, creativity or other dependent variables and effects that leaders have on followers. However, there is a tendency amongst theorists of followers/ship to either replace leader-centrism with follower-centrism or to keep the dualism in place but give primacy to followers (Collinson, 2006).

This means that the emergent field of followers/ship studies mimics leader-centric studies in homogenizing its subjects, so reducing people given the identity of 'follower' to a one-dimensional object, much like a minor cartoon character that exists only as a foil to the main characters (Ford et al., 2008). Critical thinkers accuse dominant approaches to the study of both leadership and followership of ignoring context, complexities, multiple and shifting identities, and, most of all, power dynamics (Ford et al., 2008; Collinson, 2014). That is, as we will see, the emergent body of literature on followers/ship recognizes the active role of the follower in working with the leader, but it has inherited leadership theories' uncritical stance, notably in ignoring context, identities and power.

Let us start with an early example of thinking about followers/ship, that of Burns (1978) who advocated a values-based and shared model between leaders and followers in which leaders and followers morally elevate each other. Burns argued that if leaders recognized the higher-order needs of followers they would be able to develop 'a relationship of mutual stimulation and elevation that converts followers into leaders and may convert leaders into moral agents' (Burns, 1978, p. 4). This did not actually tell us much about followers, only that they might have 'higher order needs'.

Kelley (1992) developed one of the first explicit theories of followership through introducing the concept of exemplary followers, that is, followers who are active, independent and critical thinkers. These followers, he argued, tend to have strong values and to be the courageous conscience of the organization. Kelley's approach is therefore normative – it tells us how followers should behave. It does not tell us how they do behave. This applies also to Challeff (1998) who argued that leaders and followers have complementary roles in which they serve a common purpose.

More famously, Meindl (1995) advanced the case for a follower-centred approach to leadership studies. He supports the 'romance of leadership notion' (Meindl et al., 1985) that 'embraces the phenomenological significance of leadership to people's organizational experiences' (1995, p. 330), and sees it as a 'point of departure' for emphasizing followers and contexts for understanding leadership. The romance of leadership, he observes, is about how followers think about, and thus construct and represent, leaders in their minds; it is also about how the relationship between leaders and followers is constructed. This is important: Meindl opens the door to exploring leader/follower interactions not from the leader's avowed aims and actions, but from how the follower interprets those aims and actions.

 STOP AND REFLECT 8.4

What is the difference between intended actions and how those actions are understood? Can you think of a time when you aimed to do something but your actions were totally misinterpreted by someone else? Or where you misinterpreted what someone else was aiming to do? This is what Meindl was discussing: what a leader thinks they are doing may be very different from how followers perceive their actions or statements.

This implies that (a) charisma does not emanate from a leader but exists in the minds of followers who see the leader as charismatic; (b) it is interactions between followers that influence how a leader is regarded; and (c) context is important. Thus 'Leadership is considered to have emerged when followers construct their experiences in terms of leadership concepts' (Meindl, 1995, p. 332). That is, 'the leader' is no more than a manager, a supervisor or a bossy person until staff identify their relationship with that person as one between leader(s) and follower(s). Leadership emerges from the subjective perspectives of followers, Meindl argued, concluding that this allows for future research based on the formulation of testable hypotheses. Now, we could quarrel with the assumption that subjective experiences can be explored through the testing of hypotheses: this requires quantitative methods that do not lend themselves to exploring subjectivities but instead impose meaning on people completing the survey. But Meindl's challenge to leader-centric perspectives raises important questions about the need to more explicitly consider the role of the follower in the 'construction' of leadership (Bligh et al., 2007, p. 268) (to which we would add the need to understand the effect of the construct of 'leadership' on organizational subjects). This nascent follower-centred approach to leadership (Shamir et al., 2007) recognizes the interdependence of leadership and active followership, located within a symbiotic relationship between leader and followers that is held together by trust and loyalty and rooted in the leader's commitment to ethical standards. Meindl's paper (1995) led to a burgeoning of research into followership.

A very useful overview of this post-Meindlian research is given in Bligh et al. (2011) who summarized the research undertaken into 'the romance of leadership' in the wake of Meindl's paradigm-shifting paper. These studies tend to explore how follower-attributes influence their perceptions of leaders, and they show that:

- Knowledge of successful outcomes leads to charismatic attributions, irrespective of the leader's actual charisma, suggesting that there is a halo effect.
- There is evidence that merely being given the title of leader leads followers to perceive that person differently. That is, 'followers' psychological readiness to comprehend events in terms of leadership may play an important role' in determining how leaders are regarded (Bligh et al., 2011, p. 1067) such that it is now established that followers play 'an active role in the leadership process' (p. 1068).

Bligh et al. (2011) note 'the continued importance of examining follower perceptions in evaluating leadership, and suggest caution in taking leadership ratings at face value without considering follower needs, perceptions, motivations and biases' (p. 1068). This conclusion, unfortunately, ignores Meindl's advice that individuals cannot be regarded as followers unless they themselves allocate themselves with that identity. Much of the research cited by Bligh et al. (2011) is carried out through surveys of large numbers of people, and the researchers identify people in their samples as 'followers' and thus impose the identity of followers on them.

STOP AND REFLECT 8.5

If you were asked to fill in a questionnaire that asked you, 'How does your leader influence how you feel about your job?', how would you answer?

(a) My leader makes me feel great/average/awful about my job.
(b) Hey, hang on a minute – you are implying I relate to someone I call a 'leader' and therefore you are turning me into a 'follower'.

Most of us fill out forms in the ways we have been requested to do so few of us would answer (b).

Or if we are tempted to answer (b) there is no room on the survey. It forces us to answer a question about leadership and the leader's effects.

One outcome of the studies discussed by Bligh et al. (2011) is the emergence of implicit followership theory (IFT). IFT is defined as 'individuals' personal assumptions about the traits and behaviours that characterize followers' (Sy, 2010, p. 74). These are 'lay' or 'naïve' theories, but are believed to influence relationships in practice, because leaders are understood to compare followers to an ideal(ized) follower that exists in their minds, and treat the follower accordingly, regardless of how that person actually behaves. There is also a body of work labelled implicit leadership theory (ILT) that explores leaders' unspoken assumptions about leadership. Studies into these unspoken, unarticulated theories of what sort of person a leader or follower is are not very complimentary to followers. De Vries and van Gelder (2005), for example, argue that leaders are generally imagined to be wonderful, super-human people, but followers are imagined as the very opposite. Table 8.1 shows what studies of IFT suggest.

Table 8.1

Implicit theories of leaders imagine that:	Implicit theories of followers imagine that:
Leaders are efficacious and able to bring about change.	Followers are inefficacious and would not function without leaders.
Leaders are sensitive, dedicated, charismatic, intelligent, masculine and strong.	Followers are passive and dependent.
Leaders are heroic, famous and successful.	Followers are ineffectual subordinates.
Leaders are powerful, influential, prestigious, knowledgeable and have high status.	Followers are (or should be) obedient, deferential, silent and powerless.

Central to IFTs are prototypes, or 'abstract composites of the most representative member of the most commonly shared attributes of a particular category' (De Vries and van Gelder, 2005). Some prototypes are based on descriptions (how followers are) and some on norms (how followers should act). Research into IFTs has shown:

- Individual characteristics such as race, gender or culture influence IFTs.
- Context influences IFTs, so that in successful companies followers' characteristics are regarded more positively by leaders.
- They not only influence how leaders relate to followers, but they shape followers' actions accordingly. So, someone whose leader presumes they perform effectively will perform effectively.
- A leader's style may be a function of his/her predisposed assumptions about followers (e.g. a leader may become autocratic if they presume, without evidence, that their staff are incompetent). (Sy, 2010)

In sum, IFTs may influence leaders' and followers' interactions, but the ways in which they influence them are not understood. ILTs that explore followers' implicit understanding about and expectations of leaders are believed, when brought together in the organization, to socially constitute 'a dynamic leadership process' that leads to a definition of leadership as 'an ongoing, dynamic, two-way exchange between leaders and followers that is structured by both parties' implicit theories' (Shondrik et al., 2010, p. 959). This body of research, often referred to as 'the social construction of followership', hints at how complex are the interactions between leaders and followers (or those given those labels).

Meindl (1995) argued that the leader/follower relationship is a social construction, one that he thought could be explored using quantitative research methods. There is now a body of research that has attempted to build on his idea. Shondrik et al. (2010, p. 967), for example, define the social construction of followership as:

> the emergence of a leadership relationship that occurs when (1) a potential leader perceives or infers a group of individuals to be his or her followers or (2) when individuals in a group begin to view themselves as members of a larger group led by a leader. Rather than being confined to the role of a passive participant under the control of a leader, followers are able to actively construct and shape the leader's perceptions and their self-perceptions through interactions with the leader and each other.

This is more complicated than it seems, because this perspective argues that language and the visual are involved in sensemaking in what are embodied interactions between people who experience emotions and feelings, and who bring with them to the leader/follower encounter their own memories, psyches, expectations, and so on. For example, research has shown that merely being classified as a leader changes people's perceptions of that person, while how a person looks can also influence how they are perceived as leaders (or followers?). This is 'abstract' knowledge that is difficult to explore through surveys and questionnaires, but it is very active in leader/follower processes where embodied agents attempt to understand a context even as they are creating meaning within it (Shondrik et al., 2010).

Carsten et al. (2010) similarly explore the social construction of followership, arguing that the focus should be on how followers view their own, rather than their leaders', behaviours. Not to do this is to continue to place leadership at the centre of research, they argue. Their study therefore aimed to explore individuals' 'followership schemas' or 'generalised knowledge structures that develop over time through socialization and interaction with stimuli relative to leadership and followership' (p. 546), within the organizational context in which they construct follower identities. They were able to identify three contrasting categories of followers: passive (who emphasized doing things 'the leader's way'), active (who saw leadership and followership more as teamwork) and proactive (who wished to take on a role very similar to that of leadership). Passive followers emphasized deference and obedience, active followers emphasize partnership, while proactive followers emphasize constructive challenge and voice. Only passive followers appeared to feel comfortable working with authoritarian leaders. Carsten et al. (2010) therefore conclude that there is no single, homogeneous view of followership amongst people who are followers.

However, it must be noted that by asking study participants to talk about themselves as followers (or leaders), the researchers are actively positioning participants within an identity category within which they may actively constitute that identity. This leads to the question of whether research into followers/ ship actually constitutes that which it is exploring. Does 'the follower' exist as a self-identity until someone is asked to account for themselves as a follower? These questions are pertinent to Collinson's (2006) post-structuralist exploration of followership, which questions 'the notions of voluntary and freely chosen followership that inform much thinking on follower identity and followership more generally' (p. 182).

Collinson's (2006) approach points to 'an ineluctable ambiguity at the heart of identity construction' (p. 182); that is, each person is not just *one* static identity but is a self that is actively constituted and that can be many selves. We are all of us both subjects (active agents in the world that have subjectivities) and objects (we can look at ourselves and reflect on our self as if we were someone else).

STOP AND REFLECT 8.6

As you sit and read this chapter, who are you?

How different is this 'you' from the 'you' you will be when you are with your friends or family, or out socializing?

We may resist the identities that organizations (or leaders, or managers) attempt to impose on us, although most leadership theory ignores this (Ford et al., 2008). Collinson (2006) uses post-structural theories of identity to suggest that current theories of followers and followership:

- ignore the conflicts, ambiguities and tensions that may be involved in being called a follower;
- are unaware of the multiple ways in which it is possible to enact followership and constitute the identity of follower. Collinson (2006) identifies three follower identities: conformist (conforming to a blueprint of the 'ideal' follower), resistant (refusing to conform to managerial and leadership demands, or undermining them) and dramaturgical (using impression management to give the appearance of being a good follower through various tactics. However, these identities cannot be mapped onto different individuals (as in Carsten et al.'s 2010 study), because we will all conform, resist and project an imaginary self, sometimes in the same instant.

Summary

After decades in which research into followers/ship was marginal to leadership studies, there is now an increasing level of interest in followers. While much research into followers is uncritical and can be accused of creating that which it is supposedly studying, there are moves towards more sophisticated thinking that explores the complexities of interactions between 'leaders' and 'followers'. However, this body of research does not question these categories – leadership and followership are presumed to exist, somewhere out there. Kelly (2014, but see also Chapter 9) challenges this notion. He argues for a negative ontology of leadership. There have been no empirical studies of leadership and followership, he contends. There are studies of managers and staff interacting, but when does this merge into leadership and followership? How would we know leadership and followership in interaction if we saw it? Does this mean that leadership and followership does not exist in organizations? Is it nothing more than something that is researched and written about, so exists on the written page but not in the real world?

 # Leadership on screen: Identifying ways in which followership is enacted

It is time now to do your own research. It may be impossible to observe leadership and followership in action in the material world of organizations. But it definitely exists in films and television programmes.

- Try one of the *X-Men* films – who is the leader and how is that leadership practised? Who, then, are the followers, and how do you know they are followers? What makes them different from the leader?
- If you're a fan of the *X-Men* series of films and have watched them from the beginning you will have seen how one of the less important characters in the earlier films, Wolverine, played by Hugh Jackman, evolves into the major leader/hero as the series progresses. Why is this? Can you use leadership and followership to explain the emergence of Wolverine as a leader? Does his emergence as leader mean the previous leader is now a follower?
- Alternatively try one of the *Fast and Furious* films. A strong theme in these films is 'family', but one person is the leader and others the followers. What marks the followers out as followers rather than leaders?
- Alternatively, choose a film of one of Shakespeare's tragedies, such as *Hamlet*, *Macbeth* or *King Lear*. In the tragedies the leader is a figure doomed to failure and despair, but still they have followers. Why would someone continue to follow Lear after he has become mad, or Macbeth after it has become known that he is a murderer? What does Shakespeare tell us about followership?

STOP AND REFLECT 8.7

Choose a film or television programme that has a lot of adventure in it, where heroes have to struggle to survive and (usually) emerge victorious. Choose a film or programme in which the hero has a band of supporters or followers with her/him on this epic journey.

Watch this film or programme at least twice. First, watch it and make notes of its scenes and actions – who does what, when, with and to whom? Who did you identify with? Write the story of the film from the hero's (or leader's) perspective.

Next, watch the film or programme again, and note any interactions between the hero and other characters that are on his/her side. Watch it closely. Freeze-frame parts of it so that you can get an in-depth insight into what is going on on the screen. This time, what you need to do is focus on the story from the followers' perspective. After you have watched the film or programme for a second time, write its story from the perspective of a follower – what are you doing, with and to whom, and what happens to you?

Finally, write an account that summarizes the lessons of exploring the story from the hero's (leader's) perspective and from the followers' perspective. What does this tell you about leadership and followership?

For example, Jackie Ford and I (2010) examined Homer's ancient tale of the *Odyssey* from the perspective of a crew member. There are numerous films based on the *Odyssey*. We were struck by the dark side, rather than the heroism, of the great tale. We read not of Odysseus' heroism but of his selfishness, dereliction of duty, and disregard for and denigration of those for whom he had responsibility. Indeed, through exploring this darkness at the heart of the earliest account of leadership and how that account continues to inform today's metaphors and stories, we suggested that leadership does not rescue organizations from the inabilities of managers, but rather hampers passion, creativity, and much else besides. We first summarized the *Odyssey* not through Odysseus' adventures but those that befell his crew.

The adventures of Odysseus' crew

The story starts at the end of the Trojan War, when Odysseus sets out to return to his home in Ithaca. He leads several ships of soldiers who, we may presume, are similarly keen to return home. They are not to know that it is only Odysseus who will set foot once again on Ithaca, for the many adventures they will meet along the way will result in their decimation. Many men are lost in a battle at their first port of call, the island of the Cicones. The survivors return to their ships and make land next at the island of the Lotus-Eaters. The small scouting party ate the lotus and decided they wished to stay, indulging in a life of intoxicated wonder. We can only imagine their feelings after they have been dragged back to the ship and prevented from swimming back to the island. That the crew have been banned from eating is a presaging of later prohibitions: should they drink wine they will be turned to swine, and should they listen to music they will go mad. Only Odysseus, the boss, the leader, is allowed such luxuries.

On the travellers go, to the island of the Cyclops. They come across a cave and feast on some of the sheep they find there. Polyphemus, a one-eyed giant, returns to the cave and imprisons them. The men, having eaten, are punished by themselves being eaten – Polyphemus chooses two each day for his dinner. Odysseus, of course, is not one of these, and it is his cleverness, Homer tells us, that saves the skins of himself and his crew who, after Odysseus has blinded Polyphemus, are smuggled out tied to the stomachs of sheep. At Telepylos most of the remaining men are eaten, speared or stoned by giants. Only the crew on the ship with Odysseus are saved, but they are soon to arrive at Aeaea, where the enchantress Circe gives the scouting party wine that turns them into swine. We see again how Odysseus' crew are denied the pleasures of the flesh, here wine, that Odysseus is able to indulge in. He spends a year as Circe's lover while his followers wait around. On they eventually go, and the next thing they are to be denied is listening to the unbearably beautiful (albeit deadly) voices of the Sirens. Odysseus, of course, can listen as he has his men deafen themselves by stopping their ears with beeswax. At Scylla and Charybdis six men have to be eaten by the six-headed monster, the Scylla, in order that the rest can pass safely by. But when they get to the next island, Helio, all these men die. Odysseus is left alone but he makes it back to Ithaca.

Leadership contains, in this earliest recounting, a promise to followers of only horror, failure, betrayal, disappointment and denial. We are told that followers are incapable of agency unless organized by a leader, but is it not the case that without his crew Odysseus literally could not have sailed between the Greek islands? Without his crew Odysseus is revealed to be incapable. We can imagine one of his crew telling his story:

> The crew had waited interminably for Odysseus to continue the journey home to Ithaca, but Odysseus was bewitched on this enchanted island until one day we saw our chance. Circe was away. The lads begged me to go to Odysseus and to tempt him with thoughts of his home, his wife and son, so that he would agree we could leave that fated island and return to Ithaca. He eventually gave in, but blow me down if he did not find another reason for delay, and another, and another. And all along the way he was enjoying himself, while our number of men dwindled until only a few of us now remain. I have a foreboding about the future. I fear none of us will return to Ithaca.

Western culture's foundational stories, originating in Ancient Greece, therefore contain images of followership as that where people are silenced, denigrated, infantilized, disempowered, denied and are, ultimately, disposable. This leads to the question: is this true of leadership theory today? To do this, we need to explore the implicit theories of followership that inform contemporary theories of leadership.

Identifying the implicit theories of followership in leadership theory

We explored above implicit followership theory; that is, lay theories of followership held by men and women within organizations. What is missing from those accounts is any questioning of the theories of followership that are implicit in leadership theory. Our next task is therefore to learn how to dig out those implicit theories. This involves in-depth analysis of a written text, a transferable skill that you can use over and over again in your working lives.

I will:

1 outline a model for analysing theories of leadership to identify their implicit theories of followership;
2 apply this paper to a seminal paper on leadership so that you can see a 'worked example';
3 and, finally, ask you to identify a paper on leadership theory that you think is interesting, and identify for yourself the implicit theory of followership that underpins the arguments in that paper.

Method of analysis

The method of analysis I am outlining here is a basic form of deconstruction that involves the following:

(a) Summarizing the arguments of a text.

(b) Identifying the binary opposites in the text. Based on Jacques Derrida's work, the identification of the binary opposites in texts makes explicit what is implicit and shows upon what assumptions a text's arguments rest. Identifying binary opposites involves looking for the major words used in the text, and then identifying the opposites to these words. The theory is that the dominant word does not make sense without the existence of its opposite. So, for example, we would not know what 'night' was without there being 'day'; we would not know what 'woman' is if there is a not a man to compare her with (to say that she is 'not man').

(c) Writing the story that is told from the perspective of the dominant side of the binary, and then from the subordinate side.

(d) Analysing the inconsistencies between the two.

In this chapter we will read Bass and Steidlmeier's seminal account 'Ethics, character and authentic transformational leadership behavior' (1999). It will help if you download a copy of this paper to read and work through as you read the following.

Bass and Steidlmeier (1999) advocate authentic transformational leadership as an ethical organizational identity. Authentic transformational leaders (ATLs), they argue, have moral characters, values embedded in their vision that are ethically legitimate, and they lead followers in moral processes and actions. The ATL uses influence processes, while followers use empowerment processes to engage in 'dynamic self-transformation' (p. 183). Followers wish to emulate their leaders because of charisma or idealized influence, the inspirational motivation and intellectual stimulation provided by the ATL, and individualized consideration that they provide (p. 184). The authors suggest that (p. 186):

> it is a matter of modern Western moral concern that ideals not be imposed, that behavior not be coerced, and that the search for truth not be stifled. Ethical norms and behavioral ideals should not be imposed but freely embraced. Motivation should not be reduced to coercion but grow out of authentic inner commitment. Questioning and creativity should be encouraged. Followers should not be mere means to self-satisfying ends for the leader but should be treated as ends in themselves. We label as inauthentic or 'pseudo' that kind of transformational leadership that tramples upon those concerns.

They argue that both leaders and led are transformed by the relationship (p. 186), although the distinction between authentic and pseudo-transformational leadership rests on the presence or absence of moral foundations (p. 186). Bass and Steidlmeier therefore set up a distinction between authentic and pseudo-transformational leadership.

Stage one: Summarizing the paper's arguments

Our first task therefore is to read their paper in depth, and to identify the distinctions they draw between authentic and inauthentic forms of transformational leadership. These are summarized in Table 8.2.

Table 8.2 Distinctions between authentic and inauthentic transformational leadership

	Authentic transformational leadership – ideals for their followers	Inauthentic or pseudo-transformational leadership – idols of their followers
Charisma or idealized influence	Envisioning, confident, sets high standards for emulation.	Seek power and position, and indulge in fantasies of power and success.
	Values: universal brotherhood. Promote ethical policies, procedures and processes. Must 'eventuate in the internalization in all the organization's members of shared moral standards' (p. 188)	Values: grandiose, fictitious we-they relationships that divide.
		Inconsistent and unreliable. False to organization's purpose. Outer shell of authenticity but it is a mask.
Inspirational motivation	Focus on the best in people, and harmony, charity and good works.	Focuses on the worst in people, on demonic plots, conspiracies, unreal dangers, excuses and insecurities.
	Empowerment to transform the person.	Talk about empowerment but only to seek control.
	Inwardly and outwardly concerned about the good of everyone.	May give impression of concern for the good, may be idealized by their followers, but inwardly concerned only about the good for themselves.
Intellectual stimulation	Openness, with a transcendent and spiritual dimension, allows followers to question assumptions and generate more creative solutions. Altruism is a fundamental question.	Uses a logic of false assumptions to 'slay the dragons of uncertainty, take credit for other's ideas, scapegoat them for failure. Use anecdotes rather than hard evidence. Charlatans who feed on the ignorance of their followers.
	Use persuasion to convince others on the merits of issues. Bring about change in followers' values by the merit and relevancy of their ideas.	Manipulate the values of followers. Only does the right thing when it coincides with their self-interest. Intolerant of other views, substituting emotional argumentation for rational discourse.
Individualized consideration	Underscores necessity of altruism. Treats each follower as an individual, coaches and mentors. Concerned about developing their followers into leaders. Promote attainable shared goals. Helps followers to develop their leadership skills.	Concerned with maintaining the dependence of their followers. Exploit followers' feelings to maintain deference. Expect blind obedience. Encourage fantasy and magic. Foments favouritism and competition among followers. Seeks a parent–child relationship.
	Channel their need for power into the service of others.	Uses power for self-aggrandisement. Privately contemptuous of those they are 'supposed to be serving as leaders' (p. 189). Public image (that of saviours) contradicts their private selves.

	Authentic transformational leadership – ideals for their followers	Inauthentic or pseudo-transformational leadership – idols of their followers
Followers' position – stated	'[I]nner dynamics of a freely embraced change of heart in the realm of core values and motivation, open-ended intellectual stimulation and commitment to treating people as ends not mere means' (p. 192). They will learn the values of justice, equality and human rights. Will develop an inner ethical core in which self-interest is secondary. Follower–leader distinction should wither away (p. 200), as 'true consensus in aligning individual and organizational interests' (p. 207).	Leaders value racial superiority, submission and Social Darwinism so followers will too. Followers are fantasists who engage in the leaders' fantasies.
Followers' position – implicit	Empty vessels waiting to be filled with goodness by the leader/teacher, much as happens in cults. However, less valued than shareholders, senior management and continuity of the organization (p. 204), but the successful ATL develops them so that they become ATLs themselves.	Gullible vessels easily taken in by appearances, who do not realize they are being used and exploited.

Stage two: Identifying the binary opposites in the text

Bass and Steidlmeier (1999) have already done this for us, in their distinction between authentic and inauthentic leadership. Indeed, if you read their paper yourselves, you will see that the only way they can define authentic transformational leadership is through what they see as its opposite, inauthentic transformational leadership. However, they are not the only authors to have to rely on a 'binary opposite' to arrive at a definition – if you look at other seminal papers that introduce new forms of leadership, you will see they often adopt this strategy.

Stage three: Writing the story from the perspective of the authentic transformational leader

As an ATL, I wish that my followers model themselves on me, because I am a highly moral person. If they do this, then they will become my mirror-image. But if they do that then, because they are as good as me, they will become ATLs in their own turn. That means I will no longer be their leader, because we will all be leaders together.

However, how can I be sure that the followers who become my mirror-image are authentic and not wearing a mask and playing a role as if they were authentic? It is really difficult to distinguish between the two, because the inauthentic ATL wears a mask that gives the impression of authenticity. What if I foster someone who is inauthentic? There is no way in which I can distinguish between someone who is genuinely authentic and someone who is giving the impression of being authentic. I must therefore ensure that anyone who would be an ATL works very hard at proving themselves to be authentic. The true ATL must overcome all human weaknesses, therefore I must look for followers who have no such weaknesses. If they hide their human weaknesses then they are not authentic. But – wait a minute – everyone has some weaknesses. So to be authentic, followers must hide those weaknesses, and in hiding them they must be inauthentic.

What we see by rewriting the story is therefore the impossibility of being authentic. This is what is implicit in Bass and Steidlmeier's paper: they set up the pseudo-ATL and the ATL as opposites, so that if one is not authentically transformational then one must be pseudo-ATL. There is no half-way house, no position from which one can examine one's self in one's full glory as a complex, riven human being, with weaknesses as well as strengths. Philosophers and thinkers through the centuries have explored the complexities of the human psyche and soul, and the impossibility of being truly good. To be authentic requires that one examines one's self and identifies one's weaknesses and failings, and all the things that cause the terrible internal voice to continually chastise us about our failings. It is a struggle to be good, or decent, or efficient, or whatever, and even saints acknowledge their shortcomings. To not do this is to be inauthentic. Indeed, to be authentic requires that one refuses to be a role model for one's followers, and refuses to ask them for recognition of the self as ATL. Rather, we must ask them to recognize our human failing.

Therefore, to become an authentic transformational leader requires that one acknowledges that it is impossible to be an authentic transformational leader. The identity is destroyed by its own foundations.

And have you noticed that the follower disappears from Bass and Steidlmeier's paper, even though they are the ostensible object of the ATL's attention? They appear only as empty vessels waiting to be filled with the ATL's qualities. That means that the leader must not recognize followers are individuals with their own needs, identities, wishes and aspirations. Instead, the ATL must seek to make them conform to their own ideals, but there is no evidence that their own ideals are superior to everyone else's. The follower is therefore no more than an empty vessel who waits being filled by the leader's authenticity.

Conclusion

Authentic and inauthentic transformational leaders are set up by Bass and Steidlmeier (1999) as the binary opposites of each other, but within the terms of their own arguments, if analysed closely, lies the weakness that destroys that argument. The ATL has to be like a saint who is without sin, but no human being is that perfect. To claim to be authentic is therefore to tell a lie, and so to be inauthentic. Authentic transformational leadership is impossible.

The key points in this chapter were ...

- Followers have been a neglected part of leadership studies, to the extent leadership theories tend to include followers as a sort of implicit imaginary figure.
- When we critically analyse the implicit assumptions around followers in leadership theories, we often find that they are depicted as inefficacious, passive and powerless.
- In contrast to this, critical theories of followership foreground identity, context and power – all of which highlight the complexity around the social process of leadership. We can see that leadership is not merely as simple as just what the leader does.
- We can analyse leadership (and other) texts by looking for the binary opposites implicit in the arguments. We can also explore texts by writing the story from the perspectives of different people (such as the leader or followers).

Further thinking

Shondrik, S. J., Dinh, J. E. and Lord, R. G. (2010). Developments in implicit leadership theory and cognitive science: applications to improving measurement and understanding alternatives to hierarchical leadership. *The Leadership Quarterly*, 26(6), 959–978.

Questions:

1 What is the implicit theory of leadership that underpins how academics rather than managers think about leadership?
2 Think of your own experience of being a follower to a leader – could you measure that person's impact on you? If so, how?
3 How can you use your own experience of being influenced by another person that you might call 'a leader' – what lessons did you learn from them that will inform how you lead others in the future?

Kelly, S. (2014). Towards a negative ontology of leadership. *Human Relations*, 67(8), 905–922.

1   What is 'negative ontology'? The language and concepts in this paper are difficult to understand. Using a dictionary of philosophical terms or any on-line source that helps you interpret Kelly's paper, write a summary of the paper in plain English.

2   Now that you have translated this paper into plain English, what critique would you offer of Kelly's paper?

Meindl, J. R. (1995). The romance of leadership as a follower-centric theory: A social constructionist approach. *The Leadership Quarterly*, 6, 329–341.

1   Meindl claims to use a social constructionist approach. Based on your reading from other chapters of this textbook, do you agree that he is using social constructionism? Or is he closer to a functionalist, interpretive, dialogical, or critical approach? How and why?

2   Is there any 'romance' in leader/follower interactions? What happens if we introduce power into our explorations of leader/follower interactions? Does it become something shadier than 'romance'? If so, what? If you re-wrote the 'romance of leadership' through this gloomier perspective, what would your arguments be?

Contemporary Perspectives

Contents

9

LEADERSHIP AND PROCESS

Simon Kelly

Simon grew up on a diet of superhero comics and science fiction, which is probably why as an adult he is fascinated by leaders and leadership. Having finally accepted that superheroes and Jedi knights (probably) don't exist, his research explores the relationship between leadership and the heroic, and the practical and ethical potential of rethinking leadership as collective action.

What this chapter is all about …

This chapter explores some of the reasons why leadership theories often over simplify and reduce leadership to an entity or discrete 'characteristic' or 'thing' that can be supposedly seen or possessed. Alternatively, a process perspective opens up our thinking by imagining leadership as something much more complicated, distributed, and interwoven within a specific historical and organizational context.

The key questions this chapter answers are:

- How is thinking about process different to other ways of thinking?
- Why is it difficult to think in terms of process?
- What might leadership look like from a process perspective?
- Why is it important to think about leadership as process?

Introduction

As each of the chapters in this book argues, leadership is about more than special individuals and the labels that become attached to them as indexes of their personalities, strengths, weaknesses and achievements. Rather, leadership involves ongoing relationships with *others* and those others must comply and consent to being led. Without such consent and the legitimacy that comes with it, it would be impossible to hold a meaningful position of leadership for very long. The aim of this chapter is to draw attention to the importance of these relational *others* in the production and continuation of leadership. In doing so the chapter explores how *leading as process* means moving away from 'human-centric' notions of leaders, followers, and shared goals, and towards an acknowledgment of leadership's collective and open-ended character. From here it is then possible to rethink leadership as an ongoing and interconnected series of overlapping systems, practices, people, stories, institutions, histories, objects, spaces, places and technologies.

Thinking about leadership as something made up of lots of interconnecting parts rather than one large whole – that is as something *heterogeneous* rather than *homogeneous* – is quite a challenge and so requires some radical and alternative perspectives. In this chapter you will be presented with a range of different perspectives, cases, tools and techniques for how to think 'processually' and what benefit this style of thinking might have for understanding, researching and practising leadership. The chapter is structured around the following themes:

- *Turning to process thinking*: how to make a shift from thinking about entities or 'things' to thinking about movement, flow, interaction and collective activity. Here we will look at some unusual examples that illustrate both the benefits and challenges of thinking about process.
- *Leadership as socially constructed*: Here we will look at some of the alternative paradigms for studying leadership – namely that leadership is not necessarily a psychological property of a person, but is more often experienced as a complex and socially produced practice or activity.
- *Leadership in action*: Having outlined the theoretical and methodological case for researching leadership as a social process rather than psychological property, the last section of the chapter will present three case examples that illustrate the processual character of leading and being led. Here we deliberately look to some unorthodox organizational settings that explore the subtle and fluid nature of *organizing* in settings as diverse as classical orchestras, dances and commercial airlines. These three examples together demonstrate some exciting and important emerging themes in contemporary leadership research and we will examine the intellectual insights and practical benefits that an understanding of these processes might offer.

Process thinking: Achilles and the tortoise

Absolute continuity of motion is incomprehensible to the human mind. (Tolstoy, 1869/1952, p. 469)

Let's start our investigation of leadership and process from a very unusual place. In his epic Russian novel *War and Peace*, Leo Tolstoy begins one of his chapters by describing a fundamental problem with the way that we as human beings experience process. The world we are born into and in which we must live out our lives is constantly in motion, always changing and never fixed. Yet for humans it is impossible to ever experience this world directly because in order to experience process we must first interpret it and in so doing turn process into a *thing*; into an *entity*. To illustrate this fundamental problem Tolstoy recites a riddle first used by the ancient Greek philosopher Zeno of Elea, a riddle that at first sight may seem absurd. The great warrior Achilles – who in Ancient Greek mythology was part-man, part-god: a kind of superhero of the day – is in a running race with a tortoise. However, try as he might, no matter how quickly Achilles moves he cannot overtake the tortoise. As Tolstoy explains:

There is a well-known, so-called sophism of the ancients consisting in this, that Achilles could never catch up with a tortoise he was following, in spite of the fact that he travelled ten times as fast as the tortoise. By the time Achilles has covered the distance that separated him from the tortoise, the tortoise has covered one tenth of that distance ahead of him: when Achilles has covered that tenth, the tortoise has covered another one hundredth, and so on forever. This problem seemed to the ancients insoluble. The absurd answer (that Achilles could never overtake the tortoise) resulted from this: that motion was arbitrarily divided into discontinuous elements, whereas the motion both of Achilles and of the tortoise was continuous. (Tolstoy, 1869/1952, p. 469)

For Tolstoy, the problem Achilles faces is that as a human he cannot experience the world as pure process in the way that non-human animals like tortoises supposedly can. A tortoise does not reminisce about the past, or plan for the future in the present. Tortoises do not have calendars, diaries, watches, maps, satellite navigation, smartphones, tape measures or other devices that represent and divide up the passage of time and space. They do not worry about being late or missing deadlines. They just exist in the moment … they just *are*. Humans, on the other hand, are obsessed with dividing the world up into pieces of space and time that can be organized, measured and evaluated. As you read these words look around you at all of the technologies, techniques and devices you are using (including the design and organization of this book). Our world is made up of objects, technologies, documentation, spaces, lines, charts, grids, margins, traces, places and spaces, all kinds of representations that help us to make sense of the world in terms of certain measures and causal relationships. It is very difficult for us to even conceive of the world that other non-humans like animals might experience and so this ongoing world of absolute continuity of motion is not available to us except through our technologically enhanced sense-making apparatus; an apparatus that ironically takes process and literally *re-presents* it by turning it into bits of things or entities that we can understand and work on.

Yet this is not all that Tolstoy has to say on the matter. In his discussion of absolute continuity of motion he then demonstrates how we use our interpretations and representations of process to divide up space and time to perform another trick. Having divided the world up into discrete chunks we see (or at least we think we see) causal relationships between these chunks. Tolstoy gives the following example:

Whenever I look at my watch and its hands point to ten, I hear the bells of the neighbouring church; but because the bells begin to ring when the hands of the clock reach ten, I have no right to assume that the movement of the bells is caused by the position of the hands of the watch. Whenever I see the movement of a locomotive I hear the whistle and see the valves opening and wheels turning; but I have no right to conclude that the whistling and the turning of wheels are the cause of the movement of the engine. (Tolstoy, 1869/1952, p. 470)

It is not that Tolstoy is disputing that there are such things as causal relationships, but rather that causality is part of our human experience and so has to be interpreted. Like any form of interpretation this requires us to construct a version of reality in which this causal relationship makes sense. Take this example: to someone living in a pre-industrial age when the possibility of mechanical timepieces was part of an unimaginable future, it would seem as if the hands on a watch did have the almost magical ability to make the bells of a clock tower ring. In a similar way, it might be possible to produce a statistical relationship between the size of a population of storks in a particular geographical area and the number of human babies born – but this does not mean that the old story that storks carry babies to their mothers is necessarily true. Cause and effect can be based on scientific principles, but even these scientific principles still have to be interpreted and this interpretation can be made to serve a particular agenda. Whatever the case, we have a need to make sense of the world and to see patterns and relationships whether we truly understand them to be there or not. Tolstoy leaves us with one last important message that we should be very cautious about the way in which we produce and believe in certain histories, or rather historical narratives that have become accepted truths since these too are based on a view of entities and causality.

> To study the laws of history we must completely change the subject of our observation, must leave aside kings, ministers, and generals, and study the common, infinitesimally small elements by which the masses are moved. No one can say in how far it is possible for man to advance in this way toward an understanding of the laws of history; but it is evident that only along that path does the possibility of discovering the laws of history lie, and that as yet not a millionth part as much mental effort has been applied in this direction by historians as has been devoted to describing the actions of various kings, commanders, and ministers and propounding the historians' own reflections concerning these actions. (Tolstoy, 1869/1952, p. 470)

This is the problem with both the telling of histories and the telling of stories about leadership: we always want to attribute the complexity of everyday life – the potentially meaningless ebb and flow of events in time and space – to a heroic individual, a leader whose actions give history and the process of life meaning, structure and direction. As we shall see shortly, perhaps it is not the nature of leaders and leadership that should concern us, as Tolstoy suggests, but rather the *desire* for leadership that perpetuates our fascination and bewilderment for the subject. More importantly, when we tell stories about heroic individuals what else about everyday life are we forgetting or missing?

Leadership research as the study of entities *not* process

Starting a discussion of leadership and process with Greek demi-gods and tortoises might seem a little odd, but Tolstoy's philosophical musings provide an important starting point for grasping the problems and opportunities that process thinking might present for understanding the nature of leading and leadership. So what can we summarize from our discussion so far? First, when studying leadership human beings have a tendency to extract meaning from a world of continuous movement (process). By extracting this meaning we have to turn process into a thing and so press pause on the flow of movement. This action of pausing to think about the world as 'things' is precisely what makes Achilles have to stop moving and why the tortoise always creeps those precious few tenths ahead. So to extend this racing metaphor even further, we as human beings fall at the first hurdle by trying to understand process by first obliterating process and turning flow and fluidity into some*thing* else that we can understand. Second, we then look for relationships between these constructed things and attribute certain causes to certain effects. However, our desire to see entities and causal relationships may exceed our ability to really understand the nature of the world we seek to research and so the histories we construct and the stories we tell are based on *reductionism* and *reification* – the need to reduce the world and make it meaningful for whatever purpose we desire (see Gemmill and Oakley, 1992, for more on reification and leadership). If we were feeling mischievous we might even say then that our need to abstract and reduce the world of process may well serve the same function as a lamp post serves for a drunkard – *to provide support and comfort rather than illumination*.

   Moreover, as the sociologist Professor Bruno Latour (1987, p. 12) once said: 'Things do not hold because they are true; they are true because they hold.' And as we have seen with the problem of turning process into entity and entity into a causal relationship, it is possible to create truths about the world that may not necessarily be *true* in any objective or permanent sense. What Tolstoy's beautifully ambiguous discussion teaches us is that truth is more often subjective and political, and what is true about a 'thing' or a 'relationship' is only true because it has been successfully abstracted from the flow of events it was once part of and then made to hold together long enough over time and space to become a meaningful truth to someone or some group. This act of holding a truth together is particularly relevant when we look at the history of leadership research and particularly that branch of research loosely termed 'leadership psychology'. This is the highly influential set of perspectives and studies that you will come across when you browse through any of the best-known leadership textbooks.

The studies that make up the psychological perspective include early trait theory, the study of styles and behaviours, situational approaches, transformational and authentic leadership – themes visited in the first section of this book. These studies are usually characterized by a kind of theory and methodology that uses this 'entity' view of leadership. Here there is a distinct 'leader', a human being who has a certain ability to influence. In the traditional trait theory approach this ability is defined by the force of their personality either expressed through appearance, attitude or actions (Bryman, 1986; Kirkpatrick and Locke, 1991; Zaccaro, 2007). In contrast the study of 'styles and behaviours' tended to emphasize the behaviour of a leader in terms of their consideration for followers versus their direction of tasks (Stogdill, 1974; Fiedler, 1976/1997; Hersey and Blanchard, 1982). And for the transformational or authentic leader approaches it is the leader's power to inspire and garner the trust of followers as they come to accept and share in the leader's vision (Bass, 1985; Avolio and Gardner, 2005; Goffee and Jones, 2005). In other words, in each of these different approaches to leadership, the power to lead (and conversely to follow) is a form of influence that originates in the mind, body and actions of a single leader-figure; an influence that then has an effect upon followers and the goals they seek to achieve. This results in the following formula in which discrete entities exists in a specific causal relationship with one another:

$$\text{Entity A} + \text{Entity B} = \text{Outcome C}$$

$$\text{Cause} > \text{Effect} > \text{Result}$$

This is a model that leadership scholar Warren Bennis (2007) has described as the 'leadership tripod': a three-part structure made up of three components of leader, follower and a shared goal. As we have seen in Tolstoy's critique of this kind of reasoning, it is a simple step from here to take these entities and then devise ways of demonstrating their causal relationships and using scientific modes of representation to further validate these truth claims.

Good examples of this kind of entity thinking can be found in the models and charts of early styles, contingency and situational leadership studies which we saw in Chapter 3. Here the phenomenon of leadership is reduced to related and opposing component parts. So the leader's personality or behavioural characteristics are understood as existing on a spectrum of 'consideration' versus 'initiating structure' (Stogdill, 1974), or 'relationship motivated' versus 'task motivated' (Fiedler, 1976/1997), or a 'concern for people' versus a 'concern for results' (Blake and Mouton, 1985), or 'supportive behaviour' versus 'directive behaviour' (Hersey and Blanchard, 1982). This dynamic between people and task is then mapped on to some kind of square or grid to illustrate how different degrees and combinations of 'people and task' will influence follower behaviour – which in turn will influence the kinds of results that the leader might achieve. The more complex models such as Fiedler's contingency schema or Hersey and Blanchard's situational leadership matrix also include an additional set of components that represent 'situation' in this leader–follower dyad. So for Fiedler 'situation' can be made up of additional entities that may shift and change such as 'leader–member relations', 'task structure' and 'position power'. The way in which these situational factors change over time can radically influence how successful a certain leader characteristic might be. For Hersey and Blanchard the situation is represented by squares in a 2×2 matrix that indicate the lifespan of a group as it moves from requiring 'high direction/high support' through to 'low direction/low support'. Good leadership is therefore achieved by effectively matching leadership style to the changing needs of the group – in other words *discrete entities that share a causal relationship.*

These are classic studies of leadership and there is a reason for their longevity and lasting impact on leadership research. First, they offer concise and effective illustrations of the delicate relationships between the parts that make up the leadership tripod and the consequences of not reflecting upon style, action and the changing nature of the situation. Second, they provide the possibility of predictive assessments of leadership effectiveness and a diagnostic tool for improving group or organisational performance. Third, and perhaps more importantly for our discussion, these models make the world seem much more simple, visible and manageable. They provide a much-needed formula or map for navigating a very difficult and often treacherous terrain. However, as we have seen through our discussion of Tolstoy there is a danger of an unquestioning belief in the entities that we construct and the relationships we think we can see operating between them.

Leadership scholar Professor Alan Bryman (see Figure 9.1) makes this very point when he questions the assumption underpinning these influential early studies in that it is the category and special status assigned to the 'leader' in these charts, graphs and formulations that is always presumed to be the independent variable and not some other factor. In other words, if we change something about the leader (or even change the leader altogether as Frederick Fiedler recommended) then will we really have a different outcome in terms of situation, follower behaviour and result? Is it really the leader that changes things and everything else flows from this important variable, or could the reverse also be true?

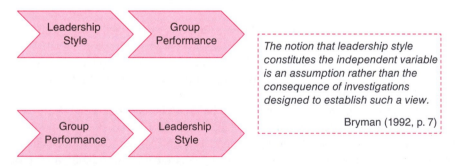

Figure 9.1   Assumptions underpinning early leadership models

Just like the whistles and valves of Tolstoy's locomotive appear to be the cause of the train's movement, so too the items on a leadership questionnaire, or the design of a chart or graph seem to indicate that individual leaders are the *cause* of leadership whereas followership is merely the *effect*. Yet other interpretations might be available and equally valid. As we will see shortly, it is very easy to disrupt this linear causal relationship by using alternative examples and cases where leadership seems to be the result of other factors such as followership, systems, teamwork, technologies, objects and language. However, this shift of perspective also requires a radical shift in mind set or what we might call a shift in 'paradigms'.

STOP AND REFLECT 9.1

Think of a moment in which you saw leadership in action. What factors might have led to the leadership you saw? In what ways might leadership have been an effect rather than a cause?

Paradigm shifting as changing the way we think

This notion of paradigms of leadership research is very nicely summarized by Richard Barker who in a research article published in the academic journal *Human Relations* in 1997 argued that what prevents leadership research from advancing and creating new and challenging theories and research studies beyond psychological readings is its dependence on a very narrow and limited worldview. In his article Barker outlines two of these worldviews or paradigms that have governed our ability to think about, study, research and practise leadership. He then offers a third paradigm that may provide an alternative opportunity for new kinds of thinking – one that has particular relevance to an understanding of process:

The feudal paradigm

Barker begins by arguing that leadership research from early writings on 'Great Men' through to the more sophisticated trait and styles studies of the twentieth century are all part of a *feudal paradigm*. This is a style of thinking and a set of assumptions based on leadership as a relationship between master and servant. Feudalism was (and in some parts of the world still is) a system of governance in which a wealthy and powerful landowner would rent out space on his land to peasant farmers. These farmers would work the land and pay the landowner in goods or taxes. It is this master/servant model that Barker argues is the underpinning assumption of leadership. Leaders are like sovereigns, kings and queens or landlords who own and can influence everything in their kingdom. This, for Barker, is the seed that has grown into the causal relationship between leaders and followers in our discussion above. The leader is the independent variable in any research study or model because the leader is the one who has all the power – in the case of the feudal paradigm this is power as decreed by God or by royal blood. Meanwhile the follower takes the position of the servant or serf who can only respond to or act upon the will of the leader-sovereign. To understand leadership, therefore, is to understand something essential about the character, behaviour or actions of this sovereign figure since the servant is merely an effect of this 'leaderful' will.

The industrial paradigm

The *industrial paradigm* according to Barker is an extension of the feudal. It is a modern expression of the same understanding that the sovereign leader holds all of the power and influence. The difference between these paradigms is that the industrial world replaces the king, queen or landlord with the engineer, manager, business owner or entrepreneur. In addition, the industrial paradigm has the application of the sciences rather than faith and religion to endorse its status and value. This is leadership as seen through the eyes of Frederick Winslow Taylor, Henry Ford or Jack Welch. Power is relocated from the castle or manor to the factory or skyscraper, and the office to the chief executive officer, but power is still held within a hierarchy in which the leader has power and influence over a largely reactive and passive group of followers. To understand the nature of leadership is still to look to the *top* of the organizational structure, to the individual rather than the group.

The emerging paradigm

At the time of writing in 1997 Barker foresaw a third possible option that he tentatively named the '*emerging paradigm*'. This was for Barker the new frontier in leadership research and the place to put forward and explore some radical alternatives to this leader-centric school of thought. The overriding characteristic of the emerging paradigm was that it should capture the relational dimensions of leadership and to reclaim the position of the follower as a more active and essential part of the practical accomplishment and experience of leadership. To paraphrase Barker, we should find new ways to put the 'ship' back into leadership:

> Consider the word leadership itself. Other words that end in the suffix –ship can be used to denote skill, such as in the words statesmanship, seamanship, or craftsmanship, or can also be used to indicate a relationship as in partnership, apprenticeship, fellowship, and in the word relationship itself. It seems we potentially have a legitimate semantic choice to use the word leadership either to indicate an ability or skill, or to indicate a relationship. (Barker, 1997, p. 347)

In his development of this third emerging paradigm Barker cautions the reader not to mistake the study of relationships with the reduction of leadership to a simple dyadic relation between leader and the led. Doing this would simply reduce and subsume leadership back within the feudal and industrial paradigms. Instead, he urges us to consider a different metaphor, that of the river and the riverbed. If leadership is the flowing water of the river then its container – the riverbed – is culture. As the river flows it is shaped and directed by the path of the riverbed, but this movement shapes the riverbed also. Both leadership and culture are in a constant state of motion, a state of becoming where neither one ever starts or stops. This for Barker is leadership in action; leadership as lived experience in which leaders, followers, situations and outcomes are all temporary effects – transient whirlpools, diversions and eddies in the ongoing movement of everyday life. And for this reason, Barker adds, 'the leadership process must be conceptualized before the leadership relationships and leadership roles'. It is this move towards understanding process as the ground on which all other theories and studies of leadership stands (or flows) that we will explore in the sections that follow.

Avoiding the fallacy of misplaced concreteness

So what place might process have in an emerging paradigm of leadership studies? One significant contribution to this theme comes in the form of Martin Wood's analysis of leadership as a problem of ontology.

STOP AND REFLECT 9.2

Barker's argument that a river-like process precedes any recognizable leadership relationship might help us to make sense of the following strange tale recounted by organizational psychologist Karl Weick:

> The young lieutenant of a small Hungarian detachment in the Alps sent a reconnaissance unit out into the icy wilderness. It began to snow immediately, snowed for two days, and the unit did not return. The lieutenant suffered, fearing that he had dispatched his own people to death. But on the third day the unit came back. Where had they been? How had they made their way? Yes, they said, we considered ourselves lost and waited for the end. And then one of us found a map in his pocket. That calmed us down. We pitched camp, lasted out the snowstorm, and then with the map we discovered our bearings. And here we are. The lieutenant borrowed this remarkable map and had a good look at it. He discovered to his astonishment that it was not a map of the Alps but of the Pyrenees. (Weick, 2001: 344–5)

- Where is the leadership in this story? Is it contained in one person? Is it even in a person?

Ontology means the nature of *being*, the reality of something – or at least what we perceive to be its essential substance. To look at leadership as ontology requires us to revisit all those taken-for-granted assumptions about what we think leadership *really* is, whether it is even 'real' in some universal sense, or if it has some other qualities that give it the *appearance* of something real.

For Wood, leadership does not have any being as such; it does not have a reality of its own. Rather what we think of as 'leadership' is an *effect* of an ongoing process. In other words, leadership is a kind of 'second order' construct, something that we use to crudely describe the indescribable processes that make up our experience of everyday life. As Wood states:

> Concrete things – for example, leaders, followers, and organizations – are surface effects. They are simple appearances we employ to give substantiality to our experience, but under whose supposed 'naturalness' the fundamentally processual nature of the real is neglected. This unwitting intellectual strategy continues to inform management studies. We may be thinking of business gurus, policy makers, political leaders, spiritual teachers, fashion icons, pop idols, and sporting heroes, but in all these senses an individual social actor is a prerequisite for 'leadership'. (2005, p. 1104)

Here, Wood is drawing on a history of process philosophy developed by such figures as Alfred North Whitehead and Henri Bergson. Whitehead in particular was a mathematician by training and in the early twentieth century he contributed to an emerging interest in studying reality as event rather than substance. As he famously stated, reality might appear stable, fixed and describable, but its ontological character is perhaps rather different: 'Nature is a dull affair, soundless, scentless, colourless; merely the hurrying of material, endlessly, meaningless' (Whitehead, 1925/1967, p. 80). In other words, in order for our perception of reality to have sound, scent and colour, and so have meaning to us, we as humans must engage in what both Whitehead and Wood describe as the *fallacy of misplaced concreteness*; that is, the act of turning event into substance, process into entity. We do this in three different ways:

1 *Reification*: We abstract the world by taking 'pieces' of it, snatching at event and placing it out of context somewhere else.
2 *Inversion*: This act of grasping at pieces of process simultaneously turns 'event' into 'substance' and so some*thing* can stand in for what was previously part of an ongoing flow of movement. So movement becomes categorized into 'types', 'descriptions', 'units', 'definitions', 'measures' and so forth.
3 *Forgetting*: Finally, we become so accustomed at reifying and inverting that we forget that we have even done it. The world appears to *already* have substance, as if it existed as an entity all along and completely independently of our own involvement or action. We even forget that we have forgotten! And this gives reification its very particular power over how we perceive reality (see also Chia, 1995, 1996).

As we have seen with Tolstoy's retelling of the tale of Achilles and the tortoise we have no choice as human beings. This act of reification, inversion and forgetting is the only way we have of experiencing and giving meaning to the world. However, for Whitehead and others, it is *remembering* that we do this that is important rather than trying to avoid it. To forget that we have forgotten our acts of reification is to commit the fallacy of misplaced concreteness: to treat something as naturally concrete rather than as something we have constructed through our own actions of sense-making and sense-giving.

This is why for Wood it is important to always question whether 'an individual social actor is a prerequisite for "leadership"'. We tend to look for special individuals not because leadership is a trait, or personality type, but because it is more palatable to reduce the process of leadership down into some*thing* or some*one* that we can study, measure, evaluate and so on. But the problem with this fallacy of misplaced leadership is that it potentially leaves out so many other things and events that might be essential for understanding the reality, the ontology, of leadership. In the following examples we explore how this remembering and critical evaluation of leadership as process might be understood in practice.

Case study: 'Show us the sound' – an aesthetic analysis of leadership in symphony orchestras

In their qualitative study of classical symphony orchestras, leadership scholars Koivunen and Wennes (2011) use a process methodology to explore how musicians work collaboratively despite the popular perception that it is the conductor that is 'the leader of the orchestra'. As their study demonstrates, being part of a symphony orchestra requires: *aesthetic judgement* – the ability to be part of a flow of sound, rhythm and musical notation; the act of *relational listening* – meaning a continuous sensitivity to the acts and actions of others (including the music as actor) and how to respond appropriately to maintain the flow of the piece you are performing; and *kinaesthetic empathy* – a bodily expression of the music and an awareness of one's own and other's bodies and physical gestures. All three elements work simultaneously as a cycle and there is no one person who has more or less 'leaderful' ability than another. Everyone is immersed in the process of making music and we might even say that if there is a 'leader' then it is in the disembodied presence of the music itself and those who are contributing and listening to it.

As the authors conclude:

Instead of continuing to support the myth of individual achievement, we should acknowledge the numerous invisible acts of enabling, supporting and facilitating that produce an outcome often mistakenly labeled 'individual achievement'. In other words, it is important to draw attention to complex webs of interaction among organization members which help leaders to achieve their outcomes. Leadership can thus be defined as a collective construction. (Koivunen and Wennes, 2011, p. 65)

1. Where do you think the 'leadership' exists in this story of symphony orchestras?
2. Does anything surprise you about the treatment of leadership in this account?
3. Have you ever experienced a similar kind of 'flow' or kinaesthetic empathy to the one described in this case? What were you doing and what kinds of processes were you paying attention to?
4. How might this kind of aesthetic leadership extend beyond orchestras into other organizational contexts? The authors talk about the flow of sound – but what else might flow between people in organizations?

Case study: Dances of leadership

Where Koivunen and Wennes (2011) look at music, Arja Ropo and Erika Sauer (2008) look at dancing. Yet here again we see some similar processual themes such as collaboration, relationality and the use of the body. In particular, Ropo and Sauer explore the differences between traditional ballroom dancing and the more contemporary idea of raves. As the authors explain, by placing these two traditions of dance side by side we might gain a unique insight into some of the assumptions we hold about leadership (see Table 9.1).

Table 9.1 Dances of leadership and underlying assumptions

Waltz (ballroom dancing)	Rave (party dancing)
Structure and rules	Fluid and open
Sequence of steps	Free movement
Man leads, woman follows	Gender irrelevant
Couples (dyad)	Individual or group

(Continued)

(Continued)

Read this extract from Ropo and Sauer (2008, p. 560) and think about the questions below:

The ballroom dance waltz is used as a metaphorical representation of a hierarchical, logical and rational understanding of leadership. The waltz metaphor describes the leader as a dominant individual who knows where to go and the dance partner as a follower or at least as someone with a lesser role in defining the dance. Raves, on the other hand represent paradigmatically different kind of a dance and therefore a different understanding of leadership. There are neither dance steps to learn, nor fixed dance partners where one leads and the other follows. Even the purpose or aim of dancing may not be known at the beginning of the dance, but it is negotiated as the raves go on. We think that raves describe the organizational life as it is often seen and felt today: chaotic, full of unexpected changes, ambiguous and changing collaborators in networks. Here leadership becomes a collective, distributed activity where the work processes and the targeted outcome is continually negotiated.

1. Think of some of the organizational contexts that you are part of. What sorts of leadership dances are you engaged in?
2. Ropo and Sauer argue that organizational life today is more like a rave. Do you agree? Why?
3. Can you think of other examples of action or activity that might help us to understand leadership as an 'aesthetic experience'?
4. What implications might these approaches to music and dance have for the theory and practice of leadership development?

Case study: Hero-making and the crash landing of Flight 1549

On 15 January 2009, US Airways Flight 1549 departed New York City's LaGuardia Airport at 3.25 p.m. en route to Charlotte, North Carolina. The co-pilot, First Officer Jeffrey Skiles, was flying the aircraft when, about ninety seconds after take-off, the Airbus A320 struck a large flock of Canada Geese, ingesting birds into both engines. 'It sounded like it was "raining birds"' the captain, Chesley 'Sully' Sullenberger III, recalled. They filled the windscreen, 'large dark birds' like a 'black and white photograph'. He felt vibrations, surprised at 'how symmetrical the loss of thrust was'; there was no yaw or sideward motion. It had to be a complete loss of both engines. 'It was the worst sickening pit of your stomach, falling through the floor feeling I've ever felt in my life,' the captain recalled. 'I knew immediately it was very bad'.

Radioing for assistance, Captain Sullenberger reported, 'Cactus 1539 [sic] hit birds. We lost thrust in both engines. We're turning back towards LaGuardia'.

Air Traffic Controller Patrick Harten immediately stopped all departures and responded, 'Do you want to try to land runway one three?', which was the shortest turn for the Airbus-turned-glider.

'We're unable. We may end up in the Hudson.'

'Okay, what do you need to land?'

'I'm not sure we can make any runway. What's over to our right, anything in New Jersey? Maybe Teterboro.'

'Off to your right is Teterboro Airport. Do you want to try and go to Teterboro?'

'Yes.'

'Cactus 1529 [sic] turn right two-eight-zero. You can land runway one at Teterboro.'

Passing through 2,000 feet and descending fast over New York City, the captain made his decision.

'We can't do it. We're gonna be in the Hudson'.

That was the last radio transmission from Cactus 1549. With both engines dead, attempts to restart futile, and the water approaching swiftly, Captain Sullenberger asked his co-pilot 'Got any ideas?' 'Actually not', he replied. Moments later the Airbus skidded across the surface of the Hudson River, sending up huge plumes of water until it came to rest just north of New York City's 39th Street ferry dock. Less than six minutes had elapsed since take-off. Within moments, an ad hoc flotilla of waterway ferries, Coast Guard vessels, and police-, fire- and tug-boats converged on the scene, expeditiously evacuating all passengers and crew safely. Only five people were seriously injured with broken bones, twenty-six were transported to local hospitals and the rest were treated for hypothermia and sent home. To many, it seemed as if a miracle had occurred. It was an unprecedented failure in an unforgiving environment with little time to prepare or react. Later, Captain Sullenberger even doubted that the emergency could be effectively mimicked in the flight simulator. (Fraher, 2011, pp. 59–60)

This dramatic and nerve-racking real-life event is retold by leadership and management scholar Amy Fraher, but Fraher is not just interested in the event itself, but in how it was reported by the news media and the consequences it had for certain key figures like Captain Sullenberger. The main title of Fraher's research article is 'Hero-making as a defence against the anxiety of responsibility and risk' and this gives some clue to her own (and our) interest in this event. As Fraher explains, following the successful emergency landing of Flight 1549 into the Hudson River in New York City, Captain Sullenberger was hailed a hero for his grace under pressure, his bravery in making a decision that risked the lives of his air crew and passengers, and his skill for being able to safely accomplish a manoeuvre that he himself admits would have been almost impossible to re-create in a flight simulator. In the days and weeks following the event Sullenberger was interviewed by all the major news networks, he appeared as a guest on top US talk shows, he was invited to appear at the Superbowl and the Oscars, and he was personally thanked by the Mayor of New York and the President of the United States.

As Fraher argues, America in its post-9/11 era desperately needed a hero and Captain Sullenberger with his years of flight experience, Air Force background, modest demeanour, impeccably smart airline uniform and silver hair provided the perfect image of the all-American hero; the classic masculine hero of an America that was almost forgotten among the corporate and political scandals, and the complexities of the war on terror that marked the late 1990s and early 2000s.

(Continued)

(Continued)

What interests Fraher, however, is how little attention was paid to the other factors that contributed to the successful landing of Flight 1549; factors that included:

- The actions of the co-pilot and the cabin crew, who worked alongside the captain to coordinate the landing, secure the aircraft and reassure and care for the passengers during and after they landed in the water.
- The air traffic control team who guided and advised the captain and co-pilot on possible routes to take and places to land. The swift action of the air traffic control team also prevented other aircraft from becoming involved in the incident by working with neighbouring airports, clearing runways and warning other planes to stay clear of the area.
- The emergency services (fire, ambulance, police) who mobilized a rescue attempt to secure the crashed plane and recover the passengers and crew as well as making sure local hospitals were aware of the incident and that possible sites for first aid might be used.
- The local ferries operating in the Hudson River also played a key part by volunteering their services and using their craft to take emergency service staff to the crash site and recover survivors before they succumbed to heart attacks and hypothermia as they entered the icy cold January water.
- After the event Captain Sullenburger also made special mention of the Crew Resource Management Training that he and his staff had received and how without this vital learning resource they would never have been able to act as quickly and decisively to manage the situation and care for their passengers.
- The good weather and clear skies were also key factors in that had it been colder, foggy or snowing then the efforts of the aircrew and emergency services and ferries would have been hampered and lives possibly lost to the crash or the freezing water.
- The time of day in which the incident occurred was also important in that it was still daylight and just before the evening rush hour. This meant that visibility was good, but also traffic on the city streets was light enough to allow emergency service vehicles to travel swiftly to and from the scene.

All of these factors contributed to the saving of all of the lives of crew and passengers that day and the construction of this event as a 'good news story' in the national media. Yet this complex process of overlapping movements of engine parts, animals, people, language, text, experience, technologies, systems, training packages, schedules, cars, ambulances, ferries, airports, hospitals, water, weather and the passage of time was reduced to a heroic narrative about the appearance, character and abilities of a single man: Captain Chesley B. Sullenberger III. Process was reduced to the simplest and most palatable story, that of a male hero saving the day. Sullenberger himself was a reluctant hero, modest and understated (making him even more heroic in the eyes of the news media) and did not enjoy this new-found fame. On several occasions he used his notoriety to draw attention to the other people, education and systems that had contributed to the saving of lives that day, but the media representation of 'Sully' (as the news media nicknamed him) as the hero of the hour was a more powerful and lasting narrative.

So what can we take from this case study?

As Fraher observes, to understand the crash landing of Flight 1549 we have to look at three separate but related issues:

1. *The importance of symbolism, hero-making and the power of a good story.* Given that no one lost their lives during the emergency landing, this event could become a positive story to inspire and lift up a nation whose self-image had been battered by nearly ten years of international terrorism and warfare. Remember, 'an individual social actor is a prerequisite for "leadership"' (Wood, 2005, p. 1104). Here Captain Sullenberger fitted this symbolic function perfectly (if reluctantly). His white older male appearance provided America with a powerful and romantic image of a golden age charisma of Gary Cooper, John F. Kennedy and John Wayne. As a result, the symbolic relevance of the event and attribution of actions, decisions and outcomes to a single individual was more important than the complex details of the event itself.

2. *The need to explore alternative stories and to find the process behind the appearance.* As Fraher argues, we can view the crash landing of Flight 1549 from a number of points of view. From the media perspective this the story of a hero saving the day. From a second perspective we can view this as an act of hero-making and symbolism, but we can also take a process perspective and look at what Fraher calls 'The untold story of collective responsibility'. If this is a tale of heroics, then perhaps the heroism lies in the teamwork of dozens of people, objects, technologies and institutions that all worked together at the same time and in the right way to achieve this happy outcome. What is required then is a method of studying complexity and process rather than individuals and their characters.

3. *Facing up to the anxiety of responsibility and risk.* Why is it, Fraher asks, that we find it much less appealing to understand and celebrate teamwork and collaboration? Is it perhaps that in doing so we have to also recognize and take responsibility for our part in the way in which the world around us works? Is it sometimes easier to look to heroes, leaders and celebrities to inspire and save us rather than taking on that responsibility ourselves?

1. In the story of Flight 1549, where do you see leadership occurring?
2. Why do you think this story is told in terms of the actions of an individual heroic leader? Do you think this heroic account is fair and accurate?
3. Why does Fraher describe this incident an example of hero-making?
4. What does heroics have to do with leadership?
5. What is the 'untold story' in Fraher's article?
6. Are there any practical implications or applications that we might take from this case study?

Conclusion: Reimagining leadership and process

This chapter has drawn attention to the sometimes unscientific and subjective character of leadership studies. Where the natural sciences try to use scientific method to discover new knowledge about the world, leadership research often uses methods that bolster certain pre-existing assumptions, ideas and ideologies – what Barker called the 'feudal' and 'industrial' paradigms in which the leader-figure is the centre of the action. From this perspective, if we want to understand what happens in the world then we should attend to those great individuals who are the makers of history. Alternatively we can take the process view as a counterpoint that reminds us that the world is often far more complicated than we can often appreciate and every attempt to understand it will always be lacking in some regard – *something will always be missed out*. This is just an unavoidable consequence of being human. We can only experience the world through interpretation and so we must always be mindful of the limits (and consequences) of our interpretations and not confuse our constructed *version* of reality with an independent 'real world'.

The turn to process thinking described in this chapter has considerable potential as it opens up new ways of thinking about and exploring leadership as a *practical* as well as an *ethical* task. Through this we can explore an array of theoretical and empirical contributions to this growing body of 'process' studies in which leadership is collective, disembodied, involving humans and non-humans, as well as other aesthetic dimensions such as sound, movement, symbolic interaction and storytelling. Yet as we come to the end of the chapter we need to think very carefully about those last two themes: symbolism and storytelling. The argument put forward in the process approach is that it will attend to the detail and complexity of everyday life – the kinds of things that are abstracted away or reified by traditional psychological theories and methods. As we have seen, there is a lot of value in looking to the processes that make up leadership interactions and activities as this reminds us that there is always more going on in the background and different stories that might be told. Recognizing this is very important as it radically changes how we think about power, organizations and society.

Yet this also leads us to an uncomfortable possibility that it doesn't really matter how close we come to understanding personality, behaviour or process, it may be that our knowledge of leadership is always incomplete and so potentially unreliable. Perhaps, as Gemmill and Oakley (1992) suggest, we should do away with the concept of leadership altogether rather than seeking to locate it elsewhere? Yet perhaps this is premature and there may be another path available. For instance, one of the potential limitations in the process approach explored in this chapter is that it tends to treat 'process' as having some substance of its own that exists in an ontological reality in which process flows on beyond the perceptive field of the human senses. The risk here is that process thinking promotes what we might call a form of *social realism*. So where leadership psychology treats leadership as a *real* part of a person's character or behaviour, process studies are in danger of seeking the *real* in action, interaction, language, movement, sound, collective activity and so on. Now consider this: what if there is no *real* – at least in the terms of the psychological or the social? What if 'process' was as much a fabrication as 'leadership'?

Let's take the following example to illustrate this point. Do you remember the story told by organizational psychologist Karl Weick earlier in the chapter? The story about the troop of Hungarian soldiers who found their way back to camp with the wrong map? This story would seem to support the process view of leadership in that no one social actor was responsible for the group finding their way back to camp, but what if this story wasn't true? What if it is entirely made up?

According to organizational researchers Basbøll and Graham (2006) there is considerable evidence to suggest that this story is either a fabrication, or at least a recycled myth whose origins may never be found. Through their research into the source of this story they find no evidence that this relates to any real group of Hungarian soldiers, or any other people that used the wrong map to find their way out of a mountain range. However, what they do find is that it first appears as a story in the poetry of a Czech poet called Miroslav Holub published in 1977. Yet the lack of any reliable source for this story has not stopped it being used and reused across the discipline of management and organization studies – and as an example in countless classes and training rooms. The story gains force not because it relates to a verifiable historical or 'real' event, but because it is a story that is told and retold over and over again: *it is a story that 'holds' over time and so becomes true*. It is the repetition of the narrative by those perceived as reliable experts that gives this story part of its power. Of course, the rest of the power of this story is simply because it is such an evocative tale of human determination, optimism and luck. It is the ability of this story to inspire and enchant that is important. As Basbøll and Graham state, this is a story that has now reached the status of myth among management and organization scholars and students. And it is precisely this theme of *myth* and the *imagination* that may be missing in both the theory and method of psychological *and* social/process perspectives on leadership.

Could it be that leadership in all its forms requires myth, imagination and storytelling to give it power and influence? Remember that everything you have read in this book has been constructed for you to read and so represents a kind of serious and very carefully written story.[1] In addition, as you cannot ever have direct knowledge of the studies, authors, places, scenarios and theories we have been describing to you, you have been encouraged to *imagine* them. Achilles and the tortoise, the leadership tripod, psychological models, the arguments and counter-arguments of different authors, business organizations, orchestras, dances and crashing planes all required your imagination to interpret and understand them. Your lack of direct experience of all of these things did not prevent you from learning about them and hopefully finding them interesting. Indeed, it is your ability to imagine that makes reading this book possible! Perhaps this is why leadership researcher Professor Keith Grint has observed that: 'Leadership is an invention … [it]… is primarily rooted in, and a product of, the imagination' (2000, p. 13).

Perhaps it is here that process studies offers an important and unexpected contribution to our knowledge of leadership – not as a means of understanding the ontological reality of process – but to provide new possibilities for how leadership might be *imagined*. Even if we may never be able to know leadership in all its complexity, this should not stop us from attempting to engage with it both *practically* and *ethically*. We may choose to think about leadership as a psychological reality, a complex social relationship, a process, or as something else entirely. Yet in whatever ways we wish to approach the topic of leadership, it is this reminder that we all have a choice about the kinds of leadership we might want to imagine (and so make possible) that is the lasting contribution of a process perspective. And finally, if we are stuck with our imaginaries and our reifications then perhaps it is best to treat them with optimism and as something productive. So where we began this chapter with a philosophical story from Leo Tolstoy about tortoises and causality, let's end it with a Woody Allen joke about chickens:

> This guy goes to his psychiatrist and says, 'Doc, my brother's crazy. He thinks he's a chicken.' And the doctor says, 'Well why don't you turn him in?' The guy says, 'I would, but I need the eggs'. (Woody Allen, *Annie Hall*, 1977)

The key points in this chapter were …

- Process thinking involves trying to resist breaking the world down into discrete entities or substances, such as leader and follower(s), or leadership as a set of traits or behaviours. Instead it looks at the wider picture and tries to imagine the world as an integrated system of ongoing events.
- Process thinking is difficult and complex. As humans we have a natural tendency for *reductionism and reification*. Reductionism means we tend to reduce the world down into something that is meaningful for our purposes. Reification means that we also tend to reduce continuous processes into concrete entities that are easier to work with.
- Leadership as a process means moving away from 'human-centric' notions of leaders, followers and shared goals, and towards an acknowledgement of leadership's collective and open-ended

---

1 Professor Emma Bell (2008) makes a similar argument in her analysis of representations of management and organization in film. As she observes, film tells a story in much the same way as a business case study. Both require a setting, characters and plot and they both have lessons to impart. As such, they are both works of fiction – just fictions written for different purposes and audiences.

character. Leadership should be understood as a complex, ongoing and interconnected series of overlapping events, systems, practices, people, stories, institutions, histories, objects, spaces, places and technologies.

- Although it is common to think about the world in non-processual terms, like entities, the important issue is that we forget we are doing this. Process thinking is important, therefore, because it reminds us to challenge such common reductionist leadership theories. It prompts us to look beyond the allure of a single heroic individual and instead pay attention to parts of leadership that are normally forgotten, such as interaction, language, movement, sound, collective activity and so on.

 # Further thinking

The following six articles voice a strong challenge to the traditional leadership paradigm by inviting us to think about leadership as a process:

Barker, R. A. (1997). How can we train leaders if we do not know what leadership is? *Human Relations*, *50*(4), 343–362.

Fraher, A. (2011). Hero-making as a defence against the anxiety of responsibility and risk: A case study of US airways flight 1549. *Organisational and Social Dynamics*, *11*(1), 59–78.

Gemmill, G. and Oakley, J. (1992). Leadership: An alienating social myth? *Human Relations*, *45*(2), 113–129.

Koivunen, N. and Wennes, G. (2011). Show us the sound! Aesthetic leadership of symphony orchestra conductors. *Leadership*, *7*(1), 51–71.

Ropo, A. and Sauer, E. (2008). Dances of leadership: Bridging theory and practice through an aesthetic approach. *Journal of Management & Organization*, *14*(5), 560–572.

Wood, M. (2005). The fallacy of misplaced leadership. *Journal of Management Studies* *42*(6), 1101–1121.

As you read through each of these, consider:

1   Is it possible to study leadership without including process?
2   Can we ever have direct experience everyday life as process?
3   What should be included in a study of leadership as process? What should be excluded?
4   What research methods should a process study draw on?
5   Can you film or take photographs of leadership as process? Give examples.
6   What practical applications might myth and the imaginary have for training and developing leadership?
7   What else might we include in Barker's emerging paradigm?

 # Leadership on screen

The following are films that capture some of the process aspects of leadership discussed in this chapter. They also remind us in different ways of the mythical and symbolic role that individual 'leaders' play when standing in for or disguising the complex and ongoing *process* of leadership.

The Wizard of Oz (1939)

Perhaps not the first film you might think about in terms of leadership. However, all the elements discussed in this chapter are here. Dorothy and her friends band together to go on a mission. They are given direction and purpose by the promise of 'The Great and Powerful Oz'. Even though they may not be best suited for the task, they muddle through until they discover that the Wizard is merely an old man operating machinery from behind a curtain. But does the absence of a physical or 'real' wizard prevent Dorothy and her companions from achieving their goals?

Monty Python's Life of Brian (1979)

What about Brian, the man mistaken for a messiah by crowds of desperate followers in Monty Python's biblical spoof? Here we see the power and influence of followership and the importance of a belief in a leader-figure that may or may not exist. Like *The Wizard of Oz*, it is the idea of leadership that produces and guides the (sometimes absurd) desires, actions and activities of groups and organizations.

The Great Dictator (1940)

Charlie Chaplin's classic film *The Great Dictator* provides some wonderful reminders of how leadership operates as a powerful symbolic construction in which the perceptions of followers, clothing, physical movement, voice and even the height of a chair are often more important that the inner qualities or physical reality of an actual leader figure.

   When watching these films, think about the importance of the (often hidden) processes that make leadership possible as well as the power of the *symbolic* and the *imaginary* for constructing the appearance of an 'all powerful' individual leader.

10

RELATIONAL LEADERSHIP

Lucia Crevani

Growing up in Italy and moving to Sweden has made Lucia somewhat 'allergic' to authority, in particular unquestioned authority, which may be why alternative takes on leadership are particularly appealing to her. She is therefore highly committed to advancing research that frames leadership as a relational achievement.

What this chapter is all about ...

The main idea is that relational leadership shifts our attention from leadership being what leaders do. Instead, it challenges us to see leadership as an emergent relational accomplishment. Thinking about leadership this way requires that we both see and practise leadership differently.

The key questions this chapter answers are:

- What is relational leadership?
- What is the difference between an entity and constructionist perspective, and why is this important?
- Why is it difficult to see leadership relationally?
- What are some ways to practise relational leadership?

Introduction

Relational leadership comprises a strand of leadership research bringing to the fore the significance of relations and relational dynamics in leadership processes. Interestingly, the idea of leadership being relational can be said to be both old and new. It is new in the sense that there has recently been an increasing interest in challenging the individualistic focus of much traditional leadership research and practice by shifting attention to relations and the social aspect of the phenomenon of leadership. But it is also an old idea, given that already in the 1980s such ideas had been articulated (Hosking, 1988; Dachler and Hosking, 1995). Why, then, did we have to wait such a long time before the larger public would start appreciating these ideas? I will return to this question later in the chapter. More fundamentally, relational leadership may be considered as an old idea since common definitions (such as those given elsewhere in this book) actually portray leadership as a social process in which influence is produced – it is when researchers actually seek to study leadership that there appears to be a tendency to limit the focus to individuals, their characteristics and their behaviours. Hence, relational leadership offers a perspective and a number of concepts that re-direct our attention to the emergent processes of co-creation that leadership may be argued to be about. For students of leadership it may mean one more perspective to add to your repertoire, or more radically a fundamentally different approach to reality itself that may re-frame how you understand other perspectives on leadership.

In this chapter, you will be introduced to relational leadership both as ideas and concepts that you can use in order to 'see' relational leadership processes in your own work, and as ideas and concepts that you can use in order to 'practise' leadership differently. The difference between the two may be difficult to grasp since management research often conflates the *description* of a phenomenon with the *prescription* about how to act. Hence the first part of the chapter is dedicated to provide concepts useful in order to understand how leadership can be described as a relational achievement – insights that enable students of leadership to reflect. In the second part, we will turn our attention to which kind of prescription for good leadership practices scholars consequently produce. Depending on what kind of organizations you are active in and on what value commitments are appealing to you, some aspects and suggestions will be mostly relevant for you. In this chapter, you will be presented with some of the main issues currently being discussed in research. In order to provide you with a structured overview, I have chosen some main concepts under which I have grouped contributions from authors that, at times, may use slightly different labels in their own work. Figure 10.1 shows how the chapter is organized along the two possibilities of 'seeing' and 'practising' relational leadership, each of them exemplified with three important leadership practices.

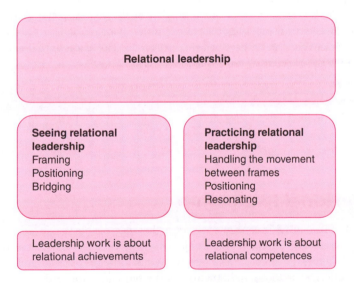

Figure 10.1   How the chapter is structured in order to distinguish between the analytical possibility to see leadership work and the more active choice to practice leadership relationally

STOP AND REFLECT 10.1

Let me introduce one example at this point. You may be familiar with the brand Gore-Tex, one globally known fabric. The company itself, W. L. Gore and Associates, has also attracted some attention for how they work with innovation, but also for how the organization is said not to be based on a traditional hierarchy.

You can listen to a short description of the organization given by the Chief Executive Officer (CEO) Terri Kelly in an interview conducted by Gary Hammel, Professor at London Business School (www.youtube.com/watch?v=47yk2upT7tM). Briefly, what she says is that this company is not organized around hero-leaders, but rather around what needs to be done and how people best can contribute to it. There are no titles and all employees are associates. Leaders are not appointed by the higher management, but rather chosen by the organization. Part of the interview also deals with why and how Bill Gore started the company more than 50 years ago.

So, Terri Kelly tells the story of an organization that is led without relying on a fixed hierarchy. Authority is not guaranteed by titles. All people are considered as key contributors to shaping the organization and its results. What makes this interview interesting is that we can glimpse some important themes for this chapter: the focus on relations and on the emergence of relational forms of leadership, the importance of language (titles and associates), the significance of focusing on the work that is being done and how that work is shaped by the contribution of several people. Ironically, approximately half of the YouTube interview is dedicated to celebrating Bill Gore and his work. The importance of his relations with other people at his previous employer is mentioned, and the influence some organization theory scholars might have had is acknowledged. But considerable focus is given to this single individual who not only innovated material products, but also created new forms of management and leadership in organizations. Hence, even in a context in which collectivity is publicly celebrated, stories of individual heroes are still deployed when making sense of an organization and its development. Such tension introduces us to the challenges of viewing leadership relationally and of practising leadership relationally.

This all raises fascinating questions: What does leadership without managers mean? How can direction be set without formal appointments and titles? This chapter will address these questions by referring to the concept of relational leadership and returning to Gore as a case study to critically discuss at the end of the chapter.

Seeing relational leadership

The aim of this section is to provide concepts and ideas that may enable you to 'see' relational leadership in a variety of work situations in which you are or will be involved. In this sense relational leadership is not a new model to apply, but rather it is a perspective that moves your attention to a different set of situations and interactions than those traditionally considered 'sites' for leadership. In other words, you will be able to name another set of practices and achievements as 'leadership', expanding the boundaries of what is considered leadership by including more people and more interactions. For all students of leadership, this means that we offer you the means to become aware of what is already going on in organizing processes, but often not recognized (or named) in terms of leadership. As you will see, the importance of the 'everyday', even the 'trivial', will be emphasized. Furthermore, given that relational dynamics often take place in conversations, communication, dialogue and language are central aspects to pay attention to (Fairhurst and Uhl-Bien, 2012).

What is the 'relational' in relational leadership?

Let's now dig deeper into the theoretical concepts we work with and discuss what 'relational' means and what consequences this has for how we understand leadership. In order to examine such a question we need to take a step back and actually start by re-considering reality as such – what in research we call *ontology*.

DEFINITION: ONTOLOGY

Ontology refers to the worldview a researcher adopts and therefore to 'what is real' and 'what is it that does exist'. This is a matter of assumptions. We have no way of 'testing' which ontological position is right and which wrong. But different assumptions lead to very different takes on the phenomena under study and should be explicitly discussed when doing research.

Although we all may agree on the fact that people are real, that they materially exist, we can still debate the extent to which individuals shape the relations they participate in and/or the degree to which relations shape the individuals they connect. In other words, are we looking at stable individuals who enter an interaction in a given situation, interact, leave the interaction and remain the same individuals as before, or do we have individuals who are constructed through their interactions in a situation that is also under construction? The more we assume that individuals not only shape the interactions they engage in, but also are simultaneously shaped by such social engagements, the more we move towards what has been called a *constructionist* perspective in the range of possible approaches (cf. Dachler and Hosking, 1995).

We thus have a scale of approaches that Uhl-Bien and Ospina (2012) usefully classify along the dimension entity-constructionist perspectives. Figure 10.2 provides an overview of the differences and the issues raised, as well as of some influential scholars. I will come back to these questions in a moment, after some more considerations about ontology.

What holds these scholars together is the firm conviction that relations are central to life, work and, in particular, leadership work. Scholars on the constructionist side challenge the common assumptions that we, human beings, grow by increasing our independence from other people (e.g. Dachler and Hosking, 1995; Fletcher, 2004) – think, for example, of the common narrative of a child increasingly gaining autonomy. But what if it was interdependence what fuelled our growth instead? Maybe the child does not grow by separation from his/her parents, but by an increasingly strong mesh of interdependences with an increasing number of people. In other words, before we can discuss what leadership is about, we need to explore our assumptions about the social world in general and their consequences. In this sense, relational leadership does not only challenge the individualistic focus of leadership research, but at a more profound level questions how we see ourselves in the world. It is therefore no surprise that it has taken time for this perspective to be accepted.

STOP AND REFLECT 10.2

Think of your own life story. Can you think of situations or episodes in which you grew as a person thanks to increased independence? And can you think of situations or episodes in which you grew as a person thanks to being interdependent on other people? When your independence increased, did any new interdependence emerge at the same time (or existing ones got stronger)? Discuss these questions with other students or with your friends.

Talking of interdependence instead of independence also brings another crucial issue to the fore: gender constructions (Dachler and Hosking, 1995; Fletcher, 2004). Although there certainly are some biological differences between male and female bodies, it is recognized that *social constructions of gender* play a fundamental role in how men and women act and interact, as well as in how they are expected to act and interact – everything from which clothes are deemed appropriate in which situations to who is to take care of different tasks. Even the meaning given to certain actions are influenced by gender constructions (Fletcher, 1998, 2004).

DEFINITION: SOCIAL CONSTRUCTION OF GENDER

Social constructionism is a theoretical approach based on an ontological position that considers social realities as continuously being brought to life in meaning-making processes over time, thus not having any 'objective' existence in themselves. Meanings, institutions and social practices are therefore never fixed and are always under reconstruction. This applies also to gender, which is conceptualized as one of the most pervasive social constructions in our societies, rather than as an essential category. Hence, the meanings (what is feminine, for instance) and practices (what is to act as a woman, for example) related to gender are not fixed but are contested and possible to change.

The typical traits attributed to successful leaders are closely related to the social construction of a certain kind of masculinity, which has made it difficult to see actors not conforming to such a masculinity as potential leaders – such constructions are, on the other hand, in practice contested and ambiguous (Wahl, 1998; Ford, 2006). More fundamentally, many of the current constructions of masculinity may be argued to be about celebrating independence and silencing interdependence (Dachler and Hosking, 1995). This poses a challenge in itself to both seeing and practising leadership relationally. Taking a relational perspective implies, at least partly, taking issues with identity constructions based on those masculinities celebrating independence and dominance. This consideration also helps to understand why traditional individualistic understandings of leadership have been so long-lived.

	Entity perspective		Constructionist perspective
Starting point	Individuals are stable entities that enter relationships		Meshes of relations are fundamental – both actors and reality itself exist and are known in relations
Focus	Individual properties and the quality of the relation bewteen individuals		Relations and interaction- what goes on and what is co-constructed
Leardership is about	Leaders' interpersonal relationships with followers and handing them properly		Relating, co-creation and emergence throughout the organisation
Example of issues	How to increase innovation by attending to the relationship between leader and followers		How to reflect on the practices one is involved in order to enhance mutual learning
Example of authors	Graen, Gersten and Day, Hollander, Shamir, Seers and Chopin	Uhl-Bien, Fletcher	Hosking, Gergen, Ospina, Carroll, Simpson, Cunliffe, Barge, Fairhurst, Drath

Figure 10.2   An illustration of the entity and constructionist perspectives, and some of the differences between them

What is relational leadership?

Having defined what 'relational' may mean, we can now discuss what relational leadership thus implies. Coming back to Figure 10.2, scholars working within the entity perspective maintain that leadership cannot be reduced to what a leader does and is necessarily about the relation between the leader and the followers. Leaders and followers are treated as stable entities that have different roles and the impact the leader has on the follower is a function of the quality of the relation between the two (Uhl-Bien, 2006). Hence the focus is on individuals, their perceptions, behaviours and intentions, as they engage in relationships they instrumentally use in order to achieve (supposedly) common goals. The influence exercised in such relationships is two-way rather than the traditional one-way conception of traditional accounts (cf. Graen and Uhl-Bien, 1995; Uhl-Bien and Ospina, 2012).

The constructionist perspective turns traditional conceptions upside down, insisting that leadership is emergent and ongoing throughout the organization. Whether managers are part of such processes is an open question, rather than an assumption. The focus is on processes in which influence is interactionally achieved leading to restructuring of organizing practices and relations (Hosking, 1988; Dachler and Hosking, 1995; Drath, 2001; Uhl-Bien, 2006), to moving with engagement into the future (Hersted and Gergen, 2013). Reality has no objective meaning in itself; it is given meaning by ongoing processes of meaning making and negotiation in interactions (Barge and Fairhurst, 2008). For example, once you have read through the book, you may understand leadership in a different way than before, the meaning of 'leadership' being reconstructed in your interactions with the book and other students. Hence, actors and contexts are constantly under reconstructions 'in ways that either expand or contract the space of possible of action' (Holmberg, 2000, p. 181; Endrissat and von Arx, 2013). Leadership work is thus about social processes of co-creation in which emergent coordination and change are produced and our attention should be on the interactions and relations in which such processes unfold – they may happen everywhere at work and involve very different actors than the ones we usually limit our attention to (Uhl-Bien, 2006; Crevani et al., 2010).

What do we look at in order to see relational leadership?

The example of Gore introduced us to the need for, but also the challenges in, applying a relational perspective, something particularly true for the constructionist perspective, which is the most radical one. An entity perspective on relational leadership may in fact be easily applied to Gore, by focusing on the quality of the relations characterizing this particular organization, and thus explaining the successful work practices leading to strong performance. But could there be more to be said about how it is to work if all co-workers are valued as contributing to the ongoing organizing processes? Scholars promoting the constructionist perspective would argue for that and for the need of a whole new vocabulary for talking about practices contributing to setting directions and about leadership in a more emergent and collaborative fashion (Barge and Fairhurst, 2008; Crevani, 2011; Carroll and Simpson, 2012). This is the real challenge. As the current leadership discourse has been narrowly focused on individual properties, we actually lack the means to think of alternatives and thus to make those alternatives visible. Therefore, I will now focus on the constructionist approach and present three examples of leadership practices that open up for alternative understandings of what leadership is about. The three practices are presented as separate, but when they take place in conversations and relations they are intertwined.

Framing

Figure 10.3   Framing

Framing is a metaphorical expression conveying the idea of putting a situation into perspective. Figure 10.3 gives an example of framing: the person taking the picture is trying to find the best angle since her picture will inevitably capture only a small fragment of what is going on around her. She is thus selecting some relevant aspects to show to those who will later look at the picture. They will not be able to see everything that was going on, rather only part of it. Framing is therefore about focusing the camera, bringing some aspects to the fore and at the same time relegating other aspects to the backstage. This is necessary in our lives as the complexity of reality is too much to handle and we need to focus on certain aspects in order to make sense of them and be able to act. In a similar way, a focused picture may say more about the situation than if we had a thousand pictures of the scene from different points of view with no idea of what to look for. The meaningfulness of a picture depends on the fact that the person with the camera is not only deciding on what to portray, but also how to portray it – which angle, which light, which instant, what to have in the centre, what to have in focus, and so on. Hence framing is not only about selecting certain aspects, but also, and most importantly, about actively influencing the production of the picture in order to put certain meanings into it. The same situations may gain different meanings depending on how the picture is framed: is it, for instance, a celebration or a critique of urban life?

The concept of frame appears in different strands of theory, but most scholars refer to the work of Goffman (1974) and his definition of a frame in terms of the definition of a situation in accordance with some organizing principle that governs the events taking place and our involvement in them. Framing has to do with creating a context for making sense of situations in particular ways (Fairhurst, 2011). A frame therefore has consequences for what becomes possible to say and to do. Depending on the framing, only certain actions will make sense and only certain kinds of relations to other people/organizations are sanctioned. It is important to bear in mind that frames are neither static nor given objects. It is what we say and do when drawing on certain frames that re-makes them 'real' over and over – which means that, with time, frames will also change.

What has framing to do with leadership, then? Think of an organization that has got stuck in how the problems they are supposed to work on and the solutions they are supposed to deliver are defined (Foldy et al., 2008). It might, for instance, be a question of difficulties in retaining female employees in a construction company despite some efforts made. The problem may have been framed in terms of women not being suited for such type of jobs and the solution implemented in terms of special training for women in order to 'fix' them. A change of framing might open for new actions with potentially different results. So, for example, what if we were to frame the problem in terms of a macho culture that not only excludes women, but is also potentially harmful for men. The actions to take would become very different now, such as initiatives aimed at 'fixing' the men instead.

A practice in which leadership work takes place is therefore the practice of framing. In particular, the collective space of action may be expanded when a group or an organization moves between different frames. Framing may be thought of as processes in which reality itself is being constructed. Moving between frames therefore means to stretch and extend the social reality we are co-creating (Barge and Fairhurst, 2008; Carroll and Simpson, 2012). You can think of it in terms of repertoire or palette of frames that you help each other in creating. By developing a repertoire of frames and shifting from one frame to another, power to shape reality and one's organization direction in it is enacted. When different frames are brought into a conversation it is possible to recognize which meanings are shared and which are not, something that leads to re-constructing situations and ourselves.

Concluding, the practices in which frames are created and the movement between frames are important leadership practices. While in hierarchical organizations the higher management may be in a position to more forcefully influence some of these constructions, it is nonetheless in specific, local and contextual interactions throughout the organization that frames are given meaning.

STOP AND REFLECT 10.3

Recognizing which frames we contribute to create and sustain is not an easy task. One way of approaching this task is to look for the metaphors (and families of metaphors) that are at play when we discuss issues.

Pause for a moment and consider a project you have been involved in. Discuss that project with other people. What kind of metaphors emerged during these conversations? Which families of metaphors can you identify? One example may just be 'family' with the connected 'brothers', 'sisters' or 'family celebration', for instance. Another very different example may be 'prison', with the related 'cage' or 'surveillance'. Once you have a few families of metaphors, try to analyse whether different metaphors open up for different courses of action and forms of relation with people inside/outside the project. For instance, if 'family' is the metaphor, the relations between the people involved are portrayed as tight and possibly friendly. With 'prison', the space of action is framed as too limited and relations with some people as clearly hostile. This difference may impact which actions make sense: in the first case, helping each other and discussing openly problems may be possible, while in the second case this kind of action may not even be considered as an option.

Positioning

Figure 10.4   Positioning

Positioning may be thought of in terms of dancing. Look at Figure 10.4: in each instant the gesture performed by one dancer is accompanied by the gesture performed by the partner. In each of the snapshots, the two actors are positioned relative to each other in a specific way that expresses the relation between the two at that moment. As in this dance, even in conversations those who are talking position themselves all the time and the picture helps in representing this moment-by-moment positioning.

Positioning refers, then, to how positions are shaped in conversations and simultaneously placed in certain kinds of relations and configurations, which have consequences for how people act (Davies and Harré, 2001). Positions also involve commitments regarding what people can do, cannot do and should do. The idea of positions differs from the idea of role since 'role' conveys the expectation of stable and defined functions, while positions are to be understood in more fluid and dynamic terms (Barge and Fairhurst, 2008). As with frames, positions exist as they are brought to life in conversations, and are therefore essentially contested and negotiated. If you think of the conversations you are taking part in, while we discuss the most diverse issues, we often also tend to produce a number of positions, more or less explicitly. It may be students and lecturers, men and women, experts, visionaries, and so on.

Positioning is an important practice in leadership work on different levels. At the level of a single conversation, it has to do with how more or less fluid positions emerge in conversational dynamics and how the people interacting take up such parts during the conversation (Hersted and Gergen, 2013). Or, in other words, how conversations are influenced by the playground taking shape as the interaction unfolds (Barge and Fairhurst, 2008). A conversation you have with your group when working in a project may, for example, take a different shape depending on whether you position yourselves as equally knowledgeable members, or as a senior person and a number of junior apprentices. In both cases, the positioning taking place is a joint and relational achievement (Hersted and Gergen, 2013). It is not enough that one member tries to position himself/herself as senior to the others. Such positioning needs somehow to be sustained by the following conversational dynamics. Also, the way we are positioned frames the talk that we produce as the interaction unfolds, as what we say may be viewed as an expression of the position we have been attributed. On the other hand, this is no deterministic process. Rather, the ongoing positioning provides the space for talk and action.

A position may also be understood as including aspects of the work one is expected to do, the task, and the kind of person one is expected to be, one's identity (Crevani, 2011). Hence, for example, the position of senior managers entails both the expectation of certain kinds of tasks to be suited for the person (for example, coordination), and of certain kind of personal characteristics (for example, authoritative). Moreover, if you think of some conversations you have participated in, you may recognize that we often position even actors not present at that moment, in relation to the ones present or to others not present.

The positions thus constructed will have to be taken into consideration, in one way or another, in the unfolding of the conversation and of subsequent conversations (cf. Gergen, 2010). For instance, if project managers are constructed as poor performers, people will probably not involve them in certain processes in which they might otherwise have played a role. As time passes, certain positions may start being taken for granted; for example, someone becomes 'an expert', which means that people will act consequentially by involving that person in certain tasks regardless of his/her formal role.

Summarizing, positioning is a practice taking place in conversations and affecting both the development of the conversation at hand and the actions and talks that become socially intelligible over time, as new conversations build on previous conversations (more or less coherently).

Bridging

Figure 10.5   Bridging

Bridging refers to practices in which actors are brought together and interdependencies are created and/ or intensified. Figure 10.5 may be one way of visualizing bridging: it is about connecting, connecting based on interdependences (each stone is dependent on the others for the bridge to hold). It is interdependence that is the 'glue'. People in organizations grow through the mesh of relations in which they are embedded. Furthermore, collective action may be viewed as based on bringing different stories, trajectories and views together (Barge and Fairhurst, 2008; Ospina and Foldy, 2010). Interdependencies are thus crucial for collective action to take place, something maybe counterintuitive for those schooled in more traditional accounts of leaders standing alone and nurturing their independence. Instead, according to this perspective, by including more actors and strengthening the meshes that connect them, collective action and achievements may gain importance over other more individual courses of action, thus increasing and strengthening the space for collective action.

Moreover, bridging is about connecting without erasing difference, and has therefore to do with mutuality, inclusiveness and multivocality (Fletcher, 2004; Ospina and Foldy, 2010).

You may think again of a group project and how, in order to move in somewhat similar directions, the people involved need to 'find each other'. It may require spending time on one-to-one connections, it may require an arena for dialogue and for surfacing different views, or it may require discussing your identities, among other possibilities (see Ospina and Foldy, 2010). You may also reflect on your friendships. How do you manage to 'reach each other'? You have probably something in common but also different opinions, different ideals, different backgrounds, and so on. How have you managed to connect without erasing such differences? What kind of discussions or episodes have been important to that end?

What do leadership practices achieve (temporarily)?

Taking a constructionist perspective means subscribing to a process view of leadership and reality (see Chapter 9) and therefore ceasing to treat leadership work as a sequence of finite stages performed by one individual. Rather, leadership work is an ongoing process. What this implies is that we will think of 'results' and 'outcomes' in a different way. Instead of identifying specific discrete results, as for example profitability or some index for innovation, and attributing these to certain leaders' properties, we will think of 'results' in more fluid and relational terms (Crevani et al., 2010). Instead of trying to take a snapshot of the situation, we want to appreciate how 'the situation' itself is unfolding. Hence, leadership work is still considered crucial for organizing, but in a different way. In other words, 'results' are themselves ongoing relational processes that leadership work produces. Looking at the literature, two sets of achievements emerge as particularly important. The first concerns the re-directing and supporting of collective action, the second is mutual learning. Leadership work may thus be described as leading to re-direction of ongoing organizing processes and re-structuring of relations (Uhl-Bien, 2006; Crevani, 2011; Uhl-Bien and Ospina, 2012). Leadership work in this sense is neither grandiose nor exceptional. It is accomplished as work is carried out, and it is thus pervasive in organizations. Leadership work performed in the practices of framing, positioning and bridging also leads to certain forms of mutual learning that increase the space of action for the people involved. Mutual learning is produced as different possibilities of meaning making are brought together, articulated and tried out (Fletcher, 2004; Barge and Fairhurst, 2008; Carroll and Simpson, 2012). This is also a process in which certain kinds of alignment may be achieved (Drath et al., 2008) thus building some common ground for sustaining concerted action.

Naming these as *re-directing* and *mutual learning* achievements should not lead you to think of them as something that can be 'finished' and 'finalized'– we are talking of ongoing processes, temporary achievements. However, although fluid, at times ambiguous and frequently contested, these processes are also processes in which power is enacted. Power relations and their structuring are central aspects to take into account and we may observe highly asymmetrical situations, in which relational dynamics grant more space of action to certain actors and limit the space for others, although focus on these issues varies among scholars.

What is noteworthy is that relational leadership scholars are often frustrated that traditional leadership ideals may oppress and/or limit people in organizations. Bringing to the fore practices usually overlooked may encourage the pursuit of more democratic and empowering processes. In this endeavour, power asymmetries are highlighted as a feature of traditional accounts of leadership, to which the relational approaches offer a more inclusive alternative (cf. Dachler and Hosking, 1995; Fletcher, 2004). Hence, a relational perspective often brings to the fore the 'power to' or 'power with', rather than the 'power over' dynamics (Follett, 1924).

DEFINITION: RELATIONAL PERSPECTIVES ON POWER

Follett's view is relational in the sense that individuals develop by relating to each other. Conflicts are inevitable but may be productive. People who work together are able to do things in concert with others and are therefore capable of co-actively constituting power that is legitimate to them, 'power with'. As a contrast to 'power with', 'power over' means, simply, that people are made to do what they otherwise would not do.

On the other hand, even in relational dynamics in which interdependence is fostered, power asymmetries may be reconstructed. For instance, framing can constrain people's space of action by disciplining them and limiting their possibility to act. Also, certain frames may be more easily mobilized than others, thus reproducing patterns of action that may re-establish power differences. When it comes to positioning, not only the space of action granted to different positions may vary considerably, but also processes of positioning imply in themselves either the reproduction or the restructuring of power relations.

 ## STOP AND REFLECT 10.4

Before proceeding, take a few moments to reflect on what you have learned so far. The following questions might help you:

- Can you find different images that may symbolize the three leadership practices introduced? Which aspects do they capture?
- Can you describe examples of conversations or situations in which framing, positioning and/or bridging has taken place? Reflect on whether the situations/conversations you have in mind are instances of 'power over' or 'power to'. If it is difficult to identify examples, you can go on analysing the project you had started working with at the end of the section on 'framing'. You should already have identified frames, can you analyse positions being constructed and positioning taking place? And have there been instances of bridging?

Practicing relational leadership

In the first part of this chapter, you have read about how to start seeing leadership relationally, that is how to make sense of existing processes in a different way. We can now turn to how you may *practise* leadership in a relational way, how to interact with others in order to change the practices of leadership.

What is the 'relational' in relational leadership?

Let us therefore discuss again what 'relational' in relational leadership may mean (see Figure 10.6). Keeping our focus on the constructionist perspective, we can now ask if relations are to be treated as means or ends. Or, in other words, does 'relational' imply that relational practices should be developed because a more competent engagement in those practices enhances leadership work or does 'relational' imply that relational practices should be developed because they are inherently ethical practices? This difference may be somehow difficult to grasp given the usual focus on instrumentality in leadership, which may have permeated your education and your experience of organizational life. Instrumentality means that we focus on the most efficient means to achieve some outcome, without taking aspects such as values and ethics into consideration. If you plan your project according to certain criteria, for example, it is often because they are supposed to guide your work in a way that assures the efficient use of your time and competence. You do not follow those criteria because they are criteria that guide your work in a way that enhances human life and growth. But once you have started thinking of yourself as an interdependent self, always becoming and growing in relation to others, thus intimately connected to 'others', the thought that we should also take responsibility for such relations and that fostering relationality may be something to pursue for the sake of humanity, rather than for enhancing organizing processes, is not so far-fetched any more. Would it, for example, be so strange to think of other participants in a project as human beings with whom to engage in an effort to help each other learn and grow?

Hence, once more it is possible to discern a range of understandings of relationality, going from 'relational' as 'done in relations' – what I will label relational achievement – to a more ethically motivated position of relating as caring and mutual responsibility – what I will name relational responsibility. Translating relational to *relational achievement* means that relations are valued since they are what reality is made of and since it is in relational dynamics that work, in particular leadership work, is carried out (e.g. Carroll et al., 2008; Crevani et al., 2010; Carroll and Simpson, 2012). In this sense, the handling of relational dynamics is crucial and may be developed. At the other end of the spectrum, relational translated into *relational responsibility* involves an ethical dimension of taking responsibility for the relation and for 'the other' to whom one is connected, and co-evolving with, in such relation. Even in this case, relational competence should be developed, but the reason for that is the imperative of more fully taking 'the other' into consideration when acting and interacting (e.g. McNamee and Gergen, 1999; Cunliffe and Eriksen, 2011; Hosking, 2011). In both cases, trust and inclusion are central aspects, and communication should not only be understood in terms of what is being said, but also in terms of emotional and aesthetic engagements (see, for example, Koivunen, 2003; Soila-Wadman and Köping, 2009).

What does it mean to practise relational leadership?

Having discussed what relational may mean, we turn now to what practising relational leadership may imply (see Figure 10.6 for a summary). Starting in the *relational achievement* end, relational leadership should unfold in collective acts. Leadership work should, in other words, be carried out in interactions involving several people based on dialogue forms that encourage and value, and to some extent align, different contributions in order to direct collective action. Perfect alignment is not necessarily a condition to be strived for, since it would mean reducing possibilities to one line of action at the expense of multivocality (Barge and Fairhurst, 2008; Crevani et al., 2010; Ospina and Foldy, 2010). Such ideas are rather similar to what Joe Raelin calls leaderful practice (Raelin, 2011). An important aspect of leadership work is thus to be able to be in conversation, to recognize how conversations are developing and to handle such developments by being sensibly responsive. The aim is to create space for the gradual emergence of coherent but open performances that support multiple positions rather than imposing one dominant rationality (Hosking, 2011).

At the other end of the range of relationality, leadership is 'being-in-relation-to others' (Cunliffe and Eriksen, 2011, p. 1430; see also Hosking, 2011). In this sense, the focus on respecting and supporting a multiplicity of voices is even more accentuated, as it is one way of coming into a respectful relation with others. Hence, what have been called 'living conversations' are important (Cunliffe and Eriksen, 2011) – conversations should be formed in terms of *talking with* rather than *talking to* people and should be kept open. Such an endeavour takes a moral connotation – Cunliffe and Eriksen talk, for example, of relational integrity in the sense that we should think of ourselves as accountable to others for our action and for the nature of the relations through which we grow in interdependence with others.

	Relational achievement	Relational responsibility
Starting point	We need to focus on, and develop, relational practices rather than individual behaviours and competences	We need to develop ethical ways of engaging with others in which we are accountable to the other
Leadership is about	Relational practices	Ethical practices
Example of issues	How can dialogical practices in which we harness difference be trained and developed?	How can we develop organisations in which we take care of one another in order to respect difference?
Example of authors	Fairhurst, Carroll, Simpson Raelin, Ospina, Barge	Hosking, Gergen, Cunliffe

Figure 10.6   The range of relational leadership understandings along the dimension relational achievement–relational responsibility

Four versions of relational leadership

Having discussed the meaning of relational and relational leadership along two dimensions, the *entity–constructionist perspective* dimension in the first part of the chapter, and the *relational achievement–responsibility* dimension above, we have now four ways of describing how to practise leadership, what to focus on and why to focus on that – see Figure 10.7. This is no exhaustive overview, but can be considered a map useful for becoming aware of some of the possibilities for practising leadership. Such a map should make clear for you that there are different meanings connected to the same label 'relational leadership', which implies that it is important to understand that for each of these meanings the practice of leadership is slightly different, the competences to be developed are different and the motives for doing so are different. If not openly discussed, divergent meanings may give rise to significant clashes. You can, for instance, think of a manager subscribing to the 'relating between people' version and a subordinate convinced that a 'relating grows people' version of leadership will be developed. Not only is the worldview completely different, but so are the values attached to it.

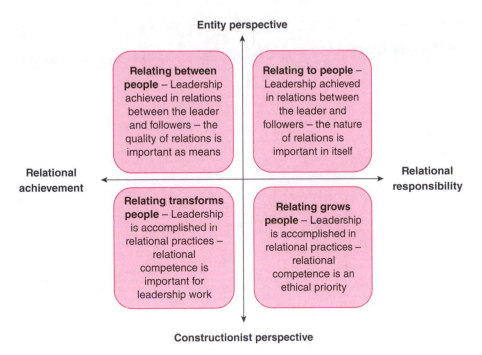

Figure 10.7   A map with four possible versions of relational leadership

What do we need to do in order to practise relational leadership?

Now that we have discussed definitions of relational leadership, we can dig deeper into how to practise leadership. We will focus on the constructionist perspective, which implies the most radical change. When it comes to the other dimension, that is relational achievement versus responsibility, the three practices are relevant in both cases. The difference lies in why they are important to people doing leadership and, consequently, which aspects within the practice may be crucial. Even in this part we will focus on three examples of practices that mirror the ones in the 'seeing leadership' part. You can find more examples in the literature (cf. Uhl-Bien and Ospina, 2012).

Movement between frames

As we saw in the first part of this chapter, framing is an important practice in relational leadership work. If you want to practise relational leadership you could therefore work on how to sensibly handle framing movements in interactions. While there may be meetings or conversations particularly organized for this aim (Ospina and Foldy, 2010), it is also important to recognize that handling movements between frames could become a practice that permeates conversations throughout the organization.

Moving between frames requires reflection on what kind of frames are currently mobilized, whether it is at the level of specific conversations or more in general at an organizational level. Constraining and disempowering frames should be contested and challenged (Ospina and Foldy, 2010). But more

Figure 10.8   Movement between frames (Acknowledgement: Pearl T. Rapalje/Koduckgirl)

generally, moving between frames is a practice to develop since it is in the movement that new meanings and new avenues are created (Barge and Fairhurst, 2008; Carroll and Simpson, 2012). Figure 10.8 is one way of visualizing the moments in which there is movement between different frames, going back to the photo metaphor introduced when talking of 'framing'. This is no task for one single person, but is a collective endeavour; it is a process of co-creation and learning. It is also a process that may be highly emotional; as Carroll and Simpson (2012) put it, we 'can see that assumptions cut right through rational, logical and detached selves to reveal and inflame what is "felt"' (p. 1302). Our engagement with and attachment to concepts, stances and positions are more or less forcefully revealed and possibly contested when different frames are brought into the conversation. If you remember the example of framing introduced in the first part of this chapter, moving from 'we have to fix the women' to 'we have to fix the men' will probably give rise to intense discussions revealing different kind of assumptions (about gender, about work, etc.) on which different people normally act. Moving framing should also be recognized as an exercise and negotiation of power.

One way to work on framing is to be more aware of the metaphors we use and to support each other in finding alternative ones, given the pervasive presence of metaphors in our conversations. For instance, at times people speak of organizations as machines that you can more or less easily tweak. Such a metaphor has a number of implications; for instance, that you can design processes that will work the way you have planned and that the people actually working are interchangeable. Adding other metaphors opens up for other assumptions and courses of action. For example, seeing an organization as an organism means recognizing the systemic nature of the organization, but also that some processes may have a life of their own and emerge in an unplanned way. Seeing an organization as a culture means recognizing that people are crucial and what guides them may be values and norms rather than formal instructions. The more alternatives, the more insight we gain on the phenomenon we are trying to makes sense of, although of course this also means learning to handle the uncertainty that several perspectives imply, compared with one limited view of the situation at hand.

STOP AND REFLECT 10.5

Working with stories may also be a viable path (Barge, 2012). For example, think of a project or, more in general, some aspect of your life (you like rock music or you love to travel, etc.). Starting from the current situation, try to describe when the story that leads to today starts and how: what the critical turning points were, who the people that had an impact were, and so on. In other words, how come you are now in the situation you are? What I am asking you to do is to create a plot for this project/aspect of your life. After that, try to elicit the other possible plots: try to see what happens if you pick other points in time (before and after) as the starting point and see if the story that describes how things have developed from that point to now changes as a consequence of the new beginning. Ask someone else to do the same exercise. What story does she or he tell? Finally, go on finding multiple possible stories that lead to the current situation. This exercise may appear difficult to begin with, but it helps you in developing how to move between frames.

Positioning

Figure 10.9   Positioning

To consciously work with positioning may be challenging due to the quick and often unreflected nature of the conversational moves in which positionings unfold. Figure 10.9 shows two dancers flying together and helping each other in that effort. Building on the dance metaphor previously introduced, this picture is a metaphor of a practice of positioning resulting in people mutually expanding their space of action, thus empowering each other.

Hence, working with 'positioning' as a practice may require reflecting on and engaging with the pattern that the conversation takes, a pattern that should avoid producing dominant positions that limit others' space. People should therefore try to address one another in terms that allow for multivocality and invite the others to join in the conversation (Hosking, 2011). Responsive listening becomes an important competence to this purpose (Barge, 2012). Obviously, there is also a need to become sensitive to when, and how, the positioning that is taking place marginalizes certain voices and views. Or, in other words, there is a need to recognize the exercise of power in conversation. Complete power symmetry may be not achievable, but you should strive to be careful in how the flow of the conversation may result in certain positions becoming constrained in terms of space of action. Striving for values such as compassion for the other (Raelin, 2011) is an essential part of relational responsibility, but may also serve its purpose in approaches closer to relational achievement.

Without reflection on positioning, it is difficult to advance a relational agenda. Think, for example, of a group meeting in which one participant is repeatedly positioned as not-knowledgeable. It may be the case of a male nurse that is sitting in an animated discussion with the parent of a patient and the female surgeon who has operated on the patient. This nurse may be positioned as not-knowledgeable, and thus disempowered, by the parents mobilizing his gender as not conforming to expectations about the area of knowledge (nursing) he is working with ('How can a man understand what kind of care my son needs?'). The nurse may also be disempowered by the surgeon mobilizing her professional belonging, and the consequent power asymmetries between doctors and nurses ('How can a nurse know better than a surgeon?'). On the other hand, the nurse may mobilize his gender and the connected traditional power relations in society ('Women should take care of domestic affairs, not playing doctors'). These are all power-full moves. They may happen because of deliberate choices, but also unconsciously in the flow of the conversation. Failure to recognize them and openly discuss them leads to weak premises for working with the other relational leadership practices, as the ground on which to build is 'damaged'. Arguing for an alternative frame, for example, may become difficult from such a disempowered position.

Positioning takes place in a context that is brought into being through the conversation by mobilizing and reconstructing situated meanings, as in this example gender identity and professional belonging (Barge, 2012). Hence, positioning builds on previous conversations, both in the particular organization and in society more generally. And skilful handling of positioning means being able to tune in to both the content and the consequences of what is being said (Hersted and Gergen, 2013).

 STOP AND REFLECT 10.6

If available in your country, go to a web service providing movies, TV drama, reality shows or series, and choose one you are interested in. Take a pen and follow a dialogue. Try to write down how people position themselves as they talk. Look several times at the dialogue and try to refine your analysis. Once you are satisfied, identify if there is some positioning that could be an obstacle to practising relational leadership and propose at least two ways in which, if you had been one of the participants in the conversation, you could have contributed to avoiding the problematic positioning and co-creating alternative positionings.

Resonating

Figure 10.10   Resonating

The last leadership practice that I am going to present to you mirrors the 'bridging' practice we can 'see' in organizations. *Resonating* is one way of working in order to make bridging happen. While the stones illustrating bridging are static, in order to illustrate the practice of resonating ripples may be better, as Figure 10.10 shows. As ripples meet each other, they change and interplay with each other. While this is a natural phenomenon, people may try to be open for interplay in a more conscious way. Barge talks of 'resonant positioning' (2012) and I build on the ideas he proposes. Resonating means being responsive to the emergent patterns in the conversation and being receptive to being moved or struck. Hence, it is not only about being alert for what frames are being mobilized, for example. Resonating also includes recognizing strong emotions that we may feel in the dialogue, as they signal that some note has been struck and it may be worth exploring that connection further (Barge, 2012). Resonating also means tuning to the tone of the conversation in order to connect with others in a way that opens the dialogue for multiple trajectories (Hosking, 2011). It means, therefore, striking a balance between confirming and challenging what others are saying and how they are feeling (Barge and Fairhurst, 2008).

Resonating is thus a subtle practice. It is difficult to exemplify in a written text, such as in this textbook, and it may actually be easier for you to recall some recent conversation and if you had the feeling, afterwards, that at some point the conversation left some potentially important path unexplored, because of something someone said or did – or you may have been left with the sensation of having interrupted some potential development. That could have been one moment in which resonating did not work. Or if you think of conversations that seem to lead to nowhere, every participant following his/her own path without succeeding in finding a way of at least partially joining the paths – thus failing in co-authoring the conversation. This may be another example of lack of resonating. But, on the other hand, when you face co-authoring that collapses into tight consensus on a single story or path you are witnessing lack of resonating. Relational leadership work is about producing direction in an organic fashion, not in a linear one. Potentially divergent trajectories are an important element, as well as the tension between different framings applied to a situation (Barge and Fairhurst, 2008; Carroll and Simpson, 2012; Hersted and Gergen, 2013). Hence, resonating is an act of balance guided by the respect for the other, an ethical engagement (Cunliffe and Eriksen, 2011).

STOP AND REFLECT 10.7

Now that you are familiar with the practice of relational leadership, you can try to apply what you have learned. Try to perform these three practices in a concrete situation. It may be some project work or some conversation you have with friends. If possible, you should explain to the others involved in the conversation the three practices you should jointly try to enact.

- What did you learn from your attempt? What was difficult and what went well?

Relational competence

The practices just described are just three examples of what a relational practice of leadership work may entail. Common to all practices is that you need to work on a different kind of competence than what is usually explored in leadership courses or development programmes. First of all, the 'who' obviously changes. Managers are the actors usually expected to show and develop leadership capabilities. This is not enough for improving relational leadership work since they are influential co-creators in interaction, not the only actors – which means that more people than managers need to be involved in developing leadership. With a more accentuated constructionist perspective, leadership work is not at all an individual question – leadership work is a social process of co-creation in which the practices described above may play important parts. Hence, rather than the person, it is the practice that has to be developed (Carroll et al., 2008). Of course, it is people who enact practices, but an explicit focus on the practice raises other kind of questions. It is therefore not enough that one person at a time works on how she or he acts and talks. It is the relational dynamics that have to be at the centre and you should work together with other people after having read this chapter and help each other in 'seeing' leadership and in 'practising' leadership relationally. It is when the abstract notions meet concrete situations that the full potential of relational leadership may be deployed. Hence, the kind of competence we are talking about is partially individual and partially collective and situated, which also means that there is no universal recipe of how to do. Rather, this competence grows by being in relation and learning to reflect on such being in relation.

Relational competence should also be understood as being about ordinary situations and everyday conversations, rather than being related to some specific occurrences in which to exercise leadership. Finally, especially if subscribing to relational responsibility, this is no value-neutral competence in which certain learned skills are applied without questioning their ethical aspects and the power effects they may contribute to.

Concluding with some questions

This chapter has provided you with an introduction to relational leadership, both in the form of lenses to analyse current practices through and of suggestions on how develop such relational practices. Figure 10.7 provides a map of the alternative views you can find in the literature, views that imply somewhat different meaning given to the concept of 'relational'. This map orients you in the existing literature and enables you to find the approach that better fits your values and work. The chapter also provides more detailed descriptions of six leadership practices, but you are invited to read additional literature for other suggestions.

Case study: W. L. Gore and Associates

As a first application of what you have learnt, you are now invited to look closer at W. L. Gore and Associates, the company introduced at the beginning of this chapter, and to use this case in order to reflect on concepts and ideas related to relational leadership. You can find information about the company on the internet, for example at www.managementexchange.com/blog/no-more-heroes. You are also invited to watch the YouTube clip cited in the introductory section again.

Once you have read or watched more information on the organization, try to answer the following questions.

1   What kind of notions does relational leadership as a perspective challenge? Can you exemplify by referring to what the people working at W. L. Gore and Associates say?
2   Listen to the interview mentioned at the beginning of this chapter. In which quadrant of the diagram in Figure 10.7 would you place Terri Kelly's story, and why?
3   If you now embrace a fully constructionist perspective, where would you look for leadership practices and how would you describe them? If you were the CEO, could you provide a different account if you were interviewed and what would you say?
4   If you were to launch an initiative for developing relational leadership practices in the organization, what would you suggest you and your co-workers need to work with, how and why?

Finally, the stories told by people employed by the organization are, for obvious reasons, avoiding the subject of power and power relations. For example, peer evaluation and leaders chosen by their peers may sound like very democratic practices. But we have seen that in relational dynamics power is at play. Describe some practices in which you expect power to be enacted and how.

The key points in this chapter were ...

- Relational leadership is not necessarily a different kind of leadership; rather it is a different lens over what counts as leadership that can lead to different practices. It extends our view further than simply individuals who are designated as leaders, and looks to the social processes involved in producing leadership.

- Entity and constructionist perspectives refer to how we see the nature of reality, including people. Entity perspectives see individuals as stable entities, who grow by increasing in independence. Constructionist perspectives see individuals who are constantly in the process of constructing and being constructed by the mesh of relations that connect them (the world around them, you could say). This is important because it fundamentally alters what we recognize as leadership. An entity perspective sees leaders and followers as stable roles, whereas a constructionist perspective sees leadership as an emergent co-creation between people.

- Entity perspectives are the most prevalent way of thinking about leadership currently. To see leadership relationally, we need a new vocabulary that can reflect a constructionist perspective.

- There are three practices of leadership that we can use to see and work with relational leadership:

  - Framing – a frame is a perspective constructing a situation. We can become conscious of the frames we are using as well as provide alternatives and learn to move between them.

  - Positioning – positions (such as junior, senior, insider) are produced in conversations and need to be understood in relation to each other. We can work with these by becoming aware of the way the conversations we take part in (or other conversations) are positioning ourselves in ways that marginalize or empower both ourselves and others.

  - Bridging and resonating – rather than being independent, people are constantly leaning on each other in the organization, like parts of a bridge. We can be conscious of this by thinking of conversations as ripples in water, resonating off one another in ways that build movement without collapsing difference.

 # Further thinking

The following papers present analyses of leadership that can be considered coherent with a relational perspective. Some of them use the word 'relational' explicitly, others not. After reading them, have a go at answering the questions below.

Carroll, B., Levy, L. and Richmond, D. (2008). Leadership as practice: Challenging the competency paradigm. *Leadership*, 4(4), 363–379.

Carroll, B. and Simpson, B. (2012). Capturing sociality in the movement between frames: An illustration from leadership development. *Human Relations*, 65(10), 1283–1309.

Cunliffe, A. L. and Eriksen, M. (2011). Relational leadership. *Human Relations*, 64(11), 1425–1449.

Hosking, D. M. (2011b). Telling tales of relations: Appreciating relational constructionism. *Organization Studies*, 32(1), 47–65.

Koivunen, N. and Wennes, G. (2011). Show us the sound! Aesthetic leadership of symphony orchestra conductors. *Leadership*, 7(1): 51–71.

Soila-Wadman, M. and Köping, A.-S. (2009). Aesthetic relations in place of the lone hero in arts leadership. *International Journal of Arts Management*, 12(1), 31–43.

Questions guiding your reflection:

1   How do the researchers approach the cases they analyse? Which methods do they apply? Which approach is more appealing to you and why? How would you design your own research?
2   Are the concepts introduced in this chapter useful in order to 'see' relational leadership in the situations described by the articles? Does the analysis provided by the researchers add other dimensions?
3   The articles also provide a range of ways of thinking relationality. Is it about language and communication; about reflection; about feelings for the other; about using our senses in order to relate; or about spirituality, to name some of the questions they generate? What does this mean for studying and practicing leadership relationally? How can we take materiality, emotions, the senses, and so on, into consideration? Look also at the other chapters in this book in order to enrich your discussion.
4   Finally, in this chapter, Crevani describes six leadership practices. The labels given to these practices are metaphors and the images illustrate such metaphors. After having read the articles above, can you identify more relational leadership practices, label them and find images that might depict them?

 # Leadership on screen

While the focus of 'practising relational leadership' is on more inclusive and multivocal forms of leadership, the dynamics of framing, positioning and bridging can also be observed in processes that are neither democratic not inclusive. For instance, recent successful series as *The Shield* or *Game of Thrones* that have been criticized for their violence and their gendered views provide examples of such dynamics. This reminds us of the importance of being aware of power effects in leadership work. Other popular series have focused on friendships and work, often in a hospital setting, such as *Grey's Anatomy* or *Scrubs*, and contain elements of relational dynamics as doing work and being in relation are intertwined. It is also worth noting that some relational dynamics may be portrayed as instrumentally deployed by the 'great architect', as in *House of Cards,* which means that relational dynamics are not necessarily the same thing as relational leadership. Finally, the popular trilogy of *The Hunger Games* provides us with instances of relational dynamics and one example of construction of a leader as a symbol (rather than a leader intentionally influencing people).

LEADERSHIP WITHOUT LEADERS

UNDERSTANDING ANARCHIST ORGANIZING THROUGH THE LENS OF CRITICAL LEADERSHIP STUDIES

Neil Sutherland

After spending his formative years touring across the world in DIY punk bands, Neil has taken the not-so-obvious career progression of writing about leadership. Disappointed with the seeming lack of interest in the exciting and innovative organizing processes of 'alternative' groups – like those he encountered on his travels – Neil set out to investigate them himself. Some insights are presented in this chapter.

What this chapter is all about …

The main idea is that mainstream leadership concepts focus on what leaders do, rather than what leadership is. Consequently, such theories cannot understand how leaderless organizations continue to function. Anarchist organizations – those that defy all norms of hierarchical organization – push the boundaries of what we know about leadership.

The key questions this chapter answers are:

- What is anarchism and why is it interesting for leadership?
- Are leaders essential for organizational functioning?
- What is critical leadership studies?
- What is leadership if it is not the actions of leaders?

Introduction

Although there has long since been a strong undercurrent of anarchism in the UK, in the last few years there has been a surge of interest in 'leaderless' anarchist social movement organizations (SMOs). Whilst anarchist groups have been organizing against capitalism and the state in a grassroots, non-hierarchical manner for years, the anarchist-centric organizing principles of the 2010/2011 student protests (initially targeting the Labour government's further education spending cuts, and later the increase in the cap on tuition fees by the Conservative/Liberal Democrat coalition government) and the 2011/2012 'Occupy' movement (set up to protest against social and economic equality) gained unprecedented exposure. Since then, the movement has showed no signs of slowing down, with a whole host of anarchist groups springing up, and national demonstrations and actions receiving increasing interest. Whilst the mainstream media have been keen to disregard these groups as 'chaotic hijackers' (*Daily Mail*, 2010), others have been more interested in trying to understand their radical organizing principles, which stand in stark contrast to the structures of more 'conventional' organizations: stressing the importance of leaderlessness, horizontality, widespread participation, democracy and anti-authoritarianism. One particularly interesting topic of debate has been centred on questions around leadership, with a variety of commentators asking: how does leadership happen in 'leaderless' groups?

STOP AND REFLECT 11.1

Perhaps you are interested in such questions, have read about these ideas in newspapers, magazines or blogs or, alternatively, have not yet given them much thought. Before we begin, then, let us take stock of your current understandings with an activity. Think about the following questions:

- What is leadership?
- What do you know about the organizing principles of modern SMOs, such as the Occupy movement and protest groups? How do they get things done? How are they different to 'conventional' business organizations?
- Do you think that organizations that do not have formal, individual and permanent leaders can still 'do' leadership?

When approaching the third question, try to articulate your own understandings. You will probably have a gut reaction to the statement, but why do you think this? What does it tell you about your underlying understandings of what leadership is?

Although a variety of theorists have attempted to investigate the phenomenon of leadership within SMOs in the past, they have all worked from the same assumption and definition: that leadership is the *resulting product* of individual, permanent and stable leader's actions, and thus an absence of *leaders* also implies an absence of leader*ship*. Generally speaking, previous studies concentrated their efforts on examining centralized and bureaucratic Marxist organizations, and their understandings draw from 'mainstream' theories of leadership in organization studies – conceptualizing leadership as something 'that leaders do', and something that disappears when these permanent leaders are not present. As such, mainstream-inspired leadership researchers attempted to understand leadership by focusing on 'successful leaders' personas, thoughts and actions' (Collinson, 2005, p. 1423). Ultimately, these theorists generally conclude by suggesting that individual leaders are not only necessary, but *essential* for organizational functioning, and are solely responsible for the overall vision, inspiration, transformation and achievement of organizations. However, a variety of scholars have noted that modern-day SMOs are no longer organized in the same way as those of the 1960s and 1970s, and are now characterized by decentralization, radical democracy, anti-hierarchy, anti-authoritarianism, participation and leaderlessness. In short, they tend to be structured around *anarchist* organizing principles. At this point, it is worth returning to the third question that you have just answered, asking: how do previous theories of leadership in SMOs relate to the current wave of anarchist organizations that function in the absence of leaders? In essence, they would suggest that without strong leaders at the helm, organizations are doomed to fail in their aims and goals. However, it is clear that the current wave of anarchist SMOs are still going strong and continuing to not only organize in a non-hierarchical way, but are also successfully challenging government and state initiatives. Perhaps, then, it is reasonable to assume that leadership *is* still happening, but not in the same way that mainstream scholars would recognize.

However, because so little has been written on leadership in SMOs since the 1960/1970s, it is generally assumed that the notions put forward by earlier scholars still hold true today, and no theories of leadership can explain how anarchist groups might function. I believe that we should take issue with this idea, and rather than unproblematically accepting the underlying assumptions of mainstream perspectives, instead we should work toward *re-conceptualising* and *re-defining* leadership – instead seeing it as a process that can be enacted collectively, and as something that is not the responsibility of a chosen few. Whilst this may seem a daunting task, turning to the literature on critical leadership studies (CLS) offers us an appropriate starting point. CLS is a relatively new school of thought, and although scholars draw upon a variety of approaches, there is a common view about denaturalizing the underpinnings of mainstream perspectives – that leaders are essential for organizational functioning – and, in fact, seeing a reliance on individual leaders as a potentially negative and destructive practice. However, as well as providing critiques of mainstream leadership research, another strand of CLS has been useful for advancing our understanding of what leadership actually is, instead seeing it as a socially constructed *process* that is constituted by 'meaning-making', and embedded in context and culture. Rather than taking individual leaders as the focal point, attention is instead paid to the ways in which leadership emerges more organically and discursively. Rethinking leadership in this way is valuable, as it offers an opportunity to understand how leadership may be performed in anarchist SMOs; in organizations that function in the *absence* of individual, hierarchically positioned leaders.

STOP AND REFLECT 11.2

Go back to the questions you answered at the beginning of this chapter. Now that you have a preliminary understanding about what this chapter will tackle, where does your definition of leadership 'sit'? Alongside the mainstream conceptualization – that leadership is something that individual leaders do? Or with a critical focus – of leadership as a process that can be enacted collectively?

The remainder of this chapter is structured as follows. I will begin by more formally introducing SMOs – defining *what* they are, as well as denoting the shift from Marxism to anarchism in recent years. After this, the next section will explore previous studies of leadership in SMOs, where I will also highlight some problematic elements and possible areas for advancing understandings. As has been highlighted, one such route for this is to draw upon the work conducted in the field of CLS – the focus of the third section of this chapter – which has been fundamental for moving us away from the mainstream preoccupation with individual *leaders*, and towards a conceptualization that emphasizes the importance of 'meaning-making', and the relational, dynamic and discursive qualities of leader*ship*.

Following this, the chapter will conclude with some reflections on the ways in which one anarchist SMO – the Radical Student Group (RSG) – has gone about 'collectivising' leadership, that is constructing settings where (a) any member can come forward to manage meanings and define reality, and (b) no one individual can assume a permanent and stable leading role. To do this, we will take the 'meeting' as the main point of focus, and discuss some of the participative-democratic practices and processes that were put in place, such as consensus decision-making, role rotation and collective agenda setting. At the end of this chapter therefore, you will not only have a greater understanding of what leadership *is*, but will also have looked at how actors are going about constructing settings where 'anybody can do it'.

Social movement organizations (SMOs)

DEFINITION: WHAT IS A SOCIAL MOVEMENT ORGANIZATION (SMO)?

Although there is considerable diversity when it comes to defining the key tenets of SMOs – as there are so many different organizational forms and ideological underpinnings – theorists generally agree that they pursue positive social change, engage in protest and/or campaigning activity, and are (mostly) volunteer-run.

Giddens (1984) suggests that there are four, non-mutually exclusive, areas in which SMOs operate, including: democratic focused (seeking to increase democracy and participation in the wider society); labour focused (working for control of the workplace); environmental focused (including those who advocate sustainability and other ecological issues); peace focused (such as anti-war organizations and those that oppose inter-human violence).

To begin, SMOs are defined by Smith as 'locally based, autonomous, volunteer-run, non-profit groups that engage in protest activity, and ... have memberships of volunteers who perform most, and often all, of the work/activity done' (2000, p. 7). However, whilst this definition is useful for a broad overview, there is considerable diversity when it comes to the specific organizational forms and underlying assumptions of SMOs. For example, whilst 'classic' scholars of the 1960 and 1970s focused on Marxist organizations (which tended to have centralized, hierarchical structures and clear leaders), others have noted the increasing influence of *anarchist* thought in post-1970s SMOs, with organizations now emphasizing decentralisation, horizontal decision-making, anti-hierarchy, radical democracy, widespread participation and 'leaderlessness' (e.g. Day, 2005).

STOP AND REFLECT 11.3

Pause for a moment here, and think about how this 'ideological shift' might change how leadership is understood and performed within modern groups.

- What would you expect leadership to look like in a centralized organization (such as the Marxist groups of the 1960–1970s)?
- How might this change in anti-hierarchical and radically democratic anarchist organizations, where every member is expected to participate?

The shift towards anarchism

Of course, anarchism did not emerge for the first time only 40 years ago, and in fact its origins can be traced back to the Stoics and the Cynics (Crabtree, 1992). Perhaps more notably, however, was the increase in anti-authoritarian writings and actions throughout the nineteenth and twentieth centuries from thinkers such as Proudhon, Bakunin, Kropotkin, Godwin and Goldman, as well as the surge in anarchist movements across Spain, Italy, France, the Americas, the UK and Russia. Although anarchism has never 'gone away', it is nevertheless still reasonable to suggest that more recent years *have* seen a revival in anarchist theory and practice. As has been the tradition over the years, there are a whole host of differing opinions and standpoints from contemporary anarchists, with some defending a more individualistic account; others fighting for a communitarian form; some (although, not many) attempting to 'curb' the powers of capitalism; and others looking to abolish it completely; some sticking to peaceful means of action; and others stressing the need for an active overthrow of the state. It would be beyond the scope of this chapter to wade into these various debates, and it is not my intention to do so. Therefore, whilst attempting to avoid making sweeping assertions that apply to *all* anarchist SMOs, it is still important to denote some of the underlying factors of modern movements and groups. To do this, I follow Graeber's (2002) account, suggesting that as well as ultimately aiming for an end to capitalism, hierarchical relations and the state, contemporary anarchism can be characterized as concerned with a radical form of democracy, and a focus on prefigurative politics. In fact, the two are inextricably linked:

- *Radical democracy*. It is argued that a concern with democracy, participation, freedom and equality is at the heart of what anarchism is about, that is: 'creating new forms of organisation'; 'creating and enacting networks based on principles of decentralised, non-hierarchical consensus democracy' in order to 'reinvent daily life as a whole' (Graeber, 2002, p. 70). Over the decades, activists have begun constructing diverse organizational forms, practices and processes that allow for cooperative and egalitarian social relations. Often, the underlying reason for this is an opposition to authoritative leaders, and to allow for structures that encourage 'bottom-up' engagement and widespread participation, in lieu of domineering social relations. The motivation for this is primarily because if individual, authoritative leaders are present, then a clear hierarchy would exist – of 'them' (those at the apex of the organization) and 'us' (as passive recipients of orders) – and instead of the organization being democratically steered, it would be the product of an elite who direct from the top-down. This 'anti-leaders' stance can be traced right back to the modern origins of anarchist thought, when Proudhon proclaimed: 'whoever lays his hand on me to govern is a usurper and a tyrant, and I declare him my enemy' (1849 [1993], p. 43).

- *Prefigurative politics.* Gordon defines the term as 'the modes of organisation and tactics undertaken ... accurately reflect[ing] the future society being sought by the group' (2005, p. 62). In short, rather than assuming a consequentialist outlook (which privileges ends over means), prefiguration understands the means to be *as important* as the ends. It sees them as inextricably linked, and rejects a focus on either means or ends at the expense of the other. Discussing this, Juris notes that 'radical ... activists are not only seeking to intervene within dominant public spheres; they are also challenging representative democracy, in part by developing their own democratic forms of organising and decision-making' (2008, p. 295). In short, if we are seeking to ultimately replace and provide an alternative to liberal representative democracy in the wider society, this must begin in the internal practices, processes and structures that are created in the organization's here and now practices. That is, activists are 'building a new world in the shell of the old'.

Whilst various theorists have sought to empirically investigate how contemporary SMOs organize, none have investigated how they might deal with questions of *leadership*. This is surprising, especially given that classic SMO scholars wrote in detail about leadership in 1960s/1970s Marxist movements. However, many years have passed since these texts were published, and they are now outdated and less sailent, unable to explain how leadership can be performed in the absence of leaders. In order to demonstrate that a new understanding of leadership is necessary, the next section will provide a brief overview of the literature on SMO leadership, emphasising: (a) that they work on the narrow assumption that leadership is simply something 'that leaders do'; and (b) that individual, hierarchically positioned leaders are essential for organizational functioning and success. Overall, we will see that accepting the conceptualizations put forward by previous SMO scholars is problematic, as they fail to understand the relational, dynamic and co-constructed nature of leadership. Rather, what would be more preferable is an approach that acknowledges how leadership can be performed in a more collective manner, amongst a range of actors, and not simply as a top-down phenomenon that is done *by* hierarchically positioned individuals *to* others at the bottom of the hierarchy. Only then can we really begin to understand the relationship between leadership and anarchism, rather than working on outdated assumptions and casting them off as mutually exclusive opposites.

Previous ('mainstream') approaches to leadership in SMOs

Although SMOs have received increased attention since the 1960s, scholars have noted that *leadership* is an understudied area (Morris and Staggenborg, 2002). This has not always been the case, however, as the

1960/1970s saw a spike in authors attempting to conceptualize how leadership was done. As highlighted in the previous section, theorists in this period tended to focus on Marxist organizations, which (often) had clear formal leaders. As such, they stressed the importance of centralized and hierarchical organizational forms for success, and sought to investigate individualistic strategies for 'maximising influence and power' (Buechler, 1995, p. 442). As far as leadership was concerned, there are some commonalities amongst theorists' assertions, especially about their understandings of what 'leadership' is. In short, these theories identify leadership as the resulting product of what individual leaders do. That is, they suggest that if we want to understand how leadership is done, then the only way to 'access' it is to examine how leaders work; how their personalities affect success; what specific styles, traits, behaviours and skills they have; and how they adapt themselves to different situations – all of which are approaches that will be familiar from the first section of this book. Generally speaking, this understanding draws from 'mainstream' theories of leadership in organization studies. The main ideas surrounding leadership in SMOs are summarized in Table 11.1.

Exploring these ideas in more detail, there are a variety of different ways in which previous scholars have attempted to understand SMO leadership, all of which draw strong parallels with mainstream approaches in organization studies. One of the more prominent strands of leadership research in SMO studies draws on charismatic, traitist and 'transformational' leadership theory; suggesting that charisma is an inherited and innate personality trait that sets the leader apart from ordinary people, and leads to the perception that they have 'supernatural' or 'superhuman' abilities. It is argued that this kind of leader has been necessary in the emergence of collective action throughout history, as, in times of 'economic, ethical, religious and political distress' (Gerth and Mills, 1958, p. 245), the leaders have been charismatic. Drawing on these ideas, several theorists have argued that individual, charismatic, non-democratic leaders are *essential* in any SMO, solely responsible for taking control of the overall vision, inspiration, resource mobilization, transformation and goal attainment of organizations. Heroic leaders play a central role in devising strategies and facilitating mobilisation by reducing costs and increasing advantages for followers. Leaders may also be understood as 'guardians of themes' (Bate et al., 2004, p. 62), in that they are the embodiment of the change that she/he wants to see. A clear distinction is drawn between leaders and followers here, with the leaders taking control of the organization, and followers becoming passive actors who lack agency, and only focus on following leaders.

Although 'trait-based' theories (Chapters 2 and 3) were (and continue to be) popular, others have stepped away from the idea that leaders' abilities are innate, and towards the understanding that there are specific *learned* styles and behaviours that can be extracted. Importantly, emphasis is placed on the idea that there is no 'one best way' to lead, but instead leaders' behaviour should be dependent on a variety of factors, such as the people involved, the required task and the organizational structure. In short, leaders do not possess just one set of characteristics, but are expected to have different 'faces', and should know when to use each one. Various studies of SMO leadership therefore focus on identifying the roles fulfilled by different types of movement leaders at different stages in the organization's development. McCarthy and Zald (1973), for example, posit that leaders must shift roles during different stages of a movement's life-cycle: during the first stages they must act as 'prophets' or visionaries; then as official representatives in the formalization period; and, finally, as administrators as institutionalization occurs. Similarly, Nadler and Tushman (1990) suggest that, depending on the situation, leaders display several distinct characteristics, including envisioning (creating an engaging vision of a future state);

Table 11.1 Traditional approaches to leadership in SMOs

	Examples of key SMO theorists	Underlying assumptions	Who does leadership? What attention is paid to followers?	What behaviours do leaders exhibit?
Traitist/ charismatic/ transformational	Blumer (1951); Gerth and Mills (1958); Oberschall (1973); Bate et al. (2004)	Leaders are born with innate and inherited characteristics.	Leaders alone, who are solely responsible for resource mobilisation and organization successes. Followers are passive and lack agency.	The literature is not unified, but agrees that leaders should always be in charge; providing a coherent vision; motivating others; rewarding and punishing; and directing activities.
Situational/ contingency	Zald and Ash (1966); McCarthy and Zald (1973); Nadler and Tushman (1990)	Leadership capacities can be 'taught' and developed, rather than being innate. There is no 'one best way' to lead, and particular styles are more appropriate in certain situations.	Mostly leaders alone. However, in certain situations, a more 'democratic' style may be preferable, where follower participation is encouraged.	A variety, from more democratic and ad hoc forms (in early stages of the organization's life-cycle) to increasing formalized and autocratic (as the organization grows).
Post-heroic/ distributed	Melucci (1990); Ganz (2000); Poletta (2002); Western (2008)	Leaders are not necessarily 'figureheads', and instead are more concerned with promoting widespread democracy and participation.	Followers are included much more, but the ultimate responsibility of success/failure still lies with individual leaders.	Delegation; empowerment of followers; management of emotional labour; increasing participation in decision-making periods.

energizing (stimulating energy throughout the organization through personal demonstration); and enabling (helping to facilitate processes, structures and resources). Finally, Zald and Ash (1966) highlight the importance of organizational structure in affecting the demands placed on leaders, with more exclusive organizations requiring leaders to focus on 'mobilizing' tasks, and inclusive organizations needing an 'articulating' style.

However, there has been a shift more recently as attempts have been made to explain how leadership can be performed more democratically. Paralleling the rise of 'post-heroic' and 'distributed' leadership approaches in organization studies, SMO theorists have sought to re-imagine leadership by highlighting how leaders encourage democratic practices within organizations; enabling others to get involved with decision-making and managing the emotional labour that may come about through increasing responsibility. Rather than the leader acting in an authoritarian manner, they are expected to take on a facilitative role: stepping back; delegating tasks; 'empowering' followers to be engaged with vision, learning and action; and constructing environments that allow for mutual learning. However, despite these attempts to expand the notion of leadership, the assumption that it emanates from an individual (albeit more 'democratic') leader remains, rather than being a process enacted by a multitude of organizational members. Furthermore, writing on distributed approaches in mainstream leadership studies, Collinson and Collinson (2009) note that, despite the change of focus, these forms are still fundamentally about top-down *delegation*, rather than bottom-up *engagement*. In short, followers may be 'empowered', but this is always determined by individual leaders, who also have the power to restrict or revoke such opportunities. For example, whilst Ganz notes that leadership in SMOs 'goes well beyond that of the stereotypical charismatic public persona', the development of democratic and participative structures is still seen to be the 'responsibility' (2010, p. 528) of permanent individual leaders.

After briefly looking at some of the previous approaches to SMO leadership, it can be seen that although there are many different perspectives, in general they rely on similar ideas – to reiterate: that 'leadership' is the resulting product of individual leaders' actions. Therefore, rather than seeking to ask the question 'What is leadership?' scholars have instead asked 'What do leaders do?' Although this may seem to be a subtle distinction, in fact it has much larger implications:

- First, it means that the term 'leadership' is left undefined, and leads to a situation where 'we know all too much about … leaders' but 'know far too little about leadership' (Burns, 1978, p. 1). Indeed, in many mainstream management texts that aim to provide organizations with *the* answer for effectiveness, a chapter devoted to leadership will be little more than a glorified tick-list of behaviours that have been recognized in previous 'successful' leaders. Therefore, although we might have a greater understanding of what specific leaders do, we are no closer to knowing what *leadership* itself is.
- Furthermore, because leadership is only defined by observing and examining leaders, *non*-leaders are paid very little attention, and when they *are* addressed, the theories simply refer to them as passive recipients of the leader's orders and goals who are marked by their 'susceptibility to certain leader behaviours or styles' (Collinson, 2005, p. 1424).
- This leader/follower binary, Gronn (2002) argues, remains 'sacrosanct' within mainstream leadership studies, and as a result of this, it could be seen that these perspectives function on the unitaristic assumption that some do/should have the power to 'lead', and some don't/shouldn't. Overall, the fault lines are clear here: from a mainstream perspective, individual, permanent and

stable leaders are the ones who are primarily responsible for *doing* leadership, and followers are reduced to a passive role, with leadership being done *to* them.

Mainstream conceptualizations are problematic because they offer no answers for situations in which individual, permanent and stable leaders are not present – in radically democratic SMOs, for example – because, if we only define leadership by the actions of individual leaders, then their absence would suggest the non-existence and 'disappearance' of leader*ship* as well. In part, this may be due to the context in which previous writings on SMO leadership emerged. Anarchism and 'leaderlessness' were not as influential (or widespread), but rather SMOs were traditionally organized in a much more formal, centralized and hierarchical manner (Day, 2005). Unfortunately, however, there has been little written on leadership in SMOs since the 1960/1970s, and previous theories are now outdated and less salient with the anarchistic organizing principles of contemporary SMOs. That is, they are unable to account for organizations that do not have individual, hierarchically placed, permanent and stable leaders. This leads to a situation where leadership itself is now being denounced in leaderless organizations and is seen to be incompatible with the ideologies and underpinnings of contemporary anarchist groups.

At this fork in the road, there are two options for us to take: (a) to assume the same understandings as mainstream scholars, and see that an absence of leaders also implies that looking for leader*ship* is futile; or (b) to step back and instead seek to reconceptualise what we understand 'leadership' to be. Regarding this, Fyke and Sayegh (2001) have suggested that, to date, we have relied too heavily on the idea of leadership being understood as an authoritative top-down process, and should move towards a more open definition that will allow for an understanding of how leadership can be performed in a more collective and egalitarian manner, and in the absence of leaders. Only then would we really be able to fully understand the relationship between anarchism and leadership, rather than casting them off as mutually exclusive opposites. Whilst this re-thinking and re-definition of leadership may seem to be an intimidating task, turning to the literature on CLS may provide an appropriate starting point. Although CLS is a relatively recent school of thought, and draws upon a range of approaches, scholars are united in their belief that mainstream conceptualizations of leadership are inadequate. Therefore, as well as seeking to challenge and reject the notion that individual, hierarchically positioned leaders are essential for organizational functioning and success, others have sought to actively re-conceptualize what leadership itself is: instead seeing it as a socially constructed process that can potentially be performed by a *range* of individuals.

 STOP AND REFLECT 11.4

Based on the problems of mainstream understandings outlined above, what do you think would be an appropriate way forward for starting to re-conceptualize leadership? That is, if we are no longer just going to concentrate on the actions of individual leaders, where (and why) should we re-focus our attention? Write down three or four ideas, perhaps centred around ideas of power, the importance of followers, and the move away from solely looking at what individual leaders do.

To begin this thinking process, you may find it useful to read the first half of Alvesson and Spicer's 2012 article, 'Critical leadership studies: The case for critical performativity'.

Rethinking leadership: Critical leadership studies (CLS)

DEFINITION: WHAT IS CRITICAL LEADERSHIP STUDIES (CLS)?

CLS is a relatively new school of thought; a loosely connected group who are united in their belief that mainstream perspectives of leadership are inadequate, and seek to question 'whether leadership is an overwhelmingly positive and necessary thing' (Alvesson and Spicer, 2012, p. 373).

Research aims, goals and outcomes are not homogeneous, and whilst some have been keen to identify problematic elements by bringing to light the 'dark side' of relying on individual leaders, others have worked towards proposing *new* definitions, conceptualizations of leadership that move away from the narrow focus of mainstream assumptions.

Generally speaking, CLS utilizes ideas outlined by critical management studies (CMS), which aims to challenge mainstream representations of organizational knowledge. In short, Fournier and Grey suggest that 'to be engaged in CMS means ... to say that there is something wrong with management ... and that it should be changed' (2000, p. 8). Similar to CMS, within CLS, although scholars draw upon a vast range of approaches, there is a common view about 'what is neglected, absent or deficient in mainstream leadership research' (Collinson, 2011, p. 181), and theorists have made an effort to move away from mainstream conceptualisations and expose their taken-for-granted assumptions (that is, (a) that leadership is the resulting product of leader's actions, and (b) that strong, individual leaders are *essential* for organisational functioning) as unnatural, irrational and inherently problematic.

The 'dark side' of leadership

One strand of CLS theorists have highlighted the negative and destructive potential of relying on individual leaders, and have sought to investigate the 'dark side' of this: exploring issues such as domination, conformity, abuse of power, blind commitment, over-dependence and seduction, coining terms such as 'toxic leadership' (Benson and Hogan, 2008); 'destructive leadership' (Einarsen et al., 2007); 'leadership derailment' (Tepper, 2000); and 'aversive leadership' (Bligh et al., 2007). For example, Ashforth (1994) argues that leaders can engage in behaviours such as: belittling of followers, self-aggrandisement, coercive conflict resolution, unnecessary punishments and the undermining of organizational goals. Schilling (2009) and Higgs (2009) also reported that leaders often exhibit behaviours that aim at obtaining purely personal (not organizational) goals, and will damage others through abuses of power. However, these kinds of analyses are seldom reflected on in the mainstream literature, which seems at odds with the lived experiences of people in organizations.

    ## STOP AND REFLECT 11.5

Take a moment to think: Have you ever been treated unfairly by a leader? What did they do? And, importantly, why do you think that so little of the leadership literature is concerned with highlighting these problems of poor, weak or even corrupt leaders that people encounter in their everyday life?

As discussed earlier, many have also problematized a reliance on individual leaders in SMOs for similar reasons: ideologically rejecting the notion that individuals should occupy hierarchical positions, and emphasizing the problems of relying on single leaders. From this perspective, a reliance on leaders represents an attack on individual (and collective) autonomy, meaning that instead of an organization being democratically maintained, it becomes the product of an elite who direct from the top-down and prohibit participation. This is politically and ideologically problematic from an anarchist perspective, and it is thus unsurprising that activists and theorists alike have highlighted their preference of 'leaderless' structures. Discussing the Occupy movement, Graeber notes that 'we don't want leaders' and stresses the need to construct forms of organization that allow participants to act 'autonomously' and 'as a collective' free from the constraints of powerful individuals (cited in Berret, 2011). Although approaching from different angles (and with different motivations), the underlying arguments of CLS theorists and anarchists come from similar places, with both rejecting the mainstream notion that individual leaders are necessary and essential for organizing functioning.

STOP AND REFLECT 11.6

We often hear talk of 'politics' and 'ideology' in the mainstream media, but rarely stop to think about what these words really mean. Discuss the question: What does it mean to 'ideologically' and 'politically' reject the notion that individual, permanent and stable leaders are necessary for organizational success? Why might anarchists reject mainstream assumptions? What is it that makes them ideologically and politically problematic?

To help, you may find it useful to return to the definition and explanation of prefigurative politics outlined earlier.

Toward a new understanding of leadership: The importance of meaning-making

DEFINITION: WHAT IS MEANING-MAKING?

Meaning-making refers to the process of 'making sense' of the world around us. Included within this are the various understandings and interpretations of what is right/wrong, acceptable/unacceptable, true/false. With 'making meaning' in a collective sense, actors appeal to these various values and beliefs to offer a direction and rationale to others.

Whilst there is some considerable literature on meaning-making in organization studies and other disciplines, it is rarely explicitly discussed, researched or otherwise 'brought into' leadership research. Smircich and Morgan went some way to remedying this in 1982, but it has received little empirical attention since then.

Whilst exploring the dark side of mainstream understandings is important, certain scholars argue that CLS might focus too much on this aspect; and that it runs the risk of becoming reactionary rather than proactive in developing new understandings. In short, if we are to reject the mainstream idea that leaders are necessary for organizational functioning, then what happens to leadership? Is there an alternative way of understanding it? Or does it vanish? Regarding this, Spicer and colleagues stress the need to include a 'more affirmative movement alongside the negative movement that seems to predominate in CMS today' (2009, p. 538), and Western asserts that 'critical theorists must go beyond identifying 'bad leadership practice' and aim to create and support successful ethical frameworks for leadership' (2008, p. 21). Therefore, although it may be useful to examine the destructive potential of mainstream perspectives, this alone is not enough and can lead to an altogether 'naive rejection of leadership' (Alvesson and Spicer, 2012, p. 368). Consequently, what is recommended is a move towards actively rethinking, reconstructing and reworking conceptualizations of leadership, both in theory and in practice.

Regarding this, recent years have seen a variety of CLS scholars seeking to redefine how leadership is conceptualized, suggesting that it is a socially constructed *process* which is embedded in context and culture (see Chapter 9). This line of thought was initiated by Smircich and Morgan (1982), who emphasized the importance of *meaning-making* in leadership processes and suggested that, in fact, it is the act of meaning-making that constitutes leadership. They argue that 'leadership is realised in the process whereby one or more individuals succeed in attempting to ... define the reality of others' (p. 123). Pondy provides a clarification to this, noting that leadership occurs when individuals 'make activity meaningful' and 'give others a sense of understanding about what they are doing and ... articulate it so they can communicate about the meaning of their behaviour' (1978, p. 89). Leadership thus emerges when actors 'articulat[e] and defin[e] what has previously remained implicit or unsaid, by inventing images and meanings that provide a focus for new attention, by consolidating, confronting and changing prevailing wisdom' (Smircich and Morgan, 1982, p. 258). However, although a core function of leadership is to define reality, this is only one aspect, as those engaging in leadership must also infuse actions with meaning, so that other actors personally believe that the action is *meaningful*, because it is viewed as a means for achieving meaningful organizational goals. A more encompassing definition of leadership may therefore be that 'leadership is exercised in moments when ideas expressed in talk or action are recognised by others as capable of progressing tasks or problems which are important to them' (Robinson, 2001, p. 91).

STOP AND REFLECT 11.7

Take a moment to reflect on this definition. How does it differ from what mainstream leadership theorists are saying? What is Robinson's main concern here – leaders, or leadership?

The collective enactment of leadership

After defining leadership more generally, there is an important distinction to make, as from a meaning-making perspective it can be understood that *any* actor who constructs meanings, defines the reality of others and provides the basis for organisational action is engaging in leadership; they are a 'leadership actor' – whether that be 'designated leaders, emergent leaders or followers' (Fairhurst and Grant, 2010, pp. 180–181). This perspective therefore rejects the notion that leaders should automatically be in charge of all leadership tasks by acknowledging the dialectical and co-constructed nature of leadership, viewing it as 'less the property of individuals and more as the contextualised outcome of interactive, rather than unidirectional ... processes' (Gronn, 2002). In this sense, leadership can be understood as an aspect of social behaviour, and as something that everybody has the potential to do. This contrasts with mainstream perspectives, which, to reiterate, suggest that leadership can only exist if there are leaders (that is, individuals who are formally appointed and/or have the *obligation* and *right* to consistently define the reality of others) to enact it. Rather, Collinson argues, relations between actors may be better understood as 'interdependent as well as asymmetrical, typically ambiguous, frequently shifting, potentially contradictory and often contested' (2011, p. 185). Therefore, rather than focusing solely on the actions of powerful individual leaders, a meaning-making perspective acknowledges that a range of leadership actors can do leadership.

As a side-note, it is worth noting that Alvesson and Svenningsson (2003a) and Wilkens (1983) argue that this type of leadership might be characterized as 'mundane'; not in the sense that it is unimportant, but rather that it occurs in the everyday interactions amongst actors, which receives very little attention. Whilst mainstream studies focus on 'critical' moments, that is when there is a great demand for meaning-making and it is dramatically met and leads to a significant impact on organisational performance (e.g. Deal and Kennedy, 1982; Peters and Waterman, 1982), it could be argued that what is happening here is no different than in the more mundane, less noticeable moments. Leadership exists outside of critical periods, where actors work to construct meanings; to make sense of what is happening; to evolve coherent frameworks of understanding. Conceptualizing leadership in this way enables a move away from more 'grandiose' notions (Alvesson and Svenningsson, 2003b, p. 1456), and towards understanding the 'leadership work' that occurs in everyday situations.

STOP AND REFLECT 11.8

Now that we have denaturalized the assumption that leadership can be only be performed by hierarchically positioned individuals (and instead, is something that any organisational actor can do), and might not have to be as 'glamorous' as the examples we often read about in popular writings, think: Have you ever 'done' leadership? That is, have you ever 'express[ed] ideas in talk or action' that were 'recognised by others as capable of progressing tasks or problems which are important to them' (Robinson, 2001, p. 91)?

Remember, this doesn't have to have happened in a formal work environment. It might be an example from your experiences in a university society, in friendship groups, or as part of a sports team.

The value of analysing 'alternative' organizations

Whilst CLS perspectives have been crucial for advancing our understanding of leadership, to date empirical studies have focused on businesses that favour economic efficiency, with some also considering other forms such as the military (Prince, 1998) or political arenas (Leach et al., 2005; John, 2010). Although these studies encompass various aims, methodologies and theoretical underpinnings, the empirical foci have much in common, tending to have centralized and hierarchical structures, where leadership is concentrated at the organisations apex. There has been no account of organizations that explicitly reject hierarchy and embrace radically democratic organizational structures. Partly acknowledging this gap, Collinson recently called upon CLS scholars to 'develop more nuanced accounts of the diverse economic, social, political and cultural contexts in which leadership dynamics are typically located' (2011, p. 190), and Spicer and his colleagues have urged theorists to investigate the 'many alternatives to current systems of managerial domination and exploitation' that 'currently exist and do indeed work' (2009, p. 554). I would argue that examining leadership in anarchist SMOs is a particularly fruitful endeavour, not least because previous studies of SMO leadership are often left wanting, but also because they provide an example of organizations that reject leaders on expressly political grounds, and seek to organize in the most democratic and participative way possible.

STOP AND REFLECT 11.9

In previous textbooks and studies, you are probably used to reading about the practices and processes of capitalist businesses. Why else might it be useful to examine alternative forms of organizations, such as SMOs?

From what has been discussed, it seems logical to assume that if we (a) no longer understand leadership to simply be the product of individual leaders, and (b) acknowledge that it can be performed by a range of actors, then by extension, it can also potentially recognize that leadership can be performed in the *absence* of individual, permanent and stable leaders. However, this is not something that happens 'naturally'. Although CLS conceptualizations do point to the idea that leadership can be performed in a collective manner, there is nothing to say that certain individuals cannot still monopolize leadership roles, act out in authoritarian ways and create a chasm between themselves and followers. In order to 'do' leadership more democratically, it is important for actors to devise structures that encourage engagement; and prevent individuals from becoming permanent and stable leaders. To examine this further, the next section will focus on the practices and processes that serve to collectivise and distribute leadership during the meetings of the Radical Student Group (RSG). To draw out some of these ideas, I will ask: what were some of the democratic structures that: (a) created situations where any member could come forward and 'do' leadership work; and (b) prevented any one individual from assuming a permanent leading role?

Case study: Collectivising leadership in the Radical Student Group (RSG)

The RSG was a relatively small organization with 8–10 core members, and existed as a local community group, engaging in grassroots organizing and offering solidarity to those in need. Primarily, grievances were directed at the introduction of government cuts (affecting council housing tenants, unemployed jobseekers and those working for community-centric public services), and the RSG was involved with setting up discussion groups, raising awareness, writing and distributing literature, and engaging in peaceful protest. Regarding their organizational structure, efforts were made to ensure that hierarchies did not easily emerge, and that power, roles and tasks were equally distributed. Broadly speaking therefore, 'leaderlessness', democracy and participation were *the* key factors that underpinned how the organization operated, where: 'Everybody, no matter who they are, or where they're from, can have a say and air their views. They might have been involved for years, or it might be their first meeting ... but they're still important.'

Face-to-face meetings were the main method for decision-making, were around three hours long and held on a monthly basis. Meetings were used primarily to plan for upcoming events, to debate, discuss and decide on what should be happening in the future, as well as reflecting back to past activities. Rather than relying on top-down models of decision-making (where single individuals were responsible for direction setting), instead a more collective form was stressed, and enacted through 'consensus decision-making'. This is a common method utilized in contemporary SMOs, where emphasis is placed on dialogue, discussion and deliberation amongst equals, and 'win–win' solutions are sought out, that is finding a solution that *everybody* can live with. This process encourages, and is born from, radical democracy, where every member has the opportunity to engage in some form of meaning-making, either by suggesting and defending ideas, or by preventing changes that they find unacceptable. This emphasis on cooperation, respect and trust was a crucial part of encouraging equality through democracy: making sure that everybody had a chance to participate.

1. A common critique of consensus decision-making is that it is very time consuming. On the contrary, more autocratic and directive forms are well known as being speedy. Based on the information here, and from sections earlier in the chapter, why do you think that RSG utilize these methods? Why are they 'politically and ideologically' important?

Therefore, although the RSG was technically 'leaderless', consensus decision-making processes allowed *any* member to contribute to leadership and meaning-making activity. This began from the very beginning of the meeting, where all members were encouraged to help set the agenda for discussion – either by placing, removing or altering the priority of items. This was relatively straightforward to do, as attendees always sat in a circle. Agenda setting is a fundamental leadership and meaning-making task, as it is (quite literally) a way of defining 'what we (are going to) do' and 'what we see as significant'. Indeed, in radically democratic settings, Dahl notes that 'the demos must have the exclusive opportunity to decide how matters are to be placed on the agenda' (1989, p. 113). Without full involvement of every present member, the concerns, opinions and viewpoints of all would not be considered, and may be 'ignored in any subsequent (undemocratic) discussion' (Gastil, 1993, p. 26). Consequently, no one individual ever took sole responsibility for setting the agenda, so that none could come to see the direction-setting role as their own personal responsibility.

(Continued)

(Continued)

2. Sitting in a circle is not particularly common in more 'conventional' business meetings, where instead there might be a 'top table'. Bearing in mind that democracy and participation were the fundamental underpinnings of the RSG's meetings, what might some of the reasons be for choosing to sit in this manner? Is it just symbolic? Or can it promote a more collective form?

Actors were also encouraged to engage in meaning-making through 'go-rounds'. This practice was used primarily when discussions did not include every present member, or when it was obvious that certain individuals were being left out. Therefore, before active decisions were reached, the discussion was halted and each member had the opportunity to express their opinions relating to a particular agenda point. This offered another opportunity for members to participate in meaning-making processes. Indeed, a number of researchers have suggested that even in democratic organizations, more outspoken members can sometimes take over and eclipse others. This is not to say that it is necessarily a conscious decision, where some members actively seek to dominate discussions, but, nevertheless, more confident individuals may simply find it easier to speak out, or challenge others. Go-rounds therefore ensured that there was a greater equality when it came to 'floor-time' (that is, the amount of time that every member spoke for), and that there was space for everybody to air their views on particular agenda points.

3. Even when efforts are made to construct a situation in which every member has the opportunity to participate, sometimes meetings are quiet and awkward – where nobody chooses to come forward and speak. Go-rounds are one way of dealing with this situation, but can you think of any other methods for encouraging participation?

Another way of collectivising leadership capacities through meetings was also done through role rotation. Within the RSG's form of consensus decision-making, there were two key formal roles, the facilitator and minute taker, which were both regularly rotated. The facilitator was not necessarily 'in charge' of the meeting – giving orders and making decisions – but assisted with the coordination of decision-making in a non-authoritarian way: making sure that discussions remained on-track; that overarching goals were always in sight; that everybody had an equal say; that there were no unresolved issues; and that an acceptable level of consensus was reached. This is a clear leadership role, as it involves meaning-making through direction setting, recognizing intersectionalities and establishing an orientation toward common goals or purpose. Although the facilitator was rarely actively involved in discussion, they were still expected to generate a coherent understanding of situations. Therefore, when acting as a facilitator, individuals had a greater opportunity (and, often, responsibility) to engage in leadership *during* the meeting.

The facilitator role was rotated on a meeting-by-meeting basis, with every member expected to take on the position at some point. This ensured that no member could come to see the role as their 'property', where only they had the necessary skills to perform the task. This was a significant factor for preventing temporary leadership actors becoming permanent leaders, because if role-specific skills were monopolized, it could lead to an unequal power balance. Furthermore, role rotation also ensured equality of participation as all members were expected to become temporary leadership actors at some point, rather than assuming that it took special skills or a particular type of person.

4. Do you think these practices and processes are fool-proof? That is, do you think that will always effectively stave off individual leaders? If not, when and how might leaders emerge?

5 Leading on from the previous question, if you were part of the RSG and it was clear that a certain individual was becoming a more permanent and stable leader, what would you do about it?

6. Finally, if the RSG were to grow in size, from 8–10 members to 50, what might be some of the problems that surface? Will consensus processes, role rotation and collective agenda still be possible? If not, why not, and what alternatives could be put into place?

Discussion and conclusion

Why does this happen? Revisiting prefigurative politics

From a mainstream perspective, it would require quite a dramatic leap of faith to believe that leadership (and organizing more generally) could be performed, *voluntarily*, in this collective manner. As noted earlier, a majority of mainstream studies on leadership are conducted within business organizations with centralized structures and a clear chain of command. The primary raison d'être is the pursuit of economic efficiency, and notions of hierarchy and permanently asymmetrical relationships are normalized. However, anarchist SMOs have an alternative focus for their activities, with an emphasis on *prefigurative politics*. Therefore, it can be observed that the construction and performance of a democratic type of leadership is not desired so that the organization can be economically efficient, but, rather, it is underpinned by wider concerns for ensuring that ideals of radical democracy and widespread participation are upheld to the fullest extent – which changes the focus from the *efficiency* of leadership to the *efficacy* of leadership. Key importance is attached to the intangible value of this kind of organizing, and the ability to realize each member's potential, to emphasize the positive impact that democratic participation has on development, and ultimately to 'change people and societies' (McKenzie, 2001, p. 30). Constructing non-hierarchical forms of leadership, that is, encouraging all members to engage in meaning-making, is therefore important because it reflects the future society by simultaneously creating equality, as well as challenging inequalities. In short, what is most vital to understand here is that these models of organizing are formed in order to ultimately replace modes and forms of representative democracy. Therefore, the process, or means, of this form of leadership – including its focus on radical democracy, widespread participation, inclusivity and, opportunities for *all* to be involved in meaning-making – is as important as the ideal goals, or ends, of anti-hierarchical organizations.

Some reflections on power: From domination to collectivity

The kind of discussions developed throughout this chapter also have implications for (re-)interpreting power relations in a collective context. From the perspective of mainstream approaches – where stable and permanent individual leaders are present – power can be conceptualized as 'power-over' (Lukes, 2005, p. 108). This draws on notions of unitary power, as well as Weber's definition of *Herrschaft* (or, power-as-domination), and is identified as the imposition of one will over another, through force, coercion, manipulation or authority. Power is therefore exercised exclusively *by* representatives/leaders, *over* followers – with no room for any discussion, negotiation or compromise. However, in the absence of individuals who are consciously compelling others to act, it may be fruitful to re-think power relations in directly democratic settings, and to draw on Starhawk's term 'power-with' (or, power as non-coercive influence). This is defined as the kind of power that occurs in a group of equals; that is, 'the power not to command, but to suggest and to be listened to, to begin something and see it happen'. Furthermore, Starhawk discusses power-with as 'the influence we can exert in a group of equals, our power to shape the group's course and shift its direction' (1987, p. 10–11). Understood in this way, power does not inherently imply domination and top-down control, but as non-coercive influence that can signify an 'individual or collective capacity that does not rob others of their abilities' (Gastil, 1993, p. 17). Rather than seeing power as a commodity that is exercised *over* passive subordinates, instead it is viewed as a more dynamic, discursive and relational quality embedded in social interactions (Jackson and Carter, 2007). Although some members may come to the forefront at times, no one individual ever has absolute authority on any issue, as decision-making power can be equalized amongst all through formalized consensus processes.

To summarize the main contributions of this chapter, we have worked towards reconceptualizing and redefining leadership. The primary purpose for this is to begin to think about how anarchist SMOs, who function in the absence of individual, permanent and stable leaders, 'do' leadership. As has been noted, previous studies of leadership in SMOs would suggest that leadership is not possible unless there are individual leaders to enact it, because leadership is understood as the *resulting product* of leaders' actions. However, by drawing from CLS, it has been shown that we may move towards a more open and appreciative understanding of leadership: denaturalizing the taken-for-granted assumption that individual leaders are always necessary, and stressing that – given the right context and organizational structure – leadership and meaning-making may be something that can be performed in a more collective manner. This understanding is important as it challenges the assumptions laid out in mainstream leadership theory and questions the idea that individual, often authoritative, leaders are necessary and essential for organizational functioning. This is done through simultaneously recognizing the negative and destructive potential of relying on individual leaders, as well as understanding how practical alternatives to this can be, and are being, created. Therefore, although it is often put forward that anarchism and leadership are mutually exclusive opposites, if we engage in a rethinking of what we understand leadership to be, and move away from the conceptualization of it as a top-down phenomenon performed by authoritative individuals, then it is possible to see that not only does leadership occur within radically democratic groups, but also that it is not incompatible with their processes, aims and goals.

The key points in this chapter were …

- Anarchist organizations eschew traditional notions of organization and hierarchy, yet they remain organized and effective. They therefore push the boundaries of what we know about leadership and require us to re-conceptualize leadership as something that can emerge from the collective, rather than the possession of the elite.

- Critical leadership studies is a growing body of scholarship that is committed to challenging taken-for-granted assumptions in leadership, such as the idea that leadership is the product of what leaders do. It offers a critique of the 'dark side' of leadership, as well as possible alternative conceptions and practices.
- When we focus on leadership instead of leaders, we can begin to see some of the essential processes and work that leadership involves. One example of this kind of work is meaning-making, where reality is defined and actions are made meaningful.
- If leadership is essentially a process of meaning-making, then a range of leadership actors can do leadership.

 # Further thinking

Fyke, K. and Sayegh, G. (2001). Anarchism and the struggle to move forward. *Perspectives on Anarchist Theory*, 5(2), 30–38.

Questions:

1 Fyke and Sayegh advocate a move towards a new conceptualization of leadership. In addition to the reasons discussed throughout this chapter, why else do they deem this re-thinking necessary?
2 What, according to this article, is the problem with simply denying that leadership exists in anarchist organizations? Why not reject both leaders and leadership?
3 Do you think that the sorts of leadership that Fyke and Sayegh promote are workable in any organization? Why?

Zald, M. and Ash, R. (1966). Social movement organizations: Growth, decay and change. *Social Forces*, 44(3), 327–340.

Questions:

1 What factors do Zald and Ash suggest are at the heart of the 'growth, decay and change' of SMOs? How important is leadership here?
2 There is evidence of various mainstream theories of leadership throughout the article. What statements, paragraphs and sections illustrate this? You may find it helpful to revisit the history of mainstream perspectives outlined earlier.
3 Overall, what do you think about the conceptualization of leadership being put forward here? What might be some issues associated with understanding leadership in this manner?

Smircich, L. and Morgan, G. (1982). Leadership: The management of meaning. *Journal of Applied Behavioural Studies*, 18(3), 257–273.

Questions:

1 How does this article challenge mainstream ideas of leadership? That is, what do Smircich and Morgan do to advance our understanding of leadership in action?

2   When discussing 'formalized' organizations, what is meant? What does leadership look like in such settings?
3   What do you think about the (implicit and explicit) discussions of power in this article? Are they more aligned with mainstream or critical thought?

 # Leadership on screen

Watch the film *Battle in Seattle* (2007) – especially focusing on the pre-protest planning meeting – and reflect on what you have learned about leadership and power throughout this chapter. Perhaps think about the following questions:

- Is power exercised in a top-down fashion here? Or is it more relational?
- Are there any specific ways in which leadership is collectivised during the meeting? Or are there certain people who have more of say? If so, why might this be?
- Based on your reading of the RSG's methods, could you make any recommendations to the group in the film on how to make their meetings more participatory and democratic?

12

LEADERSHIP, POST-STRUCTURALISM AND THE PERFORMATIVE TURN

Jackie Ford

Jackie fell into leadership research over 20 years ago after a decade of working as a manager and finding herself both intrigued and perplexed that a subject on which so much has been written could continue to be both confusing and lacking. Her research focuses on critical, ethical, gendered, relational and contextual ways to make sense of leaders, followers and leadership.

What this chapter is all about …

The main idea is that post-structuralism is a theoretical basis that challenges the positivist assumptions underpinning mainstream US-dominated leadership research. It calls attention to the way this big industry is shaping our ideas of what it means to be a leader in a reductionist and individualist way. In contrast, it offers a richer view of leadership that emphasizes language, other cultural practices and the material conditions of their lives.

The key questions this chapter answers are:

- What's wrong with our current mainstream theorizing on leadership?
- What is post-structuralism?
- How can post-structuralist ideas offer an alternative perspective on leaders and leadership?

Introduction

This chapter starts with a health warning. This is going to be a difficult read – and it was certainly difficult to write – as it asks you to engage with a completely different way of thinking about leaders, leadership, research and education. It's called post-structuralism – an ugly term for a beautiful way of thinking – and you have to be familiar with it and what it means if you want to understand leadership today.

As we have seen in earlier chapters, the growing fascination with leadership research and its practice in organizations has been one of the most enduring aspects of work in recent decades. Donkin (2010, p. 174) contends that throughout history the notion of leadership 'has passed through several manifestations, including the power of the military, the influence of intellectual thought in the classical period, the inherited rights of monarchy and aristocracy, electoral mandates of modern democracies and meritocratic elevation in corporations'. This leads to the question of at what point in history did generals became regarded as leaders rather than generals, philosophers as leaders rather than philosophers, politicians as leaders rather than politicians, and so on. There has been a marked change in the language used and the terms leaders and leadership have become much more pervasive in studies of organizations as well as in politics and the media more generally. What is also noteworthy is that in many traditional accounts of leaders and leadership, there seems only to be a focus on the *good* leader and on notions of *effective* leadership, with little or no critical appreciation of the dark side or the difficulties associated with poor leaders and bad leadership.

In recent decades, attention has been drawn to the perceived failure of charismatic and narcissistic organizational leaders (Collins, 2009; Tourish, 2013), at whose doors considerable responsibility can be laid for the global economic recession that started in the late 2000s. And yet both organizational and public interest continues to seek a torch-holder for corporate leadership and larger than life leader figures. In the UK, television has sought out such entrepreneurs as Lord Alan Sugar through *The Apprentice* series, which in Autumn 2014 has recruited to a tenth series. More globally, there has been considerable interest in the characters that comprise the panel of *Dragons' Den* or its counterparts around the world. Public, media and academic interest in leaders and leadership appear, if anything, on the increase and interest in researching, studying and practising leadership is at an all-time high. And yet, despite this embracing of the leadership mantra, there remains a remarkable lack of critical reflection on the leadership question. Furthermore, we have been struck by two factors worthy of further exploration that this chapter seeks to probe. First, in organizations more generally, there appears to have been a blind and naïve acceptance of the need for more effective leadership, without any critical appreciation of what this might mean in practice. Second, in the research of organizations undertaken within business and management schools, there remains the dominance of one particular approach – positivist, and largely quantitative research – which espouses that the truth is out there and through objective data collection and analysis this truth will be realized. This chapter is therefore an introduction to a particular way of critiquing leadership that has especially strong implications and relevance in the context of this current passion for leaders and leadership.

My own career journey and experiences to date lead me to argue for a more critical and reflexive account of what is happening in the organizational world under the guise of leadership. I am interested particularly in the relationships and interrelationships of people in organizations and critical of the theories that reduce them to homogeneous beings, trapped in the prevailing way of thinking (or discourses) of whatever is the latest leadership hot topic. My concern is that we are missing out on other ways in which to research, conceptualize and practise leadership. These are the questions that I hope to address below.

My own journey

I have been employed within and alongside UK (and other European) public sector organizations for the past 30 years, the last 20 of which have been from within university departments. During this time, I have maintained a long-standing fascination for (and frustration about) the ways in which organizations (via their managers and leaders) treat their employees, and this is perhaps a function of my first career in human resource management. In my final years in senior management posts in the UK National Health Service (as Director of Human Resources for a large acute hospital), I found myself experiencing considerable dissonance between the espoused notions (what people say) of what makes managers, leaders and organizations effective and what appeared to be translated into practice (what people actually do). Since embarking over two decades ago on my second career in university academia, this concern has not abated – indeed it seems to me that organizations have ever-greater expectations of their staff. This unsettling sense of rising demands and increasing pressure has emerged from research that colleagues and I have undertaken during this time, but it is also evident in discussions with undergraduate, postgraduate and doctoral students, and during consultancy assignments I have completed in organizations across public and private sector contexts. Individuals appear to be working ever-longer hours and covering many more roles than before; the rate and pace of change seems to have accelerated and targets and performance management pressures are becoming ever more significant features of working lives. The requirement (or individual ambition) to be a leader seems to add further to these burdens, notably as there is greater expectation of both uniformity and perfection in all that we do. This notion of the perfect being (the perfect leader/perfect parent/perfect student, etc.) is explored further in Ford and Collinson (2011). What I would like students of leadership studies to appreciate is that to be required to be a leader in today's organizations can be daunting, anxiety provoking and sheer hard work, and many who are called leaders are not up to the job and can have a negative effect on staff. On the other hand, there are people who we call 'leaders' who can and do make other's working lives much better and these people are to be praised, supported and encouraged.

Towards more critical thinking on leadership

As we have shown in earlier chapters, this is a really exciting time to be researching and studying leadership – never mind the challenges of actually practising it! We note from such discussions that traditional approaches to studying leadership continue to privilege the leader within hierarchical structural representations. Organization charts list leaders as those most senior (and therefore most important) in these companies. There appears to be much consensus in the leadership literature that leaders and leadership are important in today's organizations. It is taken for granted that leadership exists within organizations and that it can be improved and that its main purpose is to maximize the effectiveness and efficiency of organizations. The roles that leaders needs to undertake now include the model of a leader such that the very self (the identity) of the leader is consumed in this leader identity. In effect, we become the leader and all that this entails as an identity. But we do not believe that this is the whole picture. Such uncritical ways of seeing leadership are thus disciplinary, exclusionary and highly conservative.

Emerging and more critical theories of leadership recognize the more dispersed, flexible, fluid and decentralized forms of organizations that encourage a shared, distributive and relational leadership dynamic (as many chapters in this book have explored, but especially Chapters 10 and 11). There is more than a stirring of interest in more critical leadership studies that focus on plurality, ambiguity, complexity and heterogeneity rather than homogeneous and uni-dimensional forms, presenting us with new opportunities to understand and experience leadership from within much richer, contextual empirical studies. So, this analysis does not just stop at the pursuit of critique and theorizing about what scholars are writing. It also extends to seeking to offer some emancipatory potential: of new ways of thinking about, researching and practising leadership in organizations.

This chapter draws from a post-structuralist perspective, which gives recognition to the dwindling confidence in some of the more traditional (positivist) ways of explaining management and leadership processes and organizational phenomena (Weedon, 1997). Major criticisms of positivist writing within the management and organization studies field are that individual difference is denied, power asymmetries are unrecognized and context is ignored. This has resulted in a rather one-dimensional view on what it is to be a leader, it has meant that follower perspectives have been largely neglected and that the social, contextual and cultural context is overlooked. You may also recall from the Introduction to the book that we discussed the question of power in organizations, and explored the idea that more radical and post-structural forms seek to challenge the hierarchical 'command and control' approach that is embedded in traditional perspectives of power.

This has led to the plea for more far-reaching, critical and reflexive approaches to questioning how people come to appreciate their social and cultural environments. It is this plea that this chapter aims to address. After completing the above exercise, my guess is that you have made all sorts of assumptions about leaders as individuals – rather than necessarily about the process of leadership. Such assumptions about your idea of a good leader may well include notions of what they look like, how they sound, how they

---

 STOP AND REFLECT 12.1

What do you understand by the notion of 'effective leadership'?

- Write down your thoughts on this before you share them with anyone else.
- Discuss these thoughts with two or three others and compare and contrast your views, exploring where you agree or differ.
- What does this tell you about effective leadership?

---

act – all of which can be referred to as 'implicit leadership theory'. Often these implicit mental models are developed in our early childhood and are culturally based. They are subsequently influenced by the places in which we work and the people with whom we mix. This leads frequently to a more explicit model of what it means to be a leader in a particular organization – and one that people then seek to live up to as leaders – or in our follower roles, we judge leaders against such models and examine the extent to which they deliver (or fall short of delivering) on their leader role. Individuals in leadership roles constantly measure themselves against an image of the ideal leader. These are some of the features that will be addressed in this chapter: how we bring leaders and leadership into being in these ways. As colleagues and I have argued, the very act of leading is not a neutral activity:

> the becoming of the leader involves the psyche, the memory, interactions between selves and texts, interactions with others, interactions between different aspects of self, the local context, the geography, the culture. Leadership comes to the subject (who will be a leader) laden with the heroes of millennia of storytelling. It has a history. (Ford et al., 2008, p. 27)

Shortcomings of contemporary accounts of leadership

So, what are some of the shortcomings about leadership that lead us to challenge mainstream accounts and to propose that we look to post-structural theorizing in which to research, conceptualize and practise leadership? I have grouped my concerns within the following factors that underpin much of the critique for this chapter and form the basis to encourage a more reflexive consideration of opportunities for new ways of thinking and acting in relation to leadership studies. These concerns relate to: (i) the size and scope of the body of knowledge; (ii) the quality of much research on leadership; (iii) the definitional shortcomings of leadership; (iv) the presentation of leaders as transcendental and homogeneous beings; (v) the absence of gendered considerations; (vi) the uncritical stance of much research. The following section explores these further and the subsequent section seeks to illuminate post-structuralist, ways of conceptualizing leadership.

Size and scope

There is a huge and rising industry around leadership, with increasing numbers of workshops, journals, books and educational and development programmes (Ford, et al., 2008; Storey, 2011; Tourish, 2013). This industry crosses the public, private and not-for-profit sectors, includes a plethora of publications, workshops and training providers both in-company and stand-alone independent practitioners and management consultancies, and is evident in university business and management schools and extended curricular on undergraduate and postgraduate management-discipline programmes. Yet the vast proportion of much thinking and writing is still located within one narrow theoretical perspective (positivism), which is based largely on quantitative surveys that are designed to report data so as to improve profitability, efficiency and effectiveness in organizations (Ford et al., 2008; Ladkin, 2010). Although statistics can be extremely useful, they tell us little about people's subjective experiences, beliefs and their ideas.

Quality of the research

Research into leadership is often fragmented, poorly accomplished, at times inconsequential and frequently based on management/guru academics and practitioners who have a vested interest as they are keen to promulgate their latest solutions to the 'dilemmas of leadership' (Collinson and Grint, 2005, p. 5). Another danger of this research is that much of the literature on leadership, and most leadership theories – whilst failing to state this explicitly – are local (domestic) theories disguised as universal theories (Adler, 1999). Most commonly, these leadership theories describe US-based models and behaviours of leaders that celebrate individualistic (perhaps even iconoclastic), strong, masculine characters who can lead. The dominance of such perspectives has led to the observation that the characteristics and behaviours uncovered by such research reinforce Americans' extreme individualism and highly participative managerial climate. More recent research undertaken in the UK suggests that the distant heroic model of leadership so favoured in contemporary US writing does not fit the cultural contexts of the UK (Alimo-Metcalfe and Alban-Metcalfe, 2011). Moreover, what is increasingly being recognized is that leadership theories are too Western (Knights and O'Leary, 2006; Ladkin, 2010). There is emerging research evidence from the study of leaders and leadership in other countries and contexts that such models do not fit with other cultures too, notably following research in Africa, Indonesia and Malaysia (Bolden, 2011).

Lacking definition

As we know from earlier chapters in this book, there is no consensus on how to define leadership. Yukl (2013) notes that because leadership has so many different meanings to people, some theorists question whether it has any value at all as a scientific construct (see Alvesson, 2013). However, we believe that it has become such an authoritative discourse in both academic and organizational settings that it is too important to ignore (Collinson and Grint, 2005; Sinclair, 2005; Ford, 2006). As we have hopefully shown in the reflective exercise on effective leadership, we know that individuals have diverse views on what leadership means to them (see also Bresnen, 1995). These so-called 'implicit' leadership theories inform our view of what leadership can, does or should entail and they may also give us some personal insights into what approaches may work best for us in different circumstances. What is clear from the writings on leadership is that different theories have evolved in a somewhat piecemeal way more as a consequence of the varied perspectives of the researchers together with the aspect of the (leadership) phenomenon of most interest to them (Yukl, 2013). Thus differences amongst researchers in how they conceive leadership will lead to variations not only in the selection of phenomena to investigate, but also into how these phenomena will be interpreted. Researchers who hold a particularly (and at times narrow) view of what leadership is to them are unlikely to be receptive to potential findings that are inconsistent with their initial assumptions and research traditions.

Transcendental and homogeneous beings free of context

Many current approaches to leadership thinking erect a model of 'the leader' that is impossible for mere mortals to achieve. Notions of transformational leadership (see Chapter 4) and some of the competency frameworks for effective leaders that have been developed by organizations seem to expect a vast range of skills and behaviours of leaders across so many perspectives. Frequently, the leader is presented as a heroic and distant being, completely disconnected from everyday human experience and interaction. At the same time, leadership theories presume the existence of the 'perfect leader' (Ford and Collinson, 2011) and perhaps by implication the perfect follower. Management consultants and indeed academics, trainers and educators seek to define and fix the concept of leadership on the organization's behalf and thereby collude in the presentation of a core identity and perfect being for leaders within organizations. This view presumes a central, unitary identity, a coherent view of the self against which it is deemed possible to gauge whether an individual's actions are true or false, genuine or spurious, good or bad. Furthermore, it embeds an assumed homogeneity of approach to leadership, rather than a more fluid and multiple perspective that more recent, critical approaches present. Donna Ladkin's (2010) writings illustrate beautifully this point. She argues that such positivist writings collapse the concept of leadership into an individually based unit of analysis – rather than the collective process of leadership in which leaders, followers and their context are seen as significant. She further expresses concern that such an approach to isolating particular variables or characteristics that 'make up' leaders may miss the point. She exemplifies this through a vivid illustration of cake-making:

> A cake results from combining flour, sugar and eggs but its production depends on the type of oven in which it is baked and even the altitude at which it is cooked. Although from a natural science standpoint it may be possible to identify and measure all such factors, those approaches would still not be able to account for the 'meaning' attributed to the cake by those who eat it. The significance of a cake used as the central focus of a birthday celebration differs from that of one tucked into a rucksack for sustenance on a hiking trip. (Ladkin, 2010, p. 5)

In relation to judging whether or not the cake has been a success, we need also to consider the occasion:

> Additionally, the 'success' of a cake will be judged differently depending on its purpose: the lopsided gift proudly offered by my six-year-old niece will be judged differently from a misshapen delivery from a cake company I hired to produce the centrepiece at my wedding. (Ladkin, 2010, p. 5)

Translating this into the leadership context, what is clear is that the degree to which any act of leadership is deemed to be effective or not will depend on the specific social, cultural and historical moments, rather than some scripted and universal beliefs. This reductionist approach is the model of the leader that underpins much leadership theory, and that is presented in many leadership development programmes. It is the model leaders are taught to emulate, and it emerges from a narrow caricature that presents the dominant perspective of what a leader is and what s/he does. This model is impracticable within the social worlds in which leaders' work is too complex, and leaders themselves too multifarious, to constrain them within such an approach. The result is texts, lectures and training courses replete with 'standard accounts' of leadership, of models, characteristics, norms and competences that do not reflect the huge diversity of 'lived experience' of leadership life in all its settings. As Fineman (1997, p. 18) identifies, competencies 'strip down emotions to skeletal form, removing the fragile interplay and nuances that many would argue characterise the actual feelings and emotionalities of organisational life'. The same can be said of standard accounts of leadership characteristics. Its homogeneity is at odds with the endless variety of narratives and practices of leadership. We know that leaders are social beings who form concepts and practices of their leadership identities, through interactions with others. They are often emotional, complex and contradictory and research indicates that the limitations on the emotions they can express cause them to experience huge anxieties, insecurities and uncertainties (Ford, 2006; Ford, 2010). They are, in a nutshell, human beings with all that this involves.

Gendered accounts

Positivist, psychological and quantitative perspectives on the study of leadership continue to dominate the literature and many of these studies perpetuate an archetypal distinction between male and female, so continuing to subordinate women. The influence of feminist psychologists and psychoanalysts including Gilligan (1982) and Chodorow (1978) led to work that sought to valorize women's purported caring qualities and the perceived advantage of women in organizational settings. Judy Rosener's work (1997) identified and advocated women's ways of leading as a positive benefit in contemporary organizations. Nevertheless, questions were raised as to whether women actually gained any advantage by such approaches, or whether it merely reinforced gender stereotypes even further (Fletcher, 2004). There is considerable research evidence that suggests that leaders are seen not only as male but also as quite masculine (see also Chapters 2 and 7). There has been a passive submission to institutional discourses in which leadership theories have presented accounts of gender neutrality or displayed gender blindness but have inevitably imported masculine values and characteristics as the norm (Calas and Smircich, 1992; Collinson and Hearn, 1994; Ford, 2010). Connotations of leadership in the literature frequently take the form of the masculine competitive, aggressive, controlling and self-reliant individualist and thus the question as to whether leadership is critical in our organizations may hinge on whether we perceive a need to continue to support notions of aggressive, manipulative, logical masculine practices. Indeed, women and leadership frequently remain a separate topic in textbooks or accounts of leadership rather than as part of an integrated account (Gatrell and Swan, 2008).

Uncritical stance

One danger of much current and past research is that there is an attempt to create generalizable findings from data that need to be treated with more care. As we know from research more generally into management and organization studies, positivism has dominated as an underlying philosophy. Positivist researchers are searching for a reality and for true findings that validate a predetermined set of hypotheses. Thus positivist researchers undertake research in order to collect facts, to search for the truth and to explain and predict the organizational world. Such positivist approaches also dominate the study of leadership within organizations, which espouse that the truth is out there and through objective data collection and analysis the one true definition and understanding of leadership will be realized (Easterby-Smith et al., 1991). These approaches tend to assume that the study of organizations can be undertaken in a similar way to studies within the natural sciences, and would see leadership as existing as a social reality which can be studied in a similar way to the natural world (Boje et al., 2001). Furthermore, many studies of leadership have focused on quantitative empirical research and whilst there is evidence of a move towards methodological diversity (Bryman, 2004) there remains a dearth of qualitative and more interpretive studies. Historically, the favoured approaches adopted within the research literature are laboratory-based experiments or survey-based questionnaires, to the exclusion of contextually specific, qualitative studies. Greater attention needs therefore to be paid to the critical scrutinizing of *contextual* variables within studies of leadership, gender and managerial behaviour (Alvesson and Sveningsson, 2003a; Fletcher, 2004).

Until the last decade or so, there has been an almost total absence of theorizing on leadership that went beyond positivist approaches. We are now beginning to see a turn to critical studies of leadership that begins to redress this imbalance and to generate research and theorizing that draws from other disciplines and perspectives and that recognizes that there is a need for leadership studies that tell us something about the subjective, the personal and the interpersonal, about ideas and beliefs, about how people talk and dream about leadership, the stories and narratives they construct in their talking and dreaming. Whilst there is evidence of change, this is nevertheless a slow process (Tourish, 2011).

Critical leadership studies

So, why do we need such studies? Critical leadership scholars recognize that so much of the writing on leadership is constructed through a leader–follower pairing, with the followers being the (subordinated or inferior) other to the leader's (dominant or superior) position. A more critical and reflexive approach to the study of leadership is needed, which pays attention to situations, events, institutions, ideas, social practices and processes that may be seen as exercising a surplus repression (far too much influence) of those involved as leaders. More specifically, a post-structuralist approach offers a theoretical basis for analysing the subjectivities (the very identities) of men and women in relation to language, other cultural practices and the material conditions of their lives. This approach enables fresh light to be shed on leadership theories. The whole sense and notion of leadership itself is both historical and subject to change, and thus universal theories on leadership are open to challenge and debate. Post-structuralist thinking throws a challenge to the notion of the subject of Western philosophical tradition of the disembodied abstract individual governed by conscious and rational thought. Instead, it seeks to take apart (to deconstruct) the hegemonic (dominant) assumptions of whole and coherent subjects with a unified sense of who we are (our identity) that appear to be at the heart of leadership theory and who do not match the people that many of us have met who are supposed to be 'leaders'.

More recently, there is an emerging body of writing on what is being referred to as 'critical leadership studies' (CLS) (Ford, 2010; Collinson, 2011; Harding et al., 2011; see also Neil Sutherland's Chapter 11 in this book, which includes an excellent discussion on CLS). CLS is defined by Collinson (2011, p. 181) as 'the broad, diverse and heterogeneous perspectives that share a concern to critique the power relations and identity constructions through which leadership dynamics are often produced, frequently rationalised, sometimes resisted and occasionally transformed'. CLS scholars frequently draw from the more established field of critical management studies (CMS), which has long sought to provide a critique and challenge to the assumptions of much mainstream theorizing; to expose asymmetrical power dynamics; and to open up new ways of thinking and alternative forms of organizing and managing. Furthermore, CLS writers question the recurrent tendency in mainstream writing to privilege leaders and neglect followers – something that is also explored in Chapter 8 of this book by Nancy Harding.

This collective term of CLS does not offer a unifying theory (as that would surely be antithetical to its intentions to embrace more pluralistic and multiple ways of understanding leaders and leadership) but it seeks to provide a challenge to the central, mainstream perspectives that have until now dominated writing and thinking on leadership. These mainstream approaches have tended to underestimate the complexity and variety of leadership dynamics and have accepted without question the notion that leaders are in charge and that followers will carry out their orders. Drawing on more exploratory, interpretive and in-depth interrogation of the research and practices of management and organization studies, such critical research provides opportunities to reconsider the dominant discourses of leadership and to explore new interests and voices that shed fresh light on the research field. It enables a challenge to basic assumptions in use in mainstream management research, especially in relation to appreciating the complexity of leadership dynamics, the relationship and interrelationship between notions of leaders and followers and to seek to develop alternative ways of researching, conceptualizing and practising leadership (Alvesson and Willmott, 1992; Alvesson and Sveningsson, 2003a; Ford et al., 2008; Tourish, 2013).

Such critical approaches require the researcher to move from a positivist stance of the objective pursuit of the truth towards a more active role 'constructing the very reality s/he is attempting to investigate' (Chia, 1996, p. 42). Within the broader writing of CLS, this is what post-structuralist approaches explore. As academics in our research, we make leaders and create leadership as much as we study them. That is, we make visible something called leadership and we develop subject positions (characteristics and identities of leaders) into which those who are designated organizational leaders will step. However, we cannot assume a straightforward translation of theory into the constitution of subject positions or identities. We need to look at the social and cultural context into which we assume theories are inserted. Accepting someone as leader or recognizing leadership characteristics is as much about what we call the social and cultural context and also what we call the 'characteristics' of those labelled 'the followers'. As Alvesson (2002, p. 114) has noted, a cultural understanding of leadership requires an understanding of local meaning. He argues that leadership can be defined as 'about influencing the construction of reality – the ideas, beliefs and interpretations of what and how things can and should be done'. A social and contextually specific (local) definition of leadership enables greater receptivity to the meanings ascribed to leadership by the community employed within the organization under study. It is important therefore to explore how academic theories and research studies are translated within organizations and transformed into local understanding of leadership.

More critical approaches to the study of leadership pay attention to situations, events, institutions, ideas, social practices and processes that may be seen as creating additional repression or discursive disclosure, and some of these will be considered within this section of the chapter. Gibson Burrell (1992) suggests that the rise of management to corridors of power has allowed some talk of managers as if they were heroic figures. He describes the semantic inflation that has set in, whereby many senior executives refuse to call themselves 'managers', and instead refer to themselves as 'directors'. Indeed, I would argue that in many organizational contexts, this semantic inflation has displaced managers and management in favour of leaders and leadership.

Post-structuralist theorizing and the performative effect

Whilst critical leadership scholars draw from a plurality of theoretical perspectives to seek to open up new ways of thinking about leadership, my intention is to explore ideas from post-structuralist writings. Post-structuralist theories, which have influenced thinking in academia in the arts, humanities and social sciences, and in the cultural world in films, novels, and other forms of art, suggest the outcome of all this activity may differ from that anticipated; indeed the very acts of writing or representation may be producing something. Post-structuralist approaches recognize the significance of context and the role and power of discourse (of language) in shaping organizational and social practice. As Delbridge and Ezzamel (2005) attest:

> the constructive role of language is perhaps the defining characteristic that distinguishes poststructuralist literature from other intellectual approaches . . . where attention shifts decidedly towards an appreciation of the power of language in constituting the world, in the sense that language/discourse is taken as the means by which human actors engage, make sense of and construct the world. (p. 607)

Post-structuralist thinking

Post-structuralist perspectives maintain that people's lives are interwoven with the social world that surrounds them and that individuals are 'social selves' whose actions need to be interpreted through (rather than isolated from) their complex conditions and circumstances.

It is recognized that there are many forms of post-structuralist thought, rather than any unifying concept, but what these various forms share are fundamental assumptions about knowledge and power, language and discourse, and subjectivity, and these are explored briefly below as well as in Chapter 5. Post-structuralist thinking has been heavily influenced by Foucault's (1979) writings and his emphasis on the social, organizational and historical contingency of subjectivity (our identities) and the ways in which this is embedded through language. In Foucault's words, 'A critique is not a matter of saying that things are not right as they are. It is a matter of pointing out on what kinds of assumptions, what kinds of familiar, unchallenged, unconsidered modes of thought the practices that we accept rest.'

Knowledge and power

Post-structuralist theory rejects the notion of absolute truth and objectivity in favour of the plurality of meaning. So, for example, the dominant model of leadership for the last two decades has been transformational leadership and it is this approach that continues to underpin so many leadership development activities and models adopted within organizations. Through defining the required leadership practices and behaviours in this way, such organizations influence, constrain and manipulate their leaders by imposing the way they should perform their leadership roles – as transformational leaders and all that this requires. As feminist post-structuralists have observed, dominant conceptions of 'reality' and 'truth' in patriarchal Western society have tended to be male constructs that reflect and perpetuate male power interests (Flax, 1993; Gavey, 1997). Feminist explorations have exposed different truths and realities and these cast doubt on the notion of one reality and one truth. Similarly, from a post-structuralist perspective, knowledge is socially constructed through 'a specific kind of production with definite relations to the social and material world' (Venn, 1984, cited in Gavey, 1997, p. 52). Thus knowledge is ephemeral and inherently unstable; it is not neutral and is closely associated with power, with power generating knowledge and knowledge initiating power. So, those who are deemed to have the power to regulate what counts as truth (for example, those who are acknowledged to be leaders in organizations) are able to maintain their access to material advantages and power. Post-structuralist goals of scholarship include developing understandings or theories that are historically, socially and culturally specific and that are explicitly related to changing oppressive relations. Thus rather than the realist endeavour to discover reality, reveal the truth or uncover the facts, the post-structuralist undertaking is concerned with disrupting and displacing oppressive knowledge and meaning.

Language

The liberal humanist view inspired a scientific and rational worldview of language as transparent and expressive, merely reflecting and describing pre-existing subjectivity (who we are) and human experience (how we account for ourselves). Post-structuralist thinking is based on the understanding that language and discourse constitutes our sense of who we are, so that meaning is actively created through language and is therefore neither fixed nor essential. Post-structuralists maintain an emphasis on the material bases of power, notably social, economic and cultural arrangements and the need for change at this level of discourse. These discourses are multiple, offering competing (and potentially contradictory) ways of giving meaning to the world. They offer 'subject positions' (identities, behaviours, ways of seeing the world) for individuals to take up, and these positions vary in terms of the power they offer individuals (Hollway, 1984). So, for post-structuralism, it is through language in the shape of conflicting discourses that we perceive ourselves as conscious thinking subjects and it is language that allows us to give meaning to the world and to take action to achieve change (Weedon, 1997). For example, you might like to think about yourself as a student and how you 'become' a student. You will probably have an implicit notion of what a student is and how s/he behaves and this will have an impact on how you (and your fellow students) perform that role. Also, current leadership discourses are understood to involve strong elements of masculinity that act to strengthen male identities and thereby reproduce asymmetrical gender relations in organizational life. Connotations of leadership in the literature frequently take the form of the masculine competitive, aggressive, controlling and self-reliant individualist and thus the question as to whether leadership is critical in our organizations may hinge on whether we perceive a need to continue to support notions of aggressive, manipulative, logical masculine practices. The whole notion of leadership is arguably constructed through a leader–follower pairing, with the followers being the (subordinated) other to the leader's (dominant) position, which implies that followers are placed in a feminized position (see Ford, 2010).

Subjectivity

Constituted through language and discourse, subjectivity (who we are) refers to the 'conscious and unconscious thoughts and emotions of the individual, her sense of self and her ways of understanding her relation to the world' (Weedon, 1997, p. 32). Much mainstream research usually locates an essential and coherent identity to leaders and followers. A post-structuralist approach argues that there are no fixed entities such as leaders and followers, but rather complex human beings who bring with them to their work numerous intersecting identities which each inform the other. Such an approach denies the existence of an essential female or male nature and seeks to deconstruct the hegemonic assumptions that we are whole and coherent subjects with a unified sense of identity. However, this is not to deny the importance of particular forms of individual subjective investment, which can have a powerful impact on our identities. Nor is it to deny the significant role of material structures such as work, family, education and so on, all of which constitute and discipline our sense of self.

More simply, when something is brought into being it can come to dominate the ways in which we think so that it seems as if there is no other way of being. My stance in this chapter, which is informed by post-structuralist theories, is to acknowledge the existence of this thing called 'leadership' but to argue that it has been brought into being through the very repetition of the word, that is, through the *performative effect* of the repeated representations of the word in the huge number of texts published on leadership (Ford et al., 2008). Post-structuralist theories can be deployed in our research so as to offer a nuanced approach to studying accounts of leaders and leadership in organizations.

In post-structuralist perspectives that build on the performative effect of language, there is no such thing as a passive reading of a text or looking at a film: the 'gaze' is actively engaged both in interpreting the text (and thus the reader becomes part of the text) and in the production of the self, or subjectivity, through the very act of looking. Thus reader and text are caught up in one another – the text confers subjectivity which becomes the very identity of the leader (Harding, 2003; Ford and Harding, 2007). So, through reading the accounts of leaders and leadership, we absorb an idea of what a leader 'is', what s/he

---

DEFINITION: PERFORMATIVE EFFECT

By the performative impact of *words* we are referring back to the theories of J. L. Austin who argued that language is not neutral, nor merely descriptive, but actively brings something into being. The most famous example is the marriage ceremony: by pronouncing two people husband and wife a married couple is brought into being. Austin's work has proved influential in post-structuralist theories, notably in the works of Judith Butler (1993).

In the words of Gibson-Graham (1996), who draws upon this form of post-structuralist theorizing, such a performative effect of social representations are *constitutive* of the worlds they describe. In other words, representations bring things into existence. Thus:

> When theorists depict patriarchy, or racism, or compulsory heterosexuality, or capitalist hegemony they are not only delineating a formation they hope to see destabilized or replaced. They are also generating a representation of the social world and endowing it with performative force. To the extent that this representation becomes influential it may contribute to the hegemony of a 'hegemonic formation' and it will undoubtedly influence people's ideas about the possibilities of difference and change, including the potential for successful political interventions. (Gibson-Graham, 1996, p. x)

The word 'performative' has a particular meaning in post-structuralist theory. It is found notably in the work of Judith Butler (1993), whose argument is that forms of authoritative speech perform certain actions that cause things to have an existence. In other words, it is through acts of speaking and writing that things come into being. Sex and gender are the foci of Butler's most famous works. In these she critiques the dominant assumptions that both sex and gender are given (by biology) and unchangeable. Instead, she shows, following Foucault, that both sex and gender are achieved through discourses and the repeated performance, from minute to minute, of the actions that (per)form sex and gender.

should do, what s/he should look like and how s/he should behave. This all creates that very thing called leadership. As you know from elsewhere in this book, leadership is a topic that has a remarkable number of texts devoted to its study and dissemination, so our concern is partly with the impact of these innumerable texts upon readers. It is commonly assumed that readers of leadership books will learn about leadership and perhaps they will be inspired to become leaders and carry out the tasks of leadership, using the information they have been given.

In post-structuralist terms far more happens between reader and text. Each reader will interpret a text differently from any other reader, as they will bring to the reading their own unique histories, their own cultures, backgrounds, educational experiences, and so on. Further, the texts will work on the readers in different, but active ways – through the reading each reader will be somehow changed. The argument here is that texts are located within discourses, and such discourses have a *performative* impact (Butler, 1993). To define and describe leadership is to recognize its slippery nature, its meaning shaped by both the individuals' own experiences, personal background and reflexive thoughts and by those of all the other people involved within the local context (Smircich and Morgan, 1982; Alvesson, 2002). Nevertheless, a recognition of the social context and the socially constructed nature of leadership may still overlook a fundamental dimension in the study of organizational life, notably that this performative process of leadership is achieved through a range of exclusionary practices that aim to offer a homogeneous definition of what a leader in an organization is expected to be. Such exclusionary practices may well operate at the local level, but may also be informed by dominant (hegemonic) discourses and understandings of leadership. Local practices of leadership are both informed and constrained by both organizational as well as societal cultural meanings and dominating discourses of leadership. Furthermore, power and politics are central aspects of leadership relations that need to be addressed.

In summary, a post-structuralist approach offers a theoretical basis for analysing the identities of men and women in relation to language, other cultural practices and the material conditions of their lives. Such thinking enables fresh light to be shed on leadership theorizing, research and practice. The whole sense and notion of leadership itself is both historical and therefore subject to change, and thus universal theories on leadership are open to challenge and debate. Post-structuralist perspectives seek to deconstruct (take apart) existing metanarratives and develop new theoretical approaches, which insist on historical and geographical specificity and no longer claim universal status. Thus, universal truths around leaders and leadership are open to challenge and debate. So, what appears to the onlooker to be a confident, articulate person may in fact be someone who is quaking inside, extremely anxious because he or she has been labelled a 'leader'. A more critical and reflexive approach to the study of leadership pays attention to situations, events, institutions, ideas, social practices and processes that may be seen as exercising a surplus repression of those involved as leaders.

Of course, as readers of this book you could accuse us of doing the same thing: constituting something called 'leadership', albeit that our intent is to destabilize the taken-for-granted notions. As noted above, our aims are to offer an alternative way of thinking about leadership that will allow those charged with the task of being leaders (or studying leadership) to reflect upon how they are changed by taking on that very task. We are offering students of leadership (and many of you will be practising or aspiring leaders and managers) a language or set of ideas that you may not previously have come across, one which we hope will facilitate your reflection upon how you are treated when you are at work.

STOP AND REFLECT 12.2

At this point, it would be useful for you to stop and think about how, where and why you have performed identities as leaders. What were you doing and why were you doing it? Can you identify ways in which you have brought into being specific meanings of leaders and leadership?

Encouraging new approaches: Post-structuralism and leadership

Collinson (2005, 2006) has argued the need for a post-structuralist approach that recognizes the dynamics of leadership as a social process, and which encourages individuals and organizational members to interrelate in ways that encompass new forms of intellectual and emotional meaning. The aim is to discover more meaningful and constructive ways of learning, relating and working together. In earlier work with colleagues (Ford et al., 2008) we tease out what form such interrelationships should take when going beyond the psychometric measures. The approach is to use theories of the self (of our sense of who we are) as an ongoing project of construction.

Emerging from more critical approaches to studying leadership, our understandings of leadership need to become more inclusive, eclectic, integrated and contextually aware (Ford and Harding, 2007; Ford et al., 2008). For the concepts of leadership to have meaning, it is important that we question the stereotypes, norms and assumptions behind presentations of leadership in our organizations, especially by critiquing the cult of leadership that has become so engrained. More critical approaches need to be developed that challenge such taken for granted, hegemonic concepts of leadership and introduce other ways of seeing, interpreting and understanding *leaders and followers* themselves in relation to others around them and the practices of *leadership* within work settings. Rather than leadership being a strait-jacket, it should seek to improve interactions between people at work. It should enhance the quality of working life in general.

Leadership learning should therefore be designed in more inclusive and relational ways so that key parties to the leadership relationship are actively engaged. Such learning should encourage participants to challenge the taken for granted, normative and hegemonic assumptions of leadership and introduce other ways of seeing, interpreting and understanding themselves, their colleagues and their work contexts. A similar approach is advocated by Sinclair (2007) who has written influentially on the limitations of leadership development and leadership education and the ongoing preoccupation with heroic and leader-centric notions. She promotes an approach that combines three principles in her leadership teaching. First, reflection has become the basis of being a better leader, and participants are encouraged to delve into their history and journey as leader and follower. Second, learning comes from direct experience and the resource of the whole group can be used to this effect. Finally, leadership theory is used as a body of ideas and concepts to be examined critically both in the light of participants' experiences, but also on ethical and moral grounds. Such engagement with critical perspectives is also apparent in Carroll and Levy's (2010) innovative approaches to leadership learning and development. Their research and development through the New Zealand Leadership Institute is informed by social constructionist theory and practice. They seek to pioneer work that is 'informed and shaped by understandings of identity, dis-course and social context' (Carroll and Levy, 2010, p. 219). They also recognize the need for dynamic, relational, contextual and multiple approaches to leaders' identities and the leadership context. Similarly, Petriglieri (2011) argues that to improve leadership learning, leaders need to consider how images, assumptions and stories they carry in their minds necessarily impacts on how they approach, understand and learn from experiences. He conceptualizes leadership learning as identity workspaces in which it is important to work within three streams of research: the participants' experiences of lead-ing and following; making sense of their life stories as part of their identities; and their emotions and the unconscious (Petriglieri, 2011). Attention to emotional and unconscious research recognizes that managers experience complexities, contradictions and tensions, which needs to be reflected in learning and development approaches (Ford, 2006, 2010).

A return to the power of leaders and leadership studies

In the introductory chapter, we introduced the notion of power in studies of leadership and made it clear at the time how relevant more radical forms of power are in the understanding of post-structuralist theorizing on leadership. Luke's third face of institutional power is drawn from post-structuralist thinking, and shaped predominantly by the writings of Foucault. From this perspective, leaders sustain their dominance through *creating* and *shaping* the realities and norms for their followers, which reduces followers' resistance to these realities. It also generates situations in which individuals monitor their own behaviour (so-called 'self-surveillance') so that the rules and norms that have been devised and imposed by others become accepted by these individuals. So, those who are deemed to have the power to regulate what counts as truth (i.e. those powerful leaders in organizations?) are able to maintain their access to material advantages and power.

Conclusion

There needs to be much greater account taken of ways in which the terms 'leader' and 'leadership' have a performative impact (Butler, 1993); that is, how they bring things into being, so that externally imposed definitions or norms of 'leaders' and 'leadership' have become part of the identities and practices of managers. More attention should be given to change the ways in which leadership is spoken about. This can be realized, in part, through introducing into these ways of speaking alternative languages that allow for different possibilities of being leaders. We should challenge the unachievable norms of leadership, offering in place of a perfect being or super-hero a model of an imperfect individual in interactions with others. Through such pursuits, we should be attentive to the ways in which others are positioned as inferior, and ways in which the self can, in its turn, be reduced to an abject status, through encouraging exploration of the impact of the self on others and others on our identities as workers. A key factor is a recognition that our sense of selves are formed through interactions with others, and these interactions always take place within contexts made available through and limited by the discourses that make it possible to speak and to act. The critical voice that can inform more reflexive dialogical practices may be one way of encouraging a leadership that turns away from the demands of coordination and control, and towards relational practices that disrupt the complacency of many mainstream approaches and encourage leaders to face up to difficult issues in their working lives (Ford and Collinson, 2011). This may be possible through active interpretation of storied accounts of people's experiences together with reflection and critical debate in which many interpretations can be surfaced.

Case study: Rivalry in Silicon Valley

This case study is based on a story recounted in Fred Vogelstein's (2013) book *Dogfight* on the rivalry between Apple's Steve Jobs and Google's Executive Chairman, Eric Schmidt. It is an intriguing account of the conflict that has sprung up in recent years between Google and Apple (especially since in the earlier days of the iPhone history there was less competition and more collaboration between the two companies). A fascinating YouTube clip can be seen on the developments of the first iPhone prototype and its launch by Steve Jobs at a show in 2007 – prior to it really being ready to go. The clip is well worth a look – go onto the YouTube site and type 'Steve Jobs iPhone 2007 presentation'.

What is interesting about Vogelstein's book is the focus very much on Steve Jobs as a heroic but tyrannical leader, who ruled through fear but was still presented as the charismatic leader of Apple, who turned around the fortune of the company at a time in its history when it was showing signs of failure. He is presented in the book as one of the leadership gurus. Part of the book recounts a story that is available online as an excerpt. This explores a report from Andy Grignon, one of Apple's senior engineers who worked on the original iPhone's radios as this was being launched in 2007. What follows is a summary of this account.

Andy Grignon was a senior engineer at Apple and on the day reported in this book (8 January 2007) he was planning to attend the launch by Steve Jobs of the very first iPhone – a momentous event in the history of smartphones. Invitations to the launch event at the Macworld trade shows were highly sought after and not many employees were favoured with such a reward. Grignon was privileged on this occasion as he was the lead engineer on the design and build of the prototype IPhone and, as part of the original iPhone team, he had dedicated more than two and a half years of his working life to the project. These trade shows had seen the launch of all earlier Apple products by Jobs, including iTunes, the iMac, Safari web browser and the iPod shuffle. This meant that Apple fans were conditioned to expect great things from these annual events and Jobs did not want to disappoint. For years, fans had been pleading with Apple to build a phone inside their iPods so that they no longer had to carry two devices, and the iPhone was to be the answer to their prayers.

What made this launch particularly noteworthy is that the prototype was not yet ready for the launch but Steve Jobs had announced its arrival and had no intention of letting such a mere detail deter him from the live presentation. This placed Grignon under considerable pressure as he was conscious that his whole future with the company was on the line if things went wrong in the launch. Each of the rehearsals for the launch had gone badly wrong, with the iPhone not performing the tasks that were promised, so the tension was palpable during this live presentation. The build-up to the launch had been dramatic, and in keeping with all of Apple's product launches every endeavour was made to keep secret the detail of the product until the actual event. This was no exception – to the extent that Steve Jobs was so obsessed with preventing media leaks before the event that he had requested that all the contractors involved were made to sleep in the building overnight before the launch took place the following day.

As Grignon explained, if there were any glitches that showed up during the live launch event, Jobs would not be blaming himself for the shortcomings, but would be seeking to point the finger at people like him:

'It felt like we'd gone through the demo a hundred times and that each time something went wrong,' Grignon said. 'It wasn't a good feeling … mostly he just looked at you and very directly said in a very loud and stern voice, "You are f****** up my company," or, "If we fail, it will be because of you." He was just very intense. And you would always feel an inch tall [when he was done chewing you out].' (Vogelstein, 2013, p.17)

What the public were not aware of during the launch is that this prototype was far from ready to go to market: at this point only a hundred or so iPhones had been produced and all of these had manufacturing errors. This meant that during the launch, the public would not be able to handle the iPhone. They looked fine at a distance, and served the purpose during the demonstration, but they would not have stood up to close scrutiny.

So, why the great haste in getting this smartphone launched? In part, Jobs was determined to to keep face with Apple fans who were expecting great things of the company. Second, Jobs wanted to keep a lead over his competitors on smartphone development and to prove that Apple were ahead of the game. Third, this was the only new and innovative product that Apple were working on at the time and Jobs could not afford a delay.

1   What do you think this case study tells us about the leadership style and approach of Steve Jobs?
2   How does this compare with the leadership culture of Apple that you have gathered in your knowledge of this company (through the media accounts, reading of Jobs's biographies and other knowledge and data that you have acquired)?
3   What do you think a post-structuralist reading would add to this discussion of (i) Steve Jobs and (ii) Apple?

What I would reflect on in this discussion is the extent to which the media hype on Steve Jobs (as well as the PR team within Apple itself) had made him an enviable leadership figure and guru – someone who single-handedly saved Apple from failure when he returned there in the 1990s. This heroic image appears to have been reinforced since his death in 2013 and he has taken on an almost evangelic status since that time. This guru status and guru ideas have had an enormous impact on depictions of leadership in organizations. Indeed, it has been argued that gurus have provided senior executives with a sense of certainty and direction, by defining the managerial role in terms of the executive's responsibility for managing meaning for their employees, 'for creating employees' moral universe' (Clark and Salaman, 1998, p. 153). Thus, the gurus' role, and their appeal as organizational leaders, is the central, heroic status that their writings and prescriptions celebrate: the focus is very much on the manager as corporate leader, as organizational redeemer. The model is one of organizational hero, endowing management with a high-status leadership role in transforming the organization. The connotations with biblical imagery and prophet-like behaviours are not lost on critiques of this guru industry (see, for example, Clark and Salaman, 1998; Jackson, 1999; Collins, 2000).

Fewer questions than ever seem to be posed in relation to other significant stories that lurk behind Apple's success. Such questions that seem to be neglected are associated with some of the costs as well as the benefits to the technological advances and developments that such smartphones and computers have brought to our lives. What about the sweatshops in which many of these devices are assembled; or the surveillance society and the total loss of privacy that has grown on the back of the ability to locate and monitor the activities of such smartphone users?

The key points in this chapter were …

- Current mainstream theorizing on leadership has several problems, such as:

  o Leadership is becoming a big industry, fuelled by quantitative research that prioritizes questions of profitability, efficiency and effectiveness.
  o This industry is dominated by US-based models dressed up as universal theories. Such theories tend to emphasize individualism.
  o Our leadership definitions are heavily influenced by implicit and differing theories, but this fact is often ignored in mainstream research.
  o The result of all this is the production of simplistic individual models of leadership that fail to connect to the complex and heterogeneous real worlds of human beings.
  o Such models of leadership have also been dominated by masculine notions of competition, aggression, control and self-reliance.

- Post-structuralism offers an alternative theoretical framework that challenges the mainstream that the world is external and knowable by objective research. Instead it offers a theoretical basis for analysing the identities of men and women in relation to language, other cultural practices and the material conditions of their lives. Such thinking enables fresh light to be shed on leadership theorizing, research and practice.
- Post-structuralism looks at how leaders and leadership are constructed through the study of them. It asserts that while leadership exists, it has been brought into being through the ongoing repetition of the word (which is called the performative effect).

- It offers a more critical and reflexive approach to the power of the leadership discourse in shaping identities our understanding of leadership, and notably brings scrutiny to notions of perfect heroic leaders and their 'inferior' followers.

Further thinking

Ford, J. (2006). Discourses of leadership: Gender, identity and contradiction in a UK public sector organization. *Leadership*, 2(1), 77–99.

Questions:

1   What do you understand by the notion that there are 'competing discourses of leadership … in the day to day narratives of those employed in senior management positions' (p. xx)? How does this have an effect on the way that you might think about, study and practise leadership?
2   On reading this paper, why might dominant discourses of leadership make it more difficult for women to be accepted as leaders in organizations?
3   Ford suggests that macho-management discourse still abounds in leadership roles and behaviours. Thinking about your own experiences of work, what would you identify as the dominant discourse of leadership present in the places you have been employed? How has this impacted on you and on those around you?

Collinson, D. (2014). Dichotomies, dialectics and dilemmas: New directions for critical leadership studies. *Leadership*, 10(1), 36–55.

Questions:

1   How would you describe the three key themes of leadership literature that Collinson explores in this paper and why do you think these are important for future, more critical writing on leadership?
2   Power remains an unspoken and yet ever-present concept in relation to leaders and leadership studies. What new insights does this paper offer in relation to the study of power and the leader/follower dynamics?

Leadership on screen

The following films capture some of the post-structuralist aspects of leadership that are discussed in this chapter. They also alert us to the multiple ways of reading and understanding leadership.

Percy Jackson: Sea of Monsters (2013)

This is the second film in the Percy Jackson series that has been developed from the books written by Rick Riordan. It is based loosely on Greek mythology and continues the epic journeys of Percy the young demigod (who has superior water powers) and his demigod friends to fulfil their destiny. To save their world, Percy Jackson and his friends (Annabeth, who has superior brain cells, and Tyson, who has superior strength) must find the fabled and magical Golden Fleece. They embark on a treacherous odyssey into the unchartered waters of the Sea of Monsters ('known to humans as the Bermuda Triangle'); they do battle with terrifying creatures, an army of zombies and the ultimate evil. This all sounds like a regular day at work to me.

American Beauty (1999)

You may not initially think of *American Beauty* as a particularly great example of a post-structuralist film. The film explores the dark side of an American family and the nature and price of beauty in a culture obsessed with outward appearances. It depicts the way the media tells us what beauty is, and is about a man pursuing a high school girl because that is what the media has told him beauty really is. Kevin Spacey plays Lester Burnham, a man in his mid-40s going through an intense mid-life crisis; he's grown cynical and is convinced that he has no reason to go on. Lester's relationship with his wife Carolyn (Annette Bening) is not a warm one; while on the surface Carolyn strives to present the image that she's in full control of her life, inside she feels empty and desperate. Their teenage daughter Jane (Thora Birch) is constantly depressed, lacking in self-esteem and convinced that she's unattractive. Her problems aren't helped by her best friend Angela (Mena Suvari), an aspiring model who is quite beautiful and believes that that alone makes her a worthwhile person. Jane isn't the only one who has noticed that Angela is attractive: Lester has fallen into uncontrollable lust for her, and she becomes part of his drastic plan to change his body and change his life. Meanwhile, next door, Colonel Fitts (Chris Cooper) has spent a lifetime in the Marine Corps and can understand and tolerate no other way of life, which makes life difficult for his son Ricky (Wes Bentley), an aspiring film-maker and part-time drug dealer who is obsessed with beauty, wherever and whatever it may be. The main theme of the film is pursuing this perfect life that the media advocates; the perfect marriage, beauty, riches and the idea of the perfect, happy life. It shows the detrimental effects that this media ideology has on society and individuals in a clever and compelling way. So, what has this to do with leadership? The parallels for me relate to some of the guru theories of leadership and of the fixation on the ways in which leaders and leadership will act as saviours to all organizational (and political) ills.

13

SEEING LEADERSHIP

BECOMING SOPHISTICATED CONSUMERS OF LEADERSHIP

Owain Smolović-Jones and Brad Jackson

Owain Smolović-Jones is such a political junkie that at the age of 11 he kept a detailed scrap-book recording in some depth (including interviews with the candidates) the events of the 1989 Vale of Glamorgan parliamentary by-election. He is a Lecturer in Management at the Department of Public Leadership and Social Enterprise, The Open University, UK.

Brad Jackson has, from an early age, always prized a visit to the National Portrait Gallery every time he visits London. He is the Head of School of Government at Victoria University of Wellington, New Zealand.

What this chapter is all about …

The main idea is that the visual element of leadership is more important than is often given credit. By drawing on psychoanalytic philosophy, we can reflect on the way we produce and consume symbolic constructions of leadership – and this sheds light on new ways and different forms in which to interpret, explore and make sense of leadership.

The key questions this chapter answers are:

- How is the way in which we 'see' leadership important for the way in which we behave in leadership and respond to leaders?
- What is psychoanalytic philosophy?
- What new ideas come to you about how you understand and practice leadership?

Introduction

Imagine you are working for a major global insurance company that is searching for a new worldwide chief executive officer (CEO). There are three candidates for the job. Naturally curious about who may be your next company leader you immediately Google them and instantaneously up pops their photographs, their CVs, the annual reports of the companies that they have previously led and several media articles that have been written about them. In what order do you process these online artefacts? Do you go to the photographs first or work through the written material and only then look at the visual images?

Research suggests that you would most likely go first to the photographs of the CEOs and that these would have quite a significant influence on your thinking about the potential suitability of the CEO for the job and how you might work with her or him; more so than either you or most people would be willing to recognize, let alone admit.

In a similar vein, the next time you are waiting to board a flight, you might spend some time observing how business people read newspapers and magazines. Observe how much time they scan the photographs of the various leaders that are being depicted in a range of flattering and unflattering poses and how little time they spend reading most of the articles. Is this truly rational behaviour on their part if they are supposedly making sense of opportunities and threats that might be emerging in the marketplace?

 STOP AND REFLECT 13.1

In student elections, campaign flyers are usually plastered on every available space and other spaces besides. How is leadership potential and desirability communicated on these flyers? How much space is devoted to a photograph of the candidate and how much is devoted to the candidate's platform? How do you go about assessing the candidates? How important is it to 'look right/wrong' for the job? How much do you think that has changed over the years?

In this chapter we will tackle these questions and hope to cast some light on them by showing what we have learned from a small but intriguing body of studies that focus on images of leadership. We will specifically discuss how the way in which we 'see' leadership is important for the way in which we behave in leadership and respond to leaders. In constructing our argument, we will link the seeing of leadership closely to ideas from recent psychoanalytic philosophy. In particular we will introduce the idea of a 'gaze'. Leaders are gazed upon and in turn gaze back. Viewing leadership as a reciprocal act of seeing, we will argue, is an informative way of making sense of how we work within and with structures of power and authority.

Leadership: More than a pretty face?

The face communicates a vast amount of information – such as the mood a person is in, their intentions, and whether or not they are paying attention to us. Our ability to receive and interpret such facial information is neurologically hardwired by brain cells dedicated to processing facial information, which are located in the temporal and cerebral cortex. In fact, the human brain has cells responsive solely to the sight of heads and faces. These brain cells are intact even at infancy; with research showing that infants can readily interpret facial information at a very early age.

Faces can be either familiar or unfamiliar to us. Upon seeing a familiar face 'identity semantic codes' are processed, which remind us of previous experiences we have had with a person and provides us with information about their identity (Bruce, 1988). Alternatively, an unfamiliar face generates 'visually derived semantic codes'. These are based on the physical appearance of a person's face and provide the viewer with 'social' information about a person (Bruce, 1988). This information will include a person's age, gender, emotion, attractiveness and personality (Berry, 1990; Feingold, 1992; Ekman and Rosenberg, 1997).

Facial information is also used as the basis for judgements we make about others. For example, a child's facial appearance can have an impact on the amount of loving and caring attention they receive from their parents; teachers report attractive children to be more intelligent; attractive children are more readily accepted by their peers; and parents attribute mature-faced children with greater communication skills.

Given the central importance that the face plays in interpersonal communication, what role might the face of a leader play in fostering leadership between leaders and followers? The face communicates information used to infer social information from those we do not know and helps us to recall past experiences with those we do know. Unless a neurological 'defect' exists, facial perception and recognition is an automatic and biologically hardwired process. It is, therefore, likely that followers will attempt to process and recognize the face of leaders. Followers will most likely process identity semantic codes that remind them of past experiences they have had with the leader when the leader is familiar to them. When the leader is unfamiliar to them, followers will process visually derived semantic codes to gather social information about the leader.

In a world where a staggering amount of communication is mediated by Facebook, one should not be surprised by the ubiquity of notions of 'face' in common-sense as well as media treatments of leadership. For example, leaders should act as 'the face of the organisation' with its attendant corollary, 'If the face fits, you'll get the job'. In promoting diversity, media will often feature ethnic and gender minorities as the 'changing face of leadership'. Finally, a key function of leaders is to exhort their followers to 'face up to realities'. Recognizing the central importance that is ascribed to the face as an essential visual instrument of leadership, how have leadership scholars endeavoured to make sense of this?

Overcoming the 'blind spot' in leadership studies

In an era in which we are continually bombarded by visual images, it is remarkable that leadership studies has long suffered from a 'blind spot' when it comes to recognizing the influence that the production and consumption of visual images have on the conduct of organizational and political life. Two recent developments, though, have helped to bring the visual image into contention.

The first development has been the growing acceptance by leadership scholars of the socially constructed nature of leadership that was described by Donna Ladkin in Chapter 1. Rooted in the notion of the 'romance of leadership' (Meindl, 1985) this perspective has found its fullest expression in the accumulated works of Keith Grint. Starting with the recognition of the 'constitutive' nature of leadership, which emphasizes the leader's role in presenting a sufficiently compelling definition of the current and future situation to followers, Grint (2001) makes a persuasive case that leadership should profitably be considered not as a science, a view that most prominent leadership scholars have ascribed to, but as an art. Leadership, though, is not confined to one art but four – the philosophical arts, the visual arts, the martial arts and the performing arts. From the philosophical arts, Grint suggests that leaders can learn to create a compelling sense of identity for their organization (i.e. who are we?); from the visual arts they can learn to forge a powerful strategic vision for the organizations they lead (i.e. where are we going?); from the martial arts they can learn to develop smart organizational tactics (i.e. how will we achieve this?); and from the performing arts they can learn to persuasively communicate to their followers the organization's identity, its strategic vision and its tactics.

The second related development is what is described as 'the aesthetic turn' in organization studies, which has emphasized the need to develop ways of knowing that encompass all of the senses, including the visual (Taylor and Hansen, 2005).

DEFINITION: AESTHETIC LEADERSHIP

An aesthetic approach to leadership focuses upon the sensory experience and the felt meanings that are produced by and guide our interactions and decisions. The aesthetic approach to leadership deliberately examines the tacit dimension of leadership, an area that we rarely talk about but one that is more influential than we care to admit when we make sense or try to enact leadership. Aesthetic approaches to leadership do not seek to replace conventional approaches to leadership but rather to complement and supplement the more mainstream approaches to leadership. Instrumentality, ethics and aesthetics are all necessary elements that inform leadership practice. The aesthetic turn has also begun to make inroads into leadership studies.

One important implication when we bring the aesthetic lens to bear is that we need leaders who are endowed with aesthetic abilities in addition to the technical and ethical abilities that are so highly prized. This is brilliantly illustrated in a case study of the 'beautiful leadership' exhibited by a capella maestro Bobby McFerrin to a packed concert hall in Berlin. Donna Ladkin shows how McFerrin appears to effortlessly lead not only the orchestra that he is conducting but the whole audience through a combination of self-mastery and aligning his self to a 'beautiful goal' (Ladkin, 2008). An aesthetic appreciation of leadership has foregrounded the need for leaders to develop 'bodily knowledge' in addition to cognitive knowledge or affective influence that is the usual focus for leadership development. Bodily knowledge is a type of tacit knowledge, derived from demonstration and learning-by-doing, and is conceptually similar to the 'sixth sense' (Ropo et al., 2002). Just as the conductor of an orchestra might have a 'feel' for the music, the leader within an organization should develop a 'feel' for what other employees, customers and shareholders are sensing and experiencing.

 ## STOP AND REFLECT 13.2

As part of their assessment, our MBA students are asked to produce a visual artefact (e.g. a painting, photograph, performance art, sculpture, video) that captures their answer to the following question: 'The leadership we need to grapple with as a society in terms of the future hinges on ... [a question, a concept, a framework, a metaphor, a new way of thinking, etc.].' When we assess their artefacts and the presentations they give to introduce them, we have been stunned by the variety of artefacts they produce and the creativity and passion they channel into their assignments. We have had 'leadership maypole' dancing through which various leadership theories are creatively inter-weaved; we have had mime performances that memorably demonstrate the importance of authentic leadership; and we have had leadership maze installations that highlight the need for quite different sensemaking approaches in order to lead in complexity. What is most striking is the students' feedback that, although they were originally intimidated by the task, they were excited about the fact that they were able to communicate and comprehend their thinking, their hopes and fears about future leadership in a way that talking and writing was not able to do so. How would you go about responding to this assignment?

We might be able to consider how leadership is communicated aesthetically between leaders and followers directly and immediately within a specific place and time. But what of the leadership that is created distally through media such as paintings, sculptures and photographs? The portrayal of leaders has a long history through Neolithic sculpture and Greek coins to the commissioned oil paintings of kings and queens and their most powerful subjects. The primary purpose of the portrait is to communicate formal authority, and in some cases charismatic authority, to current as well as potentially new subjects who may never experience direct contact with this leader (Warner, 2014).

The painted portrait derives it symbolic power from the fact that, compared with a photograph of a leader, it is relatively unusual and generally more expensive to produce and difficult to copy. It also possesses a sense of permanence and prestige that is becoming increasingly rare in the age of the disposable celebrity. As with all works of art, the original portrait of a leader holds the most cachet, but the image can be distributed in alternative forms through the medium of print and the Internet. Ironically, though, this widespread distribution serves to strengthen the symbolic power of the original portrait (Griffey and Jackson, 2010).

Commissioned portraits are hybrid in form; that is, the artist draws upon and combines two or more divergent sources for inspiration and for impact. This process takes place at several levels of abstraction. At the most fundamental level, in enabling the portrait to carry out its virtual leader function, the artist brings together, at the initiative of the sponsors and the cooperation of the subject and the mediation of the curator, an actual or potential follower with a leader in a moment of quiet contemplation. At a slightly higher level of abstraction, as was noted earlier, portrait artists bring together in one visual representation the personal as well as the positional qualities of a particular leader in a way that is sometimes difficult for them to be isolated. At a higher level than this, leadership portraits are hybrids as artists selectively draw upon and integrate a number of artistic conventions from different historic periods and different cultures. Finally, at the highest level, the artist, the critic and the viewer draw upon and integrate different archetypes of leadership from specific historic periods and cultures (Griffey and Jackson, 2010).

Images are not only important for how followers make sense of leaders but also of the organizations that they lead. In the case of organizations like Apple, Microsoft and Virgin, it was very difficult to separate out the CEO from the corporate brand. The 'celebrification' of leadership in the realms of business and political leadership is a massive enterprise involving a complex web of agents that include media organisations, internal and external public relations firms and academic organizations (Guthey et al., 2009).

There are, however, real dangers imputing a corporate brand from a CEO image that is disseminated through websites, annual reports and media articles. Upon first impression, such photographs may appear to convey an impression of the kind of authentic presence that many observers consider to be crucial for establishing a strong corporate image. But a closer look at the constructed nature of both CEO identity and portrait photography lays bare the elusive nature of authenticity itself, as well the way that CEO portraits can function also to expose the corporations' 'chronic lack of authenticity' (Guthey and Jackson, 2005, p. 1057). This point is exemplified to powerful effect by the use by companies, most especially in the fast food industry, of cartoon figures or 'virtual leader constructs' (VLCs) (e.g. Ronald McDonald and Colonel Sanders). VLCs are 'virtual', first in terms of being virtuous in relation to culturally accepted archetypes of leadership excellence, and second in terms of not being actual embodied human beings (Boje and Rhodes, 2005).

There are dangers for leaders too. Photographic images of business leaders do not merely reflect the views of the business community, the commercial and organizational imperatives of the media, or the collective conceptions of organization and leadership dominant in the national culture at large. Such images also function very actively as rhetorical tools in ongoing symbolic struggles over the legitimacy of individual business leaders, and over the social legitimacy of corporate organization writ large. Visual images can play a critical role in building up the public profile of 'celebrity CEOs' but they can play an even more devastating role in the backlash that can afflict them and the organizations they lead when the business begins to under-perform or, worse, when ethical practice standards are transgressed. Media images played a critical role in the dramatic rise as well as the widely publicized and sudden fall from grace of Carly Fiorina, the Hewlett Packard CEO in 2005. Indeed, it is clear that female leaders tend to suffer a peculiarly malevolent scrutiny in the visual construction and destruction of their leadership (Guthey and Jackson, 2008).

On the other side of the coin, there is the recognition that we need to better understand how followers make aesthetically-based assessments of their experiences with leaders. A few pioneering studies point the way. For example, it is remarkable how reliable naive viewers (i.e. children!) have been found to be in predicting electoral success in US elections just by viewing candidate photographs (Antonakis and Dalgas, 2009). Another experimental study was surprised to discover how much information was derived from very short reviews of CEO portrait photographs that were previously unknown to MBA students and how willing they were to form narrative opinions – many of them quite sophisticated – regarding leader effectiveness (Nana et al., 2010). Moreover, it is equally sobering and disconcerting to note how important good looks can be at predicting CEO success (Rule and Lambady, 2008, 2009).

From leadership as discourse to 'seeing' leadership

So let's rewind a little to arguments made earlier in the book about constructionism in leadership studies. Our discussion on how leaders present themselves should make it quite clear that leaders seem to put a lot of effort into constructing their images in certain ways. We're rarely duped into accepting these portrayals at face value but, nevertheless, they remain influential. If these self-presentations were insignificant, it is unlikely that leaders would need to bother with employing public relations specialists.

For the remainder of this chapter we will draw on the work of the influential psychoanalyst and philosopher Jacques Lacan to dig deeper into how seeing can offer an important, critical perspective on leadership.

Lacan was a clinical psychoanalyst and psychiatrist from France, often regarded as one of the most significant figures in his field. Nevertheless, he was a controversial figure within the clinical community and indeed within scholarly and political circles more generally. In the clinical world he was regarded as too 'philosophical', too unconventional, not really sitting well with either the Freudian tradition within psychoanalysis or with the relatively recent movement of behavioural psychology, birthed in the USA and UK during and shortly after the Second World War (Rose, 1999).

Lacan was influenced by early constructionist philosophers, as well as by philosophers concerned with the politics of social relations and public ethics. Nevertheless, his training was clinical, heavily influenced by Freud's insights into the unconscious. Part of Lacan's genius was to choose to interpret much existing psychoanalytic thought from a broadly constructionist, political and ethical perspective, and vice versa.

Before we understand better Lacan's specific arguments on seeing, it is important for us to understand his broader argument. In Lacan's view, social relations are influenced through three key domains. The first is what he referred to as the 'symbolic'. The symbolic, put simply, is the realm of language, of words. There are close similarities here to Foucault's concept of discourse – we are conditioned by the words that we use and the meaning attached to those words.

The second of Lacan's orders is that of the 'imaginary', which can be translated as the realm of images, what we see and how we store such images in our psyches. We carry images of ourselves – or how we would like to be seen – around in our heads. We also carry images of others. When we think of a particular leader – for example Tony Blair, the former British Prime Minister, whom we will come to later – we might think of that leader in a particular setting, in a certain posture, and so on. The imaginary is another kind of construction but cannot be reduced to language alone. Sometimes we are disappointed because leaders fail to live up to the image we hold of them. And provided you are not a total ego-maniac, we are sure that you are often disappointed with yourself, because you sometimes fail to live up to your own ideal self-image.

Tony Blair became the leader of the British Labour Party in 1994. The party had been out of power since Margaret Thatcher won the 1979 general election, and had experienced a series of divisive and traumatic election defeats. Blair was a figure of hope for people inside and outside his party. He did not look or speak like a traditional political leader. He simultaneously projected an image of effectiveness and warmth. On the other hand, many in his party resented Blair for moving his party away from long-held political positions on the left. He won a landslide general election in 1997, and another in 2001. His popularity remained high, in a way rarely seen in elected politics, well into his second term of office. The mood of the country shifted, however, following his support of the US-led war in Iraq in 2003. Blair left office in 2007 and remains a divisive figure. We will explore the case of Tony Blair in much more depth later in this chapter.

But the more radical dimension of Lacan can be found in his discussion of his third domain – that of the 'real'. Key to Lacan's philosophy is the idea that we can never truly capture the whole of human experience, of our desires, through either images or words. Behind our everyday use of words and images lies something 'real'. The bad news is that, according to Lacan, we are hamstrung from birth and will never be able to fully access this 'real' – this realm of total satisfaction, of pure enjoyment.

Words and images will never get us there and yet we have no choice but to structure our experiences and relationships according to these two dominant ways of making sense of the world. Our parents push us in that direction and, anyway, it would be impossible to live anything approaching a satisfying life without entering into relations with other people (who are also speaking, seeing people) – hence we have to live in the world of symbols. But this is not the 'real' world. Language and images cannot possibly hope to capture the full meaning of the world, let alone the universe. Therefore, we are unable to gain full enjoyment from the world of the symbolic. So, sadly for us, we are doomed to live our lives as alienated beings. Our words and images will always come up lacking.

For now, simply remember this core idea: behind every image and set of words lies something 'real'. The fact that words and images can never offer a truly satisfactory construct means that we continually notice cracks in our representations and the representations of others. It is in these cracks that potential for really exciting leadership exists. And how do we notice cracks in what is presented to us? Through the act of *seeing*.

Gazing upon leadership

You may have noticed that we have started introducing words commonly associated with the emotions (e.g. enjoyment, desire) into our discussion. This is one major departure of Lacanian theory from social constructionism. Social constructionism might explain how we attach to certain discourses of meaning – through discipline and so on, but does not necessarily explain why. Lacan partially answers this concern. Lacan's position, put simply, is that we are creatures who chase enjoyment – enjoyment is what we desire. It is a simple enough proposition, at face value. But let's also recap and remind ourselves that we can never experience pure enjoyment (Lacan refers to such enjoyment as *jouissance*, a kind of wild, primal, libidinal form of enjoyment, which is destructive, as well as pleasurable). Yet we live in a system of symbols: we are cursed with being alienated from our own enjoyment, our *jouissance*. All we can do is endlessly chase this enjoyment, usually in ignorance of the fact that we will never really find it – we might brush against it, find it in part, but never completely.

It's an unsettling thought. It's even a quite traumatic thought. And it is this sense of high uncertainty, of trauma, that is at the heart of Lacan's (2004) concept of the gaze, a concept we argue is so important for thinking about and practising leadership.

Rather than simply describing this theory to you in its bare bones, we are going to unfold it with reference to a particularly well-known painting depicting leadership, or at least depicting two successful leaders. The painting we are referring to is Hans Holbein's *The Ambassadors*, created in 1533 (Figure 13.1). It is a painting that fascinated Lacan and it is also a painting that presents us with an image of a kind of leader-ideal.

Figure 13.1   *The Ambassadors*

The first thing to note about this painting is the age of the two men depicted. They are far closer in age to undergraduate students than the two grumpy old academics writing this chapter. To the left is Jean de Dinteville, aged 29 at the time, who was the French ambassador to England. To the right is Georges de Selve, aged 25, who at the time served as bishop of Lavaur and undertook many important ambassadorial missions on behalf of the French. These are successful young men, lauded in their own time in a similar way to the successful young business and sports people of today. Were such a painting to be commissioned nowadays, it would likely portray figures such as Serena Williams and Mark Zuckerberg. Holbein's ambassadors may only be a few years past their first postgraduate traineeship but, nevertheless, they are *leaders*.

Some clues as to the status of these subjects are offered. They are clothed as successful people. De Dinteville appears in all his pomp – note the fur-trimmed jacket, for example, which wouldn't be too amiss in an MTV video. In contrast, de Selve is solemn in the attire of the sixteenth-century senior clergy. Yet there is more. These are successful, wealthy men of the world. Note the shelves behind them – what they chose to display to the artist and audience, how they chose to portray themselves as leaders. There is a celestial globe, sun-dial and book on arithmetic: these are travelled, smart individuals. Note the lute and case of flutes indicating that they are cultured and well rounded. They are also pious people, hence the prominently displayed Lutheran hymn book.

Taking into account these symbols of status, it may be supposed that the leaders who gaze upon us from the picture do so as somewhat superior beings (or at least that's what they would like us to think). This in itself might generate a fair amount of anxiety in the viewer: 'I could never be like them', or even, 'Why *couldn't* I have been like them?' Likewise, we might suppose that contemporaries of these ambassadors might have been so impressed by the image that they were prepared to invest a lot of trust in these people, in much the same way as we might trust in our image of our favourite sportsperson to guide our team to victory, a talented chief executive to look after our stocks or a political leader to transform our country for the better.

But, of course, this is where our constructions start to break down. We know, at some level at least, that the world just does not work like that. This painting is an imperfect representation. The first clue is provided by the broken string on the lute, which, according to many art historians, signals the presence of religious doubt. As people of the time started to learn more about the science of our planet and universe, became more learned about the ways of other people and races, so they started to doubt their previous constructions, largely derived from religious teaching.

More dramatically, these ambassadors are imperfect people – and they want us to know this. Incredibly, at the bottom of the picture you will notice a rather imposing and distorted image of a floating skull! The image is a prominent example of an artistic technique known as *anamorphosis*, which, simply put, is a kind of trick of the eye employed by painters to surprise onlookers. Its use by Holbein is meant to act as a reminder to the viewer, and no doubt the subjects, that we are all mortal, imperfect beings, no matter how high up the social ladder we may have climbed. Ultimately, we are all flesh and bone and will all, at some point, die. It is the sixteenth-century equivalent of the colloquialism that even celebrities and royalty have to use the toilet! Returning to the skull, in order to obtain an undistorted, clear view, you have to step off to the right-hand side of the painting, to capture the image at just the correct angle. The painting is housed in London's National Gallery (which offers free entrance), so if you are ever in London, go and try it out for yourselves. It's a lot of fun to do and in fact to watch others trying to master the effect.

So why was Lacan so fascinated by this painting? The key to understanding the painting's importance for Lacan lies in the very feeling you probably experienced when your eyes hovered over the skull for the first time ... doubt, surprise, shock? We were expecting to be stared upon by two successful leaders of the time and instead we find ourselves locked in the gaze of a distorted skull. We think we are masters of our own enjoyment – we are the ones in control, looking upon this work of art at our own pace, on our own terms, and suddenly we are gripped by uncertainty (McGowan, 2003, 2008).

The effect is twofold. First, this gaze back upon us suggests that the enjoyment, as presented in the symbolism and imagery of success and wealth, does not equate to total enjoyment – these are mortal men. In fact, being an ambassador in the sixteenth century was quite a perilous occupation and often not at all glamorous (sixteenth-century long-distance travel was not particularly comfortable).

But more to the point, Lacan argues that this work of art gazes back upon us, disrupts our thinking – not in the superficial sense of us feeling mentally engaged or challenged, but in the sense of our very anchors, our fundamental assumptions, being shaken, often leaving us speechless. What does this gazing object want from us? We thought we knew – worldly 'success', maybe even to hold that position of leading. But actually this is not the case at all. We are left suspended, in a state of uncertainty. According to Lacan, this feeling, where the symbolic representations and assumptions of our world start to fall away, allows us a glimpse of the 'real' (McGowan, 2008).

STOP AND REFLECT 13.3

Pick up a newspaper and select three images of leaders that are being portrayed that day (i.e. political, business, entertainment, religious or sports leaders). What are your immediate impressions about the leadership that is being portrayed (i.e. good or bad, powerful or weak, etc.). Why are you reacting this way? Now dwell on the picture a little longer and begin to examine the less obvious elements of the picture (e.g. the background, cropping, light, props and enhancements). Who commissioned the picture, who took the picture and who selected it? To what extent did the leader and her or his associates control or influence this image? What were their motives? Why did they select the particular frame for this picture?

Getting to that point of traversing the real is hard-going though. Why is this? We have already touched upon the answer. The reason is that in our way lies a multitude of symbols and images. Pieced together, these constructions of ours actually constitute what Lacanians refer to as ideology. Ideology for Lacanians holds a wider meaning than simply the systems of belief we carry around about the way the world should work. Ideology is really shorthand for describing the underlying fantasies (the mix of images and discourses) that people concoct in the belief that the problems they experience will be solved through a certain set of actions or by a certain type of person.

In the field of leadership studies, the most common ideological fantasy can be found in this notion of a single (powerful and usually male) leader. Our fantasies of leadership are fuelled by popular culture – Hollywood films, for example (Ford et al., 2008). Think of how often in a mainstream cinematic release a single individual comes along to save the day. Yet how often does this truly happen in life? How safe a bet is it for us to invest so much in something that clearly happens so rarely, if ever? Yet so invested have we become in the figure of the powerful individual leader that we are prepared to sacrifice a lot of our critical faculties in the name of this fantasy (Grint, 2010). In other words, we feel better if someone else is taking the responsibility for leadership. *The Ambassadors* gnaws away at the credibility of this position, of this symbolic construction. Through its distorted gaze, this 'stain' on the otherwise perfect fantasy representation of leadership and power shakes us, allows us a glimpse of the traumatic 'real' behind our ideological fantasies. No one is coming to save us, to make everything ok.

We apologize if you started this chapter expecting some light relief from an otherwise challenging set of ideas which unsettled the way you thought about leadership. But part of the reason why we are so excited by the potential for *seeing* leadership is its potential to push us towards re-evaluating both the role of 'leaders' and 'followers' in leadership. In fact, *seeing* leadership might even lead us to question whether it is even helpful to think of leadership in leader–follower terms. What we are going to argue in the following case study is that through gazing upon leaders, we may learn not simply more about that particular leader but about our relationship to this leader, and so about our role in the affective dynamic of public leadership. Art, we argue, offers a unique opportunity for us to become locked in this gaze of public leadership.

Case study: Gazing upon Tony Blair

There are certain figures who tend to dominate the public life of a certain era, who capture a mood of a country or generation. You will have your own figures you relate to, in the world of politics, culture, even in sport. For a significant period of time, from the mid- to late 1990s, a wave of new-left politics seemed to sweep many Western liberal democratic states. In America Bill Clinton was elected to office. In Germany Gerhard Schroeder. And in the UK there was Tony Blair. These were new figures for the left – they not only espoused a different kind of ideology, one more centrist and more amenable to business but they also looked very different. They were visually striking leaders who thought a lot about the image they projected to the public in a way that elected politics had not really experienced to such an extent in the past.

People seemed to invest a lot of energy and emotion into the figure of Blair – he looked, sounded and felt like a break from the past. Here was a leader who represented the politics of the centre-left (compassionate, inclusive) yet who pulled it off with a confidence and authority not seen before in UK politics. Of course politics is a fickle business. One day a leader is a hero, the next vilified. The media distorts – every disagreement is a 'row' – and seems at times obsessed by trivia. But even taking account of the wildness of elected politics, the change of public perceptions of Blair by the end of his premiership was striking.

The image on the next page seems to us to be a fair representation of how most people visualize Tony Blair (Figure 13.2). It was taken by a *Guardian* photographer during Blair's final address to the Labour Party conference, held at Manchester in September 2006. Blair's body language is open, as if he is inviting all the criticism that could possibly be levelled at him confident in the knowledge that he could bat it away. Political marketing experts would also tell you that he is wearing the classic 'Number Ones', a particular type of outfit

(Continued)

(Continued)

Figure 13.2   Tony Blair during his final Labour Party conference address, 2006

male political leaders wear because psychologists have come to the conclusion that it is the combination of colours and styles that engender the most trust from onlookers (dark suit, white shirt, diagonally striped tie).

The image we hold of Blair in this time is akin to what is known in leadership studies as a *commander posture* (Grint, 2005b). Commanders are people of authority who tell others what to do and expect their orders to be followed. We tend to turn to commanders when we fear that we are in times of crisis and in fact commanders often create a feeling of 'emergency' with their deployment of language. Blair himself characterizes the post-9/11 atmosphere of global politics as one characterized by urgency: 'Above all, there was a sense of an emergency. In this time, the failure to act was indeed an action with its own consequence and that consequence might be profoundly adverse' (Blair, 2010, p. 396).

Lacan was interested in the relationship people held with authority – and authority figures. His argument is that we tend to look for guidance in our everyday lives from figures of authority – such as the commander – because such figures provide guidance on what to think and how to conduct ourselves. Such guidance is comforting and ubiquitous (life is full of people and rules telling us how we should behave). He went further in stating that we encounter such figures of authority both symbolically and visually. We invest a lot in these figures for two paradoxical reasons. The first is that they provide us with comfort: essentially they do the thinking and leading for us. So we can take a step back – blaming such leaders when things go wrong and celebrating them when things go well (Grint, 2010). The second reason is that these leaders exude a kind of power. They do not seem to be subject to the same symbolic constraints as we are – they seem more free.

So the appeal of Blair might be described by a Lacanian scholar as maintaining a balance between being a strict and certain figure of authority. On the one hand, he seemed to be in control of the law, of the formal structures of power that enabled him to govern. On the other hand, he could also project an image as someone who was also somehow more 'free' from the constraints of everyday rules than we are.

From a Lacanian perspective you will notice here that our discussion has accepted one of the basic premises of constructionism. This is not a matter simply of Blair projecting a certain image of himself and of us – the viewing public – accepting that image at face value. Rather, to a certain degree, our pre-determined image of what we expect of a public leader determines how Blair chose to project himself to us. We expected someone who was tough, certain of his decisions, and that is what we were handed back to us.

It is this relationship within leadership that we wish to explore next. It is here that images of leadership – and Lacan's gaze specifically – may help us to interpret leadership differently. Specifically, we will argue that being locked in the gaze may help us reconsider the leadership relationship from an ethical perspective.

Tony Blair gazes back

Tony Blair looked, sounded and felt like a different kind of political leader – at least in the UK. Latter-day twentieth-century America had experienced the Kennedys, Ronald Reagan and Bill Clinton. All of them were presidents who seemed to engender quite extraordinary levels of loyalty amongst their supporters. These were political leaders who had reached people in ways that exceeded more calculated judgements of competency in office. Many people seemed to relate to these leaders as much as lovers or great friends as figures of authority, in the more traditional, hierarchical sense.

These explanations, alone, however, would be unsatisfactory for Lacanian scholars. What these leaders managed to capture was more than respect and admiration – or even discipline. They evoked a sense of constructive, collective enjoyment (Lacan, 1999). These were leaders who both seemed to break the symbolic confines of their day but in a way which engendered feelings of solidarity, care for others and collective ambition. They looked like movie stars, and were often choreographed as such, and yet they were figures who also projected feelings of hope and solidarity – leaders who understood aspiration as well as injustice. They questioned what we thought we knew to be true of possibilities for political change and in so doing managed to generate a kind of challenging, yet collaborative enjoyment amongst their followers.

We will now explore some of the tensions and contradictions evident in this pathway from a collaborative sense of leadership to a more autocratic one through an analysis of a painting we find particularly striking, Alastair Adams's portrait of Tony Blair (see Figure 13.3).

If your reaction to this painting is anything like ours, you will have noted a certain feeling of intimidation wrapped up in your surprise. After all, here is a global statesman squarely gazing out at us. It is an uncomfortable feeling: what does this person, whose face, words and deeds are so well known to us, want from us? It is a feeling that makes you catch your breath. You probably already knew what you thought of Blair – you may even have voted for or against him. Yet here he is staring back at you – but why? What is there that we don't know? About him – about ourselves?

The second feeling we note is one of shock mingled with curiosity. The face we see is worn, the lines in his face are marked. If this were a landscape painting, these wrinkles might mark the lines of a cliff against which the sea dashes. They evoke the sense of a structure battered by the external world, by forces outside of his – and our – control. Let us also note the other imperfections. We see a peep of the infamous discoloured Blair tooth – the one stain on that famous Blair smile. And his eyes in this painting. Is it just us or are they slightly lopsided? If this is a face of leadership, then the act, the job of leading seems far from straightforward.

Gazing back at us from the canvas, we can't help but get a little lost in the dark depths of Blair's eyes. They are at once steely, somewhat mournful – and accusatory. 'Where were you when I needed you?' 'Why can't you understand how tough this job is?' In contrast to the triumphalist first image of Blair we analysed this is a portrait of leadership as tragedy. The 'dark side' as opposed to the "bright side" of leadership.

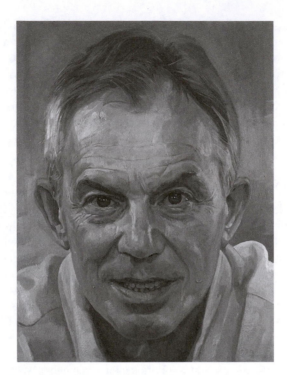

Figure 13.3   Portrait of Tony Blair

In fact, one need only study a selection of Blair's speeches and his memoirs to notice that he was particularly fascinated by the difficulty of decision-making. A common motif of Blair's oratory is a reflection upon the fact that major decisions for prime ministers are rarely straightforward. Information is incomplete. The stakes are high – usually involving people's welfare, life chances, wealth, even lives. More often than not, political leaders are not really sure that their decisions are absolutely correct. They may come across that way on the television but that is only because they think the public and, more importantly, the media, is not able to process a leader saying something akin to 'You know, this is very difficult and we are going to have to think about it and talk it through a lot more'.

Ah, but that's the job, you might say. We voters are not paid to make the big decisions – that's why we vote for political leaders. But as you are now under way with your exploration of leadership as a field of study, are you really in a position where you are happy to wash your hands of leadership, to leave it to other people? The reason this painting of Blair is so evocative is that it stares back at us, exposes the inadequacy and contradictions of this position of experiencing leadership at arm's length.

This is a haggard Blair who stares back at us. The very lines on his face, the bags under his eyes gaze at us accusingly. They expose the inadequacy of dominant thinking on leadership. We can't and shouldn't simply look upon the leadership of others from a distance: we need to be more involved, more active, more critical. But in addition, perhaps leaders such as Blair would not go too wrong if they expended more energy in exploring the limitations of their own ideological ways of seeing.

Concluding thoughts

In this chapter we have made the point that when thinking of leadership we often overlook the importance of what we see, as well as what we hear and read. In focusing on various ways in which followers visually consume leadership we encourage you to reconsider the position of followers in relation to leaders. In our quest for certainty, safety and comfort, we perhaps invest too much in our expectations in leaders. Do we expect too much from our leaders? What do we and they gain from our silence?

In this chapter we have focused a lot on big figures in elected public life. But the lessons we draw from our analysis can equally be applied to organizational life, both in paid employment and in voluntary, social groups. It is just that it is often easier to see power and authority when we think of well-known figures and historic events. Think for a moment how you relate to those who hold some authority over you, or how you relate to those over whom you hold some authority. These could be line managers or colleagues at your holiday jobs, people you work with as an intern, your teachers or your lecturers. Even those students you find yourself very often leading in group work. We wonder how much of the time you – and they – base judgements, behaviour and interactions on what you think you see.

These are assumptions of appearance. By appearance we mean the collection of normal ways of working, of behaving, of interpreting that we develop in certain groups, even in certain societies. Being quiet = not being very clever. Being confident = being very clever. Being in charge = being the person who knows best. Being a junior employee, or volunteer = not knowing much about leadership. Being a leader = being someone who *should know* the answer. Even if you know this way of seeing is limited, it is often tempting to play into caricatures for an easy life! How often do you base your behaviour on what you think someone might expect of you? Very often? How often are these assumptions, these tricks of the eye, ever challenged and questioned?

We argue that applying a gaze of leadership does challenge and question appearances. In so doing it questions dominant views about who knows best, what is right and wrong. Potentially unsettling in the extreme, the gaze takes us to unknown territory. And we have to get accustomed to this: of feeling uncomfortable about the limits of our own knowledge and capacity and also applying the same criteria to the limits of others. What's wrong with not having all the answers, with not knowing but of collectively trying to know more? At the core of this way of viewing leadership is the idea that we can never know it all but that the process of unsettling assumptions, of challenging ideas and opinions, of building new ones with others, provides a form of enjoyment. Sometimes being knocked off track by something unexpected in our gaze is the most fulfilling, liberating experience.

Ultimately, isn't this a more ethical way of viewing leadership? Of never really believing what is presented to us and, equally, never really being satisfied with what we are asking others to see. It is more accountable, for certain. We believe in adopting a gaze on leadership, as it allows us to reflect on the ethicality of leaders that goes beyond the image represented, to focus on what is 'real' (and by real, we mean beyond our dominant ways of seeing).

Adopting this perspective of seeing leadership, we believe, highlights our own ethical and responsible position as practitioners of leadership. It is up to us to recognize that our eye does not see it all – we need others to push us. It also helps us as participants and even as consumers of leadership. Those in formal positions of authority need to be kept honest by our questioning, but we also need to recognize that it is unrealistic to expect leaders to be able to really live up to our fantasies. Look for those little clues in your gaze, the little signs that things may not be as they seem – the vulnerabilities, the cracks, the uncertainty. This, we argue, is the space for leadership.

The key points in this chapter were …

- The visual element of leadership is more important than is often given credit. Visual cues, from symbolic images through to the way we read people's faces are significant in the way we understand and evaluate leadership.
- Psychoanalytic approaches seek to understand how our thoughts and emotions are formed through early experiences. Psychoanalytic philosophy – particularly that popularized by Lacan – emphasizes the reasons behind our attachment to discursive constructions. Lacanian philosophy focuses on the connections between words, images and 'the real'.
- Leadership constructions are richly symbolic and deeply imbued with fantasy. We go to great lengths both as producers and consumers of these symbolic representations to maintain these fantasies. But behind them, every now and then we catch glimpses of the real, a crack in the fantasies.
- One fantasy dominant in leadership studies is the idea of a single (powerful and usually male) leader who saves followers from their perils.

 ## Further thinking

Grint, K. (2001). *The Arts of Leadership*. Oxford: Oxford University Press.

In this seminal book on leadership, Keith Grint asks his readers to think of leadership not as a science but as an art. This intent from the author is quite striking, as most study within business school is concerned with seeking to develop a science of business studies. Thinking of leadership as an art form places it outside the dominant way of thinking about organizations promoted in most higher education institutions. Art brings to mind a couple of considerations. The first is that art is something which does not rely on hard numbers – it is about appealing to feelings, as well as cognition. The second is that art is something created, from whatever materials may be available – from the more conventional paint and canvas to something far more improvised – scrap material, a tape recorder, even the human body. And so it is with leadership, also.

In Chapter 9, Grint focuses on Martin Luther King's seminal dream speech, specifically analysing King's rhetorical strategies. But the dream speech is also visually striking, for a number of reasons. We would like you to watch the speech (it is available on YouTube), and think about the following questions:

1. What do you notice about the visuals of where the speech was delivered? How might the visual location of the speech be significant, in leadership terms?
2. What does your eye pick up about the visual composition of King's audience? What might this tell you about the kind of leadership King was trying to enact?
3. Take a good look at how King appears during the speech (how he dresses, what he does with his body). How do the visuals of his presentation contribute to (or detract from) his message?

McGowan, T. (2003). Looking for the gaze: Lacanian film theory and its vicissitudes. *Cinema Journal*, 42(3), 27–47.

You may find some of this article a little hard to trawl through but we wanted to include something for you to explore from cinema studies. McGowan's main case is that critical cinema studies have become very caught up in considerations of discipline and domination. How does the gaze of the viewer control and restrict what we see on screen, and in turn, how does what we gaze upon on the screen discipline how we think of certain social phenomena and even our fellow human beings? Why are women presented a certain way in Hollywood films, for example?

Considerations of discipline can only take us so far, however. McGowan argues that adopting a Lacanian perspective for the analysis of cinema offers a potentially enriching avenue for research, as it both highlights the limitations of our own fantasy constructions and the vulnerabilities of the structures of power we are subjected to. As an example, McGowan draws on Steven Spielberg's 1993 film *Schindler's List*, a powerful but also deeply disturbing dramatization of true events during the Second World War. It depicts the story of Oskar Schindler, played by Liam Neeson, who gradually learns of the ethical horrors and atrocities of the Nazi regime, and sets out to do as much as he can to save as many of his Jewish workers as possible. One traumatic scene takes place in the Kraków–Płaszów concentration camp. The camp head, the psychotic war criminal and mass murderer Amon Goeth (played by Ralph Fiennes), lazily awakens in the morning, stretches and leaves his naked mistress in bed. After putting on his trousers and lighting a cigarette, he nonchalantly reaches for his sniper rifle and wanders out on to the balcony. The shot then cuts to a distance perspective, and the viewer gazes upon Goeth seemingly taking aim to the left of the screen. We cut back to the balcony, viewing the scene of the prisoners at work, looking through the sights of the rifle. But then a respite. Goeth puts down the rifle. Why? Perhaps he's thought better of it. Perhaps he was never actually going to start shooting at unarmed prisoners. But no. He was actually just getting smoke in his eyes. After placing down the cigarette he brutally cuts down a woman in the work yard, which the viewer sees from Goeth's perspective. This is the stomach-churning gaze of a psychotic despot leader exercising his power at a whim.

Yet then the trauma of the scene really takes hold, as the camera angle switches down to the prison yard and the viewer is placed amidst the fleeing prisoners, in a flurry and blur of chaos and panic. Survival (and death) at the hands of this leader is random. The Holocaust was disgusting, beyond animalistic in its horror. The hero leader (Schindler) may be able to save some (over 1,000) Jews from death – but there were millions and millions more Jews, Gypsies, Slavs, disabled people and other minorities who were murdered. At the end of the scene, Goeth (pasty, pot belly on display – really a quite odious little man) stretches and ambles, bored, back into his bedroom. And so the viewer is also able to gaze upon the obscenity, but also fragility, of this supposedly monolithic power of Nazism. Beyond the symbols of power – the swastika, the propaganda films – is merely a repulsive and quite stupid little man with a gun.

So McGowan's point is that adopting a Lacanian gaze allows us to experience the cracks in our symbolic constructions (the blur, terror and confusion of the prison yard, even the obscenity of the figure of the Nazi). Life and leadership can't be easily explained or captured in symbols. We also see the return to 'normality', of the Hollywood ending (Schindler saves *some* people) and can reflect on the limitations of this perspective. Finally, we also see the fragility of power, expressed in its very brutishness and stupidity.

1. Can you think of a film that has changed the way you thought about leadership, or even a particular leader?
2. How did the film disrupt your thinking on that particular person, or series of events?

Leadership on screen

The Dark Knight (2008)

Science fiction and fantasy are often written off as serious film genres, but that is a terrible shame as these are often films that do more than any others to explore difficult, even taboo subject matter. For example, a strong case can be made that Christopher Nolan's film *The Dark Knight* is really about how we respond to and live with terrorism. What kind of leadership do we need in times such as these?

The deranged Joker figure (Heath Ledger) does not play by the conventional rules – he subverts our symbolic structures. He is not seeking positional power. Or influence. He does not even want our money ('Dynamite and gasoline are cheap!'). So what does he want? The answer is nothing other than to make us see the limitations of our relationship to leadership and the ethical foundations of our society. The film acts as a critique of both systems of leadership thought and of individual leader archetypes. But before we return to the Joker, let's first consider how the leader figures of the film respond to his various acts of criminality.

At first the answer to the terror of the Joker appears to lie in the shadowy character of Batman (Christian Bale). Batman is beyond the law but also props up the law (McGowan, 2013). He is not answerable to society in any conventional sense but is driven by a need to prop up, to support this very (fragile) society he is condemned never to fully participate within. It is a contradiction. Batman can never become a full member of Gotham society because of its adherence, at least on paper, to the law, and yet it appears that Gotham needs Batman, as a kind of unacknowledged supplement, an outside of the law which functions in a way that maintains the law (Žižek, 2009).

But to rely on this kind of law enforcement as any kind of long-term solution is unthinkable for Batman, if not for Gotham's citizens, as it would mean accepting a kind of militaristic police state. Gotham City needs a leader with credibility, who does not need to operate on the fringes of society to govern. Visually, the underground nature of Batman's work and identity is of course captured in his suit, which appears as far more weaponized in these contemporary films than in earlier television incarnations of the character. Yet we discover early on in *The Dark Knight* that the defining visual imagery of Batman (his armour) is vulnerable, as Batman is injured by a dog bite. His protective clothes need to be made more agile and flexible, we are told – perhaps a metaphor for the arguments made in favour of the 'flexible' policing of terrorism.

So if Batman does not represent the longer-term leadership future of leadership, where should the city turn? An alternative leader figure appears to be embodied in the young district attorney, Harvey Dent (Aaron Eckhart). Dent is a seemingly unshakeable, uncompromising moral leader. No compromise, no deviation from what is right. Until he experiences pain, loss and disfigurement, whereupon he becomes corrupted and conducts his own murderous rampage. Unflinching adherence to a 'pure' moral code is apparently also a fragile form of leadership – what happens when the rules change, when the system comes under pressure? Visually this fragility of 'pure' leadership is captured in a visceral manner, through Dent's facial disfigurement, the eye exploring (despite our brains urging otherwise!), the tendons, muscles, exposed jaw bone and warped flesh made visible through the burning of one side of Dent's face. Dent and the viewer are reminded in strikingly visual terms that the two extreme sides of leadership (strictly moral and unacknowledged dark arts) exist in tension.

Of course, quietly lurking in the background is the fiercely bright figure of Rachel (Maggie Gyllenhaal), the assistant district attorney. Nolan's handling of Rachel is fascinating. She appears morally strong and brave (confronting the Joker face-to-face), offering ethically sound yet pragmatic guidance to both Batman and Dent. Yet as a viewing audience we are asked to relate to her, more often than not, as the inevitable love interest of the male leads. Visually, however, this request never seems quite right. Even a cursory look at Gyllenhaal's filmography reveals that she is an actress who has studiously avoided disempowering roles. Her career has been marked by challenging, artistic films of integrity. Like her brother Jake, she is certainly an attractive screen presence. Yet her looks, again like her brother Jake's, are not those of a traditional screen beauty. The eye of the viewer experiences a dissonance – there's more to this character than male love interest!

Even in death, Rachel displays some important leadership qualities. Both Rachel and Dent have been kidnapped by the Joker, tied in separate rooms packed with explosives in different parts of Gotham. Batman only has time to rescue one. The police, with their inferior technology, cannot hope to rescue the other in time, although they try. Batman is faced with an ethical choice – the woman he loves or the leader he believes Gotham needs. He makes the wrong choice and opts for Dent. Witnessed in life through her quiet but assured and strong counsel, Rachel's leadership qualities are equally apparent in death. She looks slightly away from the camera as she talks with Dent over a speakerphone, assuring him that he will be OK, of her love for him and reminding him of his duty to the city.

At the moment when she realizes Batman has chosen to rescue Dent, the appearance of fear is quickly overtaken by an assured speech to Dent about the importance of his leadership, cruelly interrupted by the Joker's detonation. Throughout, we do not view Rachel head-on, but askance, conveying the effect that this is a character whose measure we have not quite come to terms with.

Rachel, as the ethical mediator between the darkness and light, between street-tough Batman and rigid moralizer Dent, is gone. And with it the very fabric of Gotham begins to unravel. The kind of leadership Gotham needs to navigate these difficult times – flexible but ethical, adaptive, capable of working with complexity, shades of grey – is captured in the physical awkwardness, the very presence of Gyllenhaal.

So how is the presence of this unravelling of Gotham's leadership presented visually? Through an absence. And that absence is the Joker.

The very figure of Ledger's Joker is crafted to unsettle precisely because he seems to represent nothing at all – merely a confusing emptiness. As McGowan (2013) points out, the Joker's painted mask is there to conceal the fact that there is nothing to conceal in the first place. This is a man seemingly without a past, without any positive content informing his actions. Early in the film, as the Joker prepares to murder the mobster Gambol, he provides an explanation for his psychoses rooted in childhood abuse. As horrifying as this explanation is, it nevertheless provides a kind of comfort for viewers: 'Ah, if only this child had been better cared for.' But this explanation is subsequently shattered. As Rachel confronts the Joker, she is provided with an alternative story, one where he self-mutilated in order to comfort his wife, who had been similarly mutilated by a criminal gang. What? But he said … The confusion of the viewer is matched by Nolan's visual trick of spinning the camera over and above the heads of the cast. This is a moment of uncertainty mirrored by visual confusion. Our eye is unable to fix on the point of intrigue, an explanation for the Joker's actions.

Of course there is no explanation. The Joker has nothing to hide. He is a visual representation of the inadequacy of our very systems of leadership and ethics. When we gaze upon the Joker, we gaze upon our own lack, our own emptiness (Driver, 2009, 2013). And it is this very trick of the gaze back in on the viewer which Nolan employs throughout the film, with the Joker peering into the camera, either directly or via 'home-made video'. Sometimes this gaze is front and centre of the scene, the Joker's leer and eyes gouging into the psyche of the viewer, other times as a sinister reminder of our fear, anxiety and incompleteness, floating in the background of the shot.

Nolan offers the viewer no easy conclusion to our lack of a leadership answer to the problems of Gotham (or contemporary Western society). The film ends with Batman accepting his identity as scapegoat, who will be blamed for the atrocities committed by the scarred Dent. The fantasy image of the 'perfect leader' (Dent) is one the people of Gotham need to maintain and will not be able to cope with its tarnishing. Batman thus embraces the identity of villain, accepts the burden of scapegoat, the price to pay for the childish fantasies of the city's populace.

Of course this is a bleak vision. Nolan is saying that as viewers, as citizens, we are incapable of a mature and reflective debate on the kind of ethical leadership required in an uncertain and dangerous world. He is critical of the leaders presented to the public, of course. But the accusing gaze (the Joker's gaze) falls squarely on the viewer. This is our fault. We did not deserve Rachel. And for this, she must burn.

REFERENCES

Acker, J. (1990). Hierarchies, jobs, bodies. *Gender and Society*, *4*(2), 139–158.

Ackers, P. and Preston, D. (1997). Born again? The ethics and efficacy of the conversion experience in contemporary management development. *Journal of Management Studies*, *34*(5), 677–701.

Adler, N. (1999). Global leaders: Women of influence. In G. Powell (ed.), *Handbook of Gender and Work*. Thousand Oaks, CA: Sage.

Adler, N. J. (2006). The arts and leadership: Now that we can do anything what will we do? *Academy of Management Learning & Education*, *5*(4), 486–499.

Ahonen, P., Tienari, J., Merilaninen, S. and Pullen, A. (2013). Hidden contexts and invisible power relations: A Foucauldian reading of diversity research. *Human Relations*, *67*(3), 263–286.

Alimo-Metcalfe, B. and Alban-Metcalfe, J. (2011). Leadership in public sector organisations. In J. Storey (ed.), *Leadership in Organisations: Current Issues & Key Trends*, 2nd edn. London: Routledge.

Alvesson, M. (2002). *Understanding Organizational Culture*. London: Sage.

Alvesson, M. (2013). *The Triumph of Emptiness: Consumption, Higher Education and Work Organization*. Oxford: Oxford University Press.

Alvesson, M. and Spicer, A. (2012). Critical leadership studies: The case for critical performativity. *Human Relations*, *65*(3), 367–390.

Alvesson, M. and Sveningsson, S. (2003a). The great disappearing act: Difficulties in doing 'leadership'. *The Leadership Quarterly*, *14*(3), 359–381.

Alvesson, M. and Sveningsson, S. (2003b). Managers doing leadership: The extra-ordinarization of the mundane. *Human Relations*, *56*(12), 1435–1459.

Alvesson, M. and Wilmott, H. (eds) (1992). *Critical Management Studies*. London: Sage.

Antonakis, J. and Dalgas, O. (2009). Predicting elections: Child's play. *Science 323*(5918), 1183–1183.

Ashforth, B. (1994). Petty tyranny in organisations. *Human Relations*, *47*(7), 755–778.

Avolio, B. J. and Bass, B. M. (1995). Individual consideration viewed at multiple levels of analysis: A multi-level framework for examining the diffusion of transformational leadership. *Leadership Quarterly*, *6*(2), 199–218.

Avolio, B. J. and Gardner, W. L. (2005). Authentic leadership development: Getting to the root of positive forms of leadership. *The Leadership Quarterly*. *16*(3), 315–338.

Badaracco, J. (2002). *Leading Quietly: An Unorthodox Guide to Doing the Right Thing*. Boston, MA: Harvard Business School Publishing.

Balogun, J. and Johnson, G. (2004). Organizational restructuring and middle manager sensemaking. *Academy of Management Journal*, *47*, 523–549.

Barge, K. J. (2012). Systemic constructionist leadership and working from the present moment. In M. Uhl-Bien and S. Ospina (eds), *Advancing Relational Leadership Research* (pp. 107–142). Charlotte, NC: Information Age.

Barge, K. J. and Fairhurst, G. (2008). Living leadership: A systemic constructionist approach. *Leadership*, *4*(3), 227–251.

Barker, R.A. (1997). How can we train leaders if we do not know what leadership is? *Human Relations*, *50*(4), 343–362.

Basbøll, T. and Graham, H. (2006). Substitutes for strategy research: Notes on the source of Karl Weick's anecdote of the young lieutenant and the map of the Pyrenees. *Ephemera: Theory and Politics in Organization*, *6*(2), 194–204.

Bass, B. M. (1985). *Leadership and Performance beyond Expectations*. New York: Free Press.

Bass, B. M. (1996). *A New Paradigm of Leadership: An Inquiry into Transformational Leadership*. Alexandria, VA: U.S. Army Research Institute for Behavioral and Social Sciences.

Bass, B. M. (2000). On the taming of charisma: A reply to Janice Beyer. *The Leadership Quarterly*, *10*(4), 541–553.

Bass, B. M. and Riggio, R. E. (2005). *Transformational Leadership*. London: Psychology Press.

Bass, B. M. and Steidlmeier, P. (1999). Ethics, character, and authentic transformational leadership behaviour. *Leadership Quarterly*, *10*(2), 181–217.

Bate, S., Robert, G. and Bevan, H. (2004). The next phase of healthcare improvement: What can we learn from social movements? *Quality and Safety in Health Care*, *13*(1), 62–66.

Bell, E. (2008). *Reading Management and Organization in Film*. Basingstoke: Palgrave Macmillan.

Bell, E. and Taylor, S. (2004). 'From outward bound to inward bound': The prophetic voices and discursive practices of spiritual management development. *Human Relations*, *57*(4), 439–466.

Bennis, W. G. (2007). The challenges of leadership in the modern world: An introduction to the special issue. *American Psychologist*, *62*(1), 2–5.

Bennis, W. G. and Thomas, R. J. (2002). Crucibles of leadership. *Harvard Business Review*, *80*(9), 39–45.

Benson, M. and Hogan, R. (2008). How dark side leadership personality destroys trust and degrades organisational effectiveness. *Organisations and People*, *15*(3), 10–18.

Berret, D. (2011). Intellectual roots of Wall St. protest lie in academe. Retrieved from http://chronicle.com/article/Intellectual-Roots-of-Wall/129428.

Berry, D. (1990). Taking people at face value, evidence for the kernel of truth hypothesis. *Social Cognition*, *8*, 343.

Beyer, J. M. (1999). Taming and promoting charisma to change organizations. *The Leadership Quarterly*, *10*(2), 307–330.

Blair, T. (2010). *A Journey*. London: Arrow.

Blake, R. and Mouton, J. (1964). *The Managerial Grid: The Key to Leadership Excellence*. Houston TX: Gulf Publishing.

Blake, R. and Mouton, J. (1985). *The Managerial Grid III: The Key to Leadership Excellence*. Houston, TX: Gulf Publishing.

Blanchard, H. and Johnson, S. (1983). *The One Minute Manager*. New York: Berkley Books.

Bligh, M. C. and Kohles, J. C. (2008). Leading or following? Contemporary notions of followership in academic research. Presented at the annual meeting of the Society of Industrial and Organizational Pscyhology, San Francisco, CA. April 2008.

Bligh, M., Kohles, J. and Pillai, R. (2011). Romancing leadership: Past, present and future. *The Leadership Quarterly*, *22*(6), 1058–1077.

Bligh, M., Pillai, R. and Uhl-Bien, M. (2007). The social construction of a legacy: Summarising and extending follower-centred perspectives on leadership. In B. Shamir, R. Pillai and M. Bligh (eds), *Follower-centred Perspectives on Leadership: A Tribute to the Memory of James R. Meindl* (pp. 265–277). Charlotte, NC: Information Age.

Blumer, H. (1951). Social movements. In V. Ruggiero and N. Montagna (eds), *Social Movements: A Reader* (pp. 64–72). London: Routledge

Boje, D. M. and Rhodes, C. (2005). The virtual leader construct: The mass mediatization and simulation of transformational leadership. *Leadership*, *1*(4), 407–428.

Boje, D. M. and Rhodes, C. (2006). The leadership of Ronald McDonald: Double narration and stylistic lines of transformation. *The Leadership Quarterly*, *17*(1), 94–103.

Boje, D. M., Alvarez, R. C. and Schooling, B. (2001). Reclaiming story in organisation: Narratologies and action sciences. In R. Westwood and S. Linstead (eds), *The Language of Organisation*. London: Sage.

Bolden, R. (2011). Distributed leadership in organizations: A review of theory and research. *International Journal of Management Reviews*, *13*(3), 251–269.

Bolden, R. and Kirk, P. (2012). Leadership development as a catalyst for social change: Lessons from a pan-African programme. In *Worldly Leadership: Alternative Wisdoms for a Complex World*. Basingstoke: Palgrave Macmillan.

Boltanski, L. and Chiapello, E. (2005). *The New Spirit of Capitalism*. London: Verso.

Bourjois, P. (2003). *In Search of Respect: Selling Crack in El Barrio*. New York: Cambridge University Press.

Boyatzis, R., Passarelli, A., Koenig, K., Lowe, M., Blessy, M., Stoller, J. and Phillips, M. (2012). Examination of the neural substrates activated in memories of experiences with resonant and dissonant leaders. *The Leadership Quarterly, 23*(2), 259–272.

Bresnen, M. (1995). All things to all People? Perceptions, attributions and constructions of leadership. *Leadership Quarterly*, *6*(4), 495–513.

Bruce, V. (1988), *Recognising Faces*. Hove: Lawrence Erlbaum Associates.

Bryant, S. E. (2003). The role of transformational and transactional leadership in creating, sharing and exploiting organizational knowledge. *Journal of Leadership & Organizational Studies*, *9*(4), 32–44.

Bryman, A. (1986). *Leadership and Organizations*. London: Routledge & Kegan Paul

Bryman, A. (1992). *Charisma and Leadership in Organizations*. London: Sage.

Bryman, A. (2004). Qualitative research on leadership: A critical but appreciative review. *Leadership Quarterly*, 15(5), 721–891.

Buechler, S. (1995). New social movement theories. *Sociological Quarterly*, *36*(3), 441–464.

Bürgi, P. T., Jacobs, C. J. and Roos, J. (2005). From metaphor to practice in the crafting of strategy. *Journal of Management Inquiry, 14*: 78–94.

Burgoyne, J. (2004). How certain are we that management and leadership development is effective? Seminar paper at Management Learning and Leadership Workshop, Lancaster University Management School, summer.

Burns, J. M. (1978). *Leadership*. New York: Harper & Row.

Burrell, G. (1992). The organization of pleasure. In M. Alvesson and H. Wilmott (eds), *Critical Management Studies*. London: Sage.

Burton, C. (1989). Merit and gender: Organizations and the mobilization of masculine bias. In G. Curnow and B. Page (eds), *Politicization and the Career Service*. Canberra: Canberra CAE and NSW Division of RAIPA.

Butler, J. (1993). *Bodies that Matter*. New York: Routledge.

Butler, S., Rankin, J. and Garside, J. (2013). Angela Ahrendts leaves Burberry for new job at Apple. *Guardian*. Retrieved from www.theguardian.com/business/2013/oct/15/burberry-angela-ahrendts-new-job-apple.

Cadbury, Sir A. (1992). *Report of the Committee on the Financial Aspects of Corporate Governance*. London: Gee & Co Ltd.

Calas, M. B. (1993). Deconstructing charismatic leadership: Re-reading Weber from the darker side. *The Leadership Quarterly*, *4*(3), 305–328.

Calas, M. and Smırcıch, L. (1992). Using the F word: Feminist theories and the social consequences of organizational research. In A. J. Mills and P. Tancred (eds), *Gendering Organizational Analysis*. New Park, CA: Sage.

Carroll, B. and Levy, L. (2010). Leadership development as identity construction. *Management Communication Quarterly*, *24*(2), 211–231

Carroll, B. and Nicholson, H. (2014). Resistance and struggle in leadership development. *Human Relations*. Published online first: DOI: 0018726714521644.

Carroll, B. and Simpson, B. (2012). Capturing sociality in the movement between frames: An illustration from leadership development. *Human Relations*, *65*(10), 1283–1309.

Carroll, B., Levy, L. and Richmond, D. (2008). Leadership as practice: Challenging the competency paradigm. *Leadership*, *4*(4), 363–379.

Carsten, M. K., Uhl-Bien, M., West, B. J., Patera, J. L. and McGregor, R. (2010). Exploring social constructions of followership: A qualitative study. *The Leadership Quarterly, 21*(3), 543–562.

Casey, C. (1995). *Work, Self, and Society: After Industrialism*. London: Routledge.

Challeff, I. (1998). *The Courageous Follower: Standing Up to and for Our Leaders.* San Francisco, CA: Berrett-Koehler Publishers.

Chandler, A. D. (1962). *Strategy and Structure.* Cambridge, MA: MIT Press.

Chaturvedi, S., Zyphur, M., Arvey, R., Avolio, B. and Larsson, G. (2012). The heritability of emergent leadership: Age and gender as moderating factors. *The Leadership Quarterly, 23*(2), 219–232.

Chen, C. C. and Meindl, J. R. (1991). The construction of leadership images in the popular press: The case of Donald Burr and people express. *Administrative Science Quarterly*, *36*(4), 521–551.

Chia, R. (1995). From modern to postmodern organizational analysis. *Organization Studies*, *16*(4), 579–604.

Chia, R. (1996). The problem of reflexivity in organizational research: Towards a postmodern science of organization. *Organization*, *3*(1), 31–59.

Child, J. (1984). *Organization.* London: Macmillan.

Chodorow, N. (1978). *The Reproduction of Mothering.* Berkeley, CA: University of California Press.

Clark, T. and Salaman, G. (1998). Telling tales: Management gurus' narratives and the construction of managerial identity. *Journal of Management Studies*, *35*(2), 137–161.

Cluley, R. (2012). The psychoanalytic relationship between leaders and followers. *Leadership*, *4*(2), 201–212.

Collins, D. (2000). *Management Fads and Buzzwords: Critical-Practical Perspectives*. London: Routledge.

Collins, J. (2009). *How the Mighty Fall: And Why Some Companies Never Give.* London: RH Business Books.

Collinson, D. (2005). Dialectics of leadership. *Human Relations*, *58*(11), 1419–1442.

Collinson, D. (2006). Rethinking followership: A post-structuralist analysis of follower identities. *The Leadership Quarterly*, *17*(2), 179−189.

Collinson D. (2011). Critical leadership studies. In A. Bryman, D. Collinson, K. Grint, B. Jackson and M. Uhl-Bien (eds), *The Sage Handbook of Leadership* (pp. 179–192). London: Sage.

Collinson, D. (2014). Dichotomies, dialectics and dilemmas: New directions for critical leadership studies? *Leadership*, *10*(1), 36–55.

Collinson, D. and Collinson, M. (2009). Blended Leadership. In M. Preedy, N. Bennett and C. Wise (eds) *Educational Leadership: Context, Strategy and Collaboration* (pp. 308–323). London: Sage.

Collinson, D. and Grint, K. (2005). Editorial: The leadership agenda. *Leadership, 1*(1), 5–9.

Collinson, D. and Hearn, J. (1994). Naming men as men: Implications for work, organisation and management. *Gender, Work and Organisation, 1*(1), 2–22.

Colville, I. D. and Murphy, A. J. (2006). Leadership as the enabler of strategizing and organizing. *Long Range Planning, 39,* 663–677.

Conger, J. A. and Kanungo, R. N. (1987). Toward a behavioral theory of charismatic leadership in organizational settings. *Academy of Management Review, 12*(4), 637–647.

Currie, G. and Lockett, A. (2007). A critique of transformational leadership: Moral, professional and contingent dimensions of leadership within public services organizations. *Human Relations, 60*(2), 341–370.

Costas, J. and Taheri, A. (2012). The return of the primal father in postmodernity? A Lacanian analysis of authentic leadership. *Organization Studies, 33*(9), 1195–1216.

Courpasson, D. (2000). Managerial strategies of domination: Power in soft bureaucracies. *Organization Studies, 21*(1), 141–161.

Crabtree, B. (1992). The history of anarchism. Retrieved from www.spunk.org/texts/intro/sp000282.txt.

Creaton, S. (2003). Son of Ryanair aims to realise eastern promise. *Irish Times,* 12 December, 60.

Crevani, L. (2011). Clearing for action: leadership as a relational phenomenon. Doctoral thesis, KTH Royal Institute of Technology, Stockholm.

Crevani, L., Lindgren, M. and Packendorff, J. (2010). Leadership, not leaders: On the study of leadership as practices and interactions. *Scandinavian Journal of Management, 26*(1), 77–86.

Crossley, N. (2002). *Making Sense of Social Movements*. Buckingham: Open University Press.

Cunliffe, A. L. (2009). The philosopher leader: On relationalism, ethics and reflexivity – a critical perspective to teaching leadership. *Management Learning, 40*(1), 87–101.

Cunliffe, A. L. and Eriksen, M. (2011). Relational leadership. *Human Relations, 64*(11), 1425–1449.

Dachler, H. P. and Hosking, D. M. (1995). The primacy of relations in socially constructing organizational realities. In D. M. Hosking, H. P. Dachler and K. J. Gergen (eds), *Management and Organization: Relational Alternatives to Individualism*. Aldershot: Avebury.

Daft, R. L. (2011). *Leadership*, 5th edn. London: South-Western Cengage Learning.

Dahl, R. (1989). *Democracy and Its Critics*. New Haven, CT: Yale University Press.

Daily, C. M., Dalton, D. and Canella, A. (2003). Corporate governance: Decades of dialogue and data. *Academy of Management Review, 28,* 371–382.

Daily Mail (2010). Hijacking of a very middle class protest: Anarchists cause chaos as 50,000 students take to the streets over fees. Retrieved from www.dailymail.co.uk/news/article-1328385/TUITION-FEES-PROTEST-Anarchists-cause-chaos-50k-students-streets.html.

Dalton, K. (2010). *Leadership and Management Development: Developing Tomorrow's Managers*. Harlow: FT Prentice Hall.

Davies, B. and Harré, R. (2001). Positioning: The discursive production of selves. In M. Wetherell, S. Taylor and S. J. Yates (eds), *Discourse Theory and Practice: A Reader.* London: Sage.

Day, R. (2005). *Gramsci is Dead: Anarchist Currents in the Newest Social Movements*. London: Pluto Press.

Deal, T. and Kennedy, A. (1982). *Corporate Cultures: The Rites and Rituals of Corporate Life*. Harmondsworth: Penguin Books.

Delbridge, R. and Ezzamel, M. (2005). The strength of difference: Contemporary conceptions of control. *Organization, 12*(5), 603–618.

Della Porta, D. (2006). *Democracy in Social Movements*. London: Palgrave Macmillan.

Donkin, R. (2010). *The Future of Work*. Basingstoke: Palgrave Macmillan.

Drath, W. H. (2001). *The Deep Blue Sea: Rethinking the Source of Leadership*. San Francisco, CA: Jossey–Bass.

Drath, W. H., McCauley, C. D., Palus, C. J., Van Velsor, E., O'Connor, P. M. G. and McGuire, J. B. (2008). Direction, alignment, commitment: Toward a more integrative ontology of leadership. *The Leadership Quarterly, 19*(6): 635–653.

Driver, M. (2009). Struggling with lack: A Lacanian perspective on organizational identity. *Organization Studies, 30*(1), 55–72.

Driver, M. (2013). The lack of power or the power of lack in leadership as a discursively constructed identity. *Organization Studies, 34*(3), 407–422.

Du Gay, P. (1996). *Consumption and Identity at Work*. London: Sage.

Durisin, B. and Puzone, F. (2009). Maturation of corporate governance research, 1993−2007: An assessment. *Corporate Governance: an International Review, 17*: 266−291.

Eagly, A. (2011). Female leadership advantage and disadvantage: Resolving the contradiction. In D. Collinson, K. Grint and B. Jackson (eds), *Leadership Vol. IV: 2005–2009*. London: Sage

Easterby-Smith, M., Thorpe, R. and Lowe, A. (1991). *Management Research: An Introduction*. London: Sage.

Einarsen, S. Aasland, M. and Skogstad, A. (2007). Destructive leadership behaviour: A definition and conceptual model. *The Leadership Quarterly, 18*(3), 207–216.

Ekman, P. and Rosenberg, E. (1997). *What the Face Reveals*. New York: Oxford University Press

Endrissat, N. and von Arx, W. (2013). Leadership practices and context: Two sides of the same coin. *Leadership, 9*(2), 278–304.

Ernst, C. and Chrobot-Mason, D. (2010). *Boundary Spanning Leadership: Six Practices for Solving Problems, Driving Innovation, and Transforming Organizations*. New York: McGraw Hill.

Evans, M. M. (2012). (Be)Longing: Enacting indigenous arts leadership. PhD thesis, Melbourne Business School.

Eveline, J. (1994). *The Politics of Advantage*. *Australian Feminist Studies, 9*(19), 129–154.

Fairhurst, G. T. (2007). *Discursive Leadership: In Conversation with Leadership Psychology*. Los Angeles, CA: Sage.

Fairhurst, G. T. (2009). Considering context in discursive leadership research. *Human Relations, 62*(11), 1587–1605.

Fairhurst, G. T. (2011). *The Power of Framing*. San Francisco, CA : Jossey-Bass.

Fairhurst, G. T. and Grant, D. (2010). The social construction of leadership: A sailing guide. *Management Communication Quarterly, 24*(2), 171–210.

Fairhurst, G. T. and Uhl-Bien, M. (2012). Organizational discourse analysis (ODA): Examining leadership as a relational process. *The Leadership* Quarterly, 23(6), 1043–1062.

Fayol, G. H. (1949). *General and Industrial Management*. London: Pitman.

Feingold, A. (1992). Good-looking people are not what we think. *Psychological Bulletin, 111*(2), 304–304

Ferguson, K. (1984). *The Feminist Case against Bureaucracy*. Philadelphia, PA: Temple University Press.

Fiedler, F. E. (1967). *A Theory of Leadership Effectiveness*. New York: McGraw-Hill.

Fiedler, F. E. (1972). The effects of leadership training and experience: A contingency model interpretation. *Administrative Science Quarterly*, *17*(4), 453–470.

Fiedler, F. E. (1976/1997). Situational control and a dynamic theory of leadership. In K. Grint (ed.), *Leadership: Classical, Contemporary and Critical Approaches* (pp. 126–148). Oxford: Oxford University Press.

Financial Reporting Council (2010). *UK Corporate Governance Code*. London: Financial Reporting Council. Available at: www.frc.org.uk/Our-Work/Codes-Standards/Corporate-governance/UK-Corporate-Governance-Code.aspx (accessed 14.01.15).

Financial Reporting Council (2012). *The Combined Code on Corporate Governance*. London: FRC.

Fineman, S. (1997). Emotion and management learning. *Management Learning*, *28*(1), 13–25.

Fitzsimmons, T. W., Callan, V. J. and Paulsen, N. (2014). Gender disparity in the C-suite: Do male and female CEOs differ in how they reached the top? *The Leadership Quarterly*, *25*(2), 245–266.

Flax, J. (1993). *Disputed Subjects: Essays on Psychoanalysis, Politics and Philosophy*. London: Routledge.

Fletcher, J. K. (1998). Relational practice: A feminist reconstruction of work. *Journal of Management Inquiry*, *7*(2), 163–186.

Fletcher, J. K. (2004). The paradox of postheroic leadership: An essay on gender, power, and transformational change. *The Leadership Quarterly*, *15*(5), 647–661.

Foldy, E. G., Goldman, L. and Ospina, S. (2008). Sensegiving and the role of cognitive shifts in the work of leadership. *The Leadership Quarterly*, *19*(5), 514–529.

Follet, M. P. (1924). *Creative Experience*. New York: Longman, Green.

Ford, J. (2006). Discourses of leadership: Gender, identity and contradiction in a UK public sector organization. *Leadership*, *2*(1), 77–99.

Ford, J. (2010). Studying leadership critically: A psychosocial lens on leadership identities. *Leadership*, *6*(1), 1–19.

Ford, J. and Collinson, D. (2011). In search of the perfect manager? Work–life balance and managerial work. *Work, Employment and Society*, *25*(2), 257–273.

Ford, J. and Harding, N. (2007). Move over management we are all leaders now. *Management Learning*, *38*(5), 475–493.

Ford, J. and Harding, N. (2010). Telling an untold story: On being a follower rather than a leader. Paper presented at Nottingham Trent Business School Seminar Series, March.

Ford, J. and Harding, N. (2011). The impossibility of the 'true self' of authentic leadership: A critique through object relations theory. *Leadership*, *7*(4), 465–481.

Ford, J., Harding, N. and Learmonth, M. (2008). *Leadership as Identity: Constructions and Deconstructions*. Basingstoke: Palgrave Macmillan.

Fotaki, M. and Harding, N. (2013). Lacan and sexual difference in organization and management theory: Towards a hysterical academy? *Organization*, *20*(2), 153–172.

Foucault, M. (1972). *The Archaeology of Knowlege*. London: Tavistock.

Foucault, M (1979). *Discipline and Punish*. Harmondsworth: Penguin.

Foucault, M. (1980a). *The History of Sexuality, Vol. 1: An Introduction* (trans. R. Hurley). London: Penguin.

Foucault, M. (1980b). *Power/Knowledge: Selected Interviews and Other Writings by Michel Foucault, 1972–1977* (ed. C. Gordon). New York: Pantheon.

Fournier, V. and Grey, C. (2000). At the critical moment: Conditions and prospects for critical management studies. *Human Relations*, *53*(7), 7–32.

Fraher, A. (2011). Hero-making as a defence against the anxiety of responsibility and risk: A case study of US airways flight 1549. *Organisational and Social Dynamics*, *11*(1), 59–78

French, J. and Raven, B. (1959). The basis of social power. In D. Cartwright (ed.), *Studies in Social Power* (pp. 150–167). Oxford: Univa.

Freud, S. (1989). *Group Psychology and the Analysis of the Ego*. London: Norton.

Freud, S. (2002a). *The 'Wolfman' and Other Cases*. London: Penguin.

Freud, S. (2002b). *Totem and Taboo*. Abingdon: Routledge.

Fromm, E. (1941). *Escape From Freedom*. New York: Farrar & Rinehart, Inc.

Fromm, E. (1956). *The Art of Loving*. New York: Harper & Row.

Fromm, E. (1976). *To Have or To Be?* New York: Harper & Row.

Fromm, E. (2005). *To Have or to Be?* New York: Continuum Publishing.

Fyke, K. and Sayegh, G. (2001). Anarchism and the struggle to move forward. *Perspectives on Anarchist Theory*, *5*(2), 30–38.

Galbraith, J. (1971). Matrix organizational designs: How to combine functional and project forms. *Business Horizons*, *14*(1), 29–40.

Ganz, M. (2000). Why stories matter: the art and craft of social change. *Sojourners*, *38*(3), 123–134.

Ganz, M. (2010). Leading change: Leadership, organization, and social movements. In N. Nohria and R. Khurana (eds), *Handbook of Leadership Theory and Practice* (pp. 527–568). Boston, MA: Harvard Business School Publishing Corporation.

Gardner, D. and Thornhill, T. (2011). Steve Jobs' secret legacy: Dying Apple boss left plans for four years of new products. *Daily Mail*. Retrieved from www.dailymail.uk.

Garsten, C. and Grey, C. (1997). How to become oneself: Discourses of subjectivity in postbureaucratic organizations. *Organization*, *4*(2), 211–228.

Gastil, J. (1993). *Democracy in Small Groups: Participation, Decision-making and Communication*. Philadelphia, PA: New Society Publishers.

Gatrell, C. and Swan, E. (2008). *Gender and Diversity in Management*. London: Sage.

Gaventa, J. (2003). *Power after Lukes: An Overview of Theories of Power Since Lukes and their Application to Development*. Brighton: Participation Group, Institute of Development Studies.

Gavey, N. (1997). Feminist poststructuralism and discourse analysis. In M. Gergen and S. Davis (eds), *Toward a New Psychology of Gender: A Reader* (pp. 49–54). London: Routledge.

Gemmill, G. and Oakley, J. (1992). Leadership: An alienating social myth? *Human Relations*, *45*(2), 113–129.

Gemmil, G. and Oakley, J. (1997). Leadership: An alienating social myth. In K. Grint (ed.), *Leadership: Classical, Contemporary and Critical Approaches* (pp. 272–288). Oxford: Oxford University Press.

Gergen, K. J. (2010). Co-constitution, causality, and confluence: Organizing in a world without entities. In T. Hernes and S. Maitlis (eds), *Process, Sensemaking, & Organizing*. (pp. 1–26). Oxford: Oxford University Press.

Gerth, H. and Mills, C. (1958). *From Max Weber*. Oxford: Oxford University Press.

Gibson-Graham, J. K. (1996). *The End of Capitalism (as We Knew It): A Feminist Critique Of Political Economy*. Cambridge: Blackwell.

Giddens, A. (1984). *The Constitution of Society: Outline of the Theory of Structuration*. Oxford: Polity Press.

Giddens, A. (1998). *The Third Way: The Renewal of Social Democracy*. Cambridge, UK: Polity Press.

Gilligan, C. (1982). *In a Different Voice*. Cambridge, MA: Harvard University Press.

Goffee, R. and Jones, G. (2005). Managing authenticity. *Harvard Business Review*, *83*(12), 85–94.

Goffman, E. (1974). *Frame Analysis: An Essay on the Organization of Experience*. London: Harper & Row

Goldman, D. (1996). *Emotional Intelligence: Why It Can Matter More than IQ*. New York: Bloomsbury.

Gordon, U. (2005). Anarchism and political theory: Contemporary problems. Unpublished PhD thesis, University of Oxford.

Graeber, D. (2002). The new anarchists. *New Left Review*, *13*, 61–73.

Graen, G. and Uhl-Bien, M. (1995). Relationship-based approach to leadership: Development of leader–member exchange (LMX) theory of leadership over 25 years: Applying a multi-level multi-domain perspective. *The Leadership Quarterly*, *6*(2), 219–247.

Grey, C. (1999). We are all managers now, we always were: On the development and demise of management. *Journal of Management Studies*, *36*(5), 561–583.

Griffey, E. and Jackson, B. (2010). The portrait as leader: Commissioned portraits and the power of tradition. Leadership, 6(2): 133–157.

Grint, K. (2000). *The Arts of Leadership*. Oxford: Oxford University Press.

Grint, K. (2001). *The Arts of Leadership*. Oxford: Oxford University Press.

Grint, K. (2005a). *Leadership: Limits and Possibilities*. London: Palgrave.

Grint, K. (2005b). Problems, problems, problems: The social construction of 'leadership'. *Human Relations*, *58*(11), 1467–1494.

Grint, K. (2010). The scared in leadership: Separation, sacrifice and silence. *Organization Studies*, *31*, 89–107.

Gronn, P. (2000). Distributed properties: A new architecture of leadership. *Educational Management and Administration*, *28*(3), 317–338.

Gronn, P. (2002). Distributed leadership. In K. Leithwood, K. Hallinger and K. Seashore-Louis (eds), *Second International Handbook of Educational Leadership and Administration* (pp. 653–696). Dordrecht: Kluwer:

Guthey, E. and Jackson, B. (2005). CEO portraits and the authenticity paradox. *Journal of Management Studies*, *42*(5), 1057–1082.

Guthey, E. and Jackson, B. (2008). Revisualising images in leadership and organization studies. In Barry, D. and Hansen, H. (eds), *The Sage Handbook of New and Emerging Approaches to Management and Organization Studies* (pp. 84–97). London: Sage.

Guthey, E. and Jackson, B. (2010). The portrait as leader: Commissioned portraits and the power of tradition, *Leadership 6*(3), 133–157.

Guthey, E., Clark, T. and Jackson, B. (2009). *Demystifying Business Celebrity*. London: Routledge.

Hacker, S. and Roberts, T. (2003). *Transformational Leadership: Creating Organizations of Meaning*. Milwaukee, WI: ASQ Quality Press.

Hakel, M. (1980). Obituary: Ralph M. Stodgill (1904–1978). *American Psychologist*, *35*(1), 101.

Hambrick, D. C. (2007). Upper echelons theory: An update. *Academy of Management Review, 32*, 334–343.

Hambrick, D. C. and Mason, P. A. (1984). Upper echelons: The organization as a reflection of its top managers. *Academy of Management Review, 9*, 193–206.

Hansen, H., Ropo, A. and Sauer, E. (2007). Aesthetic leadership. *The Leadership Quarterly*, *18*(6), 544–560.

Harding, N. (2003). *The Social Construction of Management: Texts and Identities*. London: Routledge.

Harding, N., Lee, H., Ford, J. and Learmonth, M. (2011). Leadership and charisma: A desire that cannot speak its name? *Human Relations*, *64*(7), 927–950.

Harris, I. C. and Ruefli, T. W. (2000). The strategy/structure debate: An examination of the performance implications. *Journal of Management Studies, 37*(4): 587–604.

Harvey, D. (2000). *A Companion to Marx's Capital*. London: Verso.

Haslam, S. A., Reicher, S. D. and Platow, M. J. (2011). *The New Psychology of Leadership: Identity, Influence and Power*. Hove: Psychology Press.

Heckscher, C. (1994). Defining the post-bureaucratic type. In C. Heckscher and A. Donnellon (eds), *The Post-bureaucratic Organisation: New Perspectives on Organizational Change* (pp. 14–62). Thousand Oaks, CA: Sage.

Heelas, P. (1996). *The New Age Movement: The Celebration of the Self and the Sacralization of Modernity*. Oxford; Cambridge, MA: Blackwell.

Heifetz, R. and Laurie, D. (1997). The work of leadership. *Harvard Business Review*, *75*(1), 124–134.

Hersey, P. and Blanchard, K. H. (1982). *Management of Organizational Behavior: Utilizing Human Resources*, 4th edn. Englewood Cliffs, NJ: Prentice-Hall.

Hersey, P. and Blanchard, K. (1988). *Management of Organizational Behavior: Utilizing human Resources*, 5th edn. Englewood Cliffs, NJ: Prentice-Hall.

Hersted, L. and Gergen, K. J. (2013). *Relational leading*. Chagrin Falls, OH: Taos Institute Publications.

Higgs, D. (2003). *Review of the Role and Effectiveness of Non-Executive Directors*. London: The Department of Trade and Industry.

Higgs, M. (2009). The good, the bad and the ugly: Leadership and narcissism. *Journal of Change Management*, *9*(2), 165–178.

Hodgkinson, G.P. and Wright, G. (2002). Confronting strategic inertia in a top management team: Learning from failure. *Organization Studies, 23*, 949–976.

Hofstede, G. (1980). *Culture's Consequences: International Differences in Work-related Values*. Beverly Hills, CA: Sage.

Hofstede, G. (1991). *Culture and Organizations: Software of the Mind*. London: McGraw-Hill.

Hofstede, G. (2001). *Cultures Consequences: Comparing Values, Behaviours, Institutions, and Organizations Across Nations*. Thousand Oaks, CA: Sage.

Hofstede, G. (2006). What did GLOBE really measure? Researchers' minds versus respondents' minds. *Journal of International Business Studies*, *37*(6), 882–896.

Hollway, W. (1984). Gender difference and the production of subjectivity. In J. Henriques, W. Hollway, C. Urwin, C. Venn and V. Walkerdine, *Changing the Subject: Psychology, Social Regulation and Subjectivity*. London: Routledge.

Holmberg, R. (2000). Organizational learning and participation: Some critical reflections from a relational perspective. *European Journal of Work and Organizational Psychology 9*(2), 177–188.

Hosking D. M. (1988). Organizing, leadership and skilful process. *Journal of Management Studies*, *25*(2), 147–166.

Hosking, D. M. (2011). Moving relationality: Meditations on a relational approach to leadership. In A. Bryman, D. Collinson, K. Grint, B. Jackson and M. Uhl-Bien (eds), *Sage Handbook of Leadership* (pp. 455–467). London: Sage.

House, R. J., Hanges, P. J., Javidan, M., Dorfman, P. W., Gupta, V. and Associates, G. (2004). *Leadership, Culture and Organizations: The GLOBE Study of 62 Nations*. Thousand Oaks, CA: Sage.

Isaacson, W. (2011). *Steve Jobs*. New York: Little, Brown.

Jackson, B. (1999). The goose that laid the golden egg? A rhetorical critique of Stephen Covey and the effectiveness movement. *Journal of Management Studies*, *36*(3), 353–377.

Jackson, B. and Parry, K. (2011). *A Very Short, Fairly Interesting and Reasonably Cheap Book about Studying Leadership*. London: Sage.

Jackson, N. and Carter, P. (2007). *Rethinking Organisational Behaviour: A Post-structuralist Framework*. New York: Prentice-Hall.

Jackson, S. E. (2010). Making consultants earn their keep. *Journal of Business Strategy, 31*(3), 56–58.

Jago, A. (1982). Leadership: Perspectives in theory and research. *Management Science, 28*(3), 315–336.

Jarzabkowski, P., Balogun, J. and Seidl, D. (2007). Strategizing: The challenges of a practice perspective. *Human Relations, 60*, 5–27.

Jessop, B. (1992). Fordism and post-Fordism: A critical reflection. In M. Storfer and A. Scott (eds), *Pathways to Industrialization and Regional Development* (pp. 42–62). London: Routledge.

John, G. (2010). *Political Leadership in France: From Charles de Gaulle to Nicolas Sarkozy.* Basingstoke: Palgrave Macmillan.

Johnson, G., Melin, L., Langley, A. and Whittington, R. (2007). *The Practice of Strategy: Research Directions and Resources. Cambridge*: Cambridge University Press.

Johnson, S. (1998). *Who Moved My Cheese? An Amazing Way to Deal with Change in Your Work and in Your Life.* New York: Putnam.

Judge, T., Piccolo, R. and Kosalka, T. (2009). The bright and dark side of traits: A review and theoretical extension of the leader trait paradigm. *The Leadership Quarterly*, *20*(6) 855–875.

Juris, J. (2008). *Networking Futures: The Movements against Corporate Globalisation.* Durham, NC: Duke University Press.

Kaplan, R. S. and Norton, D. P. (1996). *The Balanced Scorecard: Translating Strategy into Action.* Boston, MA: Harvard Business School Publishing Corporation.

Kellerman, B. (2004). *Bad Leadership: What It Is, How It Happens, Why It Matters.* Boston, MA: Harvard Business School Publishing.

Kellerman, B. (2012). *The End of Leadership.* New York: Harper Business.

Kelley, R. E. (1992). *The Power of Followership: How to Create Leaders People Want to Follow, and Followers Who Lead Themselves.* New York: Bantam

Kelley, R. E. (1988). In praise of followers, *Harvard Business Review*. Nov–Dec, 142–148.

Kelly, S. (2014). Towards a negative ontology of leadership. *Human Relations, 67*(8), 905–922.

Keren, M. and Levhari, D. (1979). The optimum span of control in a pure hierarchy. *Organization Science*, *25*(11), 1162–1172.

Kets de Vries, M. (1998). Ties that bind the leader and the led. In J. Conger and R. Kanungo (eds), *Charismatic Leadership: The Elusive Factor in Organizational Effectiveness*. San Francisco, CA: Jossey-Bass.

Khurana, R. (2002). *Searching for a Corporate Savior: The Irrational Quest for Charismatic CEOs.* Princeton, NJ: Princeton University Press.

Kickul, J. and Neuman, G. (2000). Emergent leadership behaviours: The function of personality and cognitive ability in determining teamwork performance and KSAS. *Journal of Business and Psychology*, *15*(1), 27–51.

Kirkpatrick, S. and Locke, E. (1991). Leadership: Do traits matter? *Academy of Management Executive*, *5*(2), 48–60.

Kirton, G. and Healy, G. (2012). Lift as you rise': Union women's leadership talk. *Human Relations*, *65*(8), 979–999.

Knights, D. (2009). Power at work in organizations. In M. Alvesson, T. Bridgman and H. Wilmott (eds), *The Oxford Handbook of Critical Management Studies* (pp. 144–165). Oxford: Oxford University Press.

Knights, D. and O'Leary, M (2006). Leadership, ethics and responsibility to the other. *Journal of Business Ethics*, *67*, 125–137.

Knights, D. and Wilmott, H. (2007). *Introducing Organizational Behaviour and Management*. London: Cengage.

Koivunen, N. (2003). *Leadership in Symphony Orchestras: Discursive and Aesthetic Practices*. Tampere: Tampere University Press.

Koivunen, N. and Wennes, G. (2011). Show us the sound! Aesthetic leadership of symphony orchestra conductors. *Leadership*, 7(1), 51–71.

Kolb, D. A. (1984). *Experiential Learning: Experience as the Source of Learning and Development*. Englewood Cliffs, NJ: Prentice Hall.

Kort, E. (2008). What, after all, is leadership? 'Leadership' and plural action. *Leadership Quarterly*. 19(4), 409–425.

Kotter, J. (1990). What leaders really do. *Harvard Business Review*, 68(3), 103–111.

Kotter, J. P. (2001). What leaders really do. *Harvard Business Review*, 68(3).

Kotter, J. P. (2012). *Leading Change*. Boston, MA: Harvard Business School Press.

Kouzes, J. and Posner, R. (2012). *The Leadership Challenge*, 5th edn. San Francisco, CA: Jossey Bass.

Lacan, J. (1999). *Encore, The Seminar of Jacques Lacan Book XX: On Feminine Sexuality, the Limits of Love and Knowledge*. London: Norton.

Lacan, J. (2004). *The Four Fundamental Concepts of Psychoanalysis*. London: Norton.

Lacan, J. (2007). *Ecrits: The First Complete Edition in English*. London: Norton.

Lacan, J. (2008). *The Seminar of Jacques Lacan Book XVII: The Other Side of Psychoanalysis*. London: Norton.

Lacan, J. (2013). *On the Names-of-the-Father*. Cambridge: Polity Press.

Ladkin, D. (2006). The enchantment of the charismatic leader: Charismatic leadership as aesthetic encounter. *Leadership*, 2(2), 165–179.

Ladkin, D. (2008). Leading beautifully: How mastery, congruence, and purpose create the aesthetic of embodied leadership practice. *The Leadership Quarterly*, 19(1), 64–74.

Ladkin, D. (2010). *Rethinking Leadership: A New Look at Old Leadership Questions*. London: Edward Elgar.

Latour, B. (1987). *Science in Action*. Cambridge, MA: Harvard University Press.

Leach, M., Scoones, I. and Wynne, B. (2005). *Citizens and Science: Globalisation and the Challenge of Engagement*. London: Zed Press.

Lee, N., Senior, C. and Butler, M. (2012). Leadership research and cognitive neuroscience: The state of this union. *The Leadership Quarterly*, 23, 213–218.

Levitt, S. D. and Dubner, S. J. (2005). *Freakonomics: A Rogue Economist Explores the Hidden Side of Everything*. London: Penguin.

Lindebaum, D. (2013). Pathologizing the healthy but ineffective: Some ethical reflections on using neuroscience in leadership research. *Journal of Management Inquiry*, 22(3), 295–305.

Lindebaum, D. and Zundel, M. (2013). Not quite a revolution: Scrutinizing organizational neuroscience in leadership studies. *Human Relations*, 66(6), 857–877.

Linstead, S. and Höpfl, H. J. (eds). (1999). *The Aesthetics of Organization*. London: Sage.

Lowe, K. B., Kroeck, K. G. and Sivasubramaniam, N. (1996). Effectiveness correlates of transformational and transactional leadership: A meta-analytic review of the MLQ literature. *The Leadership Quarterly*, 7(3), 385–425.

Lukes, S. (1974). *Power: A Radical View*. London: Palgrave Macmillan.

Lukes, S. (2005). *Power: A Radical View*, 2nd edn. London: Palgrave Macmillan.

Mabey, C. (2013). Leadership development in organizations: Multiple discourses and diverse practice. *International Journal of Management Reviews*, *15*(4), 359–380.

Madoff, J. (2011). Apple's visionary redefines digital age. *The New York Times*, 5 October. Retrieved from www.nytimes.com/2011/10/06/business/steve-jobs-of-apple-dies-at-56.html?pagewanted=all&_r=0, 21 November 2014.

Manning, G. and Curtis, K. (2009). *The Art of Leadership International Edition*. London: McGraw-Hill.

Markoff, J. (2011). Apple's visionary redefined digital age. *New York Times*, 5 October. Retrieved from www.nytimes.com.

McGough, R. (2003). *All the Best: The Selected Poems of Roger McGough*. London: Penguin.

McGowan, T. (2003). Looking for the gaze: Lacanian film theory and its vicissitudes. *Cinema Journal*, *42*(3), 27–47.

McGowan, T. (2008). *The Real Gaze: Film Theory after Lacan*. Albany, NY: State University of New York Press.

McGowan, T. (2013). *The Fictional Christopher Nolan*. Austin, TX: University of Texas Press.

McKenzie, J. (2001). *Perform or Else: From Discipline to Performance*. London: Sage.

McNamee, S. and Gergen, K. J. (1999). *Relational Responsibility*. Thousand Oaks, CA: Sage.

McNulty, M. (1975). A question of managerial legitimacy. *Academy of Management Journal*, *18*(3), 579–588.

Meindl, J. R. (1995). The romance of leadership as a follower-centric theory: A social constructionist approach. *The Leadership Quarterly*, *6*(3), 329–341.

Meindl, J. R., Ehrlich, S. B. and Dukerich, J. M. (1985). The romance of leadership. *Administrative Science Quarterly*, *30*, 78–102

Melucci, A. (1985). The symbolic challenge of contemporary movements. *Social Research*, *52*(4), 789–816.

Melucci, A. (1996). *Nomads of the Present: Social Movements and Individual Needs in Contemporary Society*. Philadelphia, PA: Temple University Press.

Miles, R. E. and Snow, C. C. (1978). *Organizational Strategy, Structure, and Process*. New York: McGraw-Hill.

Mintzberg, H. (1973). *The Nature of Managerial Work*. New York: Harper & Row.

Mintzberg, H. (1998). Covert leadership: Notes on managing professionals. *Harvard Business Review*, 140–147.

Mintzberg, H. and Waters, J. (1985). Of strategies deliberate and emergent. *Strategic Management Journal, 6*, 257–272.

Mishkin, A. (2009). Why Steve Jobs could be a saviour for media companies. *Guardian*. Retrieved from www.theguardian.com.

Morris, A. and Staggenborg, S. (2002). Leadership in social movements. In D. Snow, S. Soule and H. Kriesii (eds), *The Blackwell Companion to Social Movements*. Boston, MA: Blackwell.

Morrison, J. B. and Salipante, P. (2007). Governance for broadened accountability. *Nonprofit and Voluntary Sector Quarterly, 36*, 195–217

Mouffe, C. (2009). *The Democratic Paradox*. London: Verso.

Nadler, D. and Tushman, M. (1990). Organisational frame bending: Principles for managing reorientation. *Academy of Management Executive*, *3*(3), 194–204.

Nana, E., Jackson, B. and Burch, G. (2010). Attributing leadership personality and effectiveness from the leader's face: An exploratory study. *Leadership & Organization Development Journal*, *31(*8), 720–742.

Nicholson, H. and Carroll, B. (2013). Identity undoing and power relations in leadership development. *Human Relations 66*(9), 1225–1248

Nixon, C. and Chandler, J. (2011). *Fair Cop.* Carlton: Victory Books.

Nkomo, S. M. (2011). A postcolonial and anti-colonial reading of 'African' leadership and management in organization studies: Tensions, contradictions and possibilities. *Organization 18*(3), 365–386.

Northouse, P. (2015). *Leadership: Theory and Practice.* London: Sage.

Northouse, P. G. (2013). *Leadership: Theory and Practice*, Sixth Edition. Thousand Oaks, CA: SAGE Publications.

Oberschall, A. (1973). *Social Conflicts and Social Movements.* London: Pearson Education.

O'Reilly, C. A., Caldwell, D. F., Chatman, J. A., Lapiz. M. and Self, W. (2009). How leadership matters: The effects of leaders' alignment on strategy implementation. *Leadership Quarterly, 21*, 104–113.

Osborn, R. N. and Marion, R. (2009). Contextual leadership, transformational leadership and the performance of international innovation seeking alliances. *Leadership Quarterly, 20,* 191–206.

Ospina, S. and Foldy, E. (2009). A critical review of race and ethnicity in the leadership literature: Surfacing context, power and the collective dimensions of leadership. *The Leadership Quarterly*, 20(6), 876–896.

Ospina, S. and Foldy, E. (2010). Building bridges from the margins: The work of leadership in social change organizations. *The Leadership Quarterly*, 21(2), 292–307.

Parker, M. (2004). Becoming a manager, or: The werewolf looks anxiously in the mirror, checking for unusual facial hair. *Management Learning*, *35*(1), 45–59.

Parry, K. W. and Hansen, H. (2007). The organizational story as leadership. *Leadership*, *3*(3), 281–300.

Peacock, J. (1994). The politics of portraiture. In K. Sharpe and P. Lake (eds), *Culture and Politics in Early Stuart England* (pp. 199–228). Basingstoke: Macmillan.

Pearce, C. and Conger, J. (2002). *Shared Leadership: Reframing the Hows and Whys of Leadership.* London: Sage.

Pearson, C. S. (ed.). (2012). *The Transforming Leader: New Approaches to Leadership for the Twenty-first Century.* San Francisco, CA: Berrett-Koehler Store.

Peters, T. and Waterman, R. (1982). *In Search of Excellence.* New York: Harper & Row.

Petriglieri, G. (2011). Identity workspaces for leadership development. In S. Snook, N. Nohria and R. Khurana (eds), *The Handbook for Teaching Leadership.* Thousand Oaks, CA: Sage.

Pettigrew, A. (1992). On studying managerial elites. *Strategic Management Journal, 13*, 163–182.

Plato (1941). *The Republic.* Oxford: Oxford University Press.

Podsakoff, P. and Schriesheim, C. (1985). Field studies of French and Raven's bases of power: Critique, reanalysis, and suggestions for future research. *Psychological Bulletin*, *97*, 387–411.

Poletta, F. (2002). *Freedom is an Endless Meeting: Democracy in American Social Movements.* Chicago, IL: University of Chicago Press.

Pondy, L. (1978). Leadership is a language game. In M. McCall and M. Lombardo (eds), *Leadership: Where Else Can We Go?* (pp. 87–99). Durham, NC: Duke University Press.

Porter M. E. (1979). How competitive forces shape strategy. *Harvard Business Review, 57*, 137–145.

Porter, M. E. (1980). *Competitive Strategy.* New York: Free Press.

Porter, M. E. (2008). The five forces that shape strategy. *Harvard Business Review, 86*: 78–93.

Potts, J. (2009). *A History of Charisma.* Basingstoke: Palgrave Macmillan.

Prince, L. (1998). The neglected rules: On leadership and dissent. In A. Coulson (ed.), *Trust and Contracts: Relationships in Local Government, Health and the Public Services.* Bristol: Policy Press.

Proudhon, J. (1849 [1993]). *What is Property?* London: Academy Publishing Co.

Pye, A. J. (2002). Corporate directing: Governing, strategizing and leading in action. *Corporate Governance: An International Review, 10*(3), 153–162.

Pye, A. (2005). Leadership and organizing: Sensemaking in action. *Leadership*, *1*(1), 31–49.

Raelin, J. (2007). Toward an epistemology of practice. *Academy of Management Learning and Education*, *6*(4), 495–519.

Raelin J. (2011). From leadership-as-practice to leaderful practice. *Leadership*, *7*(2), 195–211.

Rieff, P. (2007). *Charisma: The Gift of Grace, and How It Has Been Taken Away from Us.* Toronto: Random House.

Rimington, S. (2001) *Open Secret: The Autobiography of the Former Director-General of MI5*. London: Hutchinson.

Rittell, H. and Webber, M. (1973). Dilemmas in a general theory of planning. *Policy Science*, *4*(2), 155–169.

Robinson, V. (2001). Embedding leadership in task performance. In K. Wong and C. Evers (eds), *Leadership for Quality Schooling* (pp. 90–102). London: Routledge.

Ropo, A., Parviainen, J. and Koivunen, N. (2002). Aesthetics in leadership: From absent bodies to social bodily presence. In K. W. Parry and J. R. Meindl (eds), *Grounding Leadership Theory and Research: Issues and Perspectives* (pp. 21–38). Greenwich, CT: Information Age Publishing Inc.

Ropo, A. and Sauer, E. (2008). Dances of leadership: Bridging theory and practice through an aesthetic approach. *Journal of Management & Organization*, *14*(5), 560–572.

Rose, N. (1999). *Governing the Soul: The Shaping of the Private Self*. London: Free Association Books.

Rosener, J. (1990). How women lead. *Harvard Business Review*, *68*(6), 119–125.

Rosener, J. (1997). *America's Competitive Secret: Women Managers*. Oxford: Oxford University Press.

Rule, N. O. and Ambady, N. (2008). The face of success inferences from chief executive officers' appearance predict company profits. *Psychological Science*, *19*(2), 109–111.

Rule, N. O. and Ambady, N. (2009). She's got the look: Inferences from female chief executive officers' faces predict their success. *Sex Roles*, *61*(9–10), 644–652.

Schein, E. H. (1980). *Organizational Psychology*. Englewood Cliffs, NJ: Prentice Hall.

Schilling, J. (2009). From ineffectiveness to destruction: A qualitative study on the meaning of negative leadership. *Leadership*, *5*(1), 102–128.

Schyns, B. and Meindl, J. R. (2005). *Implicit Leadership Theories: Essays and Explorations*. Greenwich, CT: Information Age Publishing.

Senge, P. (2006). *The Fifth Discipline: The Art and Practice of the Learning Organization*, 2nd edn. London: Random House. Sennett, R. (1998). *The Corrosion of Character: The Personal Consequences of Work in the New Capitalism*. New York: Norton.

Sennet, R. (1998). *The Corrosion of Character: The Personal Consequences of Work in the New Capitalism*. New York: Norton.

Shamir, B., Dayan-Horesh, H. and Adler, D. (2005). Leading by biography: Towards a life-story approach to the study of leadership. *Leadership*, *1*(1), 13–29.

Shamir, B., House, R. J. and Arthur, M. B. (1993). The motivational effects of charismatic leadership: A self-concept based theory. *Organization Science*, *4*(4), 577–594.

Shamir, B. Pillai, R. Bligh, M. and Uhl-Bien, M. (2007). *Follower-Centered Perspectives on Leadership: A Tribute to the Memory of James R. Meindl.* Greenwich, CT: Information Age Publishing.

Shondrik, S. J., Dinh, J. E. and Lord, R. G. (2010). Developments in implicit leadership theory and cognitive science: Applications to improving measurement and understanding alternatives to hierarchical leadership. *The Leadership Quarterly*, *26*(6), 959–978.

Sinclair, A. (2005). Journey around leadership. Working Paper, 10 March, Melbourne: University of Melbourne.

Sinclair, A. (2007). *Leadership for the Disillusioned: Moving Beyond Myths and Heroes to Leading that Liberates.* Australia: Allen & Unwin.

Sinclair, A. and Wilson, V. (2002). *New Faces of Leadership.* Carlton: Melbourne University Press.

Skeat, W. W. (1995). *Etymological Dictionary of the English Language*. Oxford: Clarendon Press.

Smircich, L. and Morgan, G. (1982). Leadership: The management of meaning. *Journal of Applied Behavioural Studies*, *18*(3), 257–273.

Smith, D. (2000). *Grassroots Associations.* Thousand Oaks, CA: Sage.

Smith, Sir R. (2004). *Audit Committees: Combined Code Guidance*. London: Financial Reporting Council.

Soila-Wadman, M. and Köping, A.-S. (2009). Aesthetic relations in place of the lone hero in arts leadership. *International Journal of Arts Management*, *12*(1), 31–43.

Sophocles (2008). *Antigone, Oedipus the King and Electra.* Oxford: Oxford World's Classics.

Sørensen, B. M. and Spoelstra, S. (2013). Faith. In *Handbook of the Philosophical Foundations of Business Ethics* (pp. 517–525). Dordrecht: Springer Netherlands.

Sørensen, B. M., Spoelstra, S., Höpfl, H. and Critchley, S. (2012). Theology and organization. *Organization*, *19*(3), 267–279.

Spicer, A., Alvesson, M. and Karreman, D. (2009). Critical performativity: The unfinished business of critical management studies. *Human Relations*, *62*(4), 537–560.

Spisak, B. R., Homan, A. C., Grabo, A. and Van Vugt, M. (2012). Facing the situation: Testing a biosocial contingency model of leadership in intergroup relations using masculine and feminine faces. *The Leadership Quarterly*, *23*(2), 273–280.

Spoelstra, S. (2013). Leadership studies: Out of business. In J. Lemmergaard and S. L. Muhr (eds), *Critical Perspectives on Leadership: Emotion, Toxicity, and Dysfunction*. Cheltenham: Edward Elgar.

Spoelstra, S. and ten Bos, R. (2011). Leadership. In M. Painter-Morland and R. ten Bos (eds), *Business Ethics and Continental Philosophy*. Cambridge: Cambridge University Press.

Starbuck, W. (2003). The origins of organization theory. In H. Tsoukas and C. Knudsen (eds), *The Oxford Handbook of Organization Theory: Meta-Theoretical Perspectives* (pp. 143–182). Oxford: Oxford University Press.

Starhawk (1987). *Truth or Dare: Encounters with Power, Authority and Mystery*. San Francisco, CA: Harper Row.

Stavrakakis, Y. (1999). *Lacan and the Political*. Abingdon: Routledge.

Stogdill, R. (1948). Personal factors associated with leadership: A survey of the literature. *The Journal of Psychology*, *25*(1), 35–71.

Stogdill, R. (1974). *Handbook of Leadership: A Survey of Theory and Research.* New York: Free Press.

Storey, J. (ed.) (2011). *Leadership in Organizations: Current Issues and Key Trends*, 2nd edn. London: Routledge.

Strati, A. (1992). Aesthetic understanding of organizational life. *Academy of Management Review*, *17*(3), 568–581.

Sveningsson, S. and Larsson, M. (2006). Fantasies of leadership: Identity work. *Leadership*, *2*(2), 203–224.

Sy, T. (2010). What do you think of followers? Examining the content, structure, and consequences of implicit followership theories. *Organizational Behavior and Human Decision Processes*, *113*(2), 73–84.

Taylor, F. W. (1911). *The Principles of Scientific Management*. New York: Harper.

Taylor, S. S. (2002). Overcoming aesthetic muteness: Researching organizational members' aesthetic experience. *Human Relations*, *55*(7), 821–840.

Taylor, S. S. and Hansen, H. (2005). Finding form: Looking at the field of organizational aesthetics. *Journal of Management Studies*, *42*(6), 1211–1231.

Taylor, S. S. and Ladkin, D. (2009). Understanding arts-based methods in managerial development. *Academy of Management Learning and Education*, *8*(1), 55–69.

Teece, D. J., Pisano, G. and Shuen, A. (1997). Dynamic capabilities and strategic management. *Strategic Management Journal, 18*, 509–533.

Tepper, B. (2000). Consequences of abusive supervision. *Academy of Management Journal*, *43*(2), 178–190.

Thomas, P. (1967). *Down These Mean Streets*. New York: Knopf.

Tilly, C. (1998). *Durable Inequality.* Berkeley, CA: University of California Press.

Tolliday, S. and Zeitlin, J. (1987). *The Automotive Industry and Its Fit between Form and Flexibility.* New York: St. Martin's Press.

Tolstoy, L. (1869/1952). *Book Eleven: 1812, Chapter I & II. War and Peace.* Chicago, IL: William Benton, pp. 469–472.

Tourish, D. (2005). Critical upward communication: Ten commandments for improving strategy and decision making. *Long Range Planning*, *38*(5), 485–503.

Tourish, D. (2011). Leading questions: Journal rankings, academic freedom and performativity: What is, or should be, the future of leadership? *Leadership*, *7*(3), 367–381.

Tourish, D. (2013). *The Dark Side of Transformational Leadership: A Critical Perspective.* London: Routledge.

Uhl-Bien, M. (2006). Relational leadership theory: Exploring the social processes of leadership and organizing. *The Leadership Quarterly*, *17*(6), 654–676.

Uhl-Bien, M. and Ospina, S. (eds). (2012). *Advancing Relational Leadership Research.* Charlotte, NC: Information Age.

US News (2010). A design, a dream. *US News*, 31 May 2010. Available at www.usnews.com (accessed September 2013).

Vaill, P. (1991). *Managing as a Performing Art: New Ideas for a World of Chaotic Change.* New York: Jossey-Bass.

Van Knippenberg, D. and Sitkin, S. B. (2013). A critical assessment of charismatic–transformational leadership research: Back to the drawing board? *The Academy of Management Annals*, *7*(1), 1–60.

Venkatesh, S. (2008). *Gang Leader for a Day: A Rogue Sociologist Crosses the Line.* London: Penguin.

Vogelstein, F. (2013) *Dogfight.* London: William Collins.

de Vries, R. E. and van Gelder, J-L. (2005). Leadership and Need for Leadership. Testing an Implicit Followership Theory. In B. Schyns and J. R. Meindl (eds), *Implicit Leadership Theories: Essay and Explorations*. Greenwich, CT: Information Age Publishing.

Vroom, V. (1964). *Work and Motivation*. New York: John Wiley.

Vroom, V. and Jago, A. (1988). *The New Leadership: Managing participation in organizations*. Englewood Cliffs, NJ: Prentice-Hall.

Vroom, V. and Yetton, P. (1973). *Leadership and Decision Making*. Pittsburgh, PA: University of Pittsburgh Press.

Wahl, A. (1998). Deconstructing women and leadership. *International Review of Women and Leadership*, *4*(2), 46–60.

Wang, G. G., Gilley, J. W. and Sun, J. Y. (2012). The 'science of HRD research': Reshaping HRD research through scientometrics. *Human Resource Development Review*, *11*(4), 500–520.

Warner, N. O. (2014). Picturing power: The depiction of leadership in art. *Leadership and the Humanities*, *2*(1), 4–26.

Weber, M. (1947). *The Theory of Social and Economic Organization*. New York: Free Press.

Weber, M. (1978). *Economy and Society*. Berkeley, CA: University of California Press.

Weedon, C. (1997). *Feminist Practice and Poststructuralist Theory*, 2nd cdn. Oxford: Blackwell.

Weick, K. E. (1995). *Sensemaking in Organizations*. Thousand Oaks CA: Sage.

Weick, K. E. (1998). Introductory essay – improvisation as a mindset for organizational analysis. *Organization Science*, *9*(5), 543–555.

Weick, K. E. (2001). *Making Sense of the Organization*. Oxford: Blackwell.

Western, S. (2008). *Leadership: A Critical Text*. Los Angeles: Sage.

Whitehead, A. N. (1925/1967). *Science and Modern World*. Cambridge: Cambridge University Press.

Whyte, W. H. (1960). *The Organization Man*. Harmondsworth: Penguin.

Wilkens, A. (1983). Organisational Stories as symbols which control the organisation. In L. Pondy, P. Frost and G. Morgan (eds), *Organisational Symbolism* (pp. 81–92). Greenwich, CT: JAI Press.

Williams, R. (1976). *Keywords: A Vocabulary of Culture and Society*. London: Fontana Press.

Williamson, O. (1971). Hierarchical control and optimum firm size. *Journal of Political Economy*, *75*(2), 123–138.

Wood, M. (2005). The fallacy of misplaced leadership. *Journal of Management Studies*, *42*(6), 1101–1121.

Yukl, G. (2013). *Leadership in Organisations*. Upper Saddle River, NJ: Prentice Hall.

Zaccaro, S. J. (2007). Trait-based perspectives of leadership. *American Psychologist*, *62*(1), 6–16.

Zald, M. and Ash, R. (1966). Social movement organizations: Growth, decay and change. *Social Forces*, *44*(3), 327–340.

Zaleznik, A. (1977). Managers and leaders: Are they different? *Harvard Business Review*, May–June, 67–78.

Žižek, S. (2009). *The Plague of Fantasies*. London: Verso.

INDEX

Tables and Figures are indicated by page numbers in bold print. The letters 'bib' after a page number refer to bibliographical information in the 'Further thinking' sections.